Department of Economic and Social Affairs

The World's Women 2010
Trends and Statistics

United Nations
New York, 2010

Department of Economic and Social Affairs

The Department of Economic and Social Affairs of the United Nations Secretariat is a vital interface between global policies in the economic, social and environmental spheres and national action. The Department works in three main interlinked areas: (i) it compiles, generates and analyses a wide range of economic, social and environmental data and information on which States Members of the United Nations draw to review common problems and take stock of policy options; (ii) it facilitates the negotiations of Member States in many intergovernmental bodies on joint courses of action to address ongoing or emerging global challenges; and (iii) it advises interested Governments on the ways and means of translating policy frameworks developed in United Nations conferences and summits into programmes at the country level and, through technical assistance, helps build national capacities.

Note

The designations employed and the presentation of material in the present report do not imply the expression of any opinion whatsoever on the part of the Secretariat of the United Nations concerning the legal status of any country, territory, city or area or of its authorities, or concerning the delimitation of its frontiers or boundaries.

The term "country" as used in the text of this report also refers, as appropriate, to territories or areas.

The designations "developed" and "developing" countries or areas and "more developed" and "less developed" regions are intended for statistical convenience and do not necessarily express a judgement about the stage reached by a particular country or area in the development process.

Symbols of the United Nations documents are composed of capital letters combined with figures.

ST/ESA/STAT/SER.K/19

United Nations publication
Sales No. E.10.XVII.11

ISBN 978-92-1-161539-5

Message from the Secretary-General

The United Nations occupies a unique position as a global storehouse of statistical information on social and economic phenomena. Numerical profiles of women and men and their status in societies are systematically collected, compiled, processed and analyzed, providing an authoritative basis for sound policymaking at all levels – national, regional and international.

The World's Women: Trends and Statistics was first published by the United Nations in 1991. A new edition has been issued every five years since 1995, as called for specifically in the Beijing Platform for Action adopted at that year's landmark Fourth World Conference on Women. With coverage encompassing the full range of issues and concerns, it is the only publication of its kind.

The World's Women 2010 is intended to contribute to the stocktaking being done to mark the fifteenth anniversary of the Beijing Conference. It addresses critical aspects of life: population, families, health, education, work, power and decision-making, violence against women, environment and poverty. It finds that progress in ensuring the equal status of women and men has been made in many areas, including school enrolment, health and economic participation. At the same time, it makes clear that much more needs to be done, in particular to close the gender gap in public life and to prevent the many forms of violence to which women are subjected.

It is my hope that the insights and information contained in the present publication will help Governments, researchers, scholars, non-governmental organizations and concerned citizens around the world in their efforts to ensure that every single woman achieves her full potential.

Ban Ki-Moon

Preface

The Beijing Platform for Action – the pre-eminent international guideline for improving the status of women – lists, among others, specific activities related to increased availability of sex-disaggregated data. It was expected that these activities would start showing results with the passage of time. Indeed, in some areas of statistics, we are witnessing an increased stock of available statistics, such as on work and education. However, the availability of gender statistics is still sporadic and weak in many countries and areas of the world, thus limiting the comprehensive statistical analysis of social phenomena and the status of women and men.

The conceptual approach of *The World's Women 2010: Trends and Statistics* is in line with those published since 1991 – to present and analyse statistics on the status of women. It highlights the differences between the status of women and men in various areas of contemporary life; statistics on men figure as prominently as statistics on women.

Eight key areas are covered: population and families, health, education, work, power and decision-making, violence against women, environment and poverty. In each of these areas, statistics were identified, compiled, processed and analyzed, bringing to light findings on the differences between the status of girls and boys, women and men. All efforts were made to make these findings easy to interpret, with the extensive use of graphical presentation and non-technical language.

The World's Women 2010 is accompanied by a comprehensive website hosted by the Statistics Division of the Department of Economic and Social Affairs. The website displays the full range of statistics used for preparing the present publication, as well as links to numerous sources of gender statistics and references to international, regional and national compilations of relevant data.

It is my hope that the present publication will be used to advance an enabling social and economic environment that will ensure equal treatment of all women and men and significantly improve the status of women in the world. It should also serve as a model for similar statistical profiles for countries, areas, regions and provinces, thus supporting the development of policies to implement a basic United Nations principle: gender equality.

Sha Zukang
Under-Secretary-General for Economic and Social Affairs

Prepared by the United Nations Statistics Division

Paul Cheung, Director

Editors

Srdjan Mrkić, *Editor-in-Chief*
Tina Johnson
Michael Rose

Drafting team – United Nations Statistics Division

Ionica Berevoescu
María Isabel Cobos Hernández
Erlinda Go
Linda Hooper
Srdjan Mrkić
Keiko Osaki Tomita
Seiffe Tadesse

Contributors

Bosiljka Djikanovic
Athena Tapales
Joann Vanek
Macro International
International Programme on the Elimination of Child Labour, International Labour Office
UNESCO Institute for Statistics

Reviewers

Denise Brown, *Principal Statistician*, Statistics New Zealand
Jean-Michel Durr, Statistics Division, Department of Economic and Social Affairs, United Nations
Keiko Osaki Tomita, Statistics Division, Department of Economic and Social Affairs, United Nations
Division for the Advancement of Women, Department of Economic and Social Affairs, United Nations
Population Division, Department of Economic and Social Affairs, United Nations
UNESCO Institute for Statistics
Department of Statistics, International Labor Office
United Nations Environmental Programme
World Health Organization

Research and technical assistance

Xinli An, Haoyi Chen, Lisa Morrison-Puckett, Vysaul Nyirongo, Tillie Peacock, Awet Segid, Patricia Tito

Design and typesetting

Cover
Graphic Design Unit, Outreach Division, Department of Public Information
Interior
Content Design Unit, Copy Preparation and Proofreading Section, Department for General Assembly and Conference Management

Executive summary

In the Beijing Declaration adopted in 1995 by the Fourth World Conference on Women, participating Governments expressed their commitment "to advance the goals of equality, development and peace for all women everywhere in the interest of humanity". To assess whether these goals are being achieved, *The World's Women* is produced by the United Nations every five years, as called for in the Beijing Platform for Action.

The World's Women 2010: Trends and Statistics presents statistics and analysis on the status of women and men in the world, highlighting the current situation and changes over time. Analyses are based mainly on statistics from international and national statistical agencies. The report covers several broad policy areas – population and families, health, education, work, power and decision-making, violence against women, environment and poverty. The main findings are summarized below.

General population patterns, families

In today's world, there are 57 million more men than women. This surplus of men is concentrated in the youngest age groups and steadily diminishes until it disappears at about age 50, thereafter becoming a surplus of women owing to their longer life expectancy. A surplus of men characterizes the world's most populous countries – China and India – hence the large surplus of men worldwide. In most other countries, there are more women than men. The surplus of women in older age groups is significant and is increasing, with obvious implications for health care and other social needs.

People are marrying at older ages than in the past – especially women. In Europe, the average age at which women first marry is 30 or older in many countries. In some less developed countries, however, such as Mali, Niger and several other countries in sub-Saharan Africa, the average age at which women first marry is still below 20. As family-building often starts with a marriage, the consequences for fertility is obvious. Globally, fertility declined to 2.5 births per woman, but women who bear more than five children are still common in countries where women marry early. Early marriage and high fertility limit such women's opportunities for education and employment and can severely diminish their chances for advancement in life.

Once constituted, maintaining families and caring for family members lies primarily on the shoulders of women, who spend, on average, more working hours per day than men.

Health

In all regions, women live longer than men. However, social, cultural and economic factors can affect the natural advantage of women compared to men. For example, in developing countries where pregnancy and childbirth can be life-threatening, women's exposure to risks associated with pregnancy and childbirth tend to equalize life expectancies between the sexes; whereas in developed countries, the adoption of unhealthy behaviours by women, such as smoking and drinking, can also equalize life expectancy. The data reveal that, globally, non-communicable diseases are already the most important causes of death for both men and women.

Achieving the Millennium Development Goals (MDGs) that relate to health is important for improving the quality of life of all people. The past decades saw considerable reductions in child mortality worldwide, which is one of the eight MDGs. However, Africa continues to have high rates of child mortality despite intensified efforts to reduce it. Another MDG is to improve maternal health. Access to prenatal care and birth delivery attendance by skilled health personnel are essential to achieving this goal. Findings show there have been increases in the proportion of women receiving prenatal care but much still needs to be improved.

The Beijing Platform for Action recognized that social and cultural factors often increase women's vulnerability to HIV and may determine the course that the infection takes in their lives. Recent data show that in sub-Saharan Africa, North Africa and the Middle East, women account for more than half of people living with HIV/AIDS. The toll exacted by HIV/AIDS on the lives of women extends beyond their physical health to the families and communities that depend on them.

Education

There is progress – albeit slow and uneven – in the literacy status of adult women and men around the world. However, reflecting the persistent disadvantages they face, women account for two thirds of the world's 774 million adult illiterates – a proportion that is unchanged over the past two decades. Gender disparities in adult literacy rates remain wide in most regions of the world. However, there is a reason to look toward future decades with optimism as improvement in access to education eventually raises literacy levels. In almost all countries, literacy rates for the young are higher than those for adults. The vast majority of young people in the world are literate and improvements in youth literacy rates have been accompanied by declining gender disparities.

Primary enrolment of girls and boys is increasing across the world. Outstanding gains have been registered in several less developed regions of the world, particularly Africa and South-Central Asia. Yet several countries in these regions are still far from attaining universal primary education. Measurable progress has been made towards greater gender parity in primary enrolment, with gender gaps diminishing in most regions of the world. Positive global trends in primary enrolment, however, obscure uneven progress and some slippage or stagnation. While the overall progress in primary education in the past decade is encouraging, major barriers stand in the way of progress: 72 million children – 54 per cent of them girls – are out of school. The evidence indicates that much remains to be done to keep the world on track to meet the goal of universal primary education.

There is increased participation in secondary education. However, progress in secondary enrolment lags behind that in primary education. Compared to participation at the primary level, a significantly lower proportion of the official secondary-school age population attends school. In addition, gender disparities in secondary enrolment are wider and occur in more countries than at the primary level. Due to the unprecedented expansion of the tertiary student body over the past two decades, one of the most noticeable improvements in women's enrolment is registered at the tertiary level. Men's dominance in tertiary education has been reversed globally and gender disparities currently favour women, except in sub-Saharan Africa and Southern and Western Asia. The distribution of tertiary enrolment across various fields of study brings to light the gender dimension of, and inequalities in, participation in tertiary education. Gender differences in tertiary participation are apparent throughout the world, with women predominant in the fields of education, health and welfare, social sciences, humanities and art, while they remain severely underrepresented in the fields of science and engineering.

Work

Globally, women's participation in the labour market remained steady in the two decades from 1990 to 2010, hovering around 52 per cent. In contrast, global labour force participation rates for men declined steadily over the same period, from 81 to 77 per cent. In 2010, women's labour force participation rates remain below 30 per cent in Northern Africa and Western Asia; below 40 per cent in Southern Asia; and below 50 per cent in the Caribbean and Central America. The gap between participation rates of women and men has narrowed slightly in the last 20 years but remains considerable. The smallest gender gaps are in the early adult years and the widest in the prime working ages.

Employment levels in the services sector continue to grow for both women and men. In the more developed economies, the labour force – especially the female labour force – is employed predominantly in services. This sector accounts for at least three quarters of women's employment in most of the more developed regions and in Latin America and the Caribbean. In contrast, agriculture still accounts for more than half of the employment of women and men in sub-Saharan Africa (excluding Southern Africa) and of women in Southern Asia. In those regions, the majority of workers – women to a greater extent than men – are in vulnerable employment, being either own-account workers or contributing family workers.

Over the years, women have entered various traditionally male-dominated occupations. However, they are still rarely employed in jobs with status, power and authority or in traditionally male blue-collar occupations. Relative to their overall share of total employment, women are significantly underrepresented among legislators, senior officials and managers, craft and related trade workers, and plant and machine operators and assemblers; they are heavily overrepresented among clerks, professionals, and service and sales workers. Horizontal and vertical job segregation has resulted in a persistent gender pay gap everywhere. While the gender pay gap is closing slowly in some countries, it has remained unchanged in others.

In spite of the changes that have occurred in women's participation in the labour market, women continue to bear most of the responsibilities for the home: caring for children and other dependent household members, preparing meals and doing other housework. In all regions, women spend at least twice as much time as men on unpaid domestic work. Women who are employed spend an inordinate amount of time on the double burden of paid work and family responsibilities; when unpaid work is taken into account, women's total work hours are longer than men's in all regions.

Like their adult counterparts, girls are more likely than boys to perform unpaid work within their own household. In the less developed regions, many young girls aged 5-14 take on a large amount of household chores, including care-giving, cooking and cleaning, and older girls do so to an even greater extent. While boys also do household chores, their participation rate is not as high as that of girls. Moreover, girls generally work longer hours than boys, whether they are engaged in housework only, employment only or both. Long hours of work affect children's ability to participate fully in education. Analysis shows that school attendance declines as the number of hours spent on household chores increases – and declines more steeply for girls than for boys.

Power and decision-making

Around the world, a lack of gender balance in decision-making positions in government persists. Women continue to be underrepresented in national parliaments, where on average only 17 per cent of seats are occupied by women. The share of women among ministers also averages 17 per cent. The highest positions are even more elusive: only 7 of 150 elected Heads of State in the world are women, and only 11 of 192 Heads of Government. The situation is similar at the level of local government: female elected councillors are underrepresented in all regions of the world and female mayors even more so.

In the private sector, women are on most boards of directors of large companies but their number remains low compared to men. Furthermore, the "glass ceiling" has hindered women's access to leadership positions in private companies. This is especially notable in the largest corporations, which remain male-dominated. Of the 500 largest corporations in the world, only 13 have a female chief executive officer.

Violence against women

While rates of women exposed to violence vary from one region to the other, statistics indicate that violence against women is a universal phenomenon and women are subjected to different forms of violence – physical, sexual, psychological and economic – both within and outside their homes.

Perpetrators of violence against women are most often their intimate partners. Women are abused physically and sexually by intimate partners at different rates throughout the world – yet such abuse occurs in all countries or areas, without exception. Younger women are more at risk than older women and since the consequences of such violence last a lifetime it has a severely adverse impact on women's family and social life.

Female genital mutilation – the most harmful mass perpetration of violence against women – is declining for the young girls compelled to suffer it. However, it is still reported in a number of countries at high levels.

At the same time, in many regions of the world, longstanding customs put considerable pressure on women to accept being beaten by their husbands, even for trivial reasons. Whether for burning the food, venturing outside without telling their husband, neglecting children or arguing with their husband, in quite a few countries a very high percentage of women consider such behaviour sufficient grounds for being physically hit.

Environment

Poor infrastructure and housing conditions as well as natural hazards disproportionately affect women from the less developed regions in terms of unpaid work, health and survival. More than half of rural households and about a quarter of urban households in sub-Saharan Africa lack easy access to drinking water. In most of those households, the burden of water collection rests on women, thereby reducing the amount of time they can spend on other activities, whether income-earning, educational or leisure.

Lack of access to clean energy fuels and improved stoves in sub-Saharan Africa and parts of Southern and South-Eastern Asia continue to have a major impact on health. Women are more exposed than men to smoke from burning solid fuels because they spend more time near a fire while cooking and more time indoors taking care of children and household chores, thus increasing their likelihood to develop respiratory infections, pulmonary disease and lung cancer. Furthermore, several natural disasters in the less developed regions, such as the 2004 Indian Ocean tsunami, claimed more female than male lives, suggesting that more needs to be done in terms of providing equal access to information and life-skills development.

All these environmental factors will continue to disproportionately affect women as long as gender-differentiated roles and expectations in the household, family and community life are maintained. At the same time, the participation of women in environmental decision-making, particularly at a high level, remains limited, thus restricting the integration of women's issues and gender perspectives into policy-making on the environment.

Poverty

In some parts of the world, women and girls are often more burdened by the poverty of their household and their environment than men and boys. At the household level, data show that certain types of female-headed households are more likely to be poor than male-headed households of the same type. In Latin America and the Caribbean and the more developed regions households of lone mothers with children have higher poverty rates than those of lone fathers with children. In the same regions, poverty rates are higher for women than for men when living in one-person households.

At the individual level, women's lack of access to and control over resources limits their economic autonomy and increases their vulnerability to economic or environmental shocks. Compared to men, lower proportions of women have cash income in the less developed regions. Existing statutory and customary laws still restrict women's access to land and other types of property in most countries in Africa and about half the countries in Asia. Moreover, significant proportions of married women from the less developed regions have no control over household spending, including spending their own cash earnings, particularly in countries from sub-Saharan Africa and Southern Asia.

Availability of gender statistics

The World's Women 2010 has benefited from an increase in the availability of gender statistics in the last 10 years. The majority of countries are now able to produce sex-disaggregated statistics on population, enrolment, employment and parliamentary representation. In addition, gender statistics in some newer areas are becoming available. For example, statistics on child labour are now collected by a larger number of countries. Similarly, surveys on time use and on violence against women were conducted in both developed and developing countries although international standards in these two statistical fields have not yet been fully developed.

At the same time, important developments with respect to some international standards and guidelines have advanced the development of gender statistics. In 2003, the definition of informal employment was adopted, paving the way for improved measurement of informal sector and informal employment. A resolution on the statistics of child labour was adopted in December 2008, thus establishing statistical measurement standards for child labour. In recent years several international standard classifications have been established by intergovernmental bodies, including those relating to occupations, economic activity, and functioning, disability and health.

However, the preparation of *The World's Women 2010* was hampered by the fact that statistics in certain domains are not available for many countries. Furthermore, even the statistics that are available are often not comparable because concepts, definitions and methods vary from country to country. Data are also lacking in detail in many cases. Gender issues cannot be adequately reflected if existing sex-disaggregated statistics are classified into categories that are too broad or are not further disaggregated by relevant characteristics, such as age, residence or educational level. Finally, the quality of data varies across countries. One or more of the above-mentioned shortcomings are often encountered in data related to international migration, maternal mortality, causes of death, vocational education, access to and use of information and communication technologies, the informal sector and informal employment. The same is true of data on occupations, wages, unemployment and underemployment, decision makers in government and the private sector, and household poverty.

In other areas, the absence of internationally agreed measurement standards and methods has resulted in a lack of gender statistics relating to disease prevalence, home-based workers, access to credit, the worst forms of child labour, human trafficking, femicide, intrahousehold poverty, individual ownership of land and losses associated with natural disasters.

In conclusion, increasing the capacity to produce reliable, accurate and timely statistics, in particular gender statistics, remains a formidable challenge for many countries.

Technical note

The World's Women 2010: Trends and Statistics presents statistics and analysis in a format and language that non-specialists can readily understand. It is organized into eight chapters: population and families, health, education, work, power and decision-making, violence against women, environment and poverty. Each chapter highlights the current situation of women and men worldwide. Where data are available, recent trends in the last 10 or 20 years, in some cases for longer periods of time, are analysed. A selection of the statistics and indicators used in the chapters are presented at the country level in the Statistical Annex (tables 1.A to 8.A) of the report.

Statistical sources

The statistics and indicators on women and men presented in the report are based mainly on data provided by the United Nations and other international organizations that compile data from national sources and/or estimate data in a comparable manner across countries. Additional regional and official national sources and, in a few cases, academic, non-governmental or private sources, were used to supplement the available data.

The World's Women 2010 is not intended for use as a primary source for the data presented. Every effort has been made to fully cite and document the sources drawn on. The statistics presented in different editions of *The World's Women* may not be comparable, due to revisions to data, changes in methodology and differences in the countries or areas covered and the regional groupings employed. As a result, trend analysis based on data in different editions of *The World's Women* should be avoided. The reader is strongly encouraged to consult the original sources since they usually contain comparable and regularly updated data.

Countries, areas and geographical groupings

The World's Women 2010 covers 196 countries or areas with a population of at least 100,000 as of 1 July 2010. The term "countries" refers to political entities that are independent States. The term "areas" refers to geographical entities that have no independent political status; an area is thus generally a portion of one or more independent States. In chapters 1 to 8, tables and figures cover only countries or areas for which data are available. Similarly, in the Statistical Annex, tables cover only countries or areas for which data are available.

For analytical purposes, countries or areas are grouped into geographic regions and subregions, as well as into more developed and less developed regions. The geographical regions or subregions used vary slightly from one chapter to another, depending on the grouping used by the international organizations providing the data and/or the statistical clustering of countries according to selected characteristics. The more developed regions include all European countries, Australia, Canada, Japan, New Zealand and the United States of America. Countries or areas in Africa,

Latin America and the Caribbean, Asia (excluding Japan) and Oceania (excluding Australia and New Zealand) are grouped under "less developed regions". For a full listing of countries or areas covered and the groupings used in the report, see the Statistical Annex, table 9.

As in previous editions of *The World's Women*, unweighted regional and subregional averages for most of the indicators have been computed by the United Nations Statistics Division from data at the country or area level. Such averaging is indicated in annotations to tables and figures. When the availability of data for a particular indicator is limited, the number of countries or areas used to calculate averages is provided. When data are available for less than three countries in a region or subregion, no averages have been computed.

Global and regional aggregates and averages prepared by international organizations have been used for most of the indicators presented in chapter 1 (Population and families) and chapter 3 (Education) and some of the indicators in chapter 2 (Health) and elsewhere. In such instances, the global and regional statistics shown are weighted estimates covering all countries or areas (including those with population less than 100,000).

Symbols and conventions

- Two dots (..) indicate that data are not available or are not reported separately.

- A short dash (–) indicates "not applicable".

- A short dash (–) between two years (e.g. 2005–2010) indicates an average over the period unless otherwise stated. When the two-year period is followed by the words "latest available" in parenthesis (e.g. 2005–2007 (latest available)), this denotes that data refer to the latest available year in the given interval.

- A long dash (—) indicates magnitude nil or less than half of the unit employed.

- A point (.) indicates decimals. Thousands are separated by a comma (,) in numbers presented in the text and by a blank space ( ) in numbers presented in tables (including the tables in the Statistical Annex).

- A minus sign (-) before a number indicates a deficit or decrease, except as indicated.

- A slash (/) between two consecutive years (e.g. 2005/06) indicates that data collection took place over a continuous period that covered a number of months within the two-year period.

Numbers and percentages in tables may not always add to totals because of rounding.

Table of contents

Figures

Page

Page

Tables

Boxes

Chapter 1
Population and families

Key findings

- The world's population tripled in the period 1950–2010 to reach almost 7 billion.
- There are approximately 57 million more men than women in the world, yet in most countries there are more women than men.
- There is a "gender spiral", with more boys and men in younger age groups and more women in the older age groups.
- Fertility is steadily declining in all regions of the world, though it still remains high in some regions of Africa.
- Life expectancy is steadily rising, with women living longer than men.
- International migration is increasing. There are more and more women migrants, and in certain areas they outnumber men.
- The age at marriage for women continues to rise – and it remains high for men.
- In family life women overwhelmingly carry the workload, although in some countries the gap has narrowed significantly.

Introduction

Changes and trends in population growth and distribution directly affect living conditions across the globe. The first part of this chapter elaborates on general population dynamics and patterns in the various world regions and the proportion of women and men in different age groups. It also looks at fertility and ageing as well as at international migration. The second part of the chapter shifts the focus to families, first considering marriages and unions and then the sharing of family responsibilities.

A. General population patterns

1. Growth and geographical distribution

The world's population in 2010 is nearly 7 billion, almost triple what it was in 1950

The world's population in 2010 is estimated at nearly 7 billion people – more precisely at 6,908,688,378 – which is almost three times the population estimated in 1950 (that is, it has taken 60 years for the population to almost triple in size).[1] This pattern is not found in all the regions of the world, much less in all countries. In general terms, population growth was steepest in Africa and Asia and almost non-existent in Europe (see figure 1.1).

Within this period of 60 years (1950–2010), the population in Eastern Africa increased five times, while the number of people in Middle Africa increased almost as much, closely followed by the Western Africa region. The two other African regions, Northern and Southern Africa, also registered well above the world average increase in the number of people – around four times as many.

A similarly significant growth of population – around four times – is also evident in Western Asia and Central America. In European regions, however, the growth was modest, with an increase in the number of people of between 30–40 per cent. During the same period the population in Northern America doubled.

In absolute terms, the world in 1950 was home to around 2.5 billion people, reaching 3 billion in

1 United Nations, 2009a.

Figure 1.1

Number of times by which the population increased from 1950 to 2010, by region

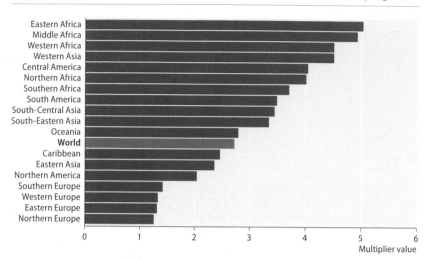

Source: United Nations, *World Population Prospects: The 2008 Revision* (2009a).

1960, 3.7 billion in 1970, over 4.4 billion in 1980, 5.3 billion in 1990 and over 6.1 billion in 2000. The difference between the number of people in 1950 and in 2010 is presented in figure 1.2.

As for the geographical distribution of the world's population in 2010 (figure 1.3), over one quarter is located in South-Central Asia (26 per cent) and a little less in Eastern Asia (23 per cent). Europe has around 11 per cent of the world's population, while South-Eastern Asia is home to 8 per cent.

Figure 1.2

The difference in the number of people in 1950 and 2010 by region

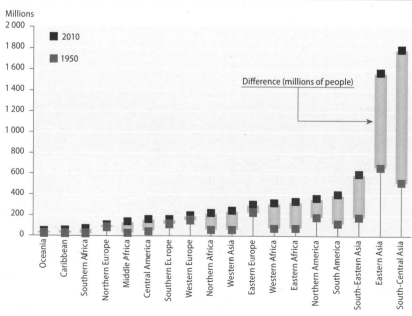

Source: United Nations, *World Population Prospects: The 2008 Revision* (2009a).

South and Northern America are next with 6 and 5 per cent, respectively, while two African regions, Eastern and Western, have 5 and 4 per cent, respectively, followed by Western Asia, Northern Africa, and Southern and Middle Africa combined (each with around 3 per cent). The share of Central America is 2 per cent, and Oceania and the Caribbean combined make up 1 per cent. Thus Asia – more specifically the South-Central, Eastern and South-Eastern regions – is inhabited by 57 per cent of all the people in the world.

2. Population distribution by sex

There is a "gender spiral", with more boys and men in the younger age groups and more women in the older age groups

There are approximately 57 million more men than women in the world in 2010. At the global level, the percentages are almost equal: 50.4 per cent men and 49.6 per cent women or, using the male/female ratio, 102 males for every 100 females. It has to be emphasized that this ratio does not apply to all age groups. In fact, there is a "gender spiral" – more boys and men are in the younger age groups and more women are in the older age groups (figure 1.4).

Moreover, this general ratio varies a great deal among the different regions of the world. Some regions have an obvious "shortage" of men while others have a "shortage" of women (figure 1.5).

Europe in general is home to many more women than men. In Eastern Europe there are 88 men per 100 women, and that ratio in other parts of Europe (Western, Southern and Northern) has a value of 96. At the other end of the spectrum, in South-Central, Western and Eastern Asia, there are approximately 106 men per 100 women. Somewhere in the middle are South-Eastern Asia, Oceania and Western Africa, where the number of men and women is almost equal.

The regional aggregates do not always reflect the distribution in individual countries. Figure 1.6 displays the number of men per 100 women for each country with a population over 100,000 in 2010. (Saudi Arabia, Oman, Bahrain, Kuwait, United Arab Emirates and Qatar have been omitted because the ratios there are heavily skewed to the men's side – that is, 121, 129, 134, 146, 204 and 307 men per 100 women, respectively – as a consequence of their sizeable foreign-born labour force made up predominantly of men.)

Figure 1.3

Geographical distribution of the world population by region, 2010

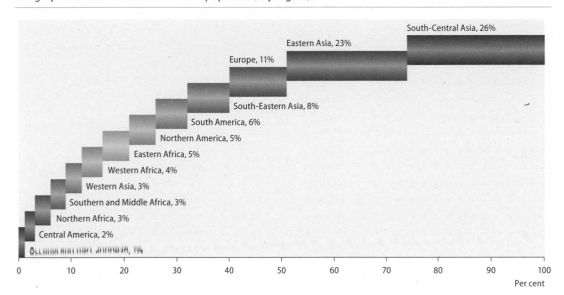

South-Central Asia, 26%

Eastern Asia, 23%

Europe, 11%

South-Eastern Asia, 8%

South America, 6%

Northern America, 5%

Eastern Africa, 5%

Western Africa, 4%

Western Asia, 3%

Southern and Middle Africa, 3%

Northern Africa, 3%

Central America, 2%

Oceania and other areas, 1%

Per cent

Source: United Nations, *World Population Prospects: The 2008 Revision* (2009a).

In the majority of countries there are more women than men, but in the most populous countries in Asia there are many more men than women

As can be seen from figure 1.6, in the significant majority of countries there are more women than men. Out of 190 countries or areas presented here,

the ratio in 117 countries was between 85 and 99 men per 100 women. In 23 countries the distribution of women and men was more or less equal. In 51 countries, however, there were more men than women, with a ratio between 101 and 111 men per 100 women.

Of the most populous countries, China (with a ratio of 108 men per 100 women), India (107), Pakistan (106) and, to a lesser extent, Bangladesh (102) are at the very top of the list of countries where the "shortage" of women might have adverse consequences in the shaping of marriages

Figure 1.4

World population 2010: Surplus of women and men by age

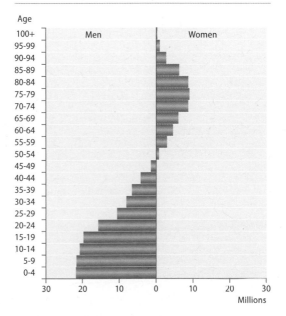

Age

Men   Women

Millions

Source: United Nations, *World Population Prospects: The 2008 Revision* (2009a).

Figure 1.5

Surplus/shortage of men per 100 women by region, 2010

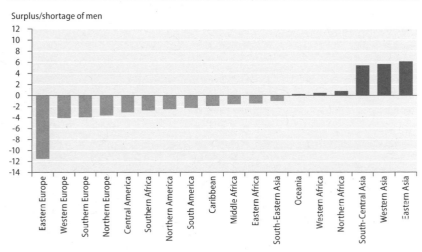

Surplus/shortage of men

Source: United Nations, *World Population Prospects: The 2008 Revision* (2009a).

Figure 1.6

Number of men per 100 women, countries or areas with total population over 100,000, 2010 (● *women*, ● *men*)

	Sex ratio	Surplus of women or men per 100 men or women		Sex ratio	Surplus of women or men per 100 men or women
Ukraine	86		Azerbaijan	96	
Latvia	86		Jamaica	96	
Estonia	86		Saint Lucia	96	
Russian Federation	86		Lebanon	96	
Netherlands Antilles	86		Channel Islands	96	
Belarus	87		Swaziland	96	
Armenia	87		Belgium	96	
Lithuania	88		Cambodia	96	
Martinique	88		Finland	96	
Georgia	89		Argentina	96	
El Salvador	89		Burundi	96	
Lesotho	90		Germany	96	
United States Virgin Islands	90		United Kingdom	96	
China, Hong Kong SAR	90		Morocco	96	
Hungary	90		Czech Republic	97	
Republic of Moldova	90		Central African Republic	97	
Kazakhstan	91		Thailand	97	
China, Macao SAR	91		Montenegro	97	
Cape Verde	92		Sri Lanka	97	
Guadeloupe	92		Colombia	97	
Puerto Rico	92		Eritrea	97	
Aruba	92		Brazil	97	
Bosnia and Herzegovina	93		Mexico	97	
Croatia	93		Turkmenistan	97	
Poland	93		Angola	97	
Uruguay	93		South Africa	97	
Bulgaria	93		Albania	97	
Zimbabwe	94		Namibia	97	
Portugal	94		Spain	97	
Rwanda	94		Kyrgyzstan	97	
Slovakia	94		Tajikistan	97	
Barbados	94		United States of America	97	
Trinidad and Tobago	94		Mali	98	
Romania	95		Dem. People's Rep. of Korea	98	
France	95		Haiti	98	
Italy	95		New Zealand	98	
Japan	95		Viet Nam	98	
Mozambique	95		Mongolia	98	
Cyprus	95		Chile	98	
Sierra Leone	95		Serbia	98	
Guatemala	95		Nicaragua	98	
Réunion	95		Togo	98	
Austria	95		Republic of Korea	98	
Switzerland	95		Mauritius	98	
Myanmar	95		Sao Tome and Principe	98	
Slovenia	96		Canada	98	
Bahamas	96		Guinea-Bissau	98	

	Sex ratio	Surplus of women or men per 100 men or women
Senegal	98	● ●
Dem. Republic of the Congo	98	● ●
Greece	98	● ●
Denmark	98	● ●
Netherlands	98	● ●
Gambia	98	● ●
Somalia	98	● ●
Equatorial Guinea	98	● ●
Israel	98	● ●
Luxembourg	99	●
Sweden	99	●
Nepal	99	●
Uzbekistan	99	●
Liberia	99	●
Chad	99	●
Australia	99	●
Malawi	99	●
Norway	99	●
Ethiopia	99	●
Madagascar	99	●
Malta	99	●
Bolivia (Plurinational State of)	99	●
United Republic of Tanzania	100	
French Guiana	100	
Zambia	100	
Indonesia	100	
Lao People's Dem. Republic	100	
Congo	100	
The former Yugoslav Republic of Macedonia	100	
Burkina Faso	100	
Gabon	100	
Honduras	100	
Djibouti	100	
Kenya	100	
Cameroon	100	
Botswana	100	
Mayotte	100	
Grenada	100	
Ecuador	100	
Ireland	100	
Niger	100	
Uganda	100	
Suriname	100	
Peru	100	
New Caledonia	100	
Cuba	100	
Nigeria	101	●
Comoros	101	●

	Sex ratio	Surplus of women or men per 100 men or women
Venezuela (Bolivarian Rep. of)	101	●
Turkey	101	●
Dominican Republic	101	●
Singapore	101	●
Tunisia	101	●
Egypt	101	●
Sudan	101	●
Philippines	101	●
Belize	102	● ●
Panama	102	● ●
Paraguay	102	● ●
Maldives	102	● ●
Algeria	102	● ●
Saint Vincent and the Grenadines	102	● ●
Syrian Arab Republic	102	● ●
Benin	102	● ●
Guinea	102	● ●
Yemen	102	● ●
Iraq	102	● ●
Bangladesh	102	● ●
Tonga	103	● ● ●
Ghana	103	● ● ●
Mauritania	103	● ● ●
Fiji	103	● ● ●
Malaysia	103	● ● ●
Costa Rica	103	● ● ●
Papua New Guinea	103	● ● ●
Iran (Islamic Republic of)	103	● ● ●
Guam	103	● ● ●
Côte d'Ivoire	104	● ● ● ●
Occupied Palestinian Territory	104	● ● ● ●
Timor-Leste	104	● ● ● ●
Vanuatu	104	● ● ● ●
Micronesia (Fed. States of)	104	● ● ● ●
French Polynesia	104	● ● ● ●
Jordan	105	● ● ● ● ●
Guyana	106	● ● ● ● ●
Iceland	106	● ● ● ● ●
Pakistan	106	● ● ● ● ●
Brunei Darussalam	106	● ● ● ● ●
India	107	● ● ● ● ● ●
Libyan Arab Jamahiriya	107	● ● ● ● ● ●
Solomon Islands	107	● ● ● ● ● ●
Afghanistan	107	● ● ● ● ● ●
China	108	● ● ● ● ● ● ●
Samoa	108	● ● ● ● ● ● ●
Bhutan	111	● ● ● ● ● ● ● ● ●
Western Sahara	112	● ● ● ● ● ● ● ● ● ●

Source: United Nations, *World Population Prospects: The 2008 Revision* (2009a).
Note: The figure excludes Bahrain, Kuwait, Oman, Qatar, Saudi Arabia and the United Arab Emirates where the sex ratio exceeds 121.

Figure 1.7
Surplus of women and men by age, China, 2000 and the Russian Federation, 2006

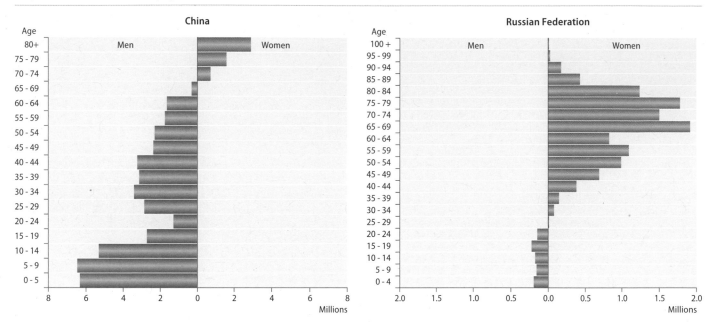

Source: United Nations, *Demographic Yearbook 2006* (2008).   Note: Scales differ for the two graphs.

and families in the medium and long term. And the fact that there is such an imbalance in those populous countries affects the overall distribution at the world level as well.

Such a disparity in the balance of women and men in some countries might be a consequence of a preference for having sons rather than daughters, and early detection of the sex of the foetus may lead to increased abortions of female foetuses. For example, an in-depth analysis of a survey of 1.1 million households in India in 1998 found that prenatal sex determination followed by selective abortion of female foetuses is the most plausible explanation for the high sex ratio at birth in that country.[2] The adjusted sex ratio for the second birth when the preceding child was a girl was 132 boys per 100 girls.[3]

The adverse consequences of sex disparity in young ages are expected to be long term and difficult to remedy – lack of women of spousal age negatively affects the formation of families. For example, figure 1.7 displays the number of women and men exceeding the 50:50 ratio by age in China at the latest population census, which took place in 2000, as well as the same statistics for the Russian Federation in 2006.

The figure points to the fact that in 2000 the total number of excess boys and young men up to 20 years of age in China was almost 21 million. As time goes by, this disparity will be reflected in the older ages as well; that will make matching women and men as spouses as well as starting families much more difficult. It might also eventually have adverse consequences on the fertility of the population as a whole, and might result in policy incentives for women of child-bearing age to have more children in order to maintain the necessary levels of population. On the other hand, there will be a multitude of single-person male households with specific needs – at the same time representing a highly mobile population unattached to families.

Sex ratio at birth

Sex ratio at birth is usually expressed as the number of male newborns per 100 female newborns. The most recent estimates for 2005–2010 (United Nations 2009a) show that, globally, the sex ratio is 107 baby boys per 100 baby girls. Regional differences, however, are evident. In Africa the sex ratio is 103 while in Asia it increases to 109 (and in Eastern Asia to 117). In Europe the sex ratio is 106 male newborns per 100 female newborns, while in Latin America and the Caribbean it is 105 – the same as in Northern America and Oceania.

2 Jha and others, 2006.
3 *Ibid.*

A very different set of circumstances is faced by countries or areas where there is a substantial surplus of women. For example, in 2006 there were almost 10.5 million more women than men in the Russian Federation. The gender spiral (figure 1.7) clearly illustrates that there are more boys and men in the early ages – up to 24 years – but that starting at age of 30 and in the older age categories the number of women is significantly higher than the number of men. One of the factors for the discrepancy in older years is the relatively low life expectancy for men at 60.4 years of age in 2006 compared to that for women at 73.2 years.[4] This difference has an impact on a range of services that need to be provided in terms of public health, social protection and so forth. It also fosters increased mobility of the female population.

Are there significant differences in sex ratios in urban and rural areas? In the case of China, while the general pattern is similar – more boys and men – there are still differences in specific age groups (figure 1.8). At younger ages, up to 10 years, the ratio is very high overall (around 120 boys per 100 girls) and is still higher in rural than in urban areas (122:117). At other ages, with the exception of the population in the 30–45 age group, the sex ratio is also higher in rural than urban areas (thus exacerbating the shortage of women in these areas). It is only at older ages that the sex ratio in urban areas exceeds the sex ratio in rural areas.

Statistics on the differences in sex ratios for urban and rural areas of the Russian Federation indicate that there are proportionally more women in urban areas, as seen in figure 1.8. Namely, in urban areas the number of men per 100 women is already below 100 in the 25–29 age group, while in rural areas this occurs only in the 50–54 age group, thus indicating a significant surplus of women in urban areas.

In some other parts of the world, statistics register exactly the opposite – the surplus of women is much more likely to be found in rural areas. For example, as seen in figure 1.8, scores of men of working age are enumerated in urban areas in Kenya. In the most productive age group (20–45) there are around 700 000 surplus men in urban areas and the number of men per 100 women exceeds 200 in some age groups, while at the same time and in the same age groups there is a surplus

Figure 1.8

Sex ratio by age, urban and rural areas. China, 2000; Kenya, 2005; and the Russian Federation, 2006

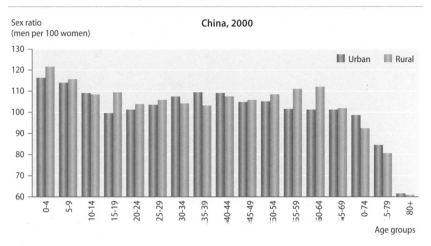

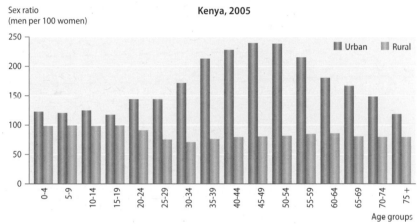

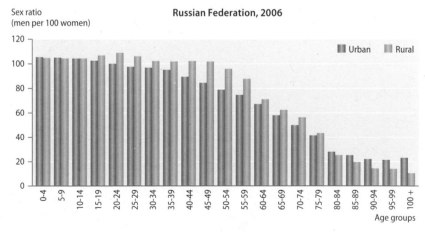

Source: United Nations, *Demographic Yearbook 2006* (2008).
Note: Data presented on different scales for sex ratio to better highlight urban/rural differences.

of approximately 1 million women in rural areas.[5] This distribution has an adverse effect in regard to the living conditions of women stranded in rural

4 United Nations, 2008.

5 *Ibid.*

Figure 1.9
World total fertility rate (*births per woman*), **1950 to 2010**

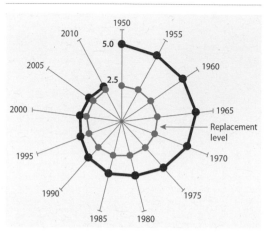

Source: United Nations,
*World Population Prospects: The
2008 Revision* (2009a).

areas where production is almost exclusively linked to agriculture, infrastructure is scarce, and education and basic public health services are lacking.

It should be emphasized that the definitions of urban and rural areas vary significantly among countries. Even within a single country there are often significant differences, and not all rural areas are alike. Presenting statistics in such broad categories shows general patterns; however, to assess the disparities in the distribution of women and men and hence to be able to fine-tune regional and local population policies, more specific data would be needed.

3. Fertility

Fertility, understood in terms of childbearing, is dependant of many factual and societal circum-

stances, such as cultural traditions, education and the overall level of development of the society and community. Two key proximate determinants of fertility are also the age of entry into union and the availability of contraception. The most commonly used measure of fertility is the total fertility rate (TFR) – the number of children that a woman would have over her childbearing years if, at each age, she experienced the age-specific fertility rate. The age-specific rate, in turn, is the number of births to women of a given age group per 1,000 women in that age group.

The total fertility rate in the world was halved between 1950 and 2010

In the period 1950–2010 the TFR in the world was halved from around 5 children to around 2.5 (figure 1.9). The replacement level is the number of children needed per woman for a population to replace itself. It is generally taken to be a TFR between 2.10 and 2.33 children per woman, depending on the impact of infant and child mortality – the lower the levels of these two phenomena, the lower the value of the replacement level. Populations below the replacement level ultimately confront the danger of extinction; populations with much higher TFR than the replacement level face the challenges of successfully sustaining the growing number of their members.

Although this general trend of women having fewer children is evident in all regions of the world, it has not had the same intensity everywhere. In some regions the TFR declined drastically – for example, in Central America the 1950 TFR was around 6.7 children while 60 years later it is 2.4 children, just above the replacement level (figure 1.10). Similarly, in Eastern Asia the 1950 TFR was around 6 children per woman but the 2010 level is well below the replacement line at 1.7 – a drop of more than 4 children per woman. Northern Africa is another example of this trend, with the 1950 TFR of 6.8 children going down to 2.8 children in 2010 – again a decrease of almost 4 children per woman.

Figure 1.10 provides an overview of the 2010 TFR and the decline compared to 1950. In some cases the decline was relatively small in absolute terms, as is the case in all European regions, but it has to be emphasized that the rates were already quite low at the beginning of this period at between 2.4 and 2.8 children per woman. On the other hand, in some regions of Africa, such as Middle, Eastern and Western Africa, the decline was also relatively

Figure 1.10
Total fertility rate by region, 1950 and 2010

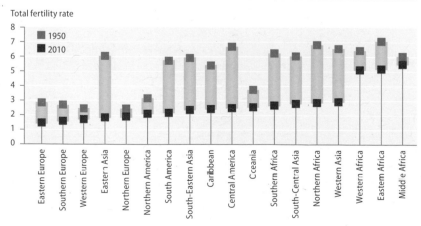

Source: United Nations, *World Population Prospects: The 2008 Revision* (2009a).

modest but the TFR remains quite high at just over 5 children per woman.

This trend of declining fertility, although universal, was not evenly distributed and has resulted in countries finding themselves in very different situations after the first decade of the twenty-first century, as shown in table 1.1.

The group of countries or areas where the fertility rate is significantly lower than the reproduction level

has China, Macao SAR and China, Hong Kong SAR at the top with around one child per woman. The total number of countries or areas in this group is 29 (included are only countries or areas with over 100,000 inhabitants). Out of these, 24 are located in Europe. In addition, most more developed Asian countries or areas are also found here, including Japan, the Republic of Korea and Singapore.

The second group consists of 55 countries or areas, with Cuba at the top with a fertility rate

Table 1.1
Countries or areas by level of total fertility rate, 2010

Countries/areas with low fertility TFR < 1.5 29 countries	Countries/areas with fertility under replacement level TFR 1.6 – 2.1 55 countries		Countries/areas with fertility above replacement level TFR 2.1 – 5 91 countries		Countries/areas with high fertility TFR > 5 21 countries
Austria	Albania	Maldives	Algeria	Lesotho	Afghanistan
Belarus	Armenia	Martinique	Argentina	Liberia	Angola
Bosnia and	Aruba	Mauritius	Azerbaijan	Libyan Arab Jamahiriya	Benin
Herzegovina	Australia	Mexico	Bahrain	Madagascar	Burkina Faso
Bulgaria	Bahamas	Mongolia	Bangladesh	Malaysia	Chad
Channel Islands	Barbados	Montenegro	Belize	Mauritania	Democratic Republic
China, Hong Kong	Belgium	Netherlands	Bhutan	Mayotte	of the Congo
SAR	Brazil	Netherlands Antilles	Bolivia (Plurinational State of)	Micronesia (Fed. States of)	Equatorial Guinea
China, Macao SAR	Brunei Darussalam	New Caledonia	Botswana	Morocco	Ethiopia
Croatia	Canada	New Zealand	Burundi	Mozambique	Guinea
Czech Republic	Chile	Norway	Cambodia	Myanmar	Guinea-Bissau
Germany	China	Puerto Rico	Cameroon	Namibia	Malawi
Greece	Costa Rica	Republic of Moldova	Cape Verde	Nepal	Mali
Hungary	Cuba	Saint Lucia	Central African Republic	Nicaragua	Niger
Italy	Cyprus	Saint Vincent and the	Colombia	Occupied Palestinian Territory	Nigeria
Japan	Democratic People's	Grenadines	Comoros	Oman	Rwanda
Latvia	Republic of Korea	Serbia	Congo	Pakistan	Sierra Leone
Lithuania	Denmark	Sweden	Côte D'Ivoire	Panama	Somalia
Malta	Estonia	Thailand	Djibouti	Papua New Guinea	Timor-Leste
Poland	Finland	Trinidad and Tobago	Dominican Republic	Paraguay	Uganda
Portugal	France	Tunisia	Ecuador	Peru	United Republic
Republic of Korea	Georgia	Turkey	Egypt	Philippines	of Tanzania
Romania	Guadeloupe	United Arab Emirates	El Salvador	Qatar	Zambia
Russian Federation	Iceland	United Kingdom	Eritrea	Réunion	
Singapore	Indonesia	Uruguay	Fiji	Samoa	
Slovakia	Iran (Islamic	United States Virgin	French Guiana	Sao Tome and Principe	
Slovenia	Republic of)	Islands	French Polynesia	Saudi Arabia	
Spain	Ireland	United States	Gabon	Senegal	
Switzerland	Lebanon	of America	Gambia	Solomon Islands	
The former Yugoslav	Luxembourg	Viet Nam	Ghana	South Africa	
Republic of			Grenada	Sri Lanka	
Macedonia			Guam	Sudan	
Ukraine			Guatemala	Suriname	
			Guyana	Swaziland	
			Haiti	Syrian Arab Republic	
			Honduras	Tajikistan	
			India	Togo	
			Iraq	Tonga	
			Israel	Turkmenistan	
			Jamaica	Uzbekistan	
			Jordan	Vanuatu	
			Kazakhstan	Venezuela (Bolivarian	
			Kenya	Republic of)	
			Kuwait	Western Sahara	
			Kyrgyzstan	Yemen	
			Lao People's Dem. Republic	Zimbabwe	

Source: United Nations, *World Population Prospects: The 2008 Revision* (2009a)

Figure 1.11
Urban and rural fertility rates, selected countries and years

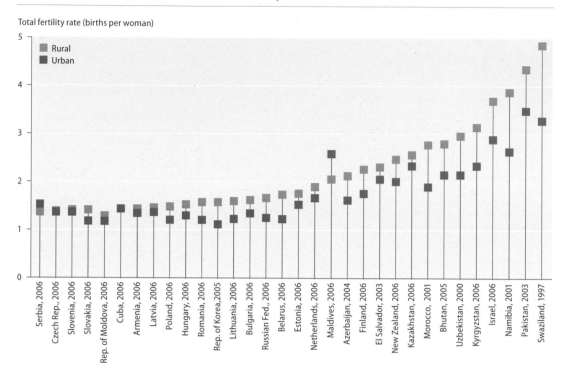

Total fertility rate (births per woman)

Source: United Nations,
Demographic Yearbook 2006 (2008).

of 1.51 children per woman. The fertility rate in this group is also below the replacement level, but not drastically so, and ranges between 1.51 to 2.1 children per woman. It is worth noting that all European countries that did not fall in the first group – low fertility – are to be found in this second group, thus pointing to the fact that there is currently no country in Europe able to ensure population replacement levels.

The third group, with a fertility level ranging from 2.1 to 5 children per woman, is made up of 91, mostly developing, countries or areas around the world, while the fourth group, with high fertility (over 5 children per woman), consists of 21 countries or areas. The fact that 19 of these 21 countries are in Africa highlights the relationship between women's access to reproductive health and other services that affect the number of births and fertility levels, especially in rural areas.

Indeed, there are generally differences in the level of fertility rates in urban compared to rural areas of a country, as illustrated by figure 1.11. This is mainly due to the relatively easy access of women in more modern urban settings to a range of services, such as education, family planning and health care, as well as their exposure to a different set of cultural and societal values. In Namibia and

Swaziland, for example, a woman in a rural area would give birth to one more child than a woman in an urban setting.

4. Ageing

People are living longer – particularly women, who tend to outlive men on average

One phenomenon that displays a constant rate of increase is the proportion of the older population. The world's population age distribution is undergoing a significant shift. Mortality is falling and people are expected to live longer than at any time in recorded history. This phenomenon particularly affects women as they tend, on average, to outlive men.

The transformation of societies from ones with a preponderance of young people towards ones where older people are becoming more numerous poses significant challenges, primarily in ensuring the right to adequate living conditions throughout the extended lifespan.

The total number of older people (aged 60 and above) went from 204 million in 1950 to approximately 760 million in 2010, an almost four-fold increase. The total number of older men increased slightly faster than the total number of women of the same age – from 92 million to 350 million for men, an increase of 3.8 times, compared to 113 million to 413 million for women, a 3.7 times increase. However, the gap between women and men, in absolute numbers, actually grew over this period (figure 1.12).

While this general trend of rising numbers of older women and men is more or less apparent in all regions, the pace of the increase varies significantly. At the world level, the share of older people in the total population grew from 8 per cent in 1950 to around 11 per cent in 2010 (figure 1.13). In several regions, however, a slight decline in the share of older population can be noticed, as in Western and Eastern Africa (by 0.3 and 0.1 percentage points, respectively) and Western Asia (by 0.1 percentage point). Some of this decline can be attributed to the influx of a younger population from abroad, such as, for example, in Western Asia, where in recent decades an increase in the number of immigrants of younger age has had an impact on the age distribution of the population.

In several regions – such as in South-Central and South-Eastern Asia, Southern and Northern Africa and Central America – the increase of the share of older population was not significant and ranged from 1–3 percentage points. The increase was higher, from 3–5 percentage points, in Eastern Europe, the Caribbean, Oceania and Northern and South America. By far the highest increase was registered in Eastern Asia (around 7 percentage points) and Northern and Western Europe (both 8 percentage points). In Southern Europe the share of older population in 1950 was around 12 per cent, and 60 years later it reached 24 per cent (an increase of 12 percentage points, the highest among all the major regions), indicating that in that region almost every fourth person is 60 years of age or older.

As women live longer than men, it is to be expected that the share of women aged 60 and above would be higher than the share of men. Indeed, women make up around 55 per cent of the total older population in the world. Yet, this percentage varies quite significantly from region to region (see figure 1.14). Although in all the regions the share of women exceeds 50 per cent, in Eastern Europe it is much higher, at 63 per cent. Southern Africa also has a high percentage of women aged 60 and above compared to men of the same age, around 59 per cent.

Population ageing usually refers to the combination of lower fertility and extended life expect-

Figure 1.12

Total number of women and men age 60 and over in the world, 1950 to 2010

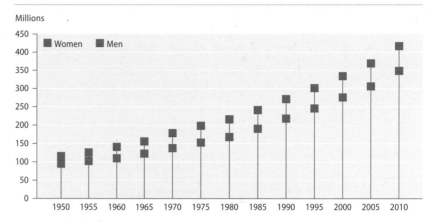

Source: United Nations, *World Population Prospects: The 2008 Revision* (2009a)

ancy. Fertility levels were elaborated on in the previous section; a short discussion on life expectancy follows below, while the detailed presentation and analysis of this issue is presented in Chapter 2 – Health.

Figure 1.13

Share of population age 60 and over in the total population by region, 1950 and 2010

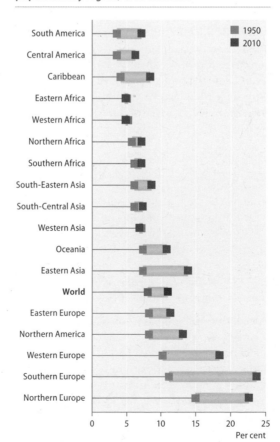

Source: United Nations, *World Population Prospects: The 2008 Revision* (2009a).

Figure 1.14

Share of women and men in the total population age 60 and above, world and regions, 2010

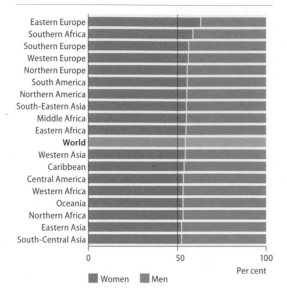

In the period 1950–2005, overall life expectancy rose from 47 years to 69 years, which indicates that the average lifespan increased around one third. This increase was almost identical for women and men, although the difference in the actual life span remains steady in favour of women (see figure 1.15). In the 1950s women were expected to live to around 48 years of age on average, compared to 45 years for men. In 2010 women's life expectancy is expected to average 71 years, while men's is expected to be around 67. In terms of the gap between women and men, the difference

Figure 1.15

Life expectancy, women and men, 1950 to 2015

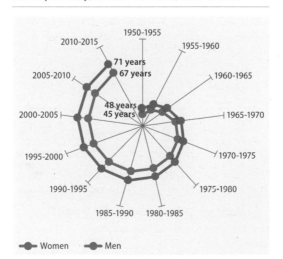

Source: United Nations,
*World Population Prospects: The
2008 Revision* (2009a).

in life expectancy can thus be seen to be growing, albeit at a very slow pace – from around three years in the 1950s to around four years in 2010.

The data indicate that there is a considerable gap in the expected life span of women and men in different regions of the world. While a woman in Middle Africa born in the period 2010–2015 is expected to live, on average, 51 years, her contemporary in Australia/New Zealand is estimated to live over 84 years on average, just slightly more than in Western, Southern and Northern Europe and in Northern America. As for men, the lowest life expectancy is estimated for men in Middle Africa, around 48 years of age, with the longest time span expected to occur in the same regions as for women, albeit lower at from 77 to 80 years of age.

Overall, life expectancy has the lowest value for both women and men in all regions of Africa, with the exception of Northern Africa. South-Central Asia is also facing lower life expectancy. All other regions of the world (including Northern Africa) are expected to witness an average life expectancy of over 70 years of age for women and over 67 for men.

5. International migration

**The number of international migrants
has been steadily increasing,
and more women are migrating**

Population movements are as old as humankind itself. These movements are the result of a whole set of different socio-economic, political and demographic circumstances. Migration of people across borders is one of the phenomena most difficult to measure in real time – without even attempting to include illegal border crossings. Consequently, one of the usually applied methods in calculating international migration is quantifying the foreign-born population in a given country, thus generating statistics on the stock of international migrants.

The total number of international migrants has been steadily increasing.[6] In 2010 it is expected to reach over 213 million people, up from around 155 million in 1990, an increase of 37 per cent (see figure 1.16).

---

6 The data for this part of the chapter are derived from United Nations, 2009b.

The composition of the migrant stock has changed over time. As societies have modernized and as education and mobility as well as employment opportunities have become more accessible to women, international migration has become much more balanced by sex. Currently, it is estimated that 105 million women make up 49 per cent of international migrant stock in general, although, as with other phenomena, regional differences exist (figure 1.17).

The participation of women in international migration was lowest in Western Asia, at around 39 per cent, followed by Southern and Northern Africa (both 43 per cent) and Southern Asia (45 per cent). At the other extreme is Eastern Europe, where the share of women international migrants was around 57 per cent, followed by Central and Eastern Asia (both 55 per cent) and Northern Europe (53 per cent).

A closer look at the trends in the participation of women in international migration reveals further differences among the regions. For example, the share of female migrants in Eastern Asia increased from 49 per cent in 1990 to 55 per cent in 2010. Similarly, in Southern Africa the share of women increased from 39 per cent in 1990 to 43 per cent in 2010. In all other regions, however, the changes in women's share were less noticeable and generally in the range of a 1 or 2 percentage points increase or decrease.

Some 75 per cent of all international migrants are located in 30 countries in the world, which identify them as the preferred destinations. The proportion of women immigrants in these countries is shown in figure 1.18.

The share of women migrants in the oil-wealthy Gulf States, such as Kuwait, Saudi Arabia and United Arab Emirates, is less than one third of the total number of migrants as the bulk of the foreign-born population are men of working age. In the United States of America the proportion of female and male migrants is almost identical, while in other more developed countries – such as Australia, Canada, France, Italy, Japan, Netherlands and the United Kingdom – women's share exceeds 50 per cent. This is probably due to settlement migration through family reunification and also the fact that migrant women have more longevity than men and increasingly migrate by themselves.

The high proportion of female migrants in Kazakhstan, the Russian Federation and Ukraine is a consequence of the dissolution of the former Soviet

Figure 1.16
International migrants by sex, the world, 1990 to 2010

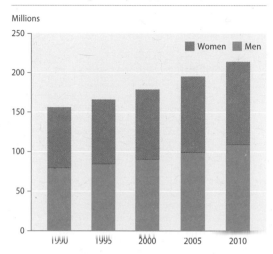

Source: United Nations, *Trends in International Migrant Stock: The 2008 Revision* (2009b)

Union, and some of these women may have not moved at all but were enumerated differently due to their place of birth.

B. Families

1. Marriages and unions

Marriage, a social construct shared by all societies and people, is the act, ceremony or process that unites two people in a relationship that, in almost all cultures, is consensual and contractual and recognized as such by law. Marriage and union are

Figure 1.17
Share of women and men in total international migrant stock by region, 2010

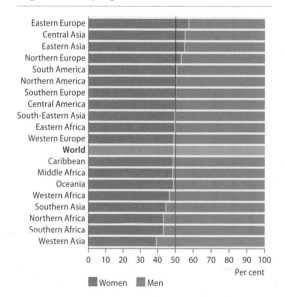

Source: United Nations, *Trends in International Migrant Stock: The 2008 Revision* (2009b).

Figure 1.18

Share of women in total immigrant stock, 30 top destination countries or areas, 2010

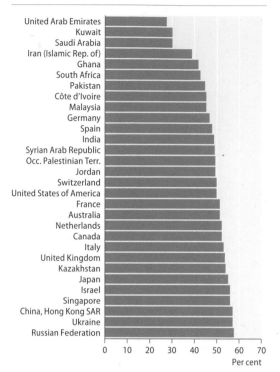

Source: United Nations, *Trends in International Migrant Stock: The 2008 Revision* (2009b).

in most cases a first step in establishing a family, often the essential unit in the composition and functioning of a society.

Young people are marrying at older ages than their parents did

---

Women and men do not enter marriage at the same age. In fact, throughout history, the average

Figure 1.19

Singulate mean age at marriage for women and men and the difference in years, countries where women marry on average at age 20 or earlier, 2002–2006 (*latest available*)

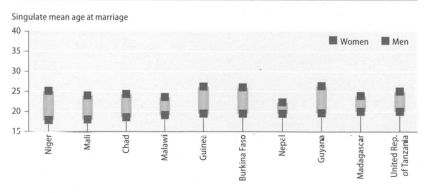

Source: United Nations, *World Marriage Data 2008* (accessed in December 2009).

age at marriage for women has always been lower, sometimes considerably so, than the average age for men. This is still apparent at the beginning of the twenty-first century, although the average age of women at first marriage is now much higher, with young people worldwide marrying at older ages than their parents did.

Substantially smaller percentages of women today marry before age 20 than in previous generations,[7] and median age at marriage is rising in nearly all regions. In developed countries, the Near East, East Asia and a few Latin American countries, women tend to marry in their early to mid-20s. Two thirds or more of young women in these regions do not marry until after age 20. In contrast, however, as many as two thirds of young women in some countries of sub-Saharan Africa marry before age 20. In several of these countries high proportions of women marry at very young ages (15 or less). In almost all developing countries women in rural areas are more likely than women in cities to marry before age 20.[8]

In addition, in a number of countries marriage has been replaced by cohabitation, which may or may not be formalized by the state. Therefore, statistics displaying singulate mean age at marriage[9] for any given year may not reflect accurately the fact of women and men living together in unions. Still, these statistics provide an overview of the marriage patterns in contemporary times.

Figure 1.19 displays statistics on the singulate age at marriage for women and men in countries where women, on average, marry at age 20 or earlier and for which these data are available. The lowest average age at first marriage for women, between 17 and 18 years, is in Niger and Mali, followed by several other countries in Africa (Chad, Malawi, Guinea, Burkina Faso, Madagascar and United Republic of Tanzania). In two countries outside of Africa, Guyana and Nepal, women marry on average when they are between 19 and 20 years old. When it comes to the singulate mean age at marriage for men in these countries, it can be seen that the differences are significant, with the exception of Nepal; for example, in Burkina Faso, Chad, Guinea,

7 McCauley and Salter, 1995.

8 Ibid.

9 Singulate mean age at marriage compares the age-specific proportion of those who are single with those who are married or widowed to calculate the average age at which the transition was made between the two states.

Guyana, Mali and Niger the difference in age at marriage between women and men is 6–7 years.

Although it may be nominally consensual, the fact that the institution of marriage is so strongly linked to tradition and the "pride" of both the bride's and groom's families often places the future bride under pressure to comply with choices that are not necessarily hers. As a UNICEF report outlines, many girls, and a smaller number of boys, enter marriage without any chance of exercising their right to choose.[10] This is more often the case with younger and less educated women. Entering into marriage at a young age almost certainly removes the girl from the educational process since assuming a wife's responsibilities usually leaves no room for schooling. This, in turn, results in less knowledge about concepts such as contraception and family planning. Early childbearing is identified with higher health risks for both mother and child.[11] Another serious concern relates to the fact that adolescent brides are an easy target for abusive partners.

Yet, the practice of girls marrying young persists in almost all societies at the beginning of this century, as figure 1.20 illustrates. It presents the data for all the countries where the percentage of girls aged 15–19 that are married or in consensual unions exceeds 5 per cent. In Niger, the share of married girls aged 15–19 is almost two thirds of the total number of girls. Almost all women there are married by age 24. In Nepal, one third of girls aged 15–19 is married, while in Zambia the same proportion is either married or living in a consensual union. India, Thailand and Uganda report over 20 per cent of all girls aged 15–19 as being married.

In some countries very young girls (15 years of age or below) enter into either marriage or a consensual union

---

Data also show that in Latin America and the Caribbean a significant number of girls aged 15–19 choose to live in consensual unions – for example, almost 24 per cent in Brazil, 20 per cent in Nicaragua, 18 per cent in Dominican Republic, around 17 per cent in Honduras and Panama, 16 per cent in Cuba and about 13 per cent in El Salvador and Peru. The proportion of young girls in these countries entering formal marriage

10 UNICEF, 2001.

11 *Ibid.*

Figure 1.20

Proportion of girls aged 15–19 who are married or in consensual unions[a]

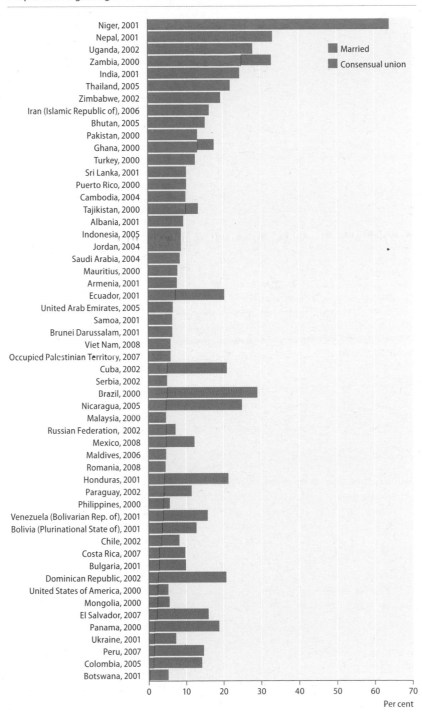

Source: United Nations, *Demographic Yearbook* data collections (2009d).
Note: a Only countries or areas where the proportion exceeds 5 per cent are shown.

ranges from 1–5 per cent, however, indicating clearly the preference of consensual unions over marriages but still entering into these relationships at a very early age.

Collecting statistics on population by age, sex and marital status reveals that in some countries very young girls (15 years of age or below) enter into either marriage or a consensual union, making them prey to all the dangers to their physical and mental health that more often than not accompany such arrangements. While the proportion of married girls aged 15 years or less is usually quite low (below 1 per cent in Brazil, Colombia, Ecuador, India, Mexico, Saudi Arabia, Sri Lanka, Thailand, Turkey and Venezuela (Bolivarian Republic of)), in some countries it ranges from 1–5 per cent (El Salvador, Ghana, Malaysia, Nepal, Nicaragua, Uganda and Zambia), while in Niger the share of such young girls that are married is around 20 per cent[12].

At the other end of the spectrum for average age of women and men entering marriage are countries where this is delayed until age 30 and above. Figure 1.21 presents singulate mean age at marriage for countries or areas where women are at least 30 years of age at that moment. The majority of these countries or areas are in Europe, such as Denmark, Finland, France, Germany, Ireland, Italy, Norway, Slovenia and Sweden. China, Hong Kong SAR and three island countries or areas – French Polynesia, Jamaica and the Netherlands Antilles – are also in that group. In contrast to the countries where women marry early and where the difference in age between women and men at first marriage is significant, in these countries the difference in age is relatively small, between one and three years at most.

2. Family responsibilities

Family life rests solidly on the shoulders of women in all areas of the world. As spouses, parents and caregivers, they take on the primary responsibility for ensuring the proper functioning of families and the provision of everyday care and maintenance. Preparing family meals, maintaining hygiene, caring for other family members and a myriad of other chores related to children consume a good part of the day for women in the world. While men are increasingly getting involved in the daily functioning of families, it is still predominantly women's responsability.

The tool of choice for assessing the amount of time people spend on various activities is the time use survey. Time use surveys occupy a specific place in contemporary national statistical systems as they can provide a wealth of data that can be used to quantify social and economic phenomena. They can help answer many crucial questions related to the differences in the status of women and men, generating much needed gender-disaggregated social statistics. Time use surveys encompass a number of areas including paid and unpaid work, division of labour within families, characteristics of family life, social connectedness, civic participation, standards of living and the differences between women's and men's participation in the labour market, education and cultural activities.[13]

> Time use studies show that women spend more time on housework and community and volunteer work than men do

Figure 1.22 illustrates differences in the use of time for women and men in terms of housework, caring for family members and community/volunteer work in several countries (the complete set of data is displayed in the Statistical Annex, table 4.C). Housework includes preparation of daily meals and washing dishes, tidying and cleaning the house, maintenance of clothing and footwear,

Figure 1.21
Singulate mean age at marriage for women and men and the difference in years, countries or areas where women marry at age 30 or later, 2002–2008 *(latest available)*

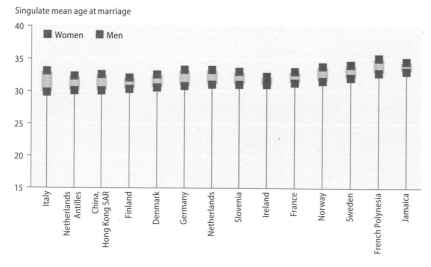

Singulate mean age at marriage

Source: United Nations, *World Marriage Data 2008* (accessed in December 2009).

12 United Nations, *Demographic Yearbook* data collection, 2009d.

13 A more detailed elaboration on differences in the use of time between women and men is presented in Chapter 4 – Work.

childcare, teaching and helping children, purchasing goods and other household management.

The figure clearly points to the fact that, as a rule, the number of hours that women spend on housework and community and volunteer work exceeds those spent by men for the same purposes. The average number of hours per day used for these activities by women ranges from around three (in Denmark) to over six (in Turkey, for example). At the same time, in several countries, men spend less than one hour on these activities – for example, in Cambodia and Pakistan[14].

It is also striking to note that the difference in the time spent by women and men per day in maintaining the household and participating in childcare and other family activities in Armenia, Iraq, Italy, Pakistan and Turkey ranges from four to five hours per day. At the other end of the spectrum, the difference in women's and men's involvement in family life ranges from one to two hours in Denmark and Sweden.

3. Family and work

As demonstrated earlier, the bulk of family care and housework continues to rest on women. However, working men are not spared. Expectations for men of long or uninterrupted hours of economic work limit their ability to be actively involved in family matters. To help both working women and men reconcile work and family responsibilities, some countries and institutions have instituted shorter work hours and family-friendly working arrangements such as flexible hours, part-time work, job-sharing, work from home and telecommuting.

The provision of public childcare is a key factor in whether mothers return to or start work outside the home

---

For mothers with young children, decisions regarding working hours – or whether to work at all – often depend on the availability of affordable and reliable childcare. In the past many workers were able to count on help from non-working relatives for childcare and other domestic tasks. Although such traditional family support still exists to a greater or lesser degree in most countries, it is becoming less available with urbanization and the increased labour force participation

Figure 1.22

Average time used for housework, caring for family members and community/volunteer work, by sex, selected countries

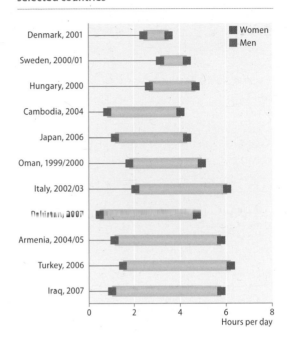

Hours per day

Source: Compiled by the United Nations Statistics Division from national statistical surveys on time use.

of women. Thus, the provision of public childcare has become a key factor for mothers contemplating returning to or starting employment. Statistics on the percentage of children in formal care or pre-school (Table 1.2) show that in countries like Czech Republic, Slovakia, Mexico, Malta, Latvia, Lithuania, Poland, Hungary and Austria this percentage does not exceed 10 per cent, thus indicating that in these countries the overwhelming number of children remain in the care of their homes in early ages, with all the implication that has primarily on mothers. On the other end of the spectrum, in Netherlands, Iceland and especially Denmark, over 50 per cent of children can be found in formal care of pre-school, thus allowing much more room for employment or other activities. Certainly the percentage of children in public childcare directly depends of its availability and affordability; therefore, this has to be taken into consideration when assessing the impact of these services to family life and responsibilities.

There are also benefits to the wide availability of affordable, reliable and high quality care for the elderly, disabled and sick. In the absence of adequate facilities or services for such persons requiring care, the task of caring for them often rests on women in the household, with similar implications in terms of demand on women's time.

---

14 See Chapter 4 – Work.

Table 1.2
Children in formal care or pre-school

Source: OECD, OECD Family
Database PF11.2: Full-time
equivalent participation rates for
children under 3 years old (2009).
For details on individual country
sources, see *http://www.oecd.org/
els/social/family/database.*
Note: Data refer to children less
than 3 years of age. Data for the
Republic of Korea and New Zealand
refer to 2008. Data for Australia
and the United States of America
refer to 2005. Data for Mexico
refer to 2009. The information
for Cyprus relates to the area
under the effective control of the
Government of Cyprus.

	Percentage of children in formal care or pre-school			Percentage of children in formal care or pre-school
Eastern Europe			**Southern Europe** (*continued*)	
Bulgaria	31		Italy	29
Hungary	10		Greece	18
Poland	9		Malta	7
Slovakia	5		**Western Europe**	
Czech Republic	3		Netherlands	54
Northern Europe			Luxembourg	43
Denmark	63		France	43
Iceland	56		Belgium	42
Sweden	45		Germany	14
Norway	42		Austria	10
United Kingdom	40		**Other more developed regions**	
Finland	26		New Zealand	38
Ireland	25		United States of America	31
Estonia	18		Japan	28
Latvia	8		Australia	25
Lithuania	8		Canada	24
Southern Europe			**Less developed regions**	
Portugal	44		Cyprus	20
Spain	34		Republic of Korea	31
Slovenia	33		Mexico	6

Chapter 2
Health

Key findings

- Women live longer than men in all regions.
- Two out of every five deaths of both women and men in Africa are still caused by infectious and parasitic diseases.
- Women are more likely than men to die from cardiovascular diseases, especially in Europe.
- Breast cancer among women and lung cancer among men top the list of new cancer cases globally.
- Women constitute the majority of HIV-positive adults in sub-Saharan Africa, North Africa and the Middle East.
- The vast majority of the over half a million maternal deaths in 2005 occurred in developing countries.
- The proportion of pregnant women receiving prenatal care is on the rise in many regions.
- Despite intensified efforts for reduction, Africa remains the region with the highest child mortality.
- Data reveal no significant disparity in the proportion of underweight girls and boys.

Introduction

Health is a state of complete physical, mental and social well-being and not merely the absence of disease or infirmity.[1] The 1995 Beijing Platform for Action emphasizes that women have the right to the enjoyment of the highest attainable standard of physical and mental health.[2] Equipping women with the necessary knowledge and skills to fulfil their health potential is essential to their own well-being as well as that of their children and families. Tackling gender inequalities in the provision of health services will enable all women and men to enjoy healthier lives and ultimately lead to greater gender equality in all areas.

The Millennium Development Goals (MDGs) were adopted in 2000 by UN Member States. Three of the eight MDGs are directly related to health.[3] The three goals are Goal 4 – reduce child mortality, Goal 5 – improve maternal health and

Goal 6 – combat HIV/AIDS, malaria and other diseases. Other goals and targets are indirectly related to health, for example, Goal 1 – eradicate extreme poverty and hunger. Not all of the 20 MDG indicators related to health include a gender dimension, which limits their usefulness in terms of evaluating and comparing the health of women and men, or girls and boys, over time and across countries.

The health status of women and men is known to be different during their life courses. This can be partly explained by their biological and physical differences. At the same time, gender norms and values in a given culture, coupled with the resulting socio-economic status and behavioural choices of women and men, can also give rise to gender inequalities in health and access to health care. This chapter reviews the statistical evidence on the global health situation of women and men with particular attention to the sex differentials. Among the dimensions explored from a gender perspective are life expectancy, causes of death, health risk factors and morbidity, HIV and AIDS,

---

1 WHO, 1948
2 United Nations, 1995a, para. 89.
3 WHO, 2005.

Table 2.1

Life expectancy at birth by region and sex, 1990–1995, 2000–2005 and 2005–2010

	Women			Men		
	1990–1995	2000–2005	2005–2010	1990–1995	2000–2005	2005–2010
Africa						
Northern Africa	68	72	73	64	68	69
Southern Africa	64	51	52	59	49	51
Eastern, Middle and Western Africa	54	55	57	50	52	54
Asia						
Eastern Asia	74	76	77	69	71	72
South-Eastern Asia	66	70	72	62	66	67
Southern Asia	59	65	67	57	62	64
Central Asia	68	70	70	61	61	62
Western Asia	72	75	76	67	71	72
Latin America and the Caribbean						
Caribbean	75	76	77	69	71	72
Central America	73	76	77	67	70	71
South America	72	75	76	66	69	70
Oceania	68	71	73	64	67	68
More developed regions						
Eastern Europe	75	76	77	66	68	69
Western Europe	80	82	83	74	76	78
Other more developed regions	80	83	83	74	77	78

Source: Computed by the United Nations Statistics Division based on data from United Nations, *World Population Prospects: The 2008 Revision* (2009).
Note: Unweighted averages.

reproductive health and the health of children. It should be noted that sometimes the geographical regions employed in this chapter are different from those used elsewhere in this report due to the groupings used in the sources of data. This is indicated in the text where relevant.

A. Life expectancy at birth

1. Levels of and trends in life expectancy at birth

As discussed briefly in Chapter 1 – Population and families, the world witnessed remarkable declines in mortality in the latter half of the twentieth century. This was due to a number of interrelated factors. Overall improvements in living conditions and nutrition, together with advances in medicine and medical treatments, accounted for the reduction everywhere. In addition, improvements in public health in developing countries meant that fewer people died of infectious and parasitic diseases. Expanded immunization programmes also protected a growing number of children from childhood diseases, contributing to significant reductions in infant and child mortality.[4]

Life expectancy at birth denotes the average number of years a newborn child can expect to live given the current levels of mortality in a country. Derived from age-specific mortality rates, it is an indicator that can provide a picture of the overall health status of populations and also allows for investigating the longevity of women and men separately.

It is well known that women live longer than men. This biological advantage for women begins at birth. However, societal, cultural and economic factors can affect the natural advantage females have over males. Studies show that "the gender gap in mortality is smaller in developing countries… because in many of these countries, women have much lower social status than men" and are exposed to risks associated with childbirth, factors that can equalize life expectancies.[5] In developed countries, the gap in life expectancy at birth may decrease as women adopt unhealthy behaviours similar to those of men,[6] such as smoking and drinking.

Women live longer than men in all regions

Table 2.1 shows the life expectancy at birth for women and men since 1990–1995 to quantify

---

4 United Nations, 2001.

5 Yin, 2007.

6 Ibid.

recent sex differentials in health. As seen in the table, women's life expectancy at birth exceeded men's in all regions and time periods observed. In 2005–2010, life expectancy at birth was highest in the more developed regions (excluding Eastern Europe) at around 83 years for women and 78 years for men. Women's life expectancy in three regions/sub-regions – Latin America and the Caribbean, Eastern Asia and Western Asia – ranged between 76 and 77 years, while men's was between 70 and 72 years. Life expectancy at birth was the lowest in Southern Africa (52 years for women and 51 years for men) and the rest of sub-Saharan Africa (57 and 54 years, respectively).

Since 1990–1995, life expectancy at birth has increased for both women and men worldwide, with relatively large gains in Northern Africa, South-Eastern Asia and Southern Asia (see table 2.1). The exception to this trend is Southern Africa, which experienced marked decreases in life expectancy during the 1990s due to the spread of the HIV/AIDS epidemic and resulting increases in mortality (see box 2.1). More recently, however, there have been some improvements in life expectancy for women and men in the region due to the development and enhanced availability of medical treatments for HIV, which have led to lower mortality. Hence, life expectancy at birth

Box 2.1 .

Life expectancy dropped sharply in Southern Africa during the 1990s

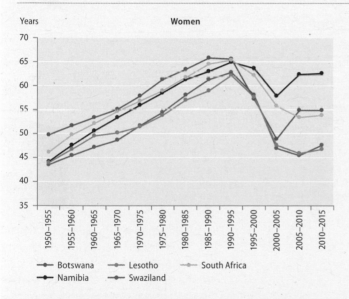
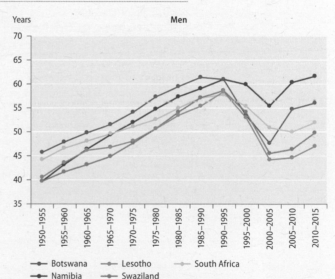

Source: United Nations, *World Population Prospects: The 2008 Revision* (2009).

HIV/AIDS, which emerged in the 1980s, had a devastating impact in various regions during the 1990s. This was particularly striking in Southern Africa, resulting in sharp drops in life expectancy in all five countries in the region. By the early 1990s, life expectancy at birth in these countries had reached over 60 years for women and 55 years for men. Within a decade, however, the figure for women declined approximately 7 years in Namibia, 10 years in South Africa and more than 15 years in Botswana, Lesotho and Swaziland.

Men's expectation of life also severely suffered during the same period in these countries. The most affected were men in Lesotho, where the life expectancy dropped by about 14 years in the period 1990–1995 to 2000–2005, and approximately the same declines took place in Botswana and Swaziland. Life expectancy for men in South Africa in the same period fell 7 years and in Namibia around 5 years.

By the late 2000s, the life expectancy at birth for men started showing signs of recovery in all five countries. For women, however, only Botswana and Namibia recorded an increase, and a declining trend continued in Lesotho, South Africa and Swaziland. Consequently, the life expectancy at birth for women in Lesotho and Swaziland fell almost to the level it had been in the late 1950s.

for women in the Southern Africa region, which dropped from 64 to 51 years between1990–1995 and 2000–2005, slightly recovered to 52 years by 2005–2010. The trend was the same for men in the region: the figure declined from 59 to 49 years between 1990–1995 and 2000–2005, followed by a modest rise to 51 years in 2005–2010.

Following the collapse of communist regimes, the region of Eastern Europe and the former USSR saw dramatic decreases in longevity during the late 1980s and early 1990s.[7] Between the 1990–1995 and 2005–2010 periods, however, there was a noticeable recovery. The increase was more pronounced for men and ranged from one to five years for most countries. Research shows that this was mainly due to reductions in cardiovascular mortality.[8]

As shown in table 2.1, there were varying trends in sex differences in life expectancy at birth at the sub-regional level. Between 1990–1995 and 2005–2010, half of the sub-regions listed narrowed the gender gaps in life expectancy at birth (Southern Africa, rest of sub-Saharan Africa, Western Asia, Eastern Asia, Caribbean, Eastern Europe, Western Europe and Other more developed regions). In these regions, larger increases in life expectancy for men than women contributed to the convergence except for Southern Africa. In contrast, in two regions (Southern Asia and Oceania) sex differences became wider over time due to larger gains made by women than men. Five regions that showed no change in the difference between female and male life expectancy were South-Eastern Asia, Central America, South America and Central Asia.

2. Sex differentials in life expectancy at the country level

At the level of countries or areas, women in Japan could expect to live longer than women in any other country in the world, namely 86 years (see figure 2.1). The highest life expectancy at birth for men, however, was only 80 years, recorded in Iceland. Both women and men in China, Hong Kong SAR had the second highest life expectancies in the world (85 and 79 years, respectively).

The countries or areas with the lowest life expectancies at birth for both women and men were concentrated in Africa, along with Afghanistan (see figure 2.2). The lowest life expectancies for women and men were in Afghanistan (44 years for both) and in Zimbabwe (44 years for women and 43 years for men). In contrast to the high life expectancy countries or areas, where sex differentials were noticeably large with greater advantage for women, the gaps were relatively small in countries or areas with low life expectancies.

> There are large gaps between women and men in the Russian Federation and the former Soviet republics in terms of their life expectancy

In 2005–2010, the largest sex difference in life expectancy in the world was found in the Russian Federation, where women lived on average 13 years longer than men (73 vs. 60 years). Several other countries of the former USSR also showed differences greater than 10 years between male and female life expectancy at birth (see Statistical Annex). At the opposite end of the spectrum, women in Swaziland lived a little under one year more than men; women and men in Afghanistan lived approximately the same number of years (about 44, as noted above). Other countries with close parity in life expectancy by sex included Botswana, Kenya and Zimbabwe in Africa and Pakistan in Asia.

B. Causes of death

The Tenth revision of the International Classification of Diseases (ICD-10), endorsed in 1990, is internationally recommended for registering

Figure 2.1
World's highest life expectancies at birth by sex, 2005–2010

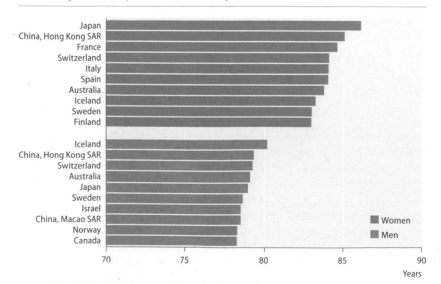

Source: United Nations, *World Population Prospects: The 2008 Revision* (2009).

7 Notzon and others, 1998.
8 Meslé, 2004.

causes of death. Over 100 countries reported detailed information on deaths to the World Health Organization (WHO) in 2007.[9] However, data on causes of death in developing countries are far from complete, and considerable uncertainty exists as to their quality. The following discussion focuses on the differences in the causes of death by sex, primarily using data available from WHO.

1. Deaths grouped by broad causes

In the ICD, deaths are grouped into three overarching categories by cause: (1) deaths from communicable, maternal, perinatal and nutritional conditions; (2) deaths from non-communicable diseases; and (3) deaths from injuries. Using these three broad categories, figure 2.3 depicts the percentage distribution of the causes of death for women and men for 1990, 2000 and 2004 when the most recent data are available. The figure shows that, by 1990, non-communicable diseases were already the most important causes of death for both sexes at the world level. In 2004, they caused 62 per cent of female deaths and 58 per cent of male deaths, while deaths from communicable diseases represented nearly a third of female and male deaths and those from injuries made up 7 per cent of deaths for females and 12 per cent for males. Thus, while the overall patterns of causes of death are similar for women and men, women are more likely than men to die from non-communicable diseases and less likely to die from injuries.

On a global level, women and men exhibited a similar trend in the causes of death between 1990 and 2004: the likelihood of dying from a non-communicable disease slightly increased over time while that from a communicable disease declined. This trend is in line with the so-called "epidemiologic transition theory", which stipulates a transition in which "degenerative and man-made diseases"[10] displace pandemics of infection as the primary causes of morbidity and mortality.[11] While the use of such broad cause groups can help attest to the transition, it is important to recognize that deaths attributable to traditional communicable diseases coexist today with those attributable to non-communicable diseases. Also, with lifestyle or behavioural changes, such as increases in tobacco and alcohol use, the number of deaths caused by non-communicable diseases could

increase further. During the period, the proportion of women and men that died from injuries remained almost unchanged.

2. Leading causes of death

Delving further into specific causes of death and how these are distributed by cause and sex leads to a better understanding of the health situation

---

Figure 2.2

World's lowest life expectancies at birth by sex, 2005–2010

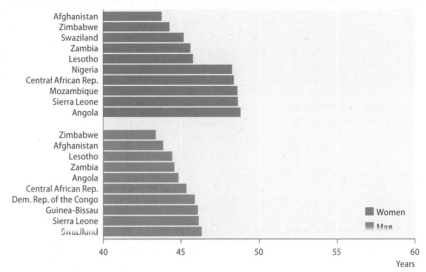

Source: United Nations, *World Population Prospects: The 2008 Revision* (2009).

Figure 2.3

Distribution of deaths by three major categories of cause of death and by sex, world, 1990, 2000 and 2004

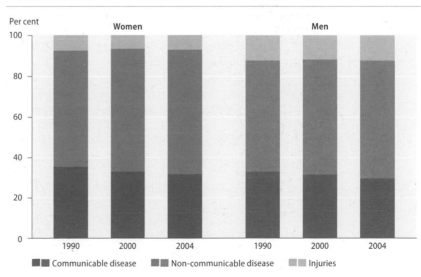

Sources: Murray and Lopez, *The Global Burden of Disease* (1996), annex table 6I; WHO, *Global Burden of Disease: 2004 update* (2008).

---

9 WHO, 2009a.

10 Omran, 1971.

11 Ibid.

Figure 2.4

Distribution of deaths by selected causes and by sex, world and regions, 2004

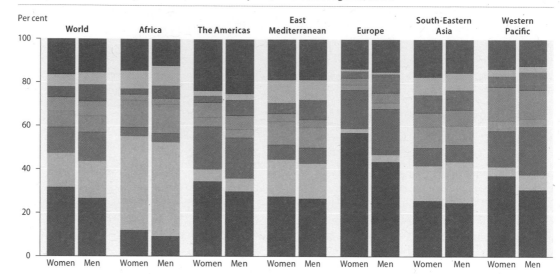

Source: Computed by the United Nations Statistics Division based on data from WHO, *Global Burden of Disease: 2004 Update* (2008).
Note: Unweighted averages. Other causes includes Congenital anomalies, Diabetes mellitus, Digestive diseases, Endocrine disorders, Genitourinary diseases, Intentional injuries, Maternal conditions, Musculoskeletal diseases, Neuropsychiatric conditions, Nutritional deficiencies, Oral conditions, Other neoplasms, Sense organ diseases and Skin diseases.

for women and men. Using lower levels of classification, figure 2.4 highlights the differences in the main causes of death by region[12] and by sex. Globally, cardiovascular disease was the leading cause of death in 2004, causing approximately 32 per cent of female deaths and 27 per cent of male deaths. Infectious and parasitic diseases, including diarrhoea and HIV/AIDS, were the second leading cause of death for both women and men, accounting for about 17 per cent of the total for each. Cancers (or *malignant neoplasms* in medical terminology) ranked third for both sexes in terms of importance, but claimed slightly more deaths among men than women.

The distribution of deaths by cause varies significantly among geographical regions

---

However, there were considerable variations in the causes of death across major geographical regions, which may stem from differences in demographic structure and prevalence of diseases as well as behavioural factors that are specific to a region. Thus, for example, Africa stands out for its disproportionately high incidence of deaths due to infec-

tious and parasitic diseases (43 per cent for both women and men in 2004). In 2007, sub-Saharan Africa saw an estimated 1.5 million AIDS deaths[13] (see also the section of HIV/AIDS in this chapter). The risk of dying from malaria is also high in Africa. In 2008, there were 243 million malaria cases, causing 863,000 deaths globally, with one out of every 10 cases occurring in sub-Saharan Africa.[14]

The second leading cause of death in Africa after infectious and parasitic diseases was respiratory infections (13 per cent for both women and men), followed by cardiovascular diseases (12 per cent for women and 9 per cent for men). Hence, the overall patterns of leading causes of death showed little differences by sex in Africa, though women were somewhat more likely to die from cardiovascular diseases and men were more likely than women to die from unintentional injuries. It should be noted that deaths related to maternal conditions accounted for 5 per cent of the total female deaths in Africa as opposed to only 2 per cent of female deaths worldwide (data not shown).

In Europe, by contrast, the share of deaths caused by infectious and parasitic diseases was almost negligible, and sex differentials in causes of death

---

12 Throughout the causes of death section, the regional grouping is based on the WHO regions, which do not correspond directly to the regional groupings based on the UNSD classification used elsewhere in the chapter.

13 UNAIDS, 2008a.
14 WHO, 2009b.

were more pronounced. The majority of female deaths (57 per cent) in this region were attributable to cardiovascular diseases, while for males these accounted for 44 per cent of the total. Higher female than male mortality from cardiovascular diseases may be partly due to the fact that many women in the region survive to the ages at which such diseases take their largest toll.[15] Cancer was the second leading cause of death for both sexes in Europe. Unintentional injuries ranked third as a cause of death in terms of importance but affected more men than women.

Women in Europe are more likely than men to die from cardiovascular diseases

The distribution of deaths by cause is somewhat similar between the Americas and Western Pacific, with cardiovascular diseases as the most important cause of death and cancer as the second for both sexes. As was the case for Europe, cardiovascular diseases led to higher mortality among women than men. The likelihood of dying from respiratory diseases is higher in Western Pacific than in any other region, and such deaths made up 16 per cent of the total deaths for women there and 13 per cent for men.

In Eastern Mediterranean and South-Eastern Asia, causes of death were more diverse than in other regions: while cardiovascular diseases and infectious and parasitic diseases were the two leading causes, neither constituted more than 30 per cent of the total. In South-Eastern Asia, the share of deaths caused by infectious and parasitic diseases was higher for men (19 per cent) than women (16 per cent).

3. Cancer morbidity and mortality

Cancer is a group of diseases characterized by uncontrolled growth and spread of abnormal cells. While people of all ages are affected, the risk usually increases with age and the number of cases is rising worldwide partly because of ageing populations. Already, it is the third leading cause of death at the global level, accounting for about 12 per cent of female deaths in 2004 and 13 per cent of male deaths in 2004 (see previous section).

The most recent global estimates on new cancer cases and cancer deaths were produced by Garcia and others by applying age-specific cancer rates from GLOBOCAN 2002[16] to the corresponding age-specific population for 2007.[17] According to the estimates, there were more than 12 million new cancer cases in the world that year. An estimated 7.6 million people also died of cancer in 2007 – more than 20,000 people every day. Men outnumber women in terms of both new cancer cases and cancer deaths. Looking in depth at data on cancer morbidity and mortality reveals marked sex differences in terms of cancer site.

Breast cancer for women and lung cancer for men head the list in new cases of cancer

The percentage distribution of the number of new cases and deaths attributed to cancer site for women and men is summarized in table 2.2. Around the world, the two most commonly diagnosed cancers among women are related to their reproductive functions. Breast cancer was the most common, accounting for 23 per cent of new cases, which was more than double the second most common – cervix uteri cancer – which made up 10 per cent. Other common cancer sites among women included colon/rectum, lung/bronchus, ovarian and stomach. In the more developed regions, breast cancer (27 per cent), colon/rectum cancer (14 per cent), lung/bronchus cancer (8 per cent) taken together represented nearly half of newly diagnosed cancers. Cancer of the cervix, which is linked to chronic infectious conditions and therefore preventable, was less common in the more developed regions and ranked only seventh in terms of importance accounting for only 4 per cent of new cases.

Among men at the global level, lung cancers including bronchus cancers had the highest incidence, representing 17 per cent of total new cases, followed by prostate cancer (12 per cent) and colon/rectum cancer and stomach cancer (10 per cent each). Lung cancer, which is considered highly related to tobacco use, was equally common in the more developed and less developed regions. The incidence of prostate cancer was notably high among men in the more developed regions, with the largest proportion or 19 per cent of the total. Indeed, nearly three quarters of recorded prostate cancer cases occurred in the more developed countries, which could be partly due to improved detection.

---

15 United Nations, 2001.

16 GLOBOCAN 2002 is a project of WHO to estimate the incidence and prevalence of and mortality from 27 cancers for all countries in the world in 2002.

17 Garcia and others, 2007.

Table 2.2

Number of new cancer cases and cancer deaths and percentage distribution by site, for women and men, 2007

	World		More developed regions		Less developed regions	
	New cases	Deaths	New cases	Deaths	New cases	Deaths
Women						
Breast	23	14	27	16	19	13
Cervix uteri	10	9	4	3	15	13
Colon/Rectum	9	9	14	13	6	6
Lung/Bronchus	8	11	8	14	7	10
Ovary	4	4	4	5	4	4
Stomach	7	9	5	7	8	10
Other sites	40	44	38	42	42	45
Total	100	100	100	100	100	100
Number (in thousand)	5 717	3 314	2 479	1 272	3 168	2 022
Men						
Colon/Rectum	10	7	13	11	6	5
Esophagus	5	7	..	3	8	9
Liver	8	11	3	5	12	15
Lung/Bronchius	17	22	18	28	16	19
Prostate	12	6	19	9	5	4
Stomach	10	12	7	9	14	14
Other sites	38	35	40	36	39	34
Total	100	100	100	100	100	100
Number (in thousand)	6 615	4 335	2 948	1 648	3 587	2 658

Source: Computed by the United Nations Statistics Division from Garcia and others, *Global Cancer Facts and Figures* (2007), p. 3.
Note: Unweighted averages. The total number excludes non-melanoma skin cancer. Estimates for regions combined do not sum to worldwide totals. Due to rounding, the sum of categories might not equal 100. New cases of esophagus cancer for men in more developed regions included in the other sites category.

The distribution of cancer deaths by site is somewhat different from that of new cases, as it reflects, in addition to the degree of awareness and detection practices, the availability and quality of medical treatments, which vary by type of cancer. Worldwide, breast cancer topped the cancer deaths among women with an estimated 465,000 deaths annually. It contributed 14 per cent of total cancer deaths, despite making up 23 per cent of new cancer cases, suggesting that it has a relatively lower mortality rate than other cancers. If it is caught early enough, women (or men) have a high survival rate, which emphasizes the importance of early detection through the use of medical tools such as mammography screening.[18]

In the more developed regions, cancer deaths among women were primarily from breast cancer, lung/bronchus cancer and colon/rectum cancer. Breast cancers in high-income countries could be associated with factors such as increasing longevity, being overweight, the use of hormone replacement therapy, lack of breastfeeding practices and low fer-

tility.[19] In the less developed regions, breast and cervix uteri cancers are the most common, contributing about 13 per cent each to the total cancer deaths. Cervix cancer can be prevented by regular screening examinations using a PAP smear and the removal of any pre-cancerous lesions. While PAP smears are relatively easy to administer in low resource settings compared to technologically intensive mammography, such services are not yet readily available in many developing countries.

For men, lung cancer accounted for the largest share or 22 per cent of total cancer deaths globally. In the more developed regions, deaths due to lung cancer made up as much as 28 per cent of cancer deaths, more than colon/rectum cancer. In the less developed regions, one out of five cancer deaths were caused by lung/bronchus cancer, while liver and stomach cancers were also common cancer sites.

C. Morbidity and health risk factors

Morbidity refers to a diseased state, disability or poor health due to any cause. It is well known that demographic, socio-economic and environmental

---

18 "Mammography is a low-dose x-ray procedure that allows visualization of the internal structure of the breast" and is considered highly accurate. See American Cancer Society, 2007.

19 WHO, 2008b.

factors as well as biological risk factors affect the types of diseases individuals develop. In addition, some behavioural factors can be linked to increases in morbidity. For instance, alcohol consumption, tobacco use, lack of physical activity and poor nutrition status can result in negative health outcomes. The research shows that men are more likely than women to gravitate toward higher risk behaviours such as cigarette smoking, heavy drinking and gun use.[20] This section addresses sex differentials in selected health risk factors, namely alcohol consumption and tobacco use, as well as morbidity due to obesity and diabetes.

1. Alcohol consumption

Sex-disaggregated data on alcohol consumption are not widely available as the measurement of alcohol use can be challenging to obtain due to different cultural norms, drink sizes and the amount of alcohol used in the drinks.[21] Nonetheless, it is important to discuss alcohol consumption from a gender perspective as it affects the health of women and men differently through chronic illness or accidents.[22] For example, an extreme effect is seen in the Russian Federation where, according to a recent study, alcohol associated excess in mortality accounts for 59 per cent of deaths in men and 33 per cent of deaths in women aged 15–54 years.[23]

Alcohol is addictive for both women and men. However, men tend to consume more than women in all regions of the world.[24] According to data[25] available from WHO, the percentages of current drinkers[26] were more similar between women and men in the more developed regions than in the less developed ones.[27] For example, 81 per cent of women and 89 per cent of men in Eastern Europe were reported as drinkers in 2000. The largest gender differences in alcohol consumption were found in the sub-region of the Western Pacific[28], where 30 per cent of women and 84 per cent of men were

current drinkers. The lowest percentages of women and men who drink alcohol were found in regions where the majority of the population was Muslim. Thus, only 1 per cent of females in the Eastern Mediterranean region[29] were reported to be current drinkers compared to 17 per cent of men.

Men are more likely than women to be current drinkers in all countries and at all ages

Figure 2.5 shows the percentage of current drinkers by sex and age group in selected developing countries in the early 2000s.[30] The proportion varied greatly among the eight countries observed. However, it revealed that men were more likely than women to be current drinkers in all the countries and at all ages. Striking gender differences in alcohol consumption characterized India and Sri Lanka, where less than 10 per cent of women in all age groups were current drinkers compared to between 24 and 40 per cent of Indian men and over 50 per cent of Sri Lankan men. While there was a general trend that the percentage of current drinkers declined with age, older age groups were reported to be drinking more than younger ones in Nigeria and Uganda. Argentinean women and men had the highest levels of current drinkers among the eight countries.

Engagement of young people in heavy alcohol consumption is often a public health concern. Research shows that in general boys drink more than girls. For example, in the Czech Republic almost a third of males aged 18–24 years consumed five or more standard drinks in one sitting at least once a week, compared to only 9 per cent of 18–24 year old females.[31] Boys were not only more likely than girls to drink but also to drink heavily, except in several European countries where levels of drinking among young females had risen to or surpassed those among young males.[32]

2. Tobacco use

Similar to alcohol consumption, tobacco use is more common among men than women. In many countries women have traditionally not smoked or used tobacco as frequently as men. However,

20 Yin, 2007.
21 Bloomfield and others, 2003.
22 WHO, 2004.
23 Zaridze and others, 2009.
24 Wilsnack and others, 2005.
25 Throughout the section on alcohol consumption, the regional grouping is based on the WHO regions.
26 Current drinkers are defined as people who have taken an alcoholic drink in the past 12 months.
27 Wilsnack and others, 2005.
28 WHO sub-region Western Pacific B (e.g. China, Philippines and Viet Nam).
29 WHO sub-region Eastern Mediterranean D (e.g. Afghanistan, Pakistan).
30 Data are from Obot and Room, 2005. This was a collaborative effort to better understand the gender dimensions of alcohol use in various cultural settings.
31 WHO, 2004.
32 Jernigan, 2001.

Figure 2.5
Current drinkers by age group and sex, selected developing countries, early 2000s

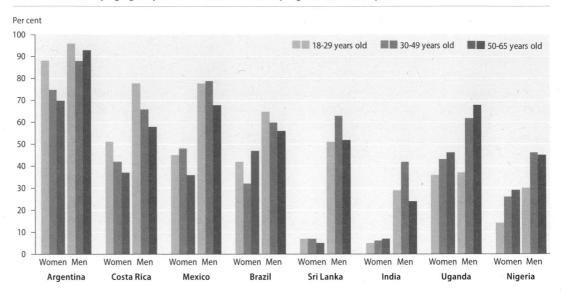

Per cent

18-29 years old   30-49 years old   50-65 years old

Women Men — Argentina | Women Men — Costa Rica | Women Men — Mexico | Women Men — Brazil | Women Men — Sri Lanka | Women Men — India | Women Men — Uganda | Women Men — Nigeria

Source: Room and Selin, Problems from men's and women's drinking in eight developing countries (2005), p. 214.

the rise in tobacco use among younger females in high-population countries is one of the most ominous potential developments of what is described by WHO as an epidemic.[33] In particular, smoking during pregnancy can harm both a women and her unborn baby, causing a number of problems including preterm delivery, low birth weight and sudden infant death syndrome. Many smoking cessation programmes, therefore, target pregnant women as a priority population.

The gender gap in tobacco use is small in the more developed regions and in South America

As figure 2.6 clearly depicts, males are more likely to smoke than females regardless of the world[34] region. The proportion of smokers among persons aged 15 years and over ranged from 10 per cent in Central America to 52 per cent in Eastern Asia for males and from less than 1 per cent in Northern Africa to 23 per cent in Western Europe for females. The highest prevalence rates of female smokers apart from Western Europe were Eastern Europe (21 per cent), South America (17 per cent) and Other more developed regions (16 per cent). For males, tobacco use exceeded 30 per cent in

many regions: Eastern Asia (52 per cent), Eastern Europe (43 per cent), South-Eastern Asia (36 per cent) and Central Asia (32 per cent). The largest differences between the percentage of females and males smoking cigarettes were found in Eastern Asia, South-Eastern Asia, Northern Africa and Central Asia. The gender gap in tobacco use was relatively small in the more developed regions and in South America.

While there are still significant differences between females and males in the level of smoking in many regions, a recent WHO study found alarming increases in tobacco use among women, particularly in Eastern, Central and Southern Europe.[35] It was found that in most European Union countries, teenage girls were as likely to smoke as boys, if not more so. At the country level, more women than men reported smoking cigarettes in Sweden. For example, an estimated 18 per cent of Swedish females and 15 per cent of Swedish males smoked cigarettes daily.[36]

Figure 2.7 displays the prevalence of smoking in ten selected countries of Eastern and South-Eastern Asia. Among these countries, the proportion of men who smoke cigarettes daily ranged from 30 per cent in Thailand to 58 per cent in Indonesia. The prevalence of smoking in China is 57 per cent, which yields over 300 million male smokers there.[37] In contrast, the prevalence of smoking among females

---

33 WHO, 2008c.

34 For this analysis, prevalence of daily cigarette smokers (at least 1 cigarette per day) was used. Data are age-standardized estimates considered comparable across countries; they are taken from Appendix III of WHO, 2008c. Estimates prepared are based on the latest available surveys on tobacco use prevalence from 135 Member States. (See the Technical Note II and Appendix III of the above report for more detailed information on the data criteria and selection).

35 WHO, 2008c.

36 Ibid.

37 Ibid.

Figure 2.6
Smoking prevalence among persons aged 15 or over, by sex and region, 2008

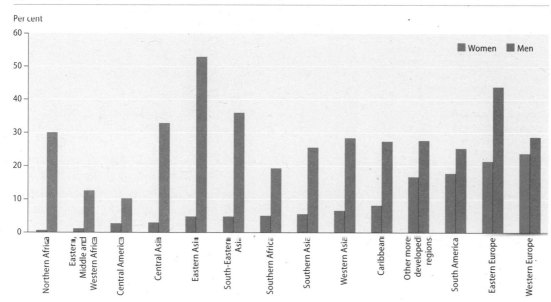

Per cent

Source: Computed by the United Nations Statistics Division based on data from WHO, *WHO Report on the Global Tobacco Epidemic, 2008* (2008).
Note: Unweighted averages.

Figure 2.7
Smoking prevalence by sex, selected countries in Eastern and South-Eastern Asia, 2008

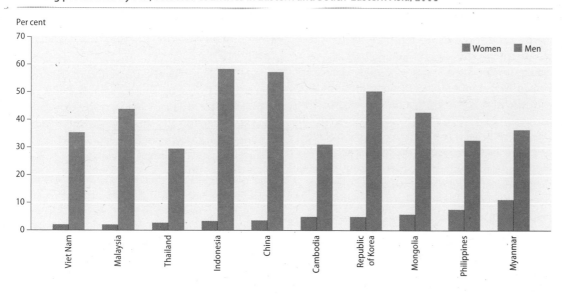

Per cent

Source: WHO, *WHO Report on the Global Tobacco Epidemic, 2008* (2008).

in these countries remained low, ranging from just 2 per cent in Viet Nam to 11 per cent in Myanmar.

3. Obesity

Obesity,[38] often the result of sedentary lifestyles and unbalanced diets, puts an individual at increased risk for many diseases and health prob-

lems including hypertension and diabetes. Once considered as a problem of the developed countries, obesity can be seen today in many parts of the world. WHO estimates that globally in 2005 there were approximately 1.6 billion adults (aged 15 years and over) who were overweight and at least 400 million obese adults.[39] It is projected that the number will continue to grow to about 2.3 billion and more than 700 million, respectively, by 2015.

---

[38] A person is classified as obese if her or his body mass index (BMI), defined as a person's weight in kilograms divided by height in meters squared, exceeds 30 (for an adult aged 18 years and older).

[39] WHO, 2006.

Figure 2.8
Prevalence of obesity for countries with over 20 per cent of women who are obese, 2000–2008 (*latest available*)

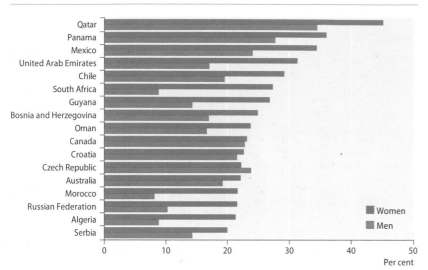

Source: International Obesity Task Force, Global Prevalence of Adult Obesity (2009).

Obesity has become a serious health problem for women in the Arab countries

Figure 2.8 displays data[40] for 17 countries where the prevalence of obesity exceeded 20 per cent among women aged 25–64 years old. Qatar and United Arab Emirates were among the countries with the highest levels of adult obesity, with 45 per cent and 31 per cent of females considered obese, respectively. In the Arab countries, obesity is seen as a serious health problem for women as lifestyles change to become more urban and sedentary; cultural and social factors may also play a role in that women and girls are not encouraged to engage in sports.[41]

Three of the top five countries with high prevalence of obesity are located in Latin America. In Panama and Mexico, 36 and 34 per cent of women respectively were considered obese, though there was also a significant percentage of men who were obese in both countries (28 per cent in Panama and 24 per cent in Mexico).

In all the countries observed, except the Czech Republic, more females than males were classi-

fied as obese. The largest sex difference was seen in South Africa, where 27 per cent of women and 9 per cent of men were classified as obese. In contrast, the difference in obesity rate by sex was not significant in countries such as Canada and Croatia.

4. Diabetes

The number of people with diabetes is projected to rise in the future

Diabetes is a group of heterogeneous disorders with the common elements of hyperglycaemia and glucose intolerance due to insulin deficiency, impaired effectiveness of insulin action, or both. Diabetes is becoming a major global health concern. Worldwide, an estimated 285 million people have diabetes in 2010, and the number is projected to rise to 439 million by 2030.[42] It is a significant health concern for developed countries but even more so for developing countries, where 70 per cent of cases are estimated to be found. The rapidly growing global diabetes epidemic also means that pre-gestational and gestational diabetes contribute substantially to 'high-risk' pregnancies; these may already be a leading cause of high-risk pregnancies in some countries.

Figure 2.9 shows the sex differences in the prevalence of diabetes by sub-regions in 2007. The prevalence for women varied greatly from a low of 3 per cent in sub-Saharan Africa (excluding Southern Africa) to a high of over 11 per cent in Central America and the Caribbean.

The data exhibit higher prevalence of diabetes for women than men in the majority of regions. For instance, in the Caribbean, the percentage of women who had diabetes was 4 percentage points higher than that of men. The sub-regions where more men than women had diabetes included Other more developed regions (excluding Eastern and Western Europe) and Central Asia.

D. HIV and AIDS

Since it was first recognized in the early 1980s, HIV/AIDS has been a critical health issue for women and men. The epidemic continues to undermine development efforts worldwide as it most often afflicts populations already beset by poverty. It particularly affects the working-age population, preventing women and men from

---

40 Global prevalence of adult obesity data from national surveys is collected and compiled by the International Obesity Task Force, which is part of the International Association for the Study of Obesity. For more details, see *http://www.iotf.org/database/documents/GlobalPrevalenceofAdultObesityJuly2009.pdf* and *http://www.iaso.org.*

41 UNDP, 2005a.

42 International Diabetes Federation, 2009.

Figure 2.9
Prevalence of diabetes by region and sex, 2007

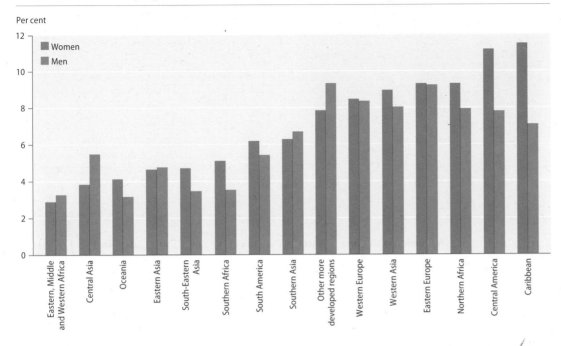

Per cent

Source: Computed by the United Nations Statistics Division based on data from International Diabetes Federation, *Diabetes Atlas* (2008)
Note: Unweighted averages.

making full contributions to development and impoverishing families. At the household level, the epidemic increases the burden of care and erodes savings. MDG 6 calls for halting and beginning to reverse the spread of HIV/AIDS by 2015.

1. Prevalence of HIV/AIDS

About half of adults living with HIV are women

The estimates produced for 2001 and 2007 by UNAIDS[43] show that the prevalence of HIV appeared to be stabilizing (see table 2.3). Worldwide[44], a total of 33 million adults and children were estimated to be living with HIV in 2007, a modest increase from 30 million in 2001. During this period, the percentage of adults aged 15–49 years with HIV remained the same at 0.8 per cent of the population, and approximately half of them were women. Increased access to antiretroviral drugs, especially in developing countries, has made it possible for those infected with the virus to survive longer. Indeed, the annual number of deaths due to AIDS slightly declined to 2 million in 2007 from its peak of 2.2 million in 2005.

Sub-Saharan Africa, especially Southern Africa, has been the region hardest hit by the epidemic (see also the discussion in section A of this chapter on the impact of HIV/AIDS on life expectancy). In 2007, two thirds of those living with HIV in the world, or 22 million people, were found in sub-Saharan Africa. The adult HIV prevalence in the region was as high as 5 per cent, while it was below 1 per cent in most other world regions, and women accounted for almost 60 per cent of all HIV-positive adults. It should be noted that within sub-Saharan Africa there was a wide variation in the prevalence rates among countries, ranging from less than 1 per cent in Comoros to 26 per cent in Swaziland.

The modes of HIV transmission vary among regions

Other sub-regions with large population living with HIV were South and South-East Asia, where over 4 million people were estimated to be infected with the virus in 2007. Unlike sub-Saharan Africa, however, men outnumbered women among HIV-positive adults, making up 63 per cent of the total. Indeed, men constituted the majority of HIV-positive adults in all regions except sub-Saharan Africa, North Africa and the Middle East and the Caribbean.

---

43 UNAIDS, 2008a.

44 Throughout the section on HIV/AIDS, the regional grouping is based on the classification used by UNAIDS.

Table 2.3
Prevalence of HIV/AIDS by sex and region, 2001 and 2007

	Number of people living with HIV/AIDS (in thousands)		Percentage of adults (15–49 years) living with HIV/AIDS		Percentage of women among HIV-positive adults	
	2001	2007	2001	2007	2001	2007
World	29 500	33 000	0.8	0.8	51	50
Sub-Saharan Africa	20 400	22 000	5.7	5.0	59	59
North Africa and Middle East	300	380	0.3	0.3	54	54
South and South-East Asia	4 200	4 200	0.4	0.3	37	37
East Asia	490	740	0.1	0.1	27	27
Oceania	25	74	0.2	0.4	18	30
Latin America	1 400	1 700	0.5	0.5	32	32
Caribbean	210	230	1.1	1.1	46	50
Eastern Europe and Central Asia	650	1 500	0.4	0.8	28	31
Western and Central Europe	610	730	0.2	0.3	26	27
North America	1 100	1 200	0.6	0.6	17	21

Source: UNAIDS, *Report on the Global AIDS Epidemic* (2008).
Note: Oceania includes Australia, Federated States of Micronesia, Fiji, Marshall Islands, New Zealand, Palau, Papua New Guinea and Tuvalu.

According to the data,[45] heterosexual sex was the most common mode of transmission in sub-Saharan Africa, the Caribbean and Oceania. In Asia, there was no one primary mode of transmission, with injecting drug use and unprotected sex, including sex work and heterosexual sex, all important contributors. In Eastern Europe and the Middle East and North Africa, sharing needles and unprotected sex with sex workers were the most common modes of transmission, while infection was primarily transmitted in both North America and Latin America through sex between men.

Research shows that women are more vulnerable than men to contracting HIV, due both to biological susceptibility as well as to social, economic and cultural pressures.[46] Unequal gender relations within and outside the family often limit the ability of women to protect themselves from HIV infection. Refusing unprotected sex is a challenge for women who are dependent on men socially and economically and therefore have limited bargaining power. Furthermore, sex outside of the union and multiple sexual partnerships are often culturally tolerated for men (though not for women), and hence a married woman can be vulnerable to HIV infection because of her husband's concurrent sexual relations.

45 UNAIDS, 2008a.
46 Matlin and Spence, 2000.

2. Knowledge of HIV

Knowledge of HIV among young adults does not exceed 45 per cent in any of the less developed regions

Part of the differentials in the level of HIV infection can be attributed to varying knowledge about transmission and prevention. Figure 2.10 shows data on the knowledge about transmission and prevention of young adults aged 15–24 years by sub-region, derived from surveys conducted mostly in developing countries between 2005 and 2007. It should be underscored that in no region with data does the proportion of young adults, regardless of sex, who have knowledge of HIV and its prevention exceed 45 per cent. This is far below the target of 95 per cent to be achieved by 2010, which was one of the goals set at the United Nations General Assembly Special Session on HIV/AIDS in 2001.[47]

Knowledge of HIV among young women is relatively high in the Caribbean, Central America and South America, as more than 40 per cent of them were aware of the infection and its prevention. At the other end of spectrum, only 12 per cent of young women had an understanding of the virus in Western Asia. At least two out of five young men in the Caribbean, Southern Africa and South America had knowledge of HIV, whereas the level in Central Asia was about half that and as low as 20 per cent.

Central America stands out for the large gap there between young women and men with knowledge of HIV transmission and prevention. As of the mid-2000s, 44 per cent of girls had knowledge compared to 27 per cent for boys, a marked difference of 17 percentage points. A knowledge gap of more than 10 percentage points also exists in Northern Africa and Western Asia, but with young men being more knowledgeable of HIV than young women. In the other world regions, the knowledge gap by sex was relatively small.

HIV/AIDS has proven to be more than just a disease and has placed significant burdens on family members, especially women. The primary caregivers for sick patients are usually women and girls within a family. It is estimated that in Africa women account for two thirds of all caregivers

47 Declaration of Commitment on HIV/AIDS: "Global Crisis – Global Action", adopted at the United Nations General Assembly Special Session on HIV/AIDS in 2001.

Figure 2.10

Knowledge of HIV and its prevention among youth aged 15–24 years, less developed regions, 2005–2007

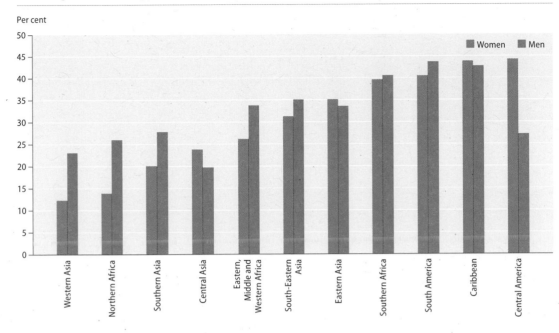

Per cent

Source: Computed by the United Nations Statistics Division based on data from UNAIDS, *Report on the Global AIDS Epidemic* (2008). Note: Unweighted averages.

for people living with HIV.[48] HIV/AIDS has also led to a large number of orphans, who are taken care of by other family members or institutions. In Africa, where 77 per cent of the world's 15 million AIDS orphans live, it is often grandmothers who take responsibility for this care.

E. Reproductive health

The reproductive years of women are from puberty through menopause, and this is the period when most women experience important life events such as entry into sexual union, marriage and childbearing. However, it is also a time of particular health risks, especially related to pregnancy and childbirth, which cause ill health and death for many women of childbearing age. The Programme of Action adopted at the International Conference on Population and Development in Cairo in 1994 acknowledges the critical importance of reproductive health to development.[49] The Beijing Platform of Action also underscores that all persons are to have access to a broad range of reproductive health services, as well as the freedom to exercise informed choice in determining the number and spacing of their children and the services needed to go safely through pregnancy and childbirth.[50]

The overall health of women during their reproductive years allows them to contribute to the economy, society and their families not just at this stage of their lifecycle but through the rest of their lives.

Goal 5 of the Millennium Development Goals calls for improving maternal health by reducing the maternal mortality ratio by three quarters and by achieving universal access to reproductive health. Each year, more than half a million women die from causes related to pregnancy and childbirth.[51] Many of them could be saved if they were provided with access to prenatal care and skilled attendants at birth as well as appropriate modern technology to deal with emergency obstetric care situations when needed. Another important way to achieve better reproductive health is to ensure that all women have access to contraceptives.

1. Prenatal and delivery care

Prenatal care is known to improve the outcome of pregnancy and birth for both mother and child. It not only monitors the health of the mother and foetus but also allows for the identification of potential complications. In addition, it can provide women with information about needed nutrition during pregnancy and breastfeeding.

---

48 UNAIDS, 2008b.

49 United Nations, 1995b.

50 United Nations, 1995a.

---

51 UNICEF, 2008a.

Table 2.4

Women receiving prenatal care, deliveries attended by a skilled attendant and deliveries in health facilities, by region, 1996 and 2000–2008 (*latest available*)

	Percentage pregnant women receiving prenatal care (at least 1 visit)		Percentage deliveries attended by a skilled attendant		Percentage deliveries in health facilities	
	1996	2000–2008	1996	2000–2008	1996	2000–2007
Africa						
Northern Africa	65	80	66	82	57	78
Southern Africa	86	92	67	78	64	72
Eastern, Middle and Western Africa	66	79	42	53	37	48
Asia						
Eastern Asia	93	94	95	98	89	94
South-Eastern Asia	77	77	64	62	52	48
Southern Asia	49	68	39	52	28	46
Central Asia	90	94	93	96	92	91
Western Asia	82	91	82	89	79	86
Latin America and the Caribbean						
Caribbean	95	96	88	92	86	79
Central America	75	90	70	82	62	76
South America	79	91	80	86	76	85
Oceania	84	..	81	81	87	..
Eastern Europe	97	97	99	100	98	99

Sources: 1996 data from United Nations, *The World's Women 2000: Trends and Statistics* (2000), p. 61, figure 3.8; 2000–2007/8 computed by United Nations Statistics Division based on data from the United Nations Statistics Division MDG database (accessed in August 2009).

Note: Unweighted averages.

As the data in table 2.4 show, the levels of prenatal care that women received varied among sub-regions. In the period 2000–2008, the overwhelming majority (over 90 per cent) of women in Southern Africa, Central and South America, the Caribbean, Eastern Asia, Central Asia, Western Asia and Eastern Europe received prenatal care at least once while pregnant. In contrast, only 68 per cent of women in Southern Asia received prenatal care during their pregnancy.

The proportion of women who receive prenatal care increased in many world regions

---

Since the mid-1990s, the percentage of women receiving prenatal care at least once during their pregnancy has increased in many regions of the world. The improvement was particularly notable in Southern Asia, where the proportion rose by 19 percentage points to reach 68 per cent in 2000–2008. An increase of over 10 percentage points was also seen in Central America, Eastern, Middle and Western Africa, Northern Africa and

South America during the same period. Against this positive trend was South-Eastern Asia, where the percentage of pregnant women who received prenatal care at least once remained at 77 per cent over the period.

Another important way to help more women survive pregnancy and childbirth is to provide them with access to skilled birth attendants such as trained nurse-midwives, trained traditional birth attendants or medical doctors. Skilled birth attendants can diagnose the need for emergency obstetric care and, if necessary, transfer the patient to a medical facility for treatment such as a caesarean section. A skilled birth attendant is essential to decrease maternal injuries, such as haemorrhages and obstructed labour, that can result in fistula or death.[52]

As the data in table 2.4 show, compared to the mid-1990s, women in the 2000s had more access to skilled birth attendants at delivery in all sub-regions except Oceania and South-Eastern Asia. Almost all women had access to a skilled birth attendant in Central Asia (96 per cent), Eastern Asia (98 per cent) and Eastern Europe (100 per cent). While some improvements were seen, still barely half of deliveries were attended by a skilled professional in Eastern, Middle and Western Africa or Southern Asia. It is estimated that an additional 350,000 midwives are needed globally to improve maternal health and allow for safer deliveries.[53]

The proportion of women who deliver a baby in health facilities increased in most regions

---

The likelihood of a woman delivering her baby in a health facility also varied across sub-regions, but it has shown an increase in most of them (see table 2.4). For the most recent period 2000–2007, births occurred almost solely in a health facility in Central Asia, Eastern Asia and Eastern Europe. In contrast, a minority took place in a health facility in Eastern, Middle and Western Africa, Southern Asia and South-Eastern Asia. It is worth noting that the proportion of women who delivered in health facilities increased markedly between 1996 and 2000–2007 in Northern Africa from 57 to 78 per cent and in Southern Asia from 28 to 46 per cent.

The availability of health facilities with access to emergency obstetrics is critical in cases where the mother experiences complications in labour and can be key to lowering the number of maternal

---

52 UNICEF, 2008b.

53 Obaid, 2009.

deaths. However, in many countries, especially in the less developed regions, lack of availability of health facilities, coupled with inadequate transportation infrastructure sometimes prevents pregnant women from getting to a medical facility and receiving the emergency care they need.

2. Maternal mortality

Most maternal deaths are caused directly by obstetric complications including post-partum haemorrhage, infections, eclampsia[54] and prolonged or obstructed labour. However, there are also significant indirect causes that heighten the risk of maternal deaths such as anaemia, iodine deficiency, malaria and HIV/AIDS.[55] Furthermore, gender inequality can also increase the chance of physical complications during pregnancy and childbirth as well as maternal mortality.[56] For instance, women may be delayed or prevented from access to obstetric care in situations where they need the permission of a male relative to do so.

The statistical challenge of maternal mortality cannot be overemphasized: obtaining reliable data on maternal deaths is extremely difficult. The reporting of maternal deaths often lacks accuracy, and there are problems of underreporting of unknown degrees. In addition, the periodicity of reporting varies, often with large intervals. Measuring maternal mortality is especially challenging in countries with poor civil registration systems, which are the primary source of data on deaths. Consequently, existing statistics are often not adequate to directly monitor the level of maternal mortality and it is necessary to rely on indirect estimates. The latest maternal mortality estimates[57] for 2005 utilize data from civil registration systems, household surveys and censuses and apply various statistical methods to develop the estimates.[58]

MDG 5 on improving maternal health is one of the goals towards which least progress has been made.[59] Gains in reducing maternal mortality remain slow in many developing countries, despite

---

54 Eclampsia is seizures (convulsions) in a pregnant woman that are not related to brain conditions.

55 UNICEF, 2008a.

56 UNDP, 2005b.

57 A Working Group, consisting of WHO, UNICEF, UNFPA and the World Bank, prepared estimates for 1990, 1995, 2000 and, most recently, 2005; however, due to changing methodologies the estimates are not compared over time in this report.

58 WHO, 2007.

59 United Nations, 2009d.

Table 2.5

Number of maternal deaths, maternal mortality ratio and lifetime risk of maternal death by region, 2005

	Number of maternal deaths	Maternal mortality ratio (MMR)	Lifetime risk of maternal death, 1 in:
World	536 000	400	92
More developed regions	960	9	7 300
CIS countries	1800	51	1 200
Less developed regions	533 000	450	75
Africa	276 000	820	26
Northern Africa	5 700	160	210
Sub-Saharan Africa	270 000	900	22
Asia	241 000	330	120
Eastern Asia	9 200	50	1 200
South-Eastern Asia	35 000	300	130
Southern Asia	188 000	490	61
Western Asia	8 300	160	170
Latin America and the Caribbean	15 000	130	290
Oceania	890	430	62

Source: WHO, *Maternal Mortality in 2005* (2007), p. 16, table 2.
Note: CIS (Commonwealth of Independent States) countries included are: Armenia, Azerbaijan, Belarus, Georgia, Kazakhstan, Kyrgyzstan, Tajikistan, Turkmenistan, Uzbekistan, the Republic of Moldova, the Russian Federation and Ukraine. Estimates for more developed regions and less developed regions exclude CIS countries

the fact that many deaths could be prevented if women had access to basic maternity and health-care services. Thus, as of 2005, there were still an estimated 536,000 women who died of complications during pregnancy, childbirth or in the six weeks following delivery (see table 2.5). Of these, the overwhelming majority (533,000) occurred in the less developed regions. Sub-Saharan Africa alone recorded 270,000 maternal deaths in 2005, indicating that half of world maternal deaths occurred in the region. The second highest number of maternal deaths was observed in Southern Asia, with 188,000 deaths in the same year.

Almost all maternal deaths occur in the less developed regions

---

The MDGs call for improvements in maternal health by reducing the maternal mortality ratio (MMR) by three quarters between 1990 and 2015. MMR is defined as the number of maternal deaths during a given time period per 100,000 live births during the same period. Globally, in 2005, the MMR was 400. There exists a striking divide in maternal mortality between the more developed and less developed regions: the MMR was as low as 9 in the former, whereas in the latter it was 450 on average. Within the less developed regions, the ratio ranged widely from 50 in Eastern Asia to 900 in sub-Saharan Africa. There were 14 countries with MMRs of at least 1,000, of which 13 were in the sub-Saharan African region. The other country was Afghanistan (see Statistical Annex).

The data on the lifetime risk of a woman dying from complications related to pregnancy or childbirth show an echo of the health inequality between women in the less developed and more developed regions. Not only is the level of MMR in less developed regions far too high, but the difference in the magnitude of risk between the more developed and less developed regions is much too wide: in the latter regions a woman had a 1 in 75 lifetime risk of maternal death, compared to 1 in 7,300 in the former. Pregnancy and childbirth were very risky for women who lived in the less developed world, especially in sub-Saharan Africa where 1 in 22 women had a lifetime risk of maternal death, as well as in Southern Asia and Oceania where the risk was 1 in some 60 women.

3. Infertility and childlessness of women

Infertility is the biological inability to have children. It has consequences for the lives of women and men in all societies. Infertility is often the result of untreated sexually transmitted infections (STIs) or can happen after a complicated childbirth or after an abortion, especially an unsafe, illegal one. Primary infertility refers to the situation when a woman has regular sexual intercourse and has not become pregnant after a specified amount of time (usually one year). Women who have secondary infertility already had a pregnancy at least once but are not able to get pregnant again. While both women and men have infertility issues, this section looks at the infertility of women.

Estimates of female infertility are derived from data on childlessness, usually from a demographic survey such as the Demographic and Health Surveys (DHS). However, voluntary childlessness can complicate estimation procedures. In the more developed regions, childlessness is higher than in the less developed regions, and there is an increasing trend in the number of women and men who remain voluntarily without children, often referred to as "childfree". In developing countries, childlessness is less frequently a matter of choice and is more often linked to infertility. In some cultures, women who do not have children can be shunned by their partners and families and sometimes even by society at large. It should be also noted that as data are retrospective and based on the results of

reproductive histories, recall bias is an issue to consider in the estimation procedure. Women might have had a live birth that resulted in an infant death many years before the survey and therefore report no live births at the time of the survey.[60] This might cause an overestimation of infertility.

Based on the analysis of data collected in 46 countries between 1994 and 2000, it was found that the overwhelming majority or 96 per cent of married women aged 40–44 had one or more surviving children.[61] However, infertility is an issue worldwide. As seen in figure 2.11, childlessness – as measured by married women aged 40–44 years who have had no fertile pregnancies – ranged from less than 1 per cent in Kyrgyzstan to 7 per cent in the Central African Republic. Relatively high levels of infertility among women, exceeding 3 per cent, were found in Cameroon, Central African Republic, Chad, Comoros, Dominican Republic and Madagascar. Infertility of women was seen in every less developed region but varied among countries in the respective region. Relatively high prevalence of primary and secondary infertility in sub-Saharan Africa can be explained by a high incidence of STIs and infections related to childbirth and abortion.

Recent estimates suggest that in mid-2002 there were 186 million ever-married women aged 25–49 in developing countries who were infertile.[62] Of those, approximately 168 million had secondary infertility and 18 million had involuntary primary infertility. Furthermore, the same study estimated that approximately 3 per cent of ever-married women aged 25–49 were childless. Due to advances in medical technology, women and men have options to treat primary and secondary infertility and achieve a pregnancy and birth, but the availability of technology varies by country and region.

4. Contraceptive use

Availability of contraceptives allows women and men to have control over the timing and the number of desired children by preventing an unintended pregnancy. The barrier methods of contraception, such as condoms, also help to protect individuals from HIV and other STIs. It is often argued that contraceptive use is a way to increase women's autonomy and to reduce their exposure to pregnancy as well as unsafe abortions. However, the balance of power between women and

60 Rutstein and Shah, 2004.

61 Ibid.

62 Ibid. Note that the estimate does not include China.

men at the couple level could shape the decision to use contraception and the type of method(s).

Data on contraceptive use, often obtained from surveys covering nationally representative samples of women of reproductive age, are available for most countries.[63] It is estimated that as of 2007 contraceptive prevalence had reached 63 per cent among married couples or those in union world-wide (see table 2.6), up only slightly from 61 per cent in 1998[64]. In developed countries, nearly 70 per cent of women aged 15–49 who were married or in union were practicing some method of contraception. Contraceptive use in the less developed regions averaged 62 per cent.

Traditional methods of contraception are more prevalent in the more developed regions

---

In both the more developed and less developed regions, the majority of women using contraception relied on modern methods (59 and 56 per cent, respectively). However, the specific methods used differed markedly between the two regions. In the less developed regions, female sterilization (22 per cent) and the intrauterine device (IUD) (15 per cent) made up the majority of contraceptive use (see table 2.6). In the more developed regions, by contrast, the most commonly used methods were the pill (18 per cent) and the male condom (16 per cent) (data not shown).[65] In Japan, condom use accounted for more than 40 per cent of methods used. Traditional methods, despite relatively low effectiveness in preventing pregnancy, were more commonly used in the more developed than less developed regions – 11 per cent vs. 6 per cent. These methods were mainly periodic abstinence and withdrawal.

The level of contraceptive use was comparable in Asia, Latin America and the Caribbean and Northern America at around 70 per cent. In these sub-regions, more than 20 per cent of women of reproductive age resorted to sterilization to prevent unwanted pregnancies. In Asia, one in every four women of reproductive age stated that they were sterilized for the reason of contraception. Indeed, female sterilization was the method used by 37 per cent of women in India and 33 per cent in China in the early 2000s.[66] While the overall use of contraception was generally high in Europe

---

63 United Nations, 2009b.

64 United Nations, 2003.

65 United Nations, 2009b.

66 Ibid.

Figure 2.11

Women aged 40–44 and married five or more years who had no fertile pregnancies, 1994–2000 (*latest available*)

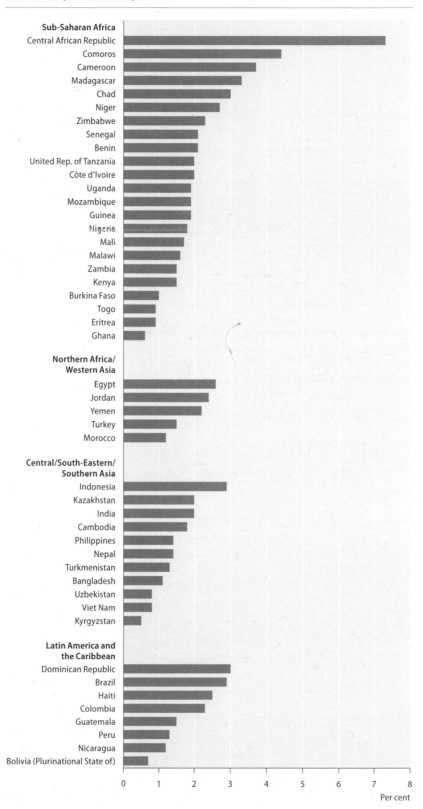

Source: Rutstein and Shah, Infecundity, infertility, and childlessness in developing countries (2004), p.10.

Table 2.6
Contraceptive prevalence among women and women with unmet need for family planning, by region, 2007

Source: United Nations, *World Contraceptive Use 2009* (2009).
Note: Contraceptive prevalence is percentage using contraception among women who are married or in union. Unmet need for family planning is the ratio of the number of women of reproductive age married or in union who are fecund, not using contraception and who report that they do not want any more children or wish to delay the next child divided by the number of women of reproductive age who are married or in union.

	Contraceptive prevalence (*per cent*)					Percentage with unmet need
		Modern method				
			Of which			
	Any method	Any modern method	Female sterilization	IUD	Any traditional method	
World	63	56	20	14	7	..
More developed regions	70	59	8	9	11	..
Less developed regions	62	56	22	15	6	11
Africa	28	22	2	5	6	22
Asia	67	61	25	18	6	9
Europe	71	56	4	14	14	..
Latin America and the Caribbean	72	64	30	7	7	11
Northern America	73	69	20	2	4	6
Oceania	59	53	12	1	6	..

at 71 per cent, the reliance on traditional methods also remained high in the region (14 per cent). Traditional methods were particularly common in countries of Eastern and Southern Europe such as Albania (38 per cent).[67]

The prevalence of contraceptive use is notably low in Africa

Africa is the region where the prevalence of contraceptive use was considerably lower, with only 28 per cent of women of reproductive age who were married or in union using any method. This is reflected, in turn, in the high level of unmet need for family planning in the region: it was estimated that 22 per cent of African women of reproductive age were in need of contraception, pointing to the gap between the desire to use contraception and the actual use.

5. Induced abortions

The number of abortions performed in developing countries shows only a negligible decline

Unwanted pregnancies due to the lack of contraception or contraceptive failure may, in some cases, result in induced abortions. Globally, there were an estimated 42 million induced abortions in 2003, compared to 46 million in 1995 (see table 2.7). During this period, the estimated number of unsafe abortions remained at around 20 million per year.[68] The majority of the declines in the abortion incidence between 1995 and 2003 took place in the more developed regions, where they fell from 10 million to 7 million, while the less developed regions registered only a modest reduction in the number, from 36 million to 35 million.

In 2003, an overwhelming majority of abortions in the world (five in six) were performed in developing countries where access to safe abortions tended to be limited. Some 26 million abortions were recorded in 2003 in Asia alone. Note, however, that this reflects the region's population size. In fact, the abortion rate, defined as the number of abortions per 1,000 women aged 15–44 years, was equally high in three less developed regions – Africa, Asia and Latin America and the Caribbean – at around 30 per 1,000 women.

The number of abortions performed in Eastern Europe had halved from 6 million in 1995 to 3 million in 2003. While greatly reduced, the abortion rate in the sub-region (44 per 1,000 women in 2003) were still notably high, even exceeding that in the less developed regions. One study[69] suggests that women in Armenia, Azerbaijan and Georgia would have an average of three abortions each if current levels prevailed throughout their

67 Ibid.

68 Singh and others, 2009.

69 Sedgh and others, 2007.

reproductive lives. A substantial proportion of women in Eastern Europe continue to depend on traditional methods of contraception (see the section on contraceptive use), and it is only recently that access to modern contraceptives has improved.[70]

It is estimated that nearly 26 per cent of the world's people live in countries whose laws prohibit abortion entirely or permit it only to save a women's life.[71] While there are only six countries and areas that do not permit abortion on any grounds – Chile, Dominican Republic[72], El Salvador, the Holy See, Malta and Nicaragua[73] – the circumstances under which abortion can be legally obtained in other countries vary widely. In countries such as India and South Africa, abortion is available on broad grounds but access to services provided by qualified personnel remains uneven.[74]

Granting women safe and legal access to abortion along with access to modern contraceptives and sex education has shown, in the long run, to reduce the number of abortions. Where restrictive abortion laws make it difficult to obtain a safe abortion, women who have an unwanted pregnancy tend to turn to unsafe abortions.[75] This may endanger their lives – unsafe abortions claim the life of approximately 68,000 women each year.[76] It is estimated that there are about 19–20 million abortions done annually by individuals without the requisite skills, of which 97 per cent are in developing countries.[77]

F. Health of children

MDG 4 calls for a reduction in child mortality. Many of the health problems that women and men face in adulthood have their origin in childhood. It is of critical importance for children to have a healthy start as this can have life-long implications for them. In particular, the well-being of girl children needs be ensured.

---

70 Singh and others, 2009.

71 Boland and Katzive, 1998.

72 United Nations, 2010.

73 United Nations, 2007.

74 Singh and others, 2009.

75 WHO defines an unsafe abortion as any procedure to terminate an unintended pregnancy done either by people lacking the necessary skills or in an environment that does not conform to minimal medical standards, or both.

76 Grimes and others, 2006.

77 Ibid.

Table 2.7

Number of abortions and abortion rate by region, 1995 and 2003

	Number of abortions (in millions)		Abortion rate	
	1995	2003	1995	2003
World	46	42	35	29
More developed regions	10	7	39	26
Less developed regions	36	35	34	29
Africa	5	6	33	29
Asia	27	26	33	29
Europe	8	4	48	28
Eastern Europe	6	3	90	44
Latin America and the Caribbean	4	4	37	31
Northern America	2	2	22	21
Oceania	<1	<1	21	17

Source: Singh and others, *Abortion Worldwide* (2009).

Note: Abortion rate is defined as the number of abortions per 1,000 women aged 15–44 years.

1. Mortality among children under 5

The past decades saw unprecedented declines of mortality in childhood, contributing greatly to the increase in life expectancy. According to United Nations estimates, mortality under age 5 dropped from 109 deaths per 1,000 live births in 1980–1985 to 71 deaths per 1,000 live births in 2005–2010, which represented a 35 per cent reduction. Despite considerable improvements in child mortality, however, 9.6 million children worldwide are still dying every year before they reach 5 years old.[78]

> Although declining, child mortality is still high in developing countries, especially in Africa

Much of the reduction in child mortality occurred in the less developed regions, where the rate fell from 122 deaths to 78 deaths per 1,000 live births between 1980–1985 and 2005–2010. Such notable improvements have been explained by a number of factors, including increased immunization coverage, higher caloric intake made possible by rising agricultural productivity, use of oral rehydration therapies during episodes of diarrhoea, use of insecticide-treated mosquito nets, better access to insecticides, more effective therapies and treatments, as well as improved water and sanitation.[79] All of these have contributed to reduce the incidence of disease at younger ages and prevent deaths when disease strikes.

---

78 United Nations, 2009c.

79 WHO, 2009a.

Table 2.8

Under 5 mortality rate per 1,000 live births by sex, 1995–2000, 2000–2005 and 2005–2010

	Girls			Boys			Difference		
	1995–2000	2000–2005	2005–2010	1995–2000	2000–2005	2005–2010	1995–2000	2000–2005	2005–2010
World	84	77	71	85	77	71	0	0	0
More developed regions	10	8	7	11	10	8	2	1	1
Less developed regions	93	85	78	93	85	78	0	0	0
Africa	156	142	130	169	154	142	13	12	12
Southern Africa	72	81	65	88	95	80	16	15	16
Asia	76	68	61	71	63	56	-5	-5	-5
Europe	11	9	8	14	12	10	3	2	2
Latin America and the Caribbean	36	28	24	45	36	31	9	8	7
Northern America	8	8	7	8	8	7	0	0	0
Oceania	36	33	30	43	36	31	7	3	2

Source: United Nations, World Population Prospects DEMOBASE (2009).

Table 2.8 displays the estimates of mortality under age 5 over the past 15 years, by region and sex. Globally, the mortality of girls and boys fell at the same pace during this period. While most regions have experienced steady declines in child mortality for both sexes, the Southern African region is distinguished by its unique trends. For both girls and boys, child mortality increased from the late 1990s to the early 2000s, registering a peak at 81 deaths per 1,000 live births for girls and 95 deaths per 1,000 per live births for boys in 2000–2005. It is likely that HIV/AIDS contributed to the increases in child mortality during the period.

Despite the considerable improvements in child mortality, the level continues to be high in the less developed regions, and the differences with the more developed regions have only slightly narrowed. In 2005–2010 the under 5 mortality of girls in the less developed regions (78 deaths per 1,000 live births) was 11 times higher than that in the more developed regions (7 deaths per 1,000), while that for boys was 78 deaths for the less developed regions and only 8 deaths for the more developed regions.

Africa is the most difficult place for children to survive. Child mortality was still highest in that region, at 130 female child deaths per 1,000 live births for girls and 142 for boys. These deaths are mainly from preventable causes such as pneumonia, diarrhoea and malaria, and many of them occur during the neonatal period. Relatively high child mortality also characterized Asia. At the other end of spectrum, the lowest child mortality was found in Northern America and Europe,

registering a rate below 10 deaths per 1,000 live births, regardless of the sex of the child.

Typically, mortality is higher among boys than girls. There are specific biological reasons which explain this. For example, male babies are more prone to congenital abnormalities that can result in higher mortality in the early years of life. However, in some countries the reverse is true. In 2005–2010, an excess of female child mortality was pronounced in Asia, especially in Afghanistan, China, India and Pakistan (see Statistical Annex).

2. Underweight

Proper nutrition is a key determinant of health for children. One estimate suggests that undernutrition is an underlying cause in more than one third of child deaths.[80] One indicator to measure the nutrition status of children in a country is the proportion of underweight children. As of 2007, 148 million children under 5 years old were considered to be underweight for their age, with two thirds of them living in Asia and a quarter in Africa.[81] Contributing factors include lack of access to nutritious foods and infection, as well as poor feeding practices. Other socio-economic factors such as low levels of family income, lack of education of parents and lack of access to health care also increase the risk of children being underweight.

Figure 2.12 displays the percentage of girls and boys under 5 years of age who are underweight.

80 Ibid.
81 UNICEF, 2008, p. 23

The data were gathered from surveys, including Multiple Indicator Cluster Surveys (MICS) and Demographic and Health Survey (DHS), conducted in 102 countries between 2000 and 2007. The percentage of underweight children varied greatly among countries where data were available. It was very high in some countries, such as Bangladesh, India and Timor-Leste, where over 40 per cent of children, both girls and boys, were found to be underweight.

The clustering of country data along the diagonal line indicates that in most countries there existed little difference in the proportion of girls and boys who were underweight, suggesting that female children enjoyed the same nutritional status as male children, although at varying levels. The exceptions to the pattern include Armenia, Bangladesh and India where girls were more underweight than boys by a margin of more than 3 per cent. On the other hand, in several African countries including Central African Republic and Comoros as well as in Timor-Leste, boys were more likely than girls to be underweight. Underlying causes of these disparities by sex need to be explored.

3. Immunization

Investing in young children entails providing preventive care such as routine vaccinations that have saved millions of lives. Vaccination rates have been steadily climbing worldwide, pushed by successful immunization campaigns. National Immunization Days had been instituted in some developing countries since the 1980s in addition to routine immunizations;[82] they began with efforts to prevent the spread of polio by immunizing all children under 5. Today, Child Health Days have proven to be a cost-effective way to raise awareness widely and scale up quality health services for children, including delivery of vaccinations.

The DHS collect information from mothers about the vaccination of their children aged 12–23 months. Using these data from 70 developing countries between 1998 and 2007, table 2.9 shows the proportion of girls and boys who received three doses of polio and DPT vaccinations.

Polio vaccination is one of the recommended childhood immunizations, and it is encouraged for children to have four doses. There was a significant variation in the coverage of polio vaccination among the less developed regions. In Northern

Figure 2.12

Percentage underweight among boys and girls under 5 years of age, 1998–2007 (*latest available*)

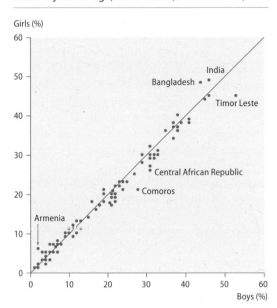

Source: Macro International, MEASURE DHS STATcompiler (2009).

Africa over 90 per cent of children received three doses. In Morocco, for example, the rate of polio immunization by 2003–2004 had reached 96 per cent for girls and 95 per cent for boys. The coverage is also generally high in Southern Asia and Central Asia, where the proportion exceeded 80 per cent for both girls and boys. However, there

Table 2.9

Proportion of girls and boys receiving three doses of polio and DPT vaccinations, by region and sex, 1998–2007 (*latest available*)

	Polio		DPT	
	Girls (%)	Boys (%)	Girls (%)	Boys (%)
Africa				
Northern Africa (3)	90	91	93	92
Southern Africa (5)	77	77	81	81
Eastern, Middle and Western Africa (31)	60	59	57	57
Asia				
Central Asia (4)	87	89	88	88
South-Eastern Asia (5)	67	67	74	74
Southern Asia (5)	86	87	78	76
Western Asia (5)	52	54	54	54
Latin America and the Caribbean				
Caribbean (3)	66	65	67	67
Central America (5)	73	72	68	72
South America (5)	70	70	74	75

Source: Computed by the United Nations Statistics Division based on data from Macro International, MEASURE DHS STATcompiler (2009).

Note: Unweighted averages; the numbers in brackets indicate the number of countries averaged.

were regions where rates could still improve. For example, barely half of children received three polio immunizations in Western Asia.

The DPT vaccine protects children from diphtheria, pertussis and tetanus (DPT), and five doses are commonly given to children between the ages of two months to five years. The immunization rates were high in Northern Africa, Southern Africa and Central Asia, with more than 85 per cent of children receiving three doses of the vaccine. The lowest rates were found in sub-Saharan Africa and Western Asia.

There exist little sex disparities in polio and DPT immunization

At the regional level, data reveal few disparities by sex of child in either polio or DPT immunization coverage. Detectable difference by sex was found only in Central America, where the DPT immunization rate for boys (72 per cent) was somewhat higher than for girls (68 per cent). At the country level, however, several countries recorded significant sex differences in immunization coverage. For instance, the polio immunization rate among girls in Madagascar in 2003–2004 was 70 per cent, which was 14 percentage points higher than that among boys. On the other hand, the proportion of children who received three doses of polio vaccination in Azerbaijan in 2006 was not only very low, but the rate for boys (24 per cent) exceeded that of girls (18 per cent) by a significant margin.

In sum, the recent statistical evidence on sex differentials in underweight and immunization coverage do not support the prevalent notion that anti-female bias might be causing better distribution of food and health treatment for boys than girls. At the country level, sex disparities in nutritional status of children and health-care provision were observed in some countries. However, the direction of disparities was not consistent.

Chapter 3
Education

Key findings

- Two thirds of the 774 million adult illiterates worldwide are women – the same proportion for the past 20 years and across most regions.
- The global youth literacy rate has increased to 89 per cent, while the gender gap has declined to 5 percentaqe points.
- Gaps between girls' and boys' primary enrolment have closed in the majority of countries, but gender parity is still a distant goal for some.
- 72 million children of primary school age are not attending school, out of which over 39 million (or 54 per cent) are girls.
- While secondary school enrolments show improvement, fewer countries are near gender parity than for primary education.
- In tertiary enrolment, men's dominance has been reversed globally and gender disparities favour women, except in sub-Saharan Africa and Southern and Western Asia.
- Women in tertiary education are significantly underrepresented in the fields of science and engineering; however, they remain predominant in education, health and welfare, social sciences, and humanities and arts.
- Worldwide, women account for slightly more than a quarter of all scientific researchers – an increase compared to previous decades but still very far from parity.
- Use of and access to the Internet grew exponentially in the past decade, narrowing the gender digital divide – however, women still do not have the same level of access as men in most countries, whether more or less developed.

Introduction

Education imparts skills and competencies that are central to human development and enhanced quality of life, bringing wide-ranging benefits to both individuals and societies. Investing in girls' and women's education in particular produces exceptionally high social and economic returns. Educated women invest more in their children and contribute to the welfare of the next generation. They are more likely to participate in the labour force, allowing them to earn an income, know and claim their rights, and attain greater influence in the household and public life. Education is essential for empowering women and for closing the gap between women and men in respect of socio-economic opportunities; it can reduce inequalities based on gender and alter the historical legacy of disadvantage faced by women.

Education has long been recognized as a fundamental right with far-reaching consequences for human development and societal progress. The right to education is proclaimed in the Universal Declaration of Human Rights and various international covenants. The importance of education for the advancement of women was highlighted in the Beijing Platform for Action,[1] in which it was identified as one of 12 critical areas of concern and affirmed as central for gender equality and women's empowerment. The Platform for Action called for eliminating discrimination in education on the basis of gender at all levels, eradicating illiteracy among women and improving women's access to vocational training, science and technology and continuing education. With the adoption of the Millennium Development Goals (MDGs),

---

1 United Nations, 1995.

Table 3.1
Number of adult illiterate women and men by region, 1990 and 2007 (*in millions*)

	Both sexes		Men		Women	
	1990	2007	1990	2007	1990	2007
World	870.1	774.4	321.3	278.5	548.8	495.9
Less developed regions	860.3	768.1	318.6	276.2	541.7	491.9
More developed regions	9.8	6.2	2.7	2.3	7.1	4.0
Africa	175.0	207.2	68.0	77.3	107.0	129.9
Eastern Africa	55.6	69.3	22.1	26.5	33.5	42.8
Middle Africa	16.9	22.9	5.7	7.3	11.2	15.6
Northern Africa	41.0	43.8	15.3	15.5	25.7	28.3
Southern Africa	5.3	4.7	2.4	2.2	2.9	2.5
Western Africa	56.1	66.5	22.5	25.9	33.6	40.7
Asia	645.0	523.6	232.4	182.1	412.6	341.5
Eastern Asia	185.6	72.2	56.0	19.7	129.6	52.4
South-Central Asia	395.5	394.6	155.7	144.6	239.8	250.0
South-Eastern Asia	42.3	34.7	14.0	11.6	28.3	23.2
Western Asia	21.5	22.1	6.8	6.3	14.8	15.8
Europe	8.6	4.8	2.2	1.6	6.4	3.2
Eastern Europe	3.9	1.6	0.7	0.5	3.3	1.1
Northern Europe	0.2	0.2	0.1	0.1	0.1	0.1
Southern Europe	3.8	2.4	1.1	0.8	2.7	1.6
Western Europe	0.6	0.6	0.3	0.3	0.3	0.3
Latin America and the Caribbean	39.9	36.5	18.0	16.4	21.9	20.1
Caribbean	3.7	3.7	1.9	1.9	1.9	1.8
Central America	10.7	10.0	4.3	4.0	6.4	6.1
South America	25.5	22.7	11.9	10.5	13.7	12.2
Northern America	0.3	0.5	0.1	0.2	0.1	0.3
Oceania	1.3	1.8	0.6	0.8	0.7	1.0

Source: UNESCO Institute for Statistics (2009a).
Note: Adult illiterates refer to women and men aged 15 and over.

the aim of eliminating gender disparities in education has been further intensified as it is essential to the Goals' achievement. Goal 3 calls for achieving gender parity in primary and secondary education, preferably by the target date of 2005, and in all levels of education no later than 2015.

A. Educational outcomes

1. Literacy

The global number of adult illiterates has declined modestly over the past two decades

Progress has been achieved in raising literacy levels for both women and men around the world. However, despite the gains registered, the number of adult illiterates is very high – and is likely to remain so – due to the impact of population growth. In 1990, an estimated 870 million adults in the world were illiterate (see table 3.1). By 2007, the number was estimated to be about 774 million, showing a slight decline by about 96 million or 11 per cent. Over the same period, the number of illiterate women declined from about 549 million to 496 million (about 10 per cent), while the number of illiterate men declined from 321 million to 279 million (13 per cent). It should be cautioned here that changes in population size strongly influence these statistics. Interpretation of headcount comparisons of illiterate populations should be made with this caveat in mind.[2]

Most sub-regions of the world have registered at least modest decreases in the size of the illiterate population, with Eastern Asia registering one of the most rapid and substantial declines, partly due to the significant advances being made in China. Contrary to these trends, however, the size of the illiterate population increased in several countries in Africa (except Southern Africa), Northern America, Oceania and Western Asia. In the period 1990–2007, Africa added over 32 million illiterates, of which about 23 million or 72 per cent were women. The growth of the illiterate population in Oceania was almost entirely the contribution of the countries of Melanesia. The sub-regions of South-Central and Western Asia likewise saw a slight rise in their female illiterate populations despite showing a reduction in the number of illiterate men. About 99 per cent of the world's illiterate population is concentrated in the less developed regions, and nearly three quarters of them live in South-Central Asia and sub-Saharan Africa, with the former accounting for over half of the total. The size of the illiterate population in South-Central Asia is primarily a reflection of the situation in the populous countries of Bangladesh, India and Pakistan.

Women comprise the majority of the illiterate population in most sub-regions of the world

Nearly two thirds of the world's illiterate population is composed of women (see figure 3.1). This proportion has held steady across several sub-regions in Africa, Asia and Europe and over the entire period between 1990 and 2007, pointing to the persistent disadvantages faced by women. With the exception of the Caribbean, women

2 UNESCO, 2003.

comprised more than half the illiterate population in every sub-region. Disparities to the disadvantage of women are particularly marked in Eastern Europe, Eastern and Western Asia and Middle Africa where women's share of the illiterate population exceeds two thirds. Where the proportion of the illiterate population is high, women are more likely than men to be illiterate.

UNESCO projections[3] point to slow overall improvements over the period to year 2015, with women continuing to account for nearly two thirds of the world's illiterate population. The largest overall reduction among women illiterates aged 15 years and older will be in East Asia and the Pacific.[4] However, in sub-Saharan Africa, where many girls still do not go to school and populations are growing fast, an increase is projected. Very little movement is expected for South-Central or Western Asia.

Literacy rates for women and men are improving but achieving universal literacy remains a significant challenge, particularly in Africa and South-Central and Western Asia

---

Focusing on literacy rather than illiteracy, it can be seen that – owing to increases in access to primary education and improved literacy programmes – significant gains have been made in raising this across the world. Between 1990 and 2007, the literacy rate increased from 76 to 84 per cent.[5] Over the same period, the global literacy rate for adult women increased from 70 to 79 per cent, while for men the rate rose from 82 to 88 per cent (see figure 3.2). Women's literacy rates in Europe and Northern America are generally well above 95 per cent, with very few exceptions. They are also generally high throughout much of Latin America and the Caribbean as well as the sub-regions of Eastern and South-Eastern Asia and Southern Africa. However, in most of sub-Saharan Africa (excluding Southern Africa) and South-Central Asia, women's literacy rates are much lower and range from about 50–60 per cent.

Most regions registered progress in raising rates for both women and men between 1990 and 2007. Rapid gains, measuring as large as 15 percentage points or more, were registered in Northern and

---

3 UNESCO Institute for Statistics, 2008.

4 These regional groupings correspond to those used by UNESCO and differ from those used in other parts of this section.

5 UNESCO Institute for Statistics, 2009b.

Box 3.1
Literacy

UNESCO defines a **literate** person as one who can with understanding both read and write a short simple statement on his (her) everyday life, and an **illiterate** person as one who cannot with understanding both read and write a short simple statement on his (her) everyday life.

One alternative and broader definition of literacy, **functional literacy** – used in some countries that have already attained universal literacy – emphasizes the use of literacy. A person is functionally literate who can engage in all those activities in which literacy is required for the effective functioning of his (her) group and community and also for enabling him (her) to continue to use reading, writing and calculation for his (her) own and the community's development. Generally, literacy also encompasses 'numeracy', the ability to make simple arithmetic calculations.

The **adult literacy rate** is the percentage of the population aged 15 and over who are literate, while the **youth literacy rate** is the percentage aged 15–24 years who are literate.

Figure 3.1
Women among adult illiterates by region, 1990 and 2007

Source: UNESCO Institute for Statistics (2009a).
Note: Adult illiterates refer to women and men aged 15 and over.

Figure 3.2
Adult literacy rates by sex and region, 1990 and 2007

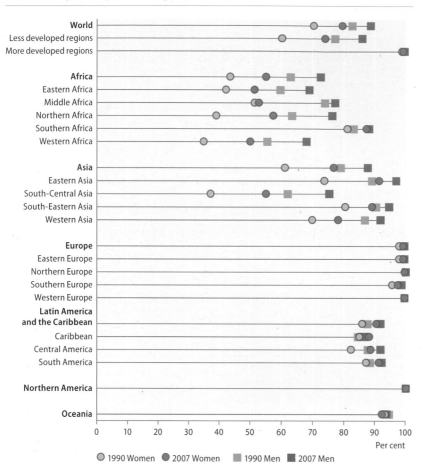

Source: UNESCO Institute for Statistics (2009a).
Note: Adult literacy rates refer to the literacy rates of women and men aged 15 and over.

Western Africa and Eastern and South-Central Asia. However, universal literacy still remains a distant goal for several less developed regions. Sub-Saharan Africa (except Southern Africa) and the sub-regions of Melanesia and South-Central Asia are the farthest from achieving this, showing a deficit greater than 30 percentage points. The sub-regions of the Caribbean, Central America, Micronesia, Southern Africa and Western Asia are next with deficits in the range of 10 to 15 percentage points. All the other sub-regions where illiteracy has not been eradicated are less than 10 percentage points away from universal literacy. To accelerate progress, governments need to show stronger political and financial commitment and attach more weight to literacy in national planning.[6]

---

6 UNESCO, 2010.

Gender gaps in adult literacy are narrowing globally but remain wide and persistent in the less developed regions

Gender gaps in adult literacy rates have decreased globally from 12 percentage points in 1990 to 9 in 2007 (see figure 3.2). For the less developed regions taken together they declined from 17 percentage points to 12, while they have narrowed, and in several cases almost closed, in the more developed regions of Europe, Northern America and Oceania as well as in Southern Africa, Eastern and South-Eastern Asia and much of Latin America and the Caribbean. In contrast, reflecting the long-term result of having no or limited educational opportunity for women, gender gaps in literacy rates remain wide and show persistence in Africa (excluding Southern Africa) and South-Central and Western Asia, ranging from 7 to 24 percentage points. Lower overall literacy rates are almost always accompanied by large differences between the rates for women and men. In those regions where progress has been slow, the disadvantages faced by women are difficult to reverse. Without sustained and effective adult literacy programmes, the majority of older women in these regions are likely to remain illiterate over the course of their lives.

Adult women's literacy rates are usually much lower in rural areas than in urban areas

National averages in literacy rates mask considerable sub-national differences. Many countries have significant urban-rural literacy gaps, with rural areas lagging behind in most cases because educational opportunities are more limited. This discrepancy is revealed by a review of literacy data from the 1990 and 2000 rounds of population censuses[7] from Africa and Asia (see figure 3.3). The urban-rural differences are larger than 30 percentage points in Egypt, Ethiopia, Morocco, Mozambique, Pakistan, Uganda, Yemen and Zambia. On the other hand, in countries where the overall literacy levels are relatively high – such as Armenia, China, Kyrgyzstan, Mongolia, Sri Lanka and Viet Nam – the urban-rural differences are less than 10 percentage points.

Literacy rates for young women and men have shown significant improvement over the past two decades and the gender gap has narrowed

---

7 United Nations, 2009.

The vast majority of young people in the world are literate. The worldwide youth literacy rate rose from 84 to 89 per cent from 1990 to 2007.[8] Over the same period, it increased from 81 to 87 per cent in the less developed regions as a whole. The global literacy rate for young women stood at 87 per cent in 2007, up from 79 per cent in 1990 (see figure 3.4). Correspondingly, young men's worldwide literacy rate stood at 91 per cent, having increased by 3 percentage points over the same period. Youth literacy is almost universal in the more developed regions of Europe, Northern America and Oceania, and rates are lower than 90 per cent only in Africa (excluding Southern Africa), South-Central Asia and the Oceania sub-regions of Melanesia and Micronesia. In parts of the world where many boys and girls do not attend school or drop out too early, youth literacy rates are much lower than the global averages. In Africa, where the rates are among the lowest in the world, only 70 per cent of young women and 79 per cent of young men are literate. The youth literacy rate is one of the indicators used to monitor progress towards MDG 2 of achieving universal primary education.[9] Many countries have made substantial progress by expanding access to education and taking measures to eliminate gender disparities. Nevertheless, many countries in these regions remain far from achieving the Goal.

Gender differences in youth literacy rates – as compared to those for adults – are not substantial in most regions (figure 3.4). Globally, the gender gap in youth literacy has declined from 9 percentage points to 5 over the period 1990–2007. Gender gaps are not significant in all the more developed regions and in several of the less developed ones. In the sub-regions of the Caribbean, Melanesia and Southern Africa gender gaps are slightly in the favour of young women (2–4 percentage points). However, gender gaps to the disadvantage of young women remain significant in the sub-regions of Africa (excluding Southern Africa), South-Central and Western Asia and Micronesia, where they range from 4–16 percentage points in favour of young men. Gender disparities in literacy are diminishing in these regions, but at a slow pace. Substantial progress in expanding school enrolments and improving school completion rates needs to be made in order to eliminate

Figure 3.3

Adult literate women in urban and rural areas in selected countries, latest census

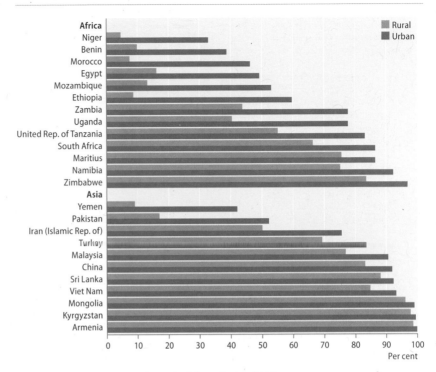

Source: United Nations, *Demographic Yearbook* data collections (2009).
Note: Latest available census is from either the 2000 or 1990 census round. Adult literates refer to those aged 15 and over.

gender disparities in youth literacy. The greatest challenge in this regard is to enrol girls and young women in school – particularly those from poor and rural households – and to ensure that, once enrolled, they remain in school.

Literacy levels of women in younger age groups are generally much higher than those in older age groups

In general, literacy levels are higher among younger age groups than among older ones, and those for younger women are often much higher than those for older women. In Europe, Northern America and other more developed countries where both the youth and adult literacy rates are very high, these differences are not very significant. However, a review of literacy data from the 2000 round of population censuses[10] for African and Asian countries shows that the percentages of young women aged 15–24 who are literate are almost always larger than those of women aged 25 and above. In countries where the overall literacy levels are relatively lower, the percentage of

---

8 UNESCO Institute for Statistics, 2009b.

9 Millennium Development Goal 2: Achieving universal primary education – Target 2.A: Ensure that, by 2015, children everywhere, boys and girls alike, will be able to complete a full course of primary schooling.

10 United Nations, 2009.

Figure 3.4
Youth literacy rates by sex and region, 1990 and 2007

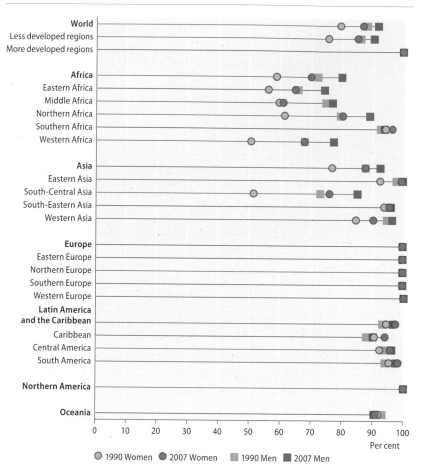

Source: UNESCO Institute for Statistics (2009a).
Note: Youth literacy rates refer to the literacy rates of young women and men aged 15–24.

cational attainment can give an indication of the stock of human capital – the knowledge and the skills available in a population. A higher level of educational attainment indicates the availability of a relatively high level of skills and knowledge in the labour force. Gender differences in educational attainment are one determinant of gender-based differences in labour market participation and outcomes. An increase in the proportion of highly educated women will likely lead to greater opportunities for more diverse and higher paying employment for women. Beyond labour markets, high levels of educational attainment also have a positive impact on broader social development goals. As noted in the Introduction, raising educational attainment is a key mechanism for empowering women. Without education of comparable quality and content to that given to men, women cannot access well paid, formal sector jobs, advance within them, participate in and be represented in government and gain political influence.[11]

Levels of educational attainment are associated with levels of socio-economic development

Figure 3.6 presents a regional comparison[12] of women's and men's educational attainment according to four levels: "no schooling", "any primary", "any secondary" and "any tertiary".[13] It is apparent from the chart that the distribution of educational attainment varies substantially across regions depending on the general level of socio-economic development. In the more developed regions, where universal primary education has been attained, the proportions of women and men with no schooling or whose highest attainment is at the primary level are low and the proportions whose highest attainment is at or above the sec-

women aged 15–24 who are literate is typically twice as high or more than that for women aged 25 and over (figure 3.5). These large differences in the rates underscore the structural difficulty of achieving rapid progress in literacy due to the preponderance of older generations in the illiterate population and the fact that the majority among this age group are women. School enrolments have a significant impact on the literacy rates for younger age groups but not for older ones, among whom the incidence of literacy is the lowest. Improving literacy levels among older age groups will not be possible without renewed urgency and larger investments in adult literacy programmes.

2. Educational attainment

Educational attainment refers to the highest level of education an individual has completed. Aggregated at the societal level, statistics on edu-

11 Lopez-Carlos and Zahidi, 2005.

12 It should be noted that the regional averages, which were computed unweighted by the population sizes of constituent countries, should not be regarded as exact because of the lack of data for some countries. However, they provide a basis for broad comparison of educational attainment across regions. It is also important to bear in mind that comparability of data is limited because of differing definitions pertaining to educational attainment used by countries and because educational systems in different countries do not necessarily impart the same amount of skills and knowledge at each level of education.

13 The educational attainment category of "no schooling" refers to all persons who have attended less than one grade at the primary level; "any primary" comprises those who completed primary education (ISCED 1) or least one grade of primary; "any secondary" includes those who attended lower secondary (ISCED 2), upper secondary (ISCED 3) or post-secondary non-tertiary (ISCED 4); and "any tertiary" comprises those who attended any tertiary education (ISCED 5-6).

ondary level are very substantial. Most countries in Europe, Northern America, Oceania and the sub-regions of the Caribbean and Central, Eastern and Western Asia display such a profile of educational attainment. Conversely, in the less developed regions where universal primary education remains a distant goal, the proportions of women and men without schooling or whose highest attainment is capped at the primary level are vast and the proportions whose attainment is at the secondary or tertiary level are dismal. This profile of educational attainment is pervasive in most of the countries in Africa and the sub-regions of Central and South America and Southern and South-Eastern Asia. The same general pattern is discernible in the chart presenting national educational attainment for countries with data (see figure 3.7).

Gender disparities in educational attainment are substantial in the less developed regions

---

There are significant differences between the educational attainment of women and men (see figures 3.6 and 3.7). In general, gender gaps across all educational attainment categories are more substantial in the less developed regions than in the more developed. Some of the largest gaps are found in Africa where on average 41 per cent of women have never attended school, compared to 24 per cent of men. In Benin, over 80 per cent of women have no schooling while for men the comparative figure is only 57 per cent. More than half the women in Malawi (55 per cent) have not attended school, while the figure is 46 per cent in Algeria and 45 per cent in the United Republic of Tanzania, all with a gender gap in the range of 20–25 percentage points in favour of men. Gender differences are also large in Southern Asia where on average 49 per cent of women have no education at all, compared to 36 per cent for men. In Bangladesh and Maldives, more than 50 per cent of women have no education. In Pakistan, 67 per cent of women have never attended school, 32 percentage points higher than for men. Most countries in Central America and South-Eastern and Western Asia show moderate gender gaps in the range of 5–10 percentage points, all in favour of men.

Substantial proportions of women and men in the less developed regions have not advanced beyond the primary level – over 30 per cent in Africa, Latin America and the Caribbean and the sub-regions of South-Eastern and Western Asia. In the case of Africa, 38 per cent and 46 per cent of

Figure 3.5

Literacy among women aged 15–24 and 25+ in selected countries or areas, 2000 census

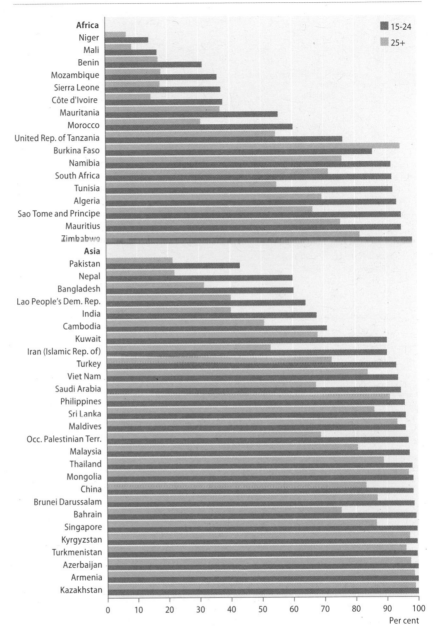

Source: United Nations, *Demographic Yearbook* data collections (2009).

women and men respectively have attained education only up to the primary level. In contrast, in Europe (except Southern Europe), the proportions are less than 15 per cent for both women and men. In Northern America they are below 10 per cent for both women and men.

Beyond primary education, 21 per cent of women in Africa on average have obtained secondary or tertiary education, compared to 30 per cent of men. The combined secondary and tertiary level

Figure 3.6

Distribution of population by the highest level of education attained, sex and region, 1995–2007 (*latest available*)

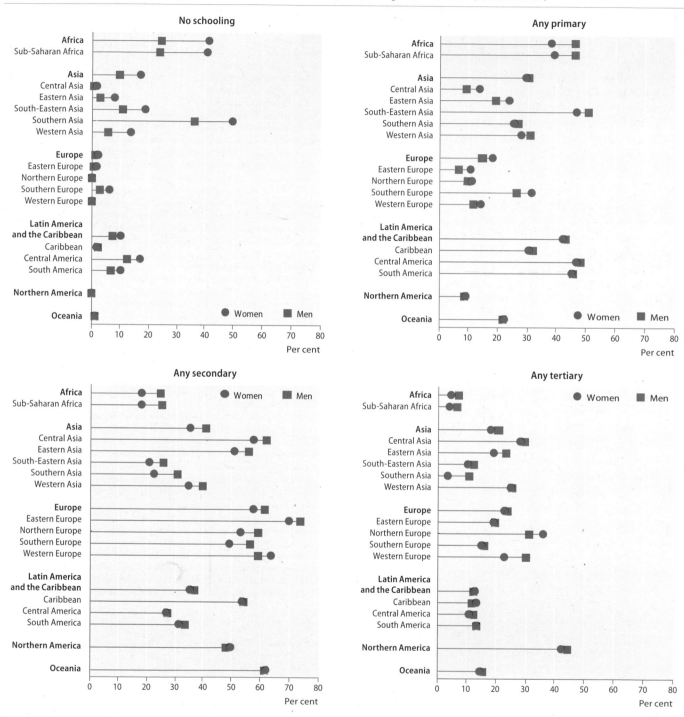

Source: Computed by the United Nations Statistics Division based on data from UNESCO Institute for Statistics (2009a) and United Nations, *Demographic Yearbook* data collections (2009).
Note: Data refer to educational attainment of population aged 25 and over. The regional averages are unweighted. The averages calculated for Africa include the values of eight countries. The averages for Oceania are based on data for four countries (Fiji, French Polynesia, New Zealand and Tonga).

attainment of women was 25 and 30 per cent in Southern and South-Eastern Asia respectively, whereas this was 41 and 37 per cent for men. In Bangladesh, Cambodia, Indonesia, Lao People's Democratic Republic, Maldives, Pakistan, Thailand and Turkey, the percentage of women with secondary or tertiary attainment was less than 25 per cent. These countries display a large gender gap

Figure 3.7

Distribution of population by sex and the highest level of education attained, 1995–2007 (*latest available*)

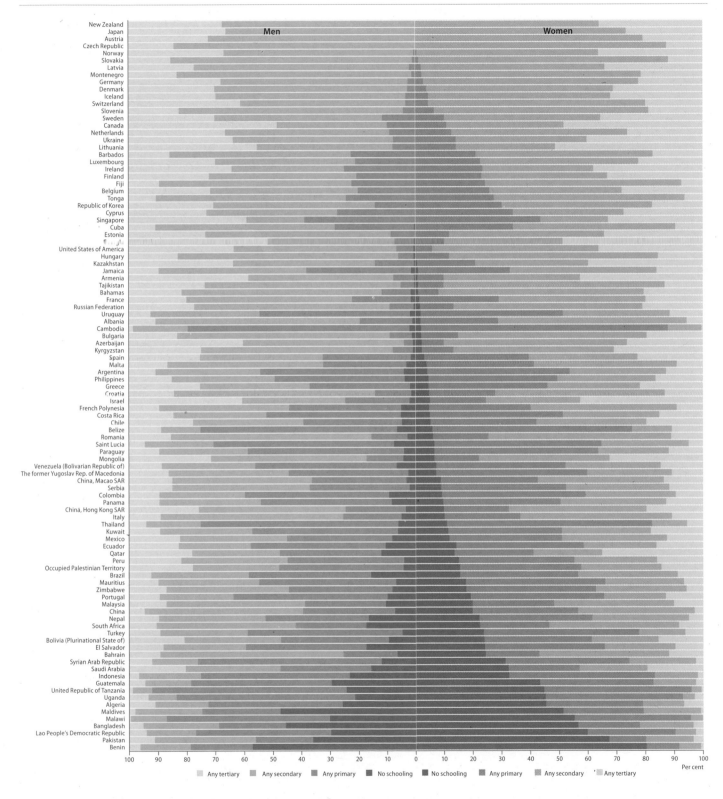

Source: Compiled by the United Nations Statistics Division from UNESCO Institute for Statistics (2009a) and United Nations, *Demographic Yearbook* data collections (2009).
Note: Data refer to educational attainment of population aged 25 and over. The population whose education level is unknown has been proportionately distributed over the four categories of educational attainment.

in the range of 10–22 percentage points, revealing a severe educational disadvantage to women.

Gender gaps across all categories of educational attainment are less pronounced in regions where levels are generally high among the population. In Europe (except Southern Europe), Northern America and several countries in Latin America and the Caribbean as well as Oceania, the proportions of women and men with combined secondary and tertiary educational attainment are almost the same, with a few exceptions. Educational attainment at the secondary and tertiary levels in Eastern Asia and Southern Europe is quite substantial at more than 60 per cent; nevertheless, these subregions display large gender gaps. China and the Republic of Korea from Eastern Asia and Albania, Croatia, Italy, Romania, Serbia and the former Yugoslav Republic of Macedonia from Southern Europe show gender gaps in the range of 10–17 percentage points, all to the disadvantage of

women. In contrast to the general pattern of gender disparities observed in both the more and less developed regions, in several Latin American and Caribbean countries (Bahamas, Jamaica, Panama, Saint Lucia, Uruguay and Venezuela (Bolivarian Republic of)) women have surpassed men in educational attainment at the secondary and tertiary levels. Moderate gender gaps are also present to the advantage of women in the Western Asian countries of Kuwait, Qatar and the Syrian Arab Republic.

B. Participation in education

1. Primary education

Participation in primary education

Primary enrolment of girls and boys is increasing across the world, but several countries are still far from attaining universal education

Enrolment in primary education has increased in most regions of the world, with several countries making rapid progress towards universal primary education. At the global level, the rate of primary-school-aged girls enrolled in school increased to 86 per cent from 79 per cent in the period 1999–2007 (see figure 3.8). Correspondingly, the rate increased for boys from 85 to 88 per cent. Out of 163 countries for which primary net enrolment data are available by sex in the period 1999–2007, girls' enrolment rates exceeded 90 per cent in 92 countries, though they were less than 75 per cent in 32 countries (see Statistical Annex).[14] Enrolment rates have improved more for girls than for boys, particularly in those regions where girls' enrolment was historically much lower. In 2007, 84 per cent of primary-school-aged girls were enrolled in the less developed regions as a whole, while the rate was 95 per cent for the more developed regions. In most developed countries of Eastern Asia, Europe, Northern America and Oceania, enrolment is nearly universal and girls' primary net enrolment rates generally stayed higher than 95 per cent during the period. The average rates for both girls and boys exceeded 90 per cent in Eastern Europe, South-Eastern Asia and much of Latin America and the Caribbean. Outstanding gains in enrolment have been registered in several less developed parts of the world, particularly Africa and South-Central Asia, partly due to the abolish-

Figure 3.8
Primary net enrolment rates by sex and region, 1999 and 2007

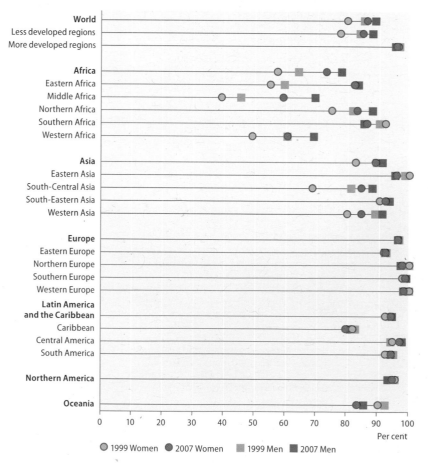

● 1999 Women   ● 2007 Women   ■ 1999 Men   ■ 2007 Men

Source: UNESCO Institute for Statistics (2009a).

14 The net enrolment rate is the enrolment of the official age group for a given level of education expressed as a percentage of the corresponding population.

ment of school fees. However, most of the countries in these regions are still far from attaining universal primary education. In Africa, despite an impressive increase of 16 percentage points in girls' primary enrolment between 1999 and 2007, only 73 per cent of primary-school-aged girls and 78 per cent of boys attended school in 2007. Two sub-regions of Africa – Middle and Western Africa – have some of the world's lowest rates with less than 60 per cent of girls of primary school age attending school. Similarly, despite a rapid rise in primary enrolment, less than 85 per cent of primary-school-aged girls in South-Central and Western Asia attended school in 2007. In contrast to the overall progress being registered in primary enrolment, a few sub-regions have seen reversals, with declines in enrolment for both girls and boys in countries in Southern Africa, Eastern Asia, the Caribbean and Oceania. In some of these cases, the declines are associated with decreasing size of the school-age population.[15]

While gender gaps in primary education have narrowed in the majority of countries across the world, gender parity is still a distant goal for several countries

---

With increased enrolment, gender gaps in primary enrolment have diminished in most regions of the world. They have narrowed even in Africa and South-Central and Western Asia, where enrolment has historically been among the lowest and the gender gaps the widest. The fast-closing gap is shown by the gender parity index (GPI) based on primary net enrolment rates – expressed as the ratio of the net enrolment for girls to that for boys – which increased from 0.93 to 0.97 globally between 1999 and 2007, although boys continue to enjoy a slightly higher enrolment than girls (see table 3.2). Out of 163 countries with data in the period, gender parity in primary education has more or less been attained in 117 of them.[16] On the other hand, 38 countries with data showed gender disparities in favour of boys, whereas disparities favouring girls were observed in only 8 countries. In the more developed regions as a whole the GPI has stayed at parity over the same period, whereas in the less developed regions as a whole the GPI has increased to that of the global average. The gap is nonexistent in Europe, Latin America and the Caribbean, Northern America and Oceania.

---

15 UNESCO, 2008.

16 Gender parity is considered to have been attained when the GPI is between 0.97 and 1.03.

Gender Parity Index

The Gender Parity Index (GPI) is commonly used to measure progress towards gender parity in education. For a given indicator, the GPI is calculated as the ratio of the value for females to that for males. A GPI value equal to one indicates parity. In general, a value less than one indicates disparity in favour of men/boys, whereas a value greater than one indicates disparity in favour of women/girls. Gender parity is considered to have been attained when the GPI lies between 0.97 and 1.03.

Gender gaps are more varied in Africa and Asia. Eastern and South-Eastern Asia have attained gender parity, whereas South-Central and Western Asia show moderate gender disparities in favour of boys. Africa shows the largest gender gap and, with the exception of the sub-regions of Eastern and Southern Africa, its GPI is well below the global average. Gender gaps are notably large in the

Table 3.2

Gender parity index (GPI) based on primary net enrolment rates by region, 1999 and 2007

	Gender parity index (GPI)	
	1999	2007
World	**0.93**	**0.97**
Less developed regions	0.92	0.97
More developed regions	1.00	1.00
Africa	**0.89**	**0.93**
Eastern Africa	0.92	0.98
Middle Africa	0.86	0.86
Northern Africa	0.92	0.94
Southern Africa	1.02	1.01
Western Africa	0.81	0.88
Asia	**0.93**	**0.97**
Eastern Asia	1.01	1.01
South-Central Asia	0.85	0.96
South-Eastern Asia	0.97	0.99
Western Asia	0.90	0.93
Europe	**0.99**	**1.00**
Eastern Europe	0.99	1.00
Northern Europe	1.00	1.01
Southern Europe	0.99	0.99
Western Europe	1.00	1.00
Latin America and the Caribbean	**0.98**	**1.00**
Caribbean	0.99	0.98
Central America	1.00	0.99
South America	0.97	1.00
Northern America	**1.00**	**1.01**
Oceania	**0.98**	**0.97**

Source: UNESCO Institute for Statistics (2009a).

Figure 3.9
Gender disparities in primary net enrolment rates, 2007

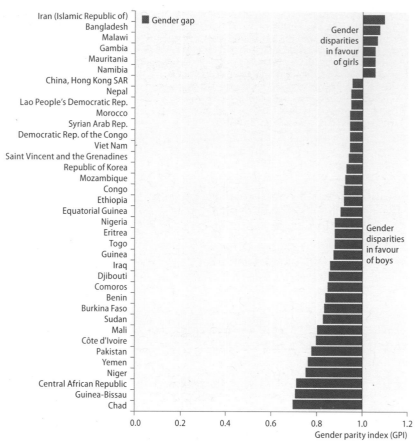

Source: UNESCO Institute for Statistics (2009a).
Note: Data presented for countries where the gender gap is 5 percentage points or larger.

sub-regions of Middle and Western Africa where the GPI is below 0.90. Although the gaps are narrowing in those regions where they had been substantial, there remain several countries in which the proportion of girls in total primary enrolment remains considerably lower than that of boys (see figure 3.9). The GPI is at or below 0.75 in Central African Republic, Chad, Guinea-Bissau and Niger. It should be noted that, although much less common, there is a gender gap in favour of girls in a few countries such as Bangladesh, Gambia, Iran (Islamic Republic of), Malawi, Mauritania and Namibia. Gender disparities are more severe in countries with a disproportionate number of poor and rural households;[17] they tend to be wider among poorer people than among the more affluent, in rural than in urban areas and, within the latter, in slum than in non-slum areas.[18]

17 United Nations Human Settlements Programme, 2006.
18 Ibid.

Out-of-school children[19]

The number of out-of-school children is declining but not fast enough

At the turn of the millennium an estimated 105 million girls and boys of primary school age around the world were not enrolled in school. This number had fallen to about 72 million by 2007, representing a decline by 33 million or 31 per cent (see table 3.3). In 2007, about 39 million girls of primary school age were not in school, compared to about 33 million boys. The expansion of access to primary education, including in some of the poorest countries, has helped reduce the number of out-of-school children, despite an overall increase in the population of children in this age group. Almost all girls and boys of primary school age out of school live in the less developed regions of the world, with nearly 70 per cent of them concentrated in sub-Saharan Africa and South and West Asia (see figure 3.10).[20] Over 32 million out-of-school children, 45 per cent of the global figure, lived in sub-Saharan Africa, and some 18 million children (about a quarter) in South and West Asia. The numbers of out-of-school children across the world are declining but not fast enough, underscoring the enormity of the challenge and the urgency of reaching poorer, more socially marginalized children who normally have less access to basic education.

While there has been progress toward gender parity in school enrolment, gender barriers remain. In 2007, girls comprised 54 per cent of the children of primary school age out of school, down from 58 per cent in 1999 (see table 3.3). The proportion of girls among these children ranges from 44 per cent in North America and Western Europe to 61 per cent in the Arab States (comprising the Middle East and North Africa). The share of out-of-school girls was the highest in the Arab States, where Egypt, Iraq and Yemen accounted for more than 70 per cent. The second-highest share of out-of-school girls is found in Central, South and West Asia, where the proportion is 58 per cent. Over the period 1999 to 2007, the regional average propor-

19 These are primary-school-age children not attending either primary or secondary education, having either not started school or dropped out before completion. They may also be in some type of non-formal education that is not recognized as fully equivalent to formal primary education.

20 The regional groupings in this section correspond to those used by UNESCO and differ from those used in other parts of this chapter.

Box 3.2
Gender parity and equality in education – what's the difference?

Gender parity and gender equality in education mean different things. The first is a purely numerical concept. Reaching gender parity in education implies that the same proportion of boys and girls – relative to their respective age groups – would enter the education system and participate in its different cycles.

Gender equality, on the other hand, means that boys and girls would experience the same advantages or disadvantages in educational access, treatment and outcomes. In so far as it goes beyond questions of numerical balance, equality is more difficult to define and measure than parity.

The achievement of full gender equality in education would imply:

- *Equality of opportunities*, in the sense that girls and boys are offered the same chances to access school, i.e. parents, teachers and society at large have no gender-biased attitudes in this respect;

- *Equality in the learning process*, i.e. girls and boys receive the same treatment and attention, follow the same curricula, enjoy teaching methods and teaching tools free of stereotypes and gender bias, are offered academic orientation and counselling not affected by gender biases, and profit from the same quantity and quality of appropriate educational infrastructures;

- *Equality of outcomes*, i.e. learning achievements, length of school careers, academic qualifications and diplomas would not differ by gender;

- *Equality of external results*, i.e. job opportunities, the time needed to find a job after leaving full-time education, the earnings of men and women with similar qualifications and experience, etc., would all be equal.

The last condition, while not strictly part of a notion of educational equality, is nevertheless entailed by it: the persistence of gender discrimination in the labour market prevents the attainment of equality of access, treatment and outcomes in education by affecting the relative costs and perceived benefits of educating girls and boys. Accordingly, if full gender equality in education were to be achieved, it is probably the case that ending labour market discrimination, in all its gendered forms, would be required.

Source: UNESCO, *EFA Global Monitoring Report 2003/4* (2003).

Table 3.3
Number of primary-school-age girls and boys out of school by sex and region, 1999 and 2007 (*in thousands*)

	1999				2007			
	Both sexes	Boys	Girls	Girls (%)	Both sexes	Boys	Girls	Girls (%)
World	105 035	44 558	60 477	58	71 791	32 677	39 115	54
Less developed regions	101 773	42 939	58 834	58	68 638	30 965	37 673	55
More developed regions	1 791	902	889	50	2 334	1 304	1 030	44
Arab States	7 980	3 249	4 731	59	5 753	2 232	3 520	61
Central and Eastern Europe	2 036	843	1 193	59	1 552	749	803	52
Central Asia	464	231	233	50	271	115	156	58
East Asia and the Pacific	5 992	2 897	3 095	52	9 039	4 683	4 357	48
East Asia	5 674	2 750	2 923	52	8 484	4 417	4 067	48
Pacific	318	147	172	54	555	266	290	52
Latin America and the Caribbean	3 538	1 618	1 920	54	2 989	1 506	1 483	50
Caribbean	493	246	247	50	621	304	318	51
Latin America	3 045	1 372	1 673	55	2 367	1 202	1 165	49
North America and Western Europe	1 420	713	707	50	1 931	1 081	850	44
South and West Asia	38 594	14 168	24 426	63	18 032	7 644	10 388	58
Sub-Saharan Africa	45 012	20 840	24 172	54	32 226	14 667	17 559	54

Source: UNESCO, *EFA Global Monitoring Report 2010* (2010).
Note: Regional groupings correspond to those used by UNESCO and differ from those used in other parts of this chapter.

Figure 3.10

Geographic distribution of primary school age children out of school, 1999 and 2007

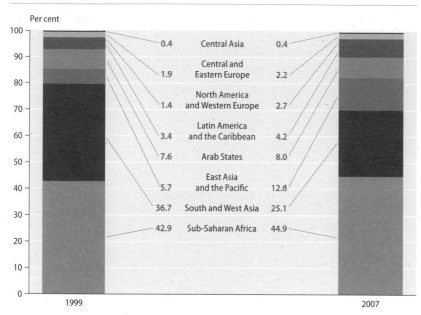

Per cent

1999		2007
0.4	Central Asia	0.4
1.9	Central and Eastern Europe	2.2
1.4	North America and Western Europe	2.7
3.4	Latin America and the Caribbean	4.2
7.6	Arab States	8.0
5.7	East Asia and the Pacific	12.6
36.7	South and West Asia	25.1
42.9	Sub-Saharan Africa	44.9

Source: UNESCO, *EFA Global Monitoring Report 2010* (2010).
Note: Regional groupings correspond to those used by UNESCO and differ from those used in other parts of this chapter.

tion in Central Asia has seen a rise while South and West Asia registered a decrease. Georgia, India, Pakistan and Tajikistan are among the countries where girls comprise more than 60 per cent of out-of-school children of primary school age. In sub-Saharan Africa as a whole, girls account for 54 per cent of such children, but in Benin, Central African Republic, Guinea, Togo and United Republic of Tanzania the proportion is well over 60 per cent.

Poverty and other barriers keep some children out of school

Many barriers stand in the way of children's schooling, including poverty, child labour, unaffordable school fees, lack of basic facilities, discrimination and low quality education. These barriers are often compounded by negative cultural practices – such as early marriage and the preference for educating boys over girls – that put education out of reach for many girls. Analysis[21] done by UNESCO based on household survey data for 80 countries, collected between 1996 and 2003 as part of Multiple Indicator Cluster Surveys (MICS) and Demographic and Health Surveys (DHS), show that household wealth is always strongly related to school attendance, with

children from the poorest households more likely to be out of school than their peers in the rest of the population. The analysis found that children of primary school age who live in the poorest 20 per cent of households are three times more likely to be out of school than children living in the richest 20 per cent. Child labour, commonly a symptom of poverty in a household, is a related phenomenon that interferes with schooling. The educational level of parents is also often a factor. The analysis showed that primary-school-age children with a mother with no education are twice as likely to be out of school than children with a mother with some education. Place of residence was also seen to influence the likelihood that a child will be out of school. The proportion is greater in rural areas than in urban areas, with 82 per cent of out-of-school children living in the former. Reasons for this include less access to education, including long distances to schools, and lack of trained teachers.

Natural disasters and civil conflicts are also barriers that disrupt the education of many children. According to the UN High Commissioner for Refugees, more than 1.5 million school-age refugee children live in less developed countries.[22] Data for 114 refugee camps in 27 countries show that full primary school enrolment has been achieved in only six out of ten camps, and that at least one in five refugee children is not part of the formal education system.[23] Ensuring that the most vulnerable and marginalized children are enrolled and remain in school requires targeted programmes and interventions aimed at poor households and strategies for developing educational systems that are inclusive, equitable and sustainable.

School progression

School progression is a critical factor in the effort to ensure that all girls and boys have access to, and complete, free and compulsory primary education of good quality. Without this, high levels of intake and enrolment do not by themselves guarantee the achievement of universal primary education. In countries with limited access to education, repeaters may keep others out of school. High levels of repetition and drop out prevent a considerable number of children from reaching secondary school at the appropriate age, which in

---

21 UNESCO Institute for Statistics, 2005a.

22 United Nations, 2008.

23 Ibid.

turn undermines efforts to improve coverage of secondary education. They also reveal problems in the internal efficiency of the educational system and possibly reflect a poor level of instruction. Repetition and drop out disproportionately affect students from low-income and socially disadvantaged groups. Ensuring equity and quality in the education system implies overcoming repetition, drop out and low learning achievement.

Repetition at the primary level is widespread in most less developed regions

Analysis of recent data shows that repetition is an extensive phenomenon in most less developed regions of the world. A considerable number of children experience difficulty progressing from one grade to the next at the primary level. The Statistical Annex presents data on primary repetition rates for girls and boys. The phenomenon of repetition affects all regions; however, it has been the most persistent and its incidence the highest in Africa. In this region, the overall primary repeater rates range between 3 and 34 per cent in 48 countries with data. In 27 countries or areas the repetition rate surpasses 10 per cent. Repeaters account for over a quarter of enrolment in Burundi, Comoros, Central African Republic, Gabon and Sao Tome and Principe (see figure 3.11). In Asia, repetition rates have improved over the past few decades. In the majority of the countries in the region they are well below 5 per cent, and they exceed 10 per cent in only 6 countries out of 46 with data: Afghanistan (16 per cent), Bangladesh (11 per cent), Cambodia (12 per cent), Lao People's Democratic Republic (17 per cent), Nepal (21 per cent) and Timor-Leste (15 per cent). In Latin America and the Caribbean, repetition rates are the highest in Brazil (20 per cent), Guatemala (12 per cent), the Netherlands Antilles (13 per cent) and Suriname (16 per cent). In the rest of the countries with data in this region, repetition rates are well below 10 per cent. The lowest repetition rates at the primary level are found in Europe and Northern America, in part due to the policy of automatic promotion that is practiced in several countries in these regions. In countries with available data, the only ones recording repetition rates of 3 per cent or more are Belgium (3 per cent), France (4 per cent), Luxembourg (4 per cent) and Portugal (10 per cent). It should be noted that repetition is not uniformly distributed across all primary school grades. In most cases, the highest rates of repetition tend to be concentrated

Figure 3.11

Proportion of repeaters among pupils in primary education, by sex, 2007

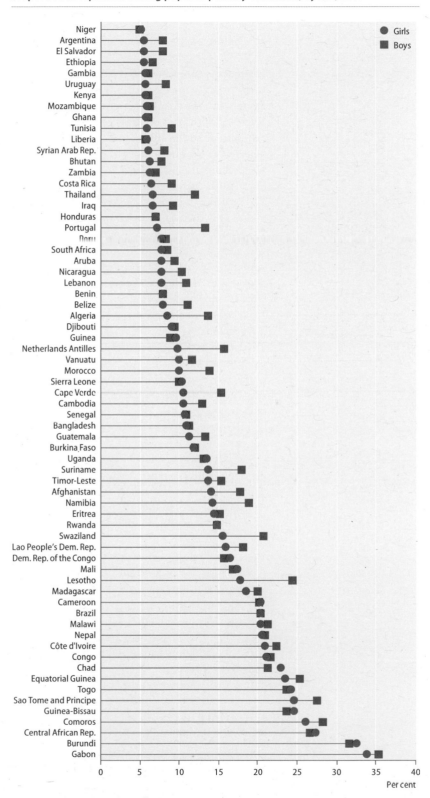

Source: UNESCO Institute for Statistics (2009a).

Note: Data presented for selected countries where the repetition rate for girls is larger than 5 per cent. Data correspond to reference year 2007 or latest available in the period 2000–2007.

in the early grades and, though not exclusively, among children from poor families, those living in rural areas and disadvantaged social groups.

Girls repeat in fewer countries than boys

In general, gender disparities in school progression at the primary level favour girls. Once enrolled in school, girls tend to do better than boys. In 158 countries with data on repetition rates by sex in the period 2000–2007, in 124 countries boys repeated at a higher rate than girls while only in 11 countries did girls repeat at a higher rate than boys. With the exception of Oman and Turkey, all the other countries where girls repeated at a higher rate are located in sub-Saharan Africa. In 23 countries repetition rates showed gender parity, with girls and boys repeating at more or less the same rate. It should be noted that in the majority of countries, the differences between the repetition rates for girls and boys are not large. However, in some countries and areas – Algeria, Lesotho, the Netherlands Antilles, Portugal, Swaziland and Thailand – gender gaps of more than 5 percentage points are observed, all to the disadvantage of boys. One study on the Middle East and North Africa suggests that the apparent similarities of repetition rates among girls and boys in these regions should be interpreted in light of the fact that the drop-out rate among girls is notably higher than among boys.[24] Thus in actual fact only a few girls are given the opportunity to repeat their grade.[25]

Survival rates to the last grade of primary show considerable variation

The survival rate to the last grade of primary school – defined as the proportion of students starting first grade who are expected to reach the last grade regardless of repetition – measures the ability and efficiency of an education system to retain students. It also indicates the magnitude of drop out. Survival rates approaching 100 per cent indicate a high level of retention or a low incidence of drop out. The survival rate to the last grade of primary school is an official indicator to track progress towards MDG 2 (which, as previously noted, calls for universal primary education by the year 2015).

Survival rates vary considerably across the world. For countries with data in the period 1999–2007, the rates ranged from 25 per cent to 100 per cent

24 Mehran, 1995.
25 Ibid.

(see Statistical Annex). Of the 147 countries with data, in 92 countries girls had higher rates than boys. Boys' rates exceeded those of girls' in 52 countries, while in 3 countries girls and boys reached the last grade of primary school in equal proportions. The survival rate was less than 50 per cent in 10 countries, while it surpassed 90 per cent in 64 countries. The lowest survival rates globally were in sub-Saharan Africa, where they were below 50 per cent in nine countries: Chad, Central African Republic, Equatorial Guinea, Madagascar, Malawi, Mozambique, Rwanda, Togo and Uganda (see figure 3.12). In these countries, more than half of all children who start attending primary school drop out before completion. Africa is also one of the regions in which almost half of the countries have higher rates for boys than girls. Asia has seen improved survival rates, with half of the countries attaining survival rates in excess of 90 per cent. In the countries of Latin America and the Caribbean with data, the rates were all above 80 per cent, except in Dominican Republic, El Salvador, Guatemala, Guyana, Nicaragua and Suriname. For the majority of the more developed countries of Europe and Northern America, rates of survival were very close to 100 per cent.

Girls and boys survived or dropped out of school in equal proportions in the majority of countries

Gender parity in survival rates has been observed in the majority of countries with data. This indicates that in those countries girls and boys survived to the last grade of primary or dropped out of school in more or less equal proportions. Out of 147 countries with data, this was the case in 81 countries. In 47 countries girls survived at a higher rate than boys, while in 19 countries the situation was reversed. Sub-Saharan Africa is where several of the countries with relatively larger gender disparities in survival rates were found. In Côte d'Ivoire, Central African Republic, Chad, Guinea, Mali, Mozambique, Niger, Sao Tome and Principe, Togo and Zambia, the rates for boys were 5 percentage points or more than those for girls. On the other hand, the rates for girls were 5 percentage points or more than those for boys in Algeria, Botswana, Cape Verde, Comoros, Ghana and Lesotho. In half of the countries in Asia, gender disparity favours boys over girls. The highest survival disparity is found in Iraq, where 39 girls per 100 drop out while the comparable figure is 22 per 100 for boys. In Latin America and the Caribbean, girls survived to the last grade of primary school at a higher rate than boys in all countries with data except in Bolivia (Plurinational State of), Guatemala and Guyana.

2. Secondary education

Participation in secondary education

Relatively fewer girls and boys attend secondary school

Less than 58 per cent of the world's girls and 60 per cent of boys in the official secondary-school age group attended secondary school in 2007 (see figure 3.13), a significantly lower proportion than enrol in primary school. Globally, secondary net enrolment increased by 8 percentage points for girls and 6 percentage points for boys over the period 1999–2007. Girls' secondary enrolment rates in Africa, Asia and Latin America and the Caribbean have registered gains ranging from 6 to 13 percentage points over the same period. Out of 144 countries for which secondary enrolment data were available by sex in the period 1999–2007, girl's enrolment rates were less than 50 per cent in 42 countries and exceeded 90 per cent in only 25 countries (see Statistical Annex). When compared to those at the primary level, secondary enrolment rates display greater variation between the more and less developed regions. Over 90 per cent of girls in the official secondary-school age group were enrolled in school in Europe (except Eastern Europe) and Northern America in 2007. Despite the gains being made, secondary school enrolment is too low in many of the less developed regions. Enrolment of secondary school-aged girls was less than 30 per cent in all sub-regions of Africa, except Northern and Southern Africa, while in South-Central Asia the rate was 44 per cent. In several of the less developed regions, a significant proportion of the secondary-school-age population is either out of school or attends primary school.[26] In Oceania, almost two thirds of boys and girls of secondary school age were out of school in 2006, while in sub-Saharan Africa 41 per cent were out of school and 34 per cent attended primary rather than secondary school; only about a quarter attended secondary school.[27]

Gender disparities occur in more countries and remain wider than those at the primary level

26 United Nations, 2008.
27 Ibid.

Figure 3.12
Survival rates to last grade of primary by sex, 2007

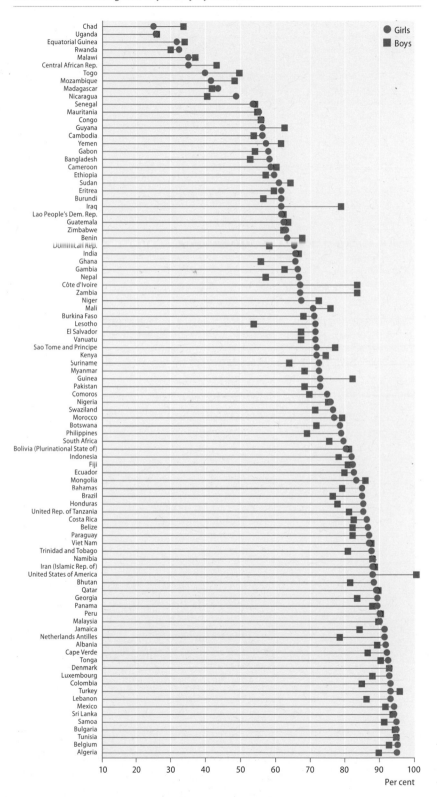

Source: UNESCO Institute for Statistics (2009a).
Note: Data presented for selected countries where the survival rate for girls is less than 95 per cent. Data correspond to reference year 2007 or latest available in the period 2000–2007.

Figure 3.13
Secondary net enrolment rates by sex and region, 1999 and 2007

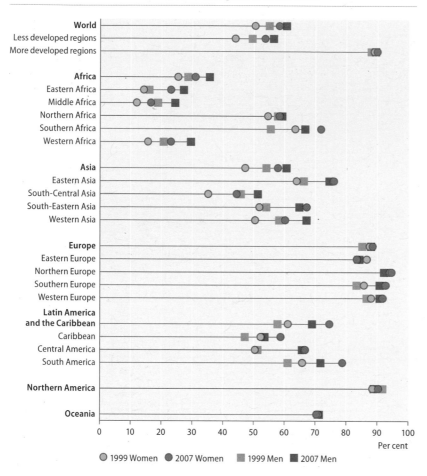

○ 1999 Women   ● 2007 Women   ▪ 1999 Men   ▪ 2007 Men

Source: UNESCO Institute for Statistics (2009a).

whereas in the less developed regions as a whole it was 0.95, significantly favouring boys. Gender disparities in secondary participation favouring girls over boys have been observed in 48 countries with data. In countries in Latin America and the Caribbean such as Argentina, Brazil, Colombia, Nicaragua, Panama, Uruguay and Venezuela (Bolivarian Republic of), where GPIs are larger than 1.10, substantially more girls are enrolled in secondary education than boys (see figure 3.14). In a number of countries in Southern Africa (Botswana, Lesotho, Namibia and South Africa), South-Eastern Asia (Malaysia, Philippines and Thailand) and Oceania (Fiji, Samoa and Tonga), enrolment rates for girls also exceed those for boys.

Table 3.4
Gender parity index based on secondary net enrolment rates by region, 1999 and 2007

	Gender parity index (GPI)	
	1999	2007
World	**0.92**	**0.96**
Less developed regions	0.89	0.95
More developed regions	1.01	1.01
Africa	**0.88**	**0.87**
Eastern Africa	0.86	0.84
Middle Africa	0.63	0.67
Northern Africa	0.94	0.98
Southern Africa	1.14	1.07
Western Africa	0.76	0.77
Asia	**0.87**	**0.95**
Eastern Asia	0.96	1.02
South-Central Asia	0.77	0.87
South-Eastern Asia	0.96	1.04
Western Asia	0.86	0.90
Europe	**1.03**	**1.01**
Eastern Europe	1.04	0.99
Northern Europe	1.01	1.03
Southern Europe	1.02	1.02
Western Europe	1.02	1.01
Latin America and the Caribbean	**1.06**	**1.07**
Caribbean	1.12	1.09
Central America	0.98	1.01
South America	1.08	1.09
Northern America	**0.96**	**1.02**
Oceania	**0.99**	**0.99**

Source: UNESCO Institute for Statistics (2009a).

The global gender parity index (GPI) based on net secondary enrolment rates has risen to 0.96 in 2007 from its corresponding value of 0.92 in 1999, showing that the gender gap at the secondary level is narrowing globally (see table 3.4). Although gender disparities in access to secondary education have improved, they remain more prevalent and wider than those at the primary level. This is so in part because gender differences at the secondary level are a reflection of cumulative gender disparities at the primary level and those at transition to secondary.[28] A smaller number of countries are near parity in secondary education than in primary education. Out of 144 countries with data, gender parity has been attained in only 54 countries, in contrast to 117 countries at the primary level. In the more developed regions in 2007, the GPI was 1.01, indicating gender parity has more or less been achieved,

28 UNESCO, 2005b.

On the other hand, gender disparities favoured boys in 42 countries with data. The proportion of girls in total secondary enrolment remains considerably lower than that of boys in many of the less developed sub-regions, most notably in Middle Africa where the GPI is 0.67, Western Africa (0.77) and Eastern Africa (0.84). Substantial gender gaps to the disadvantage of girls also remain in South-Central and Western Asia, where the GPI for secondary school in 2007 was 0.87 and 0.90, respectively. In the majority of African and Asian countries girls have substantially lower enrolment rates than boys at both the primary and secondary levels.

Participation in technical and vocational education and training (TVET)

More boys participate in TVET in all regions except Latin America and the Caribbean

Technical and vocational education and training (TVET) encompasses a wide range of fields of study – from teacher training programmes to commercial studies to technical fields in industry and engineering – and prepares learners for the acquisition of knowledge and skills for the world of work, usually in a specific trade, occupation or job requiring expertise in a particular group of techniques or technology.

Regional averages of girls' participation in TVET at the secondary level are presented in figure 3.15. The data show that this varies greatly across regions. More boys participate in TVET in all regions except Latin America and the Caribbean, where slightly more girls than boys are enrolled (54 per cent). Of the 161 countries for which data were available in the period 1999–2007, girls had lower TVET enrolment than boys in 129 of them (see Statistical Annex). Significantly more girls were enrolled than boys in half of the countries with data in Latin America and the Caribbean, including over 60 per cent in Bolivia (Plurinational State of), Jamaica and Peru. Girls in South and West Asia[29] were considerably underrepresented in TVET programmes, accounting for less than 28 per cent of total enrolment. In sub-Saharan Africa, the majority of countries displayed larger enrolment for boys. In Equatorial Guinea, Guinea, Niger, Sao Tome and Principe and Sudan,

girls' share was below 25 per cent. However, in five countries in the region (Congo, Kenya, Lesotho, Mali and Sierra Leone) girls represented over half of the TVET enrolment. The gender-based differences observed in respect of access to secondary education are, to a large extent, also reflected in the participation levels of TVET programmes.

29 The regional groupings in this section correspond to those used by UNESCO and differ from those used in other parts of the chapter.

Figure 3.14
Gender disparities in secondary net enrolment, 2007

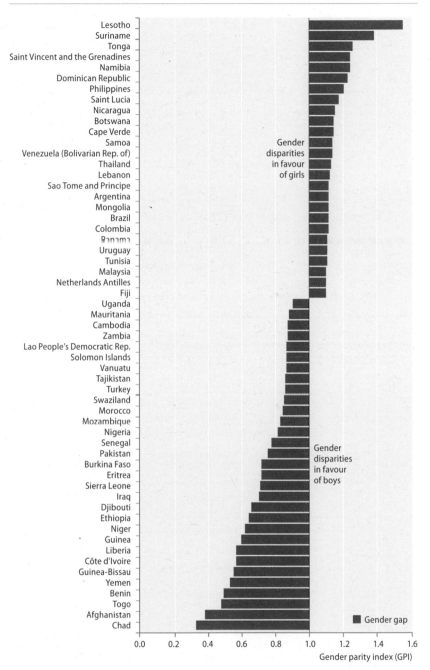

Source: UNESCO Institute for Statistics (2009a).
Note: Data presented for selected countries where the gender gap is 10 percentage points or larger.

Figure 3.15

Girls in secondary technical and vocational programmes (*percentage in total enrolment*), 2007

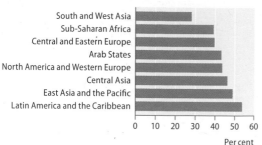

Source: UNESCO Institute for Statistics (2009b).
Note: Regional groupings correspond to those used by UNESCO and differ from those used in other parts of this chapter.

However, investigating enrolment levels alone is not sufficient to obtain a comprehensive understanding of the relationship between gender and TVET programmes. To determine the extent to which the traditional differentiation between "masculine" and "feminine" subjects remains, it is necessary to assess the enrolment of girls and boys by the different fields of study.[30]

The study of gender parity in TVET programmes is rendered even more complex when it is taken into account that – despite its important contribution to enhancing knowledge and skills as well as the employability and income of young people – the esteem attributed to vocational education in many countries still lags behind that accorded to general education.[31] In some of those countries, girls may be widely represented in TVET programmes while boys occupy a larger share of the more prestigious general education streams. As a result, vocational education indicators may appear misleadingly advantageous for girls.[32]

3. Tertiary education

Participation in tertiary education

Tertiary enrolment of women and men has seen substantial growth globally

Enrolment in tertiary education has continued to expand worldwide. From 1990 to 2007, it more than doubled from 66.9 million to 152.4 million (see table 3.5). Over the same period, tertiary enrolment in East Asia and the Pacific[33] – home

30 UNESCO, 2003.

31 UNESCO-UNEVOC, 2006.

32 Ibid.

33 The regional groupings in this section correspond to those used by UNESCO and differ from those used in other parts of the chapter.

to the largest number of tertiary students in the world – has more than quadrupled for women and almost tripled for men. This situation is in part a reflection of the rapid growth of the student body in China. Likewise, in South and West Asia the expansion of tertiary enrolment has also been substantial, mirroring that achieved in East Asia and the Pacific. Sub-Saharan Africa has experienced rapid growth too, with the total size of enrolment more than tripling over the same period. Despite this achievement, however, the region still trails other regions in the provision of tertiary level education. Enrolment has more than doubled for both women and men in Latin America and the Caribbean. In contrast, Europe and North America, which had historically high participation in tertiary education, have seen the slowest growth in enrolment over the period 1990–2007.

Men's dominance in tertiary education has been reversed globally

The global trends show that the former preponderance of men in tertiary education has been reversed. In 1990 men comprised 54 per cent of those enrolled, but the gender balance has shifted in favour of women, who accounted for 51 per cent of tertiary enrolment in 2007 (see table 3.5). The global share of women in tertiary education increased by 5 percentage points between 1990 and 2007. Out of 166 countries with available data in the period, women's share was 50 per cent or more in 102 countries. At the regional level, women's share exceeded 55 per cent in 2007 in the more developed regions of Europe and North America, and there were more women than men enrolled in the Arab States, Central Asia and Latin America and the Caribbean. In keeping with the global trend, there was also rapid growth in women's share in tertiary education in East Asia and the Pacific, South and West Asia and sub-Saharan Africa. However, in these regions, men have continued to be enrolled in larger proportions than women. In general, women in Africa were poorly represented at the tertiary level except in some Northern and Southern African countries where they were in the majority. Women's shares were among the lowest in the world in several countries in Eastern, Middle and Western Africa. In Benin, Chad, Congo, Eritrea, Gambia and Guinea-Bissau, these were below 20 per cent. Women's shares have also been relatively lower in South and West Asia. In Afghanistan, Bangladesh, Bhutan, Iraq, Nepal and Yemen, women's share was well below

Table 3.5
Number of women and men in tertiary education and women's share by region, 1990 and 2007

	1990				2007			
	Both sexes	Men	Women	Women (%)	Both sexes	Men	Women	Women (%)
World	**66 912**	**36 380**	**30 532**	**46**	**152 483**	**75 127**	**77 356**	**51**
Arab States	2 375	1 498	876	37	7 302	3 641	3 661	50
Central and Eastern Europe	13 521[a]	6 292[a]	7 229[a]	53[a]	20 750	9 372	11 378	55
Central Asia	1 545[a]	783[a]	763[a]	49[a]	2 534	1 217	1 317	52
East Asia and the Pacific	13 911	8 608	5 302	38	46 714	24 177	22 537	48
Latin America and the Caribbean	7 087	3 674	3 413	48	17 757	8 116	9 641	54
North America and Western Europe	24 935	12 034	12 902	52	34 783	15 277	19 506	56
South and West Asia	6 213	4 280	1 933	31	18 504	10 835	7 670	41
Sub-Saharan Africa	1 273	859	413	32	4 141	2 492	1 648	40

Source: UNESCO Institute for Statistics (2009a).
Note: Regional groupings correspond to those used by UNESCO and differ from those used in other parts of this chapter. Footnote "a" denotes reference year 2000. Numbers are in thousands.

40 per cent. In contrast, in the South-Eastern Asian countries of Brunei Darussalam, Indonesia, Malaysia, Myanmar, Philippines and Thailand, women's share was 50 per cent or more.

When making regional comparisons concerning tertiary participation levels, it is useful to take into account population size. The tertiary gross enrolment ratio (GER) measures changes in par-

---

Measuring participation in tertiary education

Unlike in primary and secondary education, where the target age groups consist of the official school-age populations, the notion of a target population does not readily apply to tertiary education as there are usually no official ages for attendance. Most tertiary education systems offer a wide range of programmes and pathways, allowing students to achieve a degree in just two years or to complete an advanced research degree in seven or eight years. In light of this variation, the gross enrolment ratio (GER) for tertiary education is calculated on the basis of a standard age range of five years that begins at the end of secondary education. The tertiary GER is computed as the total enrolment in tertiary education, regardless of age, expressed as a percentage of the target population made of the five-year age group following secondary school leaving. The tertiary GER is useful to compare the volume of participation in tertiary programmes. However, it is important to note that there are limitations when comparing the actual population coverage across countries due to the diversity in the duration of tertiary programmes, the enrolment of large numbers of women and men outside the target age group and the high levels of drop-outs and frequent re-enrolments.

Source: UNESCO Institute for Statistics, *Global Education Digest 2009* (2009).

---

ticipation levels relative to a target population group consisting of the five-year age group following secondary school leaving and can be used to compare the volume of participation. Due to a steady expansion of education systems across the world, tertiary GERs have increased in all regions. The global GER for women more than doubled between 1990 and 2007 from 13 per cent to 27 per cent (see figure 3.16). The average global participation of women in tertiary education has exceeded that of men's, which rose from 14 per cent to 25 per cent over the same period.

Tertiary GERs show large regional disparities. In North America and Western Europe, the GERs for women and men in 2007 were 82 per cent and 61 per cent, respectively. Similarly, countries in Central and Eastern Europe enjoy a high GER of 69 for women, 14 percentage points above the ratio for men. These regions are the global leaders in terms of women's participation in higher education. In Latin America and the Caribbean, the average GER for women increased by 21 percentage points in the period between 1990 and 2007. In 2007 women's GER stood at 37 per cent, slightly higher than the ratio for men at 31 per cent. Some of this gain was due not only to increased access but also to slower population growth.[34] In East Asia and the Pacific, GERs for women rose from 6 per cent in 1990 to 26 in 2007, a growth of 20 percentage points. Such a large increase was achieved partly due to the remarkable growth registered in China mentioned above. The region of South and West Asia, which had

---

34 UNESCO Institute for Statistics, 2009c.

Figure 3.16

Tertiary gross enrolment ratio (*GER*) by sex and region, 1990 and 2007

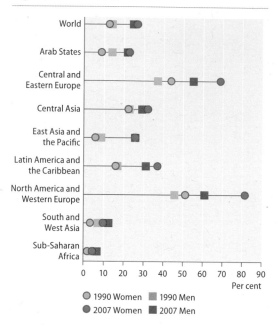

Source: UNESCO Institute for Statistics (2009a).
Note: Regional groupings correspond to those used by UNESCO and differ from those used in other parts of this chapter. For the regions of Central and Eastern Europe and Central Asia, data refer to year 2000 and 2007, respectively.

similar levels of participation to East Asia and the Pacific in the 1990s, managed to grow its GERs by only a modest 6 percentage points for both women and men over the same period. In 2007 GERs for women stood at 10 per cent while the ratio for men was slightly higher at 13 per cent. Except for Iran (Islamic Republic of), where women's GER was 34 per cent, all the other countries in the region including India had GERs of 10 per cent or less, and women's enrolment lagged behind that of men's. The average GERs for women and men in sub-Saharan Africa remain among the lowest in the world, and women in this region face significant barriers to participation in higher education.

Tertiary gender disparities favour women

In 2007 the GPI of the worldwide tertiary GER stood at 1.08, reflecting a gender distribution highly favourable to women (see figure 3.17). Two decades previously, men's participation had been higher than women's as reflected in the GPI of 0.88. Global tertiary enrolment ratios for women and men reached parity in the year 2003 but since then the global participation of women has been exceeding that of men.[35] Out of 154 countries with data, only 8 countries showed gender parity. In 54 other countries more men than women participated in tertiary education while in the

---

35 Ibid.

remaining 92 countries women were in the majority. The GPI in 2007 far exceeded the parity value of one in all the more developed regions. In North America and Western Europe it was 1.33, while Central and Eastern Europe and Latin America and the Caribbean displayed GPIs of 1.25 and 1.19 respectively. A significant gender gap in favour of men remains in those regions where a large gap already existed and where overall enrolment is much lower. Sub-Saharan Africa (0.66) and South and West Asia (0.76) were the only regions where the tertiary enrolment GPI was below one. Women in several countries in Africa and South and West Asia face severe disadvantages in tertiary education. In a few countries the GPI was less than 0.40: Afghanistan, Congo, the Democratic Republic of the Congo, Ethiopia, Guinea, Mauritania, Niger, Tajikistan and Yemen.

Tertiary enrolment by field of study

Women's choices of specific fields of study have a significant impact on their future lives, careers and roles in society. Analysis of tertiary enrolment by different fields can determine whether there is a gender pattern in their selection – that is, "masculine" and "feminine" fields of study. It can shed light on whether differences in the selection of study areas reflect individual preferences or cultural and social stereotypes. Such an analysis can also elicit information on the capacity of tertiary education systems to provide programmes in different academic disciplines and to meet the needs of labour markets and society at large.

Figure 3.18 presents data on women's enrolment among eight broad fields of study: education; health and welfare; humanities and arts; social science, business and law; science; engineering, manufacturing and construction; agriculture; and services. The chart illustrates gender differences in participation among these eight fields in relation to the proportion of women in total tertiary enrolment. It is apparent from the panels in the chart that gender patterns vary distinctly by field of study.

Women still dominate traditionally "feminine" fields of study and are underrepresented in science and engineering fields

---

The fields in which women have traditionally been dominant – education, health and welfare, humanities and arts, and social science, business and law – are still dominated by them. In more than two out of three countries for which data were available in the period 1999–2007, women outnumbered men in enrolment in these four fields. In the panels, the countries in which women outnumber men in the respective fields of study are located above the horizontal line, which represents 50 per cent share of female enrolment. Women's participation is particularly prominent in education. Out of 120 countries with data, the share of women enrolled in this field exceeded 50 per cent in 92 countries. In 36 countries, it exceeded 75 per cent. In Armenia, Croatia, Estonia, Georgia, Lebanon and the Netherlands Antilles, women's share was greater than 90 per cent. The situation completely reverses in certain other countries where women's share in education is lower than that of men. These countries are mostly located in sub-Saharan Africa, and to some extent in Asia, where women's share in tertiary education is relatively low.

A different picture emerges when looking at women's participation in the fields of science, engineering, manufacturing, and construction, agriculture and services. Men's participation in these fields is greater than that of women in the majority of countries reporting data in the period 1999–2007. In the panels in figure 3.18, those countries in which women are outnumbered by men are located below the horizontal line. Out of 117 countries with data, men enrolled in science outnumbered women in 89 countries. In these countries, men's participation was more than women's even in some of those cases where women outnumbered men overall in tertiary enrolment. These countries represent diverse regions and tertiary education systems. In contrast, women's participation in science was more than men's in 26 countries. In most of these countries, women made up more than half of the entire tertiary enrolment. Several Arab States are represented in this group of countries, including Bahrain, where women comprised 75 per cent of those enrolled in science, Jordan and Lebanon (each 51 per cent), Oman (56 per cent), Qatar (69 per cent) and Saudi Arabia (59 per cent). Women's participation is higher in these countries in part because a large number of men pursue higher education overseas. Despite enjoying better access to tertiary education than ever before, women continue to face challenges in accessing the fields of study traditionally dominated by men. The gender patterns in participation among the eight fields of study indicate that gender-based stereotypes survive and that role models that could lead young women to challenging, better-paid careers are scarce.

Figure 3.17

Gender parity index (*GPI*) of tertiary gross enrolment ratios by region, 1990 and 2007

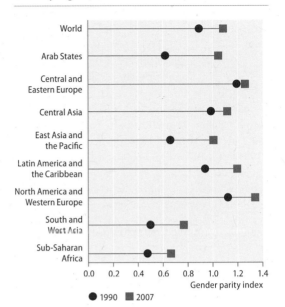

● 1990   ■ 2007

Source: UNESCO Institute for Statistics (2009a).
Note: Regional groupings correspond to those used by UNESCO and differ from those used in other parts of this chapter. For the regions of Central and Eastern Europe and Central Asia, data refer to year 2000 and 2007, respectively.

C. Teaching staff

Several factors impinge on the quality of education and the learning environment, including lack of trained teachers, limited availability of textbooks, over-crowding of classrooms, insufficient instructional time and inadequate school facilities. Quality in education depends in large part on the quality of the teaching staff. Gender balance among the staff is critical for promoting gender parity and equality in access to, and achievement in, education and for creating a supportive and non-discriminating learning environment for both women and men. There is evidence that gender balance among teaching staff is closely related to the improvement of gender parity in enrolments.[36] As the proportion of female teachers increases from low levels, girls' enrolments rise relative to boys. The "feminization" of the teaching profession, particularly in countries where women have lower socio-economic status, can serve as an empowering tool for young women to pursue their studies and for parents to choose to educate girls.[37]

Table 3.6 displays regional averages of women's share in the teaching staff by level of education for the years 1999 and 2007. Similar data is presented in figure 3.19 for countries that reported statistics

---

36 Colclough and others, 2003.

37 UNESCO, 2003.

for 2007 on women's share of the teaching staff at all levels of education. The trends show that the participation of women in the teaching profession has increased at all levels of education in most countries.

Women predominate in teaching at the primary level

Female teachers constitute the majority of primary school teachers in most regions, and their global share increased from 58 to 62 per cent between 1999 and 2007. Across the world, however, the proportions of women in the teaching staff at the primary level show a wide range. For the more developed regions as a whole, this was 84 per cent in 2007 whereas in the less developed regions it

stood at 57 per cent. It was highest in Eastern Europe at 93 per cent and lowest in Middle Africa at 32 per cent. In 98 countries out of 193 reporting data in the period 1999–2007, the proportion of female primary school teachers exceeded 75 per cent (see Statistical Annex). In some countries women represent almost the totality of primary school teachers – the proportion was larger than 90 per cent in 21 countries. In contrast, in 16 countries the participation of women in the teaching profession at the primary level was less than 30 per cent. All but two of these countries – Afghanistan and Yemen – are in sub-Saharan Africa. Low levels of female participation (below 50 per cent) are also found in some countries in South-Central Asia (Bangladesh, Bhutan, India, Nepal and Pakistan), South-Eastern Asia (Cambodia, Lao People's

Figure 3.18

Women as a percentage of enrolment in selected broad fields of study, 2007

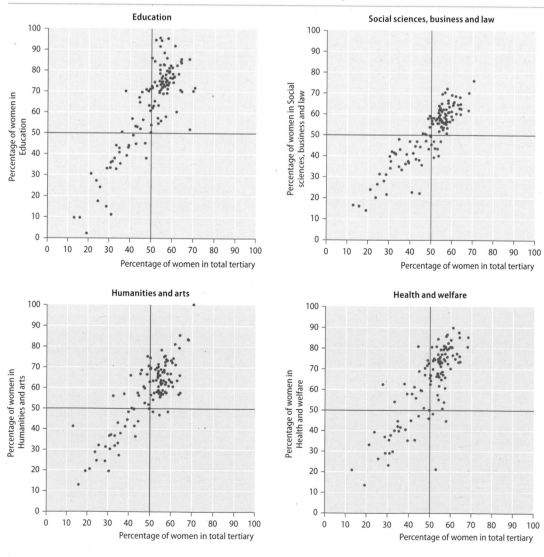

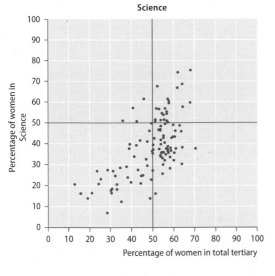

Science

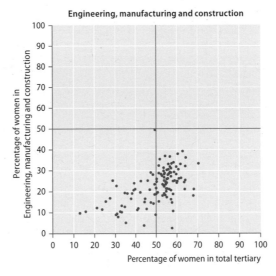

Engineering, manufacturing and construction

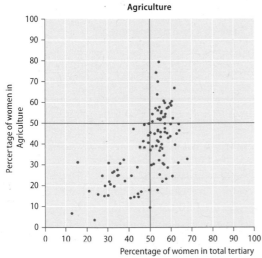

Agriculture

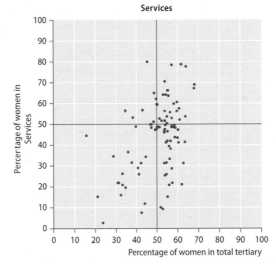

Services

Source: UNESCO Institute for Statistics (2009a).

Note: Each point represents one country. The horizontal line is a gender parity line for the respective field of study. Below the gender parity line, women's participation in the respective field of study is lower than that for men's. Above the line, women's participation exceeds men's. Data correspond to reference year 2007 or latest available in the period 1999–2007.

Democratic Republic and Timor-Leste) and Oceania (Papua New Guinea and Solomon Island) (see figure 3.19). The data show that the proportion of female primary teaching staff is lower in countries with low levels of overall enrolment.

Women's share in teaching drops significantly at higher levels

Compared to the primary level, women teachers at the secondary level constitute a lower proportion at about 52 per cent in the period from 1999 to 2007. Their share ranged from 77 per cent in Eastern Europe to 15 per cent in Middle Africa in 2007. The proportion in the less developed regions as a whole was 48 per cent, and it was 38 per cent in Africa and 46 per cent in Asia. With the exception of Northern and Southern Africa, women teachers throughout Africa were vastly outnum-

bered by men. In five African countries – Chad, Equatorial Guinea, Guinea, Guinea-Bissau and Togo – the proportion of female teachers at the secondary level was below 10 per cent.

Women constitute the lowest proportion of teachers at the tertiary level, making up only 42 per cent in both the more and less developed regions in 2007. Tertiary level data for 146 countries reported in the period 1999–2007 showed that in 125 countries (or 86 per cent) the proportion of women teachers was below 50 per cent. Outside of sub-Saharan Africa, proportions well below 30 per cent were found in several Arab countries or areas – Jordan, Kuwait, Occupied Palestinian Territory, Oman, United Arab Emirates and Yemen. Even in Northern America and Europe (except Eastern Europe), women's proportion of the teachers in tertiary education was significantly lower than 50 per cent. On the other hand, in a

Table 3.6

Women in teaching staff by level of education and region, 1999 and 2007 (*per cent*)

	Primary		Secondary		Tertiary	
	1999	2007	1999	2007	1999	2007
World	**58**	**62**	**52**	**52**	**39**	**42**
Less developed regions	52	57	48	48	39	42
More developed regions	83	84	61	63	38	42
Africa	**45**	**48**	**37**	**38**	**33**	**31**
Eastern Africa	40	44	30[a]	32	26	25
Middle Africa	25	32	16	15	10	..
Northern Africa	49	59	44	49	36	37
Southern Africa	78	76	50	53	47[a]	50[b]
Western Africa	39	41	27	26	29	17[b]
Asia	**50**	**55**	**45**	**46**	**33**[a]	**38**
Eastern Asia	54[a]	57	40[a]	44	32[a]	36
South-Central Asia	38	47	40	40[b]	33[a]	37
South-Eastern Asia	64	66	53	56	39	46
Western Asia	57	58[b]	55	54[b]	35	37
Europe	**83**	**85**	**65**	**67**	**42**	**46**
Eastern Europe	92	93	75	77	52[a]	54
Northern Europe	76	80[b]	57	62[b]	37	41[b]
Southern Europe	80	83	60	64	34	38
Western Europe	77	83	53	56	33	36
Latin America and the Caribbean	**76**	**78**	**64**	**60**	**45**	**46**
Caribbean	64	67	53	51	44	55
Central America	63	68	46	48	..	..
South America	82	83	70	65	44	42
Northern America	**85**	**87**	**57**	**63**	**41**	**44**
Oceania	**72**[a]	**75**[b]	**..**	**..**	**44**	**..**

Source: UNESCO Institute for Statistics (2009a).
Notes:
a Data refer to a year in the period 2000–2002.
b Data refer to a year in the period 2004–2006.

few countries in Eastern Europe (Belarus, Latvia, Lithuania, Republic of Moldova and Russian Federation), Latin America and the Caribbean (Argentina, Cuba and Jamaica), South-Central Asia (Georgia, Kazakhstan and Kyrgyzstan) and South-Eastern Asia (Myanmar, Philippines and Thailand), women teachers at the tertiary level have attained participation levels greater than those observed in the more developed regions.

D. Scientific and technological knowledge

Much of the improvement in human welfare over the past century can be attributed to scientific and technological innovations.[38] The diffusion of new

[38] Juma and Yee-Cheong, 2005.

information and communication technologies (ICTs) has revolutionized the role of knowledge in societies. However, there is a "knowledge divide" – the cumulative effect of the various rifts observed in the main areas that make up knowledge (access to information, education, scientific research, and cultural and linguistic diversity) – which threatens to become a factor of exclusion.[39] This divide is particularly glaring between developed and developing countries and is also found within a given society, including between women and men. Women's participation in creating, transmitting and processing knowledge – and the elimination of gender disparities in access to information and scientific and technological knowledge – is a key concern in addressing inequalities and promoting human development.

1. Research and development

Women are starkly underrepresented among researchers worldwide

Investment in research and development is vital for generating knowledge and for laying the foundation for scientific and technological innovations. Sustainable science and technology capacity development is critical for building the foundation for a knowledge-based society, and countries need to establish and maintain an indigenous science and technology workforce that not only consumes other countries' technological exports but also creates, acquires, assimilates, utilizes and diffuses science and technology knowledge.[40] Qualified researchers, professionals and technicians are required to manage the expansion of a country's science, technology and innovation capacity. However, in an age where science and technology based-knowledge is becoming a determinant of economic competitiveness, women are starkly underrepresented among researchers, professionals and technicians.[41]

Figure 3.20 presents data on women's and men's share of the total number of researchers by region. The data show that women constitute only slightly more than a quarter of all researchers worldwide. They also account for less than half of researchers in all regions and in 101 out of 115 countries with available data (see Statistical Annex). In 49 countries women's share is less than a third. In the

[39] UNESCO, 2005.
[40] UNESCO, 2007.
[41] Ibid.

Research and development

Research and development (R&D) comprise creative work undertaken on a systematic basis in order to increase the stock of knowledge, including knowledge of humanity, culture and society, and the use of this stock of knowledge to devise new applications. The term covers three activities: basic research, applied research and experimental development. Researchers are professionals engaged in the conception or creation of new knowledge, products, processes, methods and systems and also in the management of the projects concerned.

African countries of Ethiopia, Gambia, Guinea and Senegal, women account for less than 10 per cent of all researchers. In contrast, in a handful of countries in Africa (Cape Verde and Lesotho), Asia (Azerbaijan, Georgia, Kazakhstan, Philippines and Thailand), Europe (Latvia, Lithuania and the former Yugoslav Republic of Macedonia) and Latin America (Argentina, Brazil and Venezuela (Bolivarian Republic of)) women make up half or slightly more than half of researchers. Gender parity – defined here as a share of between 45 and 55 per cent for each sex – has been achieved in only 23 countries.

In Africa, the average share of women in research is 33 per cent. The proportion is higher than the world average in Northern Africa (36 per cent) whereas in sub-Saharan Africa the average is 28 per cent. In about half of the countries with available data in sub-Saharan Africa, women account for less than 30 per cent of researchers. Cape Verde, Lesotho and Tunisia are the only countries that have achieved gender parity in Africa.

In Asia as a whole, women represent 19 per cent of researchers. The countries of Central Asia have recorded the highest share worldwide (49 per cent). However, in the sub-regions of Eastern Asia and Southern Asia, the numbers are far below the global average of 29 per cent. Along with Bangladesh, India[42] and Nepal, Japan and the Republic of Korea report some of the lowest proportions of women researchers in the region (15 per cent or below). Women's participation is relatively higher in South-Eastern Asia, where the sub-regional average stands at 40 per cent and national level estimates range from 21 per cent in Cambodia to 85 per cent in Myanmar. Seven countries (Armenia, Azerbaijan, Georgia, Kazakhstan, Mongolia,

---

42 Data measured not on the basis of headcount but on full-time equivalency (FTE), a method that adjusts for part-time or part-year participation.

Figure 3.19

Women in teaching staff by level of education and country, 2007

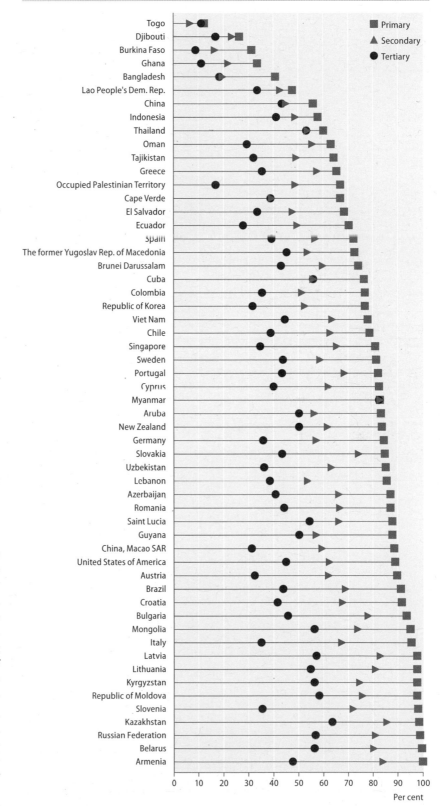

Source: UNESCO Institute for Statistics (2009a).

Figure 3.20
Women's and men's share of the total number of researchers by region, 2007 or latest available year

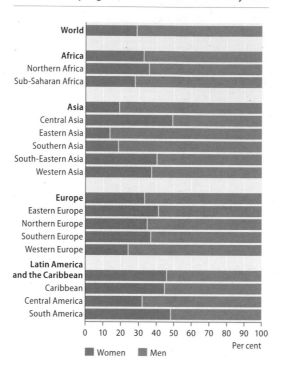

Source: UNESCO Institute for Statistics (2009a).
Note: Regional averages computed based on available data (no imputations were made for countries with missing data). Data refer to headcount of the total number of persons who are mainly or partially employed in research and development.

There is a wide range of reasons for women's underrepresentation in research and development, one major factor being that they are less likely than men to obtain tertiary level qualifications in science, engineering and technology fields required for a career in scientific research. Other factors related to working conditions and career development are also important and include work-life balance, gendered patterns and approaches to productivity, performance measurement, retention and promotion criteria and research grant awards.[43] Lack of good work-life balance policies may limit women's participation as they frequently perform paid work along with heavy family responsibilities. Once in employment, rigid employment practices and lack of opportunities for retraining can lead to skilled women leaving science and technology careers permanently.[44] Although these issues affect both men and women, women are more affected as they are more likely to have gaps in employment due to maternity leave and family care-giving demands.

2. Decision-making in research and development

Fewer women are represented on scientific boards

Women have had less opportunity than men to participate in research and development, and scientific research has in return often neglected their situations, interests and concerns. This has been the case in part because women are underdeployed in research and generally have less access than men to research and development resources.[45] Another reason is that fewer women are represented at the higher levels of personnel in scientific institutions – including advisory, funding and other decision-making bodies. Women have less chance of reaching senior levels in these institutions, including holding positions of influence through membership in scientific boards.[46]

The proportion of female members of scientific boards can serve as a useful indication for the degree to which women participate in the process of setting the science and technology agenda. Figure 3.21 displays data on the share of women on these boards in 27 countries, almost all of which

Philippines and Thailand), representing less than a quarter of those with available data in Asia, have achieved gender parity.

At 46 per cent, women's share of researchers in Latin America and the Caribbean exceeds the global average. At the level of country or area, it ranges from 18 per cent in the United States Virgin Islands to 52 per cent in Venezuela (Bolivarian Republic of). Gender parity has been attained in Argentina, Brazil, Cuba, Ecuador, Paraguay and Venezuela (Bolivarian Republic of). However, in countries or areas with small research communities such as Guatemala, Honduras and the United States Virgin Islands, women's share accounts for less than a third.

Women researchers in Europe account for 33 per cent of the total. While the regional proportion is above the global average, women account for 30 per cent or less in Austria, Belgium, Denmark, France, Germany, Luxembourg, Netherlands and Switzerland. The gender balance is much better in Eastern and Southern Europe where over 41 per cent and 37 per cent, respectively, of researchers are women. Gender parity has been achieved in Bulgaria, Croatia, Latvia, Lithuania, Republic of Moldova, Romania, Serbia and the former Yugoslav Republic of Macedonia.

43 UNESCO, 2007.
44 Ibid.
45 European Commission, 2006.
46 Ibid.

are in Europe.[47] Although the data presented lack geographical coverage and representation of regions from different development groups, they nonetheless provide evidence of the severe under-representation of women in such bodies. The scarcity of sex-disaggregated data among professorial ranks and at higher levels of personnel in scientific institutions poses a significant obstacle to the analysis of policies in science and technology from a gender perspective.

The share of women on or presiding over scientific boards is below 50 per cent in all of the 27 countries, ranging from 49 per cent in Sweden to 4 per cent in Luxembourg. With the exception of seven countries, women's share is less than 30 per cent. The situation is more balanced in Finland, Norway and Sweden, where the share of female board membership exceeds 40 per cent. The proportion of women is above 30 per cent in Croatia, Bulgaria, Denmark and Iceland.

Correcting the gender imbalance in participation in science and technology requires strategic approaches. Effective measures include popularizing science and promoting scientific literacy and the use of the tools of technology. Efforts should also be made to increase the number of women students in the scientific and technical professions. Another important step to take is enhancing women's representation at the top levels of decision-making processes in higher education institutions, scientific associations, research and development centres and major scientific and technological companies. The objective of increasing women's participation in the generation of scientific and technological knowledge cannot be achieved if women are not sufficiently involved in setting the science and technology agenda.

3. Gender digital divide

Inequalities of access to the Internet is further marginalizing women

Information and communication technologies (ICTs) are pivotal for the development of knowledge societies. Advances in this area have been

Figure 3.21

Proportion of women on scientific boards, 2007 or latest available year

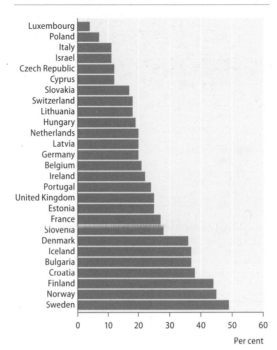

Source: European Commission, *She Figures 2006* (2006).

affecting the means of creating, transmitting and processing knowledge. The uneven distribution of access to and use of ICTs – known as the "digital divide" – has become a major barrier to development because of the risks it poses to economic and social marginalization and to the widening of the knowledge divide. The digital divide occurs along multiple and often overlapping lines: education, poverty, gender, age, disability, ethnicity and region. The gender digital divide represents a dimension in which a knowledge gap has emerged between women and men.[48] Inequalities of access to information sources, contents and infrastructures can hamper the growth of knowledge societies. If left unaddressed, this could also further marginalize women and increase societal disparities.

Use of the Internet is one indicator of access to information and sharing of knowledge. Figure 3.22 shows data on the proportion of female and male Internet users relative to their respective populations across 55 countries. The figure illustrates the limited availability of sex-disaggregated ICT statistics, particularly in the less developed regions. The figure also demonstrates that the proportion of women who use the Internet varies substantially across regions and countries. In about half of the countries or areas shown, less than 50 per cent of

47 Data on women in science in Europe have recently been made more available primarily due to the work of the Helsinki Group on women and science. Established by the European Commission in November 1999, the Group aims to promote the participation and equality of women in the sciences on a Europe-wide basis, the compilation of sex-disaggregated statistics and the building of gender-sensitive indicators.

48 Lopez-Carlos and Zahidi, 2005.

Figure 3.22

Proportion of population using the Internet, by sex and country or area, 2008 or latest available year

women use the Internet. Among these, in nine low Internet penetration countries or areas – Azerbaijan, Costa Rica, Dominican Republic, Honduras, Mexico, Occupied Palestinian Territory, Panama, Paraguay and Turkey – less than 25 per cent of women use the Internet. In contrast, the proportion of women who use the Internet is larger than 75 per cent in Denmark, Finland, Iceland, Netherlands, Norway and Sweden, all high Internet penetration countries.

The figure also provides evidence that, with some exceptions, the gender digital divide is widespread. In general, it is more pronounced among less developed countries with low Internet penetration, although it is also evident in several more developed countries with high Internet penetration. Gender gaps to the disadvantage of women – some more and others less pronounced – are present in all the regions shown. Out of the 55 countries presented, the gender gap in 28 is more than 5 percentage points. In all these countries a higher proportion of men than women use the Internet, except in Cuba where the gender disparity is in favour of women.

Gender gaps are substantial in several countries or areas. In the former Yugoslav Republic of Macedonia, Greece, Italy, the Occupied Palestinian Territory, Serbia and Sri Lanka – all with low Internet penetration – the gender gaps in favour of men range from 10 to 13 percentage points. Substantial gender gaps ranging from 10 to 22 percentage points are also present in the following relatively high Internet penetration countries/areas: Austria; China, Hong Kong SAR; Germany; Japan; Luxembourg; the Republic of Korea and Switzerland. The greatest disparity is registered in the relatively high Internet penetration country of Luxembourg, where the gender gap is 22 percentage points in favour of men. This shows that the gender digital divide is as pertinent in the more developed countries as in the less developed ones.

On the other hand, the gender gap is less pronounced or non-existent in a number of countries from both more and less developed economies. It is less than 5 percentage points in the low Internet penetration countries of Bulgaria, Costa Rica, the Dominican Republic, Honduras, Mexico, Panama, Paraguay, Poland, Romania and Uruguay as well as in the relatively high Internet penetration countries of Australia, Canada, Estonia, Finland, France, Hungary, Iceland, Ireland, Latvia, Lithuania, New Zealand, Slovenia and the United States of America.

Source: Compiled by the United Nations Statistics Division from EUROSTAT, Information Society statistics database (2009); UNECE statistical database (2009); ITU, Information Society statistical profiles 2009: Americas (2009); and national sources (as of October 2009).

Note: Data refer to use of the Internet in the last three months preceding the survey in the majority of countries presented. Use of the Internet is defined as any kind of use, whether at home, at work or from anywhere else, for private or professional purposes, using a computer or any other means. Data refer to population aged 16–74 in the majority of countries presented. The comparability of data is limited due to varying definition of Internet use and differing population age groups and lengths of period of Internet use surveyed.

Many women face barriers in accessing ICTs. One is that they are more likely than men to lack basic literacy and computer skills. Another, in the less developed regions, may be gender-based cultural attitudes. The location of information centres or cybercafés in places that women may not be comfortable frequenting or that are culturally inappropriate for them to visit causes them to have less access to those ICT facilities that do exist.[49] Even when access is not an issue, the paucity of Internet content that meets the information needs of women can lead to inequality in use. As a result of issues such as these, women's ability to benefit equally from the opportunities offered by ICTs and to contribute fully to the knowledge-based economy is limited.[50] To overcome the further marginalization of women, it is imperative to expand their access to and use of ICTs. However, while expanding access is necessary, it is not sufficient to close the gender digital gap.[51] To do this requires policies containing specific measures for targeting and addressing the gender dimensions of ICTs.

---

[49] Hafkin, 2003.

[50] Ibid.
[51] Huyer, 2005.

Chapter 4
Work

Key findings

- Globally, women's participation in the labour market remained steady in the two decades from 1990 to 2010, whereas that for men declined steadily over the same period; the gender gap in labour force participation remains considerable at all ages except the early adult years.

- Women are predominantly and increasingly employed in the services sector.

- Vulnerable employment – own-account work and contributing family work – is prevalent in many countries in Africa and Asia, especially among women.

- The informal sector is an important source of employment for both women and men in the less developed regions but more so for women.

- Occupational segregation and gender wage gaps continue to persist in all regions.

- Part-time employment is common for women in most of the more developed regions and some less developed regions, and it is increasing almost everywhere for both women and men.

- Women spend at least twice as much time as men on domestic work, and when all work – paid and unpaid – is considered, women work longer hours than men do.

- Half of the countries worldwide meet the new international standard for minimum duration of maternity leave – and two out of five meet the minimum standard for cash benefits – but there is a gap between law and practice, and many groups of women are not covered by legislation.

Introduction

Women constitute roughly half of the population of the world and thus potentially half of its work force. As a group they do as much work as men, if not more. However, the types of work they do – as well as the conditions under which they work and their access to opportunities for advancement – differ from men's. Women are often disadvantaged compared to men in access to employment opportunities and conditions of work; furthermore, many women forego or curtail employment because of family responsibilities. The removal of obstacles and inequalities that women face with respect to employment is a step towards realizing women's potential in the economy and enhancing their contribution to economic and social development.

The Beijing Declaration affirms nations' commitment to the inalienable rights of women and girls and their empowerment and equal participation in all spheres of life, including in the economic domain.[1] The Beijing Platform for Action identifies women's role in the economy as a critical area of concern, and calls attention to the need to promote and facilitate women's equal access to employment and resources, as well as the harmonization of work and family responsibilities for women and men. Furthermore, the Millennium Development Goals (MDGs) target the achievement of full and productive employment and decent work for all, including women and young people, as part of MDG 1 to eradicate extreme poverty and hunger.

Some progress has been made towards these ends, but the gains are uneven. This chapter examines trends over the last 20 years and describes the current situation of women and men in the labour force, employment conditions, the reconciliation of work and family life, and child labour.

1 United Nations, 1995.

A. Women and men in the labour force

1. Labour force participation of women and men

**Trends in women's labour force participation
are mixed but for men there
is a decrease virtually everywhere**

Globally, women's participation in the labour market remained steady in the two decades from 1990 to 2010, hovering around 52 per cent. In contrast, global labour force participation rates for men declined steadily over the same period from 81 to 77 per cent (figure 4.1). The gap between participation rates of women and men has narrowed slightly but remains at a consider-

able 25 percentage points in 2010. (For concepts related to the labour force, see box 4.1.)

Global trends, however, mask different sub-regional trends in the case of women and variations in the extent of decrease in the case of men. Between 1990 and 2010, certain sub-regions showed substantial increases in women's labour force participation rates while others showed declines. The most notable increases for women were in Northern Africa and Latin America and the Caribbean, regions or sub-regions where participation rates were initially low – below 40 per cent. Sub-Saharan Africa, the more developed regions (except Eastern Europe), Oceania (excluding Australia and New Zealand) and Southern

---

Box 4.1

Concepts related to the labour force

The "economically active population" comprises all persons of either sex who furnish, or are available to furnish, the supply of labour for the production of goods and services, during a specified time reference period. As defined by the System of National Accounts (SNA), the production of goods and services includes all production oriented to the market, some types of non-market production (including production and processing of primary products for own consumption), own-account construction and other production of fixed assets for own use. It excludes unpaid activities, such as unpaid domestic activities and volunteer community services.

Two useful measures of the economically active population are the "usually active population", measured in relation to a long reference period such as a year; and the "currently active population", measured in relation to a short reference period such as one week or one day. The currently active population, also called the "labour force", is the most widely used measure of the economically active population. The labour force comprises all persons above a specified minimum age who were either employed or unemployed during the specified reference period. The statistics on economic characteristics presented in this chapter refer to persons 15 years of age or over, unless otherwise stated.

"Employed" comprises all persons above a specified age who during the short reference period either worked for pay or profit, or contributed to a family business (farm) without receiving any remuneration (i.e., were unpaid).

"Unemployed" comprises all persons above a specified age who during a specified reference period:

- "did not have any work/job", i.e., were not employed;
- were "currently available for work", i.e., were available for paid employment or self-employment; and
- were "seeking work", i.e., had taken specific steps in a specified recent period to seek paid employment or self-employment (this condition is relaxed in situations where the conventional means of seeking employment are not relevant).

"Persons not in the labour force" (or "population not currently active") comprises all persons not classified as employed or unemployed during the reference period, as well as those below the age specified for measuring the economically active population. A person may be inactive for the following reasons:

- attending an educational institution;
- engaging in household duties;
- retired or old age; or
- other reasons, such as infirmity, disability, etc.

Source: Hussmanns and others, 1990, chapters 2 and 3.

Asia also registered some gains. In contrast, women's labour force participation decreased in the other sub-regions of Asia and in Eastern Europe; these are sub-regions where women's participation rate was above 50 per cent in 1990, with the exception of Western Asia (table 4.1).

Even with the recent increases for women, in 2010 their labour force participation rates still fall below 50 per cent in many sub-regions: less than 30 per cent in Northern Africa and Western Asia; below 40 per cent in Southern Asia; and under 50 per cent in the Caribbean and Central America. In the remaining sub-regions of the world, women's participation rates are between 50 and 70 per cent.

For men, labour force participation rates declined in all regions except South-Eastern Asia where they remained unchanged over the last two decades. The sharpest declines were in Eastern Europe, members of the Commonwealth of Independent States (CIS) located in Asia, Eastern Asia and Western Asia, where participation rates fell by more than 5 percentage points (table 4.1). By 2010, men's labour force participation rates range from 66 per cent in Eastern Europe to 83 per cent in South-Eastern Asia. In general, men in the more developed regions have much lower participation

Figure 4.1

Estimated and projected global labour force participation rate, persons aged 15 years or over, by sex, 1990–2010

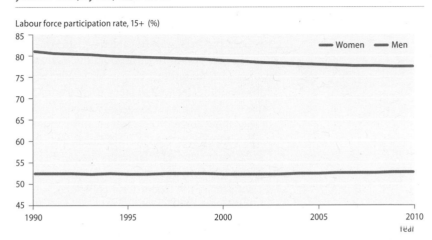

Labour force participation rate, 15+ (%)

Source: ILO, Economically Active Population Estimates and Projections 1980–2020 (accessed in June 2008).

rates than their counterparts in the less developed regions, mainly as a result of earlier withdrawal from the labour market (see section A.2, Labour force participation across age groups).

The share of women in the labour force is still far from parity in many sub-regions

Table 4.1

Estimated and projected labour force participation rate of persons aged 15 years or over by region and sex, 1990 and 2010

	Female labour force participation rate (%)			Male labour force participation rate (%)		
	1990	2010	Difference	1990	2010	Difference
Africa						
Northern Africa	23	29	6	76	74	-2
Sub-Saharan Africa	60	62	2	82	80	-2
Asia						
Eastern Asia	72	69	-3	85	79	-6
South-Eastern Asia	59	57	-2	83	83	0
Southern Asia	35	36	1	85	81	-4
Western Asia	26	23	-3	79	72	-7
CIS in Asia	68	60	-8	81	73	-8
Latin America and the Caribbean						
Caribbean	39	48	9	75	72	-3
Central America	35	43	8	84	79	-5
South America	38	59	21	81	80	-1
Oceania	62	64	2	77	75	-2
More developed regions						
Eastern Europe	58	54	-4	73	66	-7
Rest of more developed regions	50	53	3	74	69	-5

Source: Computed by the United Nations Statistics Division based on data from ILO, Economically Active Population Estimates and Projections 1980–2020 (accessed in June 2009).
Note: Western Asia excludes Armenia, Azerbaijan and Georgia; CIS in Asia includes the aforementioned countries plus Kazakhstan, Kyrgyzstan, Tajikistan, Turkmenistan and Uzbekistan.

The share of women in the labour force gives an indication of the extent of women's access to the labour market relative to men's, a value of 50 per cent indicating gender parity. Most regions of the world are still far from attaining this, but there has been progress, most notably in Latin America and the Caribbean. In this region, the increase in women's labour force participation, coupled with a corresponding decrease in men's participation (see table 4.1), led to a substantial rise in women's share of the labour force. While still far from attaining parity with men, women in Latin American and the Caribbean no longer lag far behind women in other regions. In South America, women now comprise 44 per cent of the labour force compared to only 33 per cent in 1990. Central American women are still somewhat behind, at 37 per cent (table 4.2).

Northern Africa, Southern Asia and Western Asia remain the regions where women comprise a small share of the labour force – 30 per cent or less. Women's share is highest in Eastern Europe and the CIS in Asia, where it is almost at par with men's. Not far behind are sub-Saharan Africa, Eastern Asia, South America, the more developed regions except Eastern Europe, and Oceania; in these regions, women comprise about 45 per cent of the adult labour force.

Table 4.2

Estimated and projected share of women in the adult (15+) labour force by region, 1990 and 2010

	Women's share of the adult labour force (%)	
	1990	2010
Africa		
Northern Africa	24	28
Sub-Saharan Africa	43	44
Asia		
Eastern Asia	44	45
South-Eastern Asia	42	41
Southern Asia	28	30
Western Asia	27	26
CIS in Asia	48	47
Latin America and the Caribbean		
Caribbean	35	41
Central America	30	37
South America	33	44
Oceania	43	46
More developed regions		
Eastern Europe	48	49
Rest of more developed regions	42	45

Source: Computed by the United Nations Statistics Division based on data from ILO, Economically Active Population Estimates and Projections 1980–2020 (accessed in June 2009).
Note: Western Asia excludes Armenia, Azerbaijan and Georgia; CIS in Asia includes the aforementioned countries plus Kazakhstan, Kyrgyzstan, Tajikistan, Turkmenistan and Uzbekistan.

2. Labour force participation across age groups

Trends in labour force participation across age groups

There has been a sharp decline in labour force participation among young women and men but an increase in participation among women aged 25 and older in most regions

---

With increased opportunities for secondary and higher education, women and men are entering the labour force later than in the past. Compared to 1990, there has been a decrease in labour force participation rates among persons in the age groups 15–19 and 20–24 in all regions. This is illustrated in figure 4.2 by data from six countries: Bulgaria, Chile, Italy, Japan, Malawi and Tunisia.

Women in the middle adult ages (i.e., aged 25–54) have higher labour force participation rates now compared to 1990 in most regions, as illustrated by the examples of Chile, Italy, Tunisia and, to a lesser degree, Japan. The exception is Eastern Europe, where participation of women declined after 1990, as exemplified by the case of Bulgaria. One factor that might explain this is the loss or reduction of state-sponsored social services (for example, childcare) after the collapse of the centrally planned economies, resulting in women having to withdraw from the labour force to care for their children or other family members.

Beyond age 55, the increase in women's labour force participation was smaller, except for women around the age of retirement in some countries in Eastern Europe. In Bulgaria, for example, it can be seen that the labour force participation rate of women aged 55–59 skyrocketed from 11 per cent in 1992 to 60 per cent in 2007. The prolonged time in the labour market in more recent years can be attributed in part to the end of the era of state-controlled employment and changes in retirement policies.

For men, trends in labour force participation after age 25 were relatively consistent across regions—remaining the same or declining slightly over the last two decades, with the exception of men from age 55 in Bulgaria and Chile. In these two countries, participation increased among men aged 55–69. A very sharp increase in labour force participation was recorded for men aged 60–64 in Bulgaria, a phenomenon observed for women aged 55–59 and probably for similar reasons.

Figure 4.2

Labour force participation rates by age group, by sex, for two years

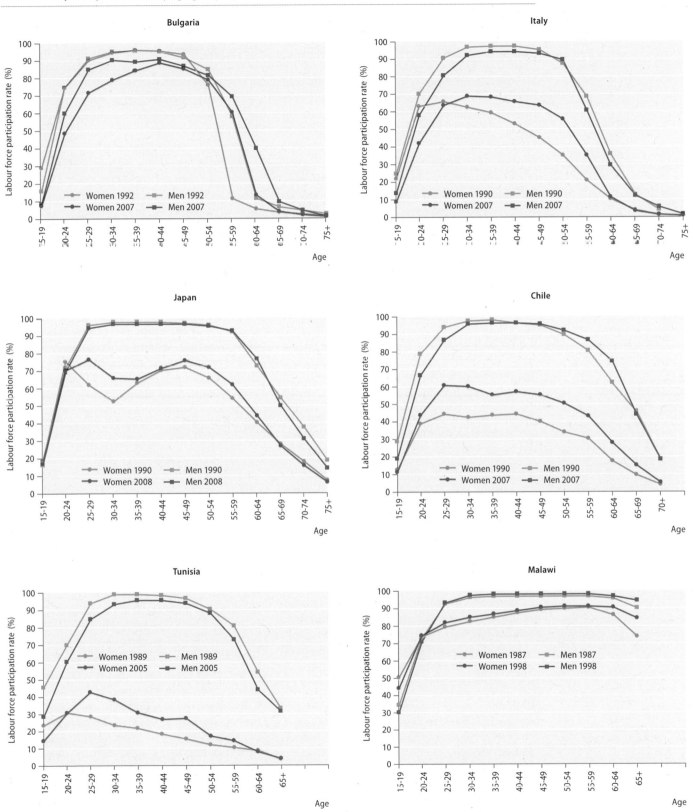

Source: ILO, LABORSTA table 1A (accessed in July 2009).

The gender gap in labour force participation is considerable at all ages except the early adult years

In general, women's labour force participation is lower than men's at all stages of the life cycle. The narrowest gender gap is in the young adult years (ages 15–19), while the widest gap is generally from ages 30–34 through 50–54, as illustrated by the cases of Chile, Italy, Japan and Tunisia (figure 4.2). Of these four countries, Tunisia stands out for having the widest gender gap at all ages, as is typical of countries in Northern Africa and Western Asia. Chile, Italy and Japan also have wide gender gaps at all ages, very prominent in the ages between 30 and 54, narrowing slowly thereafter and tailing off at the older ages without totally disappearing. Eastern Europe, exemplified by Bulgaria, has relatively narrow gender gaps at all ages. Similarly, in sub-Saharan Africa – where labour force participation of both women and men is high at all ages – the gender gap is relatively small, as for example in Malawi.

Age patterns of labour force participation

Examining the labour force participation of women and men over the life cycle, four distinct patterns can be observed: the first two apply to both women and men and the last two to women in certain sub-regions or countries.

For women and men alike, the most common pattern is one of low participation at ages 15–19, sharply higher participation at ages 20–24, then continued gradual increase with age, peaking somewhere between ages 25–35 for women (35–44 for men), maintaining the high participation rates until about age 50 and then beginning to decline. For women, this pattern indicates that those who are in the labour force remain in it during their reproductive years. The pattern described is typical for both women and men in most countries of the world (see the examples of Bulgaria, Chile and Italy), and for men in Japan and Tunisia (figure 4.2).

While the general pattern may be the same, the peak ages of labour force participation vary across countries and between the sexes, as does the pace of exit from the labour force after age 50. For women, the decline in labour force participation after age 50 can be very sharp (as in Bulgaria, Italy and, to a lesser degree, Japan) or gradual (as in Chile and Tunisia). The sharp decline of participation seen in Bulgaria, Italy and Japan is typical of coun-

tries with relatively comprehensive pension systems in place to support workers after retirement.

A second pattern is the one seen for both women and men in many sub-Saharan African countries where subsistence agriculture is a substantial sector of the economy. In such economies, private or state-sponsored pension systems such as those found in the more developed regions to support older people are not common, thus the concept of retirement is generally not present. In this pattern, labour force participation tends to be high from the early ages, peaks early, stays on a high plateau until about age 60 and then declines very slowly. This is illustrated for both women and men by the example of Malawi, where labour force participation at ages 65 and beyond remained at a high of 84 per cent for women and 94 per cent for men (figure 4.2).

A third pattern is the one seen among women in Northern Africa and Western Asia. Typified by the case of Tunisia in 2005, women's labour force participation starts at a low level at ages 15–19, peaks at ages 25–29 and drops immediately and continuously thereafter. Women in these regions have the lowest overall labour force participation rates in the world, dropping out of the labour force much earlier than women elsewhere and not returning. For some countries in the region, the age at which participation rates peak is now a little higher than in the past, as illustrated by the case of the Tunisia where the peak participation rate for women was at ages 20–24 in 1989 but rose to ages 25–29 in 2005. This is most likely the result of later marriage and childbearing.[2]

A fourth pattern, featuring a double peak, reflects the situation where it is common for women to leave the labour force to bear and raise children and re-enter it later in life. Countries such as Japan and the Republic of Korea continue to have this pattern, although the initial peak in participation rate now occurs at a later age. In Japan, for example, that peak is now at ages 25–29 as opposed to ages 20–24 in 1990. The dip in participation rates has shifted to five years older and is not as sharp as before, indicating later childbearing and childrearing as well as more women opting to continue working through those ages. A few other countries – specifically Australia, Egypt (in recent years), Indonesia, Ireland and the Philippines – have this double-peak pattern, although the dips are less pronounced and vary in location (age) and width (duration).

---

2 Fertility among young women has dropped in the last two decades in Tunisia, as shown in United Nations, *World Population Prospects: The 2008 Revision* (2009).

3. Unemployment

It is difficult to compare reported unemployment rates across countries, sometimes even within countries, because of different data sources and definitions. Even when definitions are the same, unemployment has different meanings in countries that have unemployment insurance as compared to those that do not. In the latter, most people cannot afford to be unemployed. This is the case for the majority of countries in the less developed regions, where visible unemployment may be low but is often disguised as underemployment. In addition, discouraged workers may no longer seek work and are therefore excluded from the count of unemployed. Interpretations of unemployment rates in the less developed regions should be made with these factors in mind.

Adult unemployment

Unemployment is higher among women than men

In the vast majority of countries, adult unemployment was higher among women compared to men (figure 4.3). Reported unemployment rates for women in 2007 ranged from 1.1 per cent (Thailand) to 36 per cent (the former Yugoslav Republic of Macedonia) and for men from 1.3 per cent to 35 per cent (also Thailand and the former Yugoslav Republic of Macedonia). Unemployment rates in countries around the world clustered in the range of 1–10 per cent for both women and men.

The available data suggest a consistently high female unemployment rate in at least three sub-regions: Northern Africa, the Caribbean and Southern Europe (table 4.3). Unemployment rates for women in all the three sub-regions showed notable declines but were still among the highest in 2007: 17 per cent in Northern Africa, 14 per cent in the Caribbean and 10 per cent in Southern Europe. The corresponding average unemployment rates for men in these sub-regions were 10, 8 and 6 per cent, respectively. These three sub-regions also had the highest gender gap in unemployment rate and a female-male differential of more than 5 percentage points in at least two of the three years shown.

At the other end of the spectrum, countries in Eastern Asia (China not included) had the lowest adult unemployment rates for women (averaging 3 per cent in 2007). Other sub-regions with low unemployment rates for women in 2007 include the more

developed regions outside Europe (4 per cent) and Northern Europe (5 per cent). The corresponding unemployment rates for men are close, averaging 4 per cent in all these three sub-regions, and there is no significant gender gap in adult unemployment.

Youth unemployment

Unemployment is more prevalent among the young, especially young women

---

For young people aged 15–24, unemployment is an even more acute problem. Young women and men alike are typically three times as likely as adult women and men to be unemployed. In 2007, for half of the countries of the world, young women's unemployment rates were 16 per cent or more, reaching as high as 66 per cent in Bosnia and Herzegovina. Other countries where this rate exceeded

Figure 4.3
Unemployment rates of women and men aged 15 or over, 2007

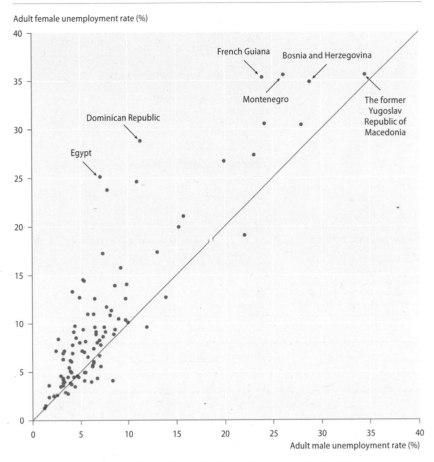

Source: ILO, Key Indicators of the Labour Market, 5th edition, table 8a (accessed in July 2009).
Note: Points above and left of the diagonal line represent countries where women's unemployment rate is higher than men's.

Table 4.3
Adult (15+) unemployment rate by region and sex, for 1990, 2000 and 2007

	Adult female unemployment rate (%)			Adult male unemployment rate (%)			Female-male differential (*percentage points*)		
	1990	2000	2007	1990	2000	2007	1990	2000	2007
Africa									
Northern Africa (3)	20	17	17	11	11	10	9	6	7
Asia									
Eastern Asia (3)	2	4	3	2	6	4	0	-2	-1
South-Eastern Asia (4)	4	6	6	4	6	5	0	0	1
Latin America and the Caribbean									
Caribbean (8)	20	16	14	13	10	8	7	6	6
Central America (6)	9	10	7	7	7	5	2	3	2
South America (7)	9	14	10	7	10	6	2	4	4
More developed regions									
Eastern Europe (9)	..	12	8	..	12	7	..	0	1
Northern Europe (8)	6	5	5	6	5	4	0	0	1
Southern Europe (4)	15	14	10	7	7	6	8	7	4
Western Europe (7)	7	6	6	4	4	5	3	2	1
Other more developed regions (5)	6	5	4	6	6	4	0	-1	0

Source: Computed by the United Nations Statistics Division based on data from ILO, Key Indicators of the Labour Market, 5th edition, table 8a (accessed in June 2009). **Note:** Unweighted averages; the numbers in brackets indicate the number of countries averaged. The average for Eastern Asia does not include China.

50 per cent in 2007 include Egypt, South Africa and the former Yugoslav Republic of Macedonia. For young men, the situation was not much better. Half of the countries had unemployment rates of at least 14 per cent, and young men's unemployment rates exceeded 50 per cent in two countries: Bos-

nia and Herzegovina (60 per cent) and the former Yugoslav Republic of Macedonia (57 per cent).[3]

Much like their adult counterparts, young women in Northern Africa and Southern Europe are the worst off, with average unemployment rates exceeding 30 per cent. In contrast, and again similar to the situation for the adult population, countries in Eastern Asia, Northern Europe and the more developed regions outside Europe were those where young women had the lowest average unemployment rates, at 10 per cent or lower. These are also the regions where young women are not disadvantaged compared to young men when it comes to unemployment (figure 4.4).

B. Employment conditions of women and men

1. Economic sector of employment

Employment in the services sector continues to grow for both women and men

For both women and men, the services sector as a source of employment continues to grow relative to the agricultural sector (see box 4.2 for the major economic sectors). This reflects the movement of the labour force globally from agriculture

Figure 4.4
Youth (aged 15–24) unemployment rate by region and sex, 2007

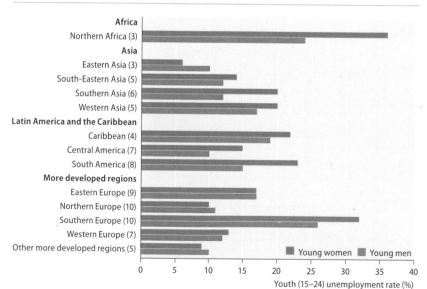

Source: Computed by the United Nations Statistics Division based on data from ILO, Key Indicators of the Labour Market, 5th edition, table 9 (accessed in July 2009).
Note: Unweighted averages; the numbers in brackets indicate the number of countries averaged. The average for Eastern Asia does not include China. Western Asia excludes Armenia, Azerbaijan and Georgia.

3 ILO, 2007, table 9.

Table 4.4
Direction of change in the sectoral share of employment between 1990 and 2007, by region and sex

	Women			Men		
	Agriculture	Industry	Services	Agriculture	Industry	Services
Asia						
Eastern Asia (3)	↓	↓	↑	↓	↓	↑
South-Eastern Asia (5)	↓	↓	↑	↓	=	↑
Southern Asia (3)	↓	↓	↑	↓	↑	↑
Western Asia (3)	↓	↓	↑	↓	=	↑
Latin America and the Caribbean						
Central America (3)	↑	↓	↑	↓	↑	↑
South America (3)	=	↓	↑	↓	=	↑
Caribbean (3)	↓	↓	↑	↓	↑	−
More developed regions						
Northern Europe (8)	↓	↓	↑	↓	↓	↑
Southern Europe (4)	↓	↓	↑	↓	=	↑
Western Europe (5)	↓	↓	↑	=	↓	↑
Other more developed regions (5)	↓	↓	↑	↓	↓	↑

Source: Computed by the United Nations Statistics Division based on data from ILO, Key Indicators of the Labour Market, 5th edition, table 4a (accessed in July 2009).
Note: Based on unweighted averages calculated for the two years; the numbers in brackets indicate the number of countries averaged. A down arrow indicates a decrease of at least 2 percentage points in the proportion employed in the given economic sector between 1990 and 2007, while an up arrow indicates an increase of at least 2 percentage points; an = sign indicates that the change in either direction is less than 2 percentage points. The average for Eastern Asia does not include China. Western Asia excludes Armenia, Azerbaijan and Georgia.

to industry and increasingly to services. The relative importance of the industrial sector as a source of employment for women continued to decline in the last two decades in all regions, whereas for men it varied from a decline in most of the more developed regions to an increase or no change in most sub-regions of Asia and Latin America and the Caribbean (table 4.4).[4]

In most regions, women work predominantly in the services sector

In more developed economies the labour force – especially the female labour force – is employed predominantly in services. This sector accounts for at least three quarters of women's employment in the more developed regions, with the exception of Eastern Europe (with 66 per cent), and in Latin America and the Caribbean. Agriculture is the least important source of women's employment in these regions, accounting for a 3–12 per cent share (table 4.5).

In Africa, the relative distribution of women's employment among the three sectors varies sharply. For the more economically advanced countries that constitute the Southern African region, the pattern is similar to that of the more

Box 4.2
Major economic sectors

The classification of employment by economic sector is done in accordance with the main economic activity carried out where the work is performed. The three major economic sectors – agriculture, industry and services – are defined as follows:

- Agriculture covers farming, animal husbandry, hunting, forestry and fishing.

- Industry comprises mining and quarrying; manufacturing; electricity, gas, steam and air conditioning supply; water supply, sewerage and waste management and remediation activities; and construction.

- Services covers wholesale and retail trade; repair of motor vehicles; transportation and storage; accommodation and food service activities; information and communication; financial and insurance activities; real estate activities; professional, scientific and technical activities; administrative and support service activities; public administration and defence; compulsory social security; education; human health and social work activities; arts, entertainment and recreation; and other service categories.

Source: United Nations, 2009a.

---

4 No analysis was made for Africa, Eastern Europe, and the CIS in Asia as data were not available for both 1990 and 2007.

Table 4.5

Sectoral distribution of employed persons, by region and sex, 2004–2007 (*latest available*)

	Women			Men		
	Agriculture (%)	Industry (%)	Services (%)	Agriculture (%)	Industry (%)	Services (%)
Africa						
Northern Africa (3)	42	16	41	28	25	47
Southern Africa (3)	19	11	70	26	25	49
Eastern, Middle and Western Africa (5)	68	6	26	71	9	20
Asia						
Eastern Asia (4)	11	13	76	13	25	62
South-Eastern Asia (6)	30	17	54	34	23	43
Southern Asia (5)	55	17	28	32	24	43
Western Asia (8)	15	8	77	8	32	59
CIS in Asia (6)	48	7	45	41	23	36
Latin America and the Caribbean						
Caribbean (7)	4	10	85	15	29	56
Central America (7)	6	16	78	30	24	46
South America (6)	10	12	78	21	27	51
More developed regions						
Eastern Europe (8)	12	22	66	14	41	45
Northern Europe (10)	3	13	84	7	37	56
Southern Europe (10)	10	17	73	11	36	53
Western Europe (6)	3	12	85	4	36	60
Other more developed regions (5)	3	11	86	5	32	63

Source: Computed by the United Nations Statistics Division based on data from ILO, Key Indicators of the Labour Market, 5th edition, table 4a (accessed in July 2009).
Note: Unweighted averages; the numbers in brackets indicate the number of countries averaged. Due to rounding, the sum of categories might not equal 100. The average for Eastern Asia does not include China. Western Asia excludes Armenia, Azerbaijan and Georgia; CIS in Asia includes the aforementioned countries plus Kazakhstan, Kyrgyzstan, Tajikistan, Turkmenistan and Uzbekistan.

developed regions, with the service sector accounting for 70 per cent of women's employment. However, unlike in the more developed regions and Latin America, agriculture (19 per cent) is still a more important source of employment than industry (11 per cent). A very different picture emerges for the countries of Northern Africa: here agriculture and services are both important sectors, each accounting for about 40 per cent of women's employment. In the rest of Africa, agriculture is still by far the sector where both women and men are concentrated – accounting for 68 per cent of all female employment and 71 per cent of all male employment.

There are also sharp differences among countries in Asia. A high proportion of women (54–77 per cent) are employed in the services sector in Eastern, South-Eastern and Western Asia, whereas among the CIS in Asia equally high proportions of employed women are in agriculture and services (more than 40 per cent each). In contrast, women are predominantly in agriculture (55 per cent) in Southern Asia. In this sub-region, the service sector accounts for only 28 per cent of female employment.

Compared to women, men tend to be more spread out across the three economic sectors. For example, in the more developed regions, Latin America and the Caribbean and Eastern and Western Asia, the service sector also predominates for men's employment but it accounts for about half to two thirds, which is substantially less than for women. In all regions, men are found in the industrial sector much more than women are. In 2007, more than 20 per cent of male employment (and as high as 41 per cent in Eastern Europe) was in the industrial sector in virtually all regions of the world. For women, the share of industry was above 20 per cent only in Eastern Europe.

2. Status in employment

To understand women's and men's situation and position in the labour market, it is essential to identify their status in employment. This entails classifying jobs on the basis of the type of explicit or implicit contract of employment an individual has with her or his employer or other persons (see box 4.3). A worker's type of contract, or status in employment, often determines the job's level of security, protection and rights.

Box 4.3
Status in employment

Employment, as defined by the 13th Conference of Labour Statisticians (Geneva, 1992), is comprised of two broad categories: "paid employment" and "self-employment".

Persons in paid employment include those who during the reference period were either (a) "at work" – i.e., performed some work for wage or salary, in cash or in kind, or (b) "with a job but did not work" – i.e., were temporarily not at work but had a formal attachment to their job, having already worked in their present job.

Persons in self-employment include those who during the reference period were: (a) "at work" – i.e., performed some work for profit or family gain, in cash or in kind, or (b) had an enterprise, such as a business or commercial enterprise, a farm or a service undertaking, but were temporarily not at work for any specific reason.

The International Classification of Status in Employment (ICSE), adopted in 1993, provides guidelines for classifying jobs in the labour market on the basis of the type of explicit or implicit contract of employment an individual has with his or her employer or other persons. Five major groups and a residual category are presented in ICSE-93: employees, employers, own-account workers, members of producer cooperatives and contributing family workers.

Employees hold paid employment jobs and are typically remunerated by wages and salaries, but may also be paid by commission from sales, or by piece-rates, bonuses or in-kind payments, such as food, housing or training.

Employers, working on their own account or with one or several partners, hold self-employment jobs and have engaged on a continuous basis one or more persons to work for them in their businesses as employees.

Own-account workers, working on their own account or with one or several partners, hold self-employment jobs and have not engaged any employees on a continuous basis.

Members of producers' cooperatives hold self-employment jobs in a cooperative producing goods and services, in which each member takes part on an equal footing with other members in all decisions relating to production, sales, investments and distribution of proceeds.

Contributing family workers (referred to in previous classifications as unpaid family workers) hold a self-employment job in a market-oriented establishment (i.e., business or farm) operated by a relative living in the same household, who cannot be regarded as a partner because their degree of commitment to the operation of the establishment is not at a level comparable to that of the head of the establishment.

For analytical purposes, employers and own-account workers are sometimes combined and referred to as "self-employed". Workers in paid employment are referred to as "wage and salaried workers". Contributing family workers, although considered part of the group "self-employed", are usually analysed separately since their jobs, unlike other self-employment jobs, are unpaid.

Source: ILO, 2003a; see also ILO, 1993a.

Wage employment is the most common form of employment, but own-account work and contributing family work are more prevalent in parts of Africa and Asia

---

Wage and salaried employees constitute the majority of employed women and men in most parts of the world. In the more developed regions, Eastern Asia, Western Asia and the Caribbean, at least 80 per cent of employed women are wage and salaried workers; furthermore, in these regions or sub-regions employed women are more likely than employed men to be in wage employment. Wage employment is also prevalent in Southern Africa for both women and men. However, wage and salaried workers are uncommon in Eastern and Western Africa and in Southern Asia, where they constitute a minority (less than 50 per cent) among both women and men who are employed. In these sub-regions, women and men are more likely to be own-account or contributing family workers (table 4.6)

Persons working on their own account contribute income to the family when secure paid jobs are not available, generating employment not just for themselves but also for their family members, who are often not paid but work as "contributing family workers". Own-account employment allows more flexibility for women, who often have to combine family responsibilities with income-earning activities. However, unlike wage and salaried workers, own-account workers face high economic risks.

Table 4.6

Distribution of employed persons by status in employment, by region and sex, 2004–2007 *(latest available)*

	Women				Men			
	Wage and salaried workers (%)	Employers (%)	Own-account workers (%)	Contributing family workers (%)	Wage and salaried workers (%)	Employers (%)	Own-account workers (%)	Contributing family workers (%)
Africa								
Northern Africa (3)	46	2	19	34	58	8	22	11
Southern Africa (3)	76	3	17	4	82	7	9	2
Eastern and Western Africa (6)	20	1	47	32	24	1	56	18
Asia								
Eastern Asia (3)	86	2	7	5	80	7	13	<1
South-Eastern Asia (6)	52	2	23	23	52	4	34	9
Southern Asia (5)	30	1	22	46	44	3	40	12
Western Asia (6)	80	1	6	12	79	5	13	2
CIS in Asia (4)	45	1	39	15	50	3	39	7
Latin America and the Caribbean								
Caribbean (5)	80	2	16	2	67	3	27	1
Central America (6)	64	3	25	7	64	6	24	6
South America (9)	62	3	28	6	62	6	28	3
More developed regions								
Eastern Europe (8)	84	2	10	4	78	4	16	1
Northern Europe (5)	93	2	4	1	84	5	10	<1
Southern Europe (9)	81	3	10	6	74	6	17	2
Western Europe (4)	89	3	6	3	84	7	8	1
Other more developed regions (4)	88	2	7	2	83	5	11	1

Source: Computed by the United Nations Statistics Division based on data from ILO, Key Indicators of the Labour Market, 5th edition, table 3 (accessed in July 2009).
Note: Unweighted averages; the numbers in brackets indicate the number of countries averaged. Due to rounding, the sum of categories might not equal 100. The average for Eastern Asia does not include China. Western Asia excludes Armenia, Azerbaijan and Georgia; CIS in Asia includes the aforementioned countries plus Kazakhstan, Kyrgyzstan, Tajikistan, Turkmenistan and Uzbekistan.

In Eastern and Western Africa, own-account workers make up 47 per cent of female employment and 56 per cent of male employment. Other sub-regions where own-account workers exceed 20 per cent of the female employed are South-Eastern Asia, Southern Asia, the CIS in Asia, Central America and South America. In the last three of these sub-regions, women are as likely as men to be own-account workers, but in virtually all other sub-regions of the world, the likelihood to be own-account workers is higher for men than women.

All over the world, women are more likely than men to be contributing family workers – more than twice as likely in most regions. In certain sub-regions, contributing family workers account for a third or more of all female workers – for example, in Southern Asia (46 per cent), Northern Africa (34 per cent) and Eastern and Western Africa (32 per cent) (table 4.6).

The distribution of workers by status in employment is closely related to the distribution of workers by economic sector of employment. Where labour is concentrated in the industry and services sectors, as in the more developed regions and the relatively more advanced economies within the less developed regions, wage employment is the prevalent form of employment. However, in regions where large numbers of workers are engaged in agriculture, own-account work and contributing family work are the prevalent forms of employment for women.

Vulnerable employment is prevalent – especially among women – in parts of Africa and Asia

An indicator for monitoring progress in achieving the new MDG target of full and productive employment and decent work for all looks at the proportion of own-account and contributing family workers in total employment (see box 4.4).[5] Workers in these two categories are also referred

5 See official list of MDG Indicators, available at *http:// unstats.un.org/unsd/mdg/Host.aspx?Content=Indicators/Official List.htm*

Box 4.4
The importance of the status in employment classification

The key dimensions underlying the International Classification of Status in Employment (ICSE) are: (1) the economic risk involved in the job and (2) the type of authority over establishments and other workers. Reflecting these dimensions, the classification provides an important basis for understanding the structure of labour markets and the effects of this structure on poverty and gender equality. Two recent developments underscore the importance of ICSE.

First, the statistical definition of informal employment was approved by the 17th International Conference of Labour Statisticians (ICLS) in 2003.[a] Informal employment as defined is a job-based concept, and an important criterion for identifying workers in informal employment is their status in employment (see also box 4.5).

Second, at least two indicators for monitoring the Millennium Development Goals (MDGs) rely on the status of employment classification. In Goal 1 (eradicate extreme poverty and hunger), a specific indicator is the proportion of own-account and contributing family workers in total employment; and in Goal 3 (promote gender equality and empower women), a new supplementary indicator was recommended that would cover all status in employment categories cross-classified by formal/informal and agricultural/non agricultural employment.[b]

The importance of an up-to-date classification of status in employment can not be over-emphasized. As conditions of employment are changing globally, there is increasing recognition that the current classification, ICSE-93, is no longer adequate. Many employment arrangements in both developed and developing countries do not fit easily into one or the other of the current status in employment categories. Thus, in 2008, the 18th ICLS recommended that the ILO Bureau of Statistics undertake methodological work for a revision of the ICSE that would better reflect contemporary realities of the labour market and the associated economic and social concerns.[c]

a ILO, 2003b.
b This indicator was recommended by the Sub-Group on Gender Indicators of the Inter-Agency and Expert Group (IAEG) on MDG Indicators to address problems with the current indicator, namely the share of women in non-agricultural wage employment, which reflects only one aspect of women's situation in the labour market.
c ILO, 2008c.

to as being in "vulnerable employment" because, unlike most employees, they are subject to a high level of job insecurity and do not have safety nets to cover them during periods when they are out of work or unable to work (due to sickness, for example). For own-account workers the returns from work are often very low and their work situation is generally more sensitive to economic fluctuations and cycles, while for contributing family workers there are no cash returns. Informality of work characterizes these types of employment (see the discussion below on the informal sector and informal employment).[6]

Employment in the two categories considered as vulnerable employment is most prevalent among women and men in Eastern and Western Africa (figure 4.5). In Northern Africa and certain sub-regions of Asia, namely South-Eastern Asia, Southern Asia and the CIS in Asia, vulnerable employment is also prevalent among employed women, exceeding 40 per cent. In these sub-regions, higher proportions of women are in vulnerable employment compared to men, mainly due to large numbers of contributing family workers among the former. Vulnerable employment is not as common (less than 20

Figure 4.5
Employed persons in vulnerable employment by region and sex, 2004-2007
(latest available)

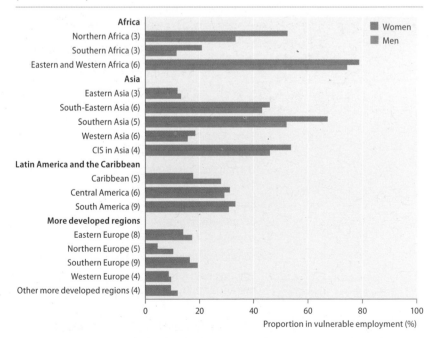

Source: Computed by the United Nations Statistics Division based on data from ILO, Key Indicators of the Labour Market, 5th edition, table 3 (accessed in July 2009).
Note: Unweighted averages; the numbers in brackets indicate the number of countries averaged. The average for Eastern Asia does not include China. Western Asia excludes Armenia, Azerbaijan and Georgia; CIS in Asia includes the aforementioned countries plus Kazakhstan, Kyrgyzstan, Tajikistan, Turkmenistan and Uzbekistan.

6 See also United Nations, 2009c.

per cent) for both women and men in the more developed regions, Eastern Asia, Western Asia and Southern Africa. As noted earlier, wage employment is the dominant form of work in those regions.

Compared to employees, own-account workers and contributing family workers, employers constitute a very small proportion of those employed. In no region in the world did employers constitute more than 3 per cent of employed women in 2007. From the available data, only three countries topped 5 per cent in the proportion of employers among the female employed: Finland, Germany and Sweden. The regional figures for men are typically twice as high as for women and range from 1 per cent to 8 per cent (table 4.6).

3. The informal sector and informal employment

In most developing countries, women who are not engaged in farming as own-account workers or contributing family workers are often employed as street vendors, independent home-based workers, industrial outworkers, contributing family workers

in non-agricultural family businesses or domestic workers in the homes of others. Many women are also engaged in waste collecting or small-scale mining and construction and a few others as employers in small-scale enterprises. Although these jobs are very different in the activities performed, modes of operations and earnings, all are part of informal employment and provide the main source of work for women outside agriculture. (See box 4.5 for categories of workers included in the definition of informal sector and informal employment.)

Informal employment is the main source of jobs for women – as well as men – in most developing countries

---

While informal employment is also an important source of employment for men in developing countries, it is more so for women. In the late 1990s, 84 per cent of women non-agricultural workers in sub-Saharan Africa were informally employed compared to 63 per cent of men; in Latin America it was 58 per cent of women compared to 48 per cent of men. In Asia the proportion of women and

---

Box 4.5
Defining informal sector and informal employment

The concepts of the informal sector and informal employment are relatively new in labour statistics, developed to better measure employment in unincorporated small or unregistered enterprises (informal sector) and employment that is not covered by legal and social protection (informal employment).

In 1993 the 15th International Conference of Labour Statisticians (ICLS) adopted a resolution setting out the statistical definition of the informal sector to refer to employment and production that takes place in unincorporated small or unregistered enterprises.[a] Ten years later, the 17th ICLS adopted the definition for the related and broader concept of informal employment.[b] Informal employment refers to all informal jobs, whether carried out in formal sector enterprises, informal sector enterprises or households. It comprises:

Persons employed in the informal sector (except those rare persons who are in the sector who may have formal employment) including:

- Own-account (self-employed) workers in their own informal enterprises;
- Employers in informal enterprises;
- Employees of informal enterprises;
- Contributing family workers working in informal sector enterprises; and
- Members of informal producers' cooperatives.

Persons in informal employment outside the informal sector, specifically:

- Employees in formal enterprises not covered by national labour legislation, social protection or entitlement to certain employment benefits such as paid annual or sick leave;
- Contributing family workers working in formal sector enterprises;
- Paid domestic workers not covered by national labour legislation, social protection or entitlement to certain employment benefits such as paid annual or sick leave; and
- Own-account workers engaged in the production of goods exclusively for own final use by their household (e.g., subsistence farming, do-it-yourself construction of own dwelling).

a For the full definition see Resolution concerning statistics of employment in the informal sector in ILO, 1993b.
b For the full definition see ILO, 2003b.

men non-agricultural workers in informal employment was roughly equal, at 65 per cent.[7] These statistics, prepared in 2001, are based on what is called a "residual estimation method". Until recently only a few countries directly measured informal employment and employment in informal enterprises, so an indirect approach based on existing published statistical data available in many developing countries was used.[8]

With the establishment of the definitions of informal sector and informal employment and the recognition of the importance of informal employment, an increasing number of countries are now collecting data on informal employment and informal sector directly through household surveys, in some cases supplemented by enterprise surveys. Not many countries have fully analysed their data, but data for seven countries in different regions are shown in table 4.7 to illustrate the importance of informal employment among women as well as men in these countries – and not just in the informal sector but also outside of it.

The proportion of women's non-agricultural employment that is informal in the seven countries ranges from a low of 18 per cent in the Republic of Moldova to a high of 89 per cent in Mali. In most of the countries, informal employment comprises more than half of women's non-agricultural employment. Further, in all of them except the Republic of Moldova informal employment is a greater source of employment for women than for men. It is noteworthy that in India and Mali nearly 90 per cent of women employed in non-agriculture are in informal employment with over 70 per cent in the informal sector. In India, these women are in jobs such as street vendors, garment makers in informal enterprises in the home and construction workers. (See also box 4.6, Improving statistics on informal employment in India.)

The relatively low rates of informal employment in the Republic of Moldova reflect the legacy of a centrally planned economy where informal activities were considered illegal and even forbidden. Now in countries of Eastern Europe and the CIS such activities have an important role in creating jobs, in providing income and in the production of goods and services. For example, if agriculture were included, the proportion of women's employment that is informal in the Republic of Moldova would rise to 38 per cent.[9]

Table 4.7

Informal employment as a percentage of total non-agricultural employment, by sex, 2003–2004 (*latest available*)

		Informal employment		Employment in the informal sector		Informal employment outside the informal sector	
		As percentage of total non-agricultural employment					
	Year	Women	Men	Women	Men	Women	Men
Brazil (urban)	2003	52[a]	50[a]	32	42	24	12
Ecuador (urban)	2004	77	73	44	36	33	37
India[b]	2004/05	88	84	73	71	15	13
Mali	2004	89[a]	74[a]	80	63	10	13
Republic of Moldova	2004	18	25	5	11	14	14
South Africa	2004	65	51	16	15	49	36
Turkey	2004	36	35	..	..	..	..

Sources: For all countries except India, ILO Department of Statistics: for Brazil, ILO estimates based on official data from various sources; for Mali and South Africa, ILO estimates computed from labour force survey micro data; for the rest, ILO estimates based on labour force survey data. For India, estimates provided by Jeemol Unni based on the Survey of Employment and Unemployment.

Notes

a The sum of the components "employment in the informal sector" and "informal employment outside the informal sector" exceeds total informal employment due to the presence of formal employment in the component "employment in the informal sector".

b Data refer to persons aged 5 or over.

Generally, women's informal jobs are more likely to be in the informal sector than outside of it. The exception again is the Republic of Moldova and, in addition, South Africa. Employment in the informal sector often is in own-account self-employment, in activities such as street vending or in small-scale production in one's home. The low rates in South Africa in part reflect the history of apartheid with its prohibition of black-owned businesses.[10]

4. Occupational segregation

Types of occupations vary considerably across regions and between the sexes

Women and men are segregated in different types of occupations. The occupation groups in which they are employed vary widely across regions. Looking at the top two occupation groups that women and men engage in, it is immediately apparent, however, that these are similar in subregions with a significant agricultural sector, where they tend to include either or both of the major

---

7 ILO, 2002.

8 For details on the residual estimation method, see ILO, 2002.

9 ILO, 2004a.

10 Under apartheid, most informal selling in urban centres and even would-be formal black-owned businesses were defined as illegal. Restrictions on black-owned businesses have been loosened since the formal ending of apartheid (ILO, 2002).

Box 4.6
Improving statistics on informal employment in India: the role of users

The importance of dialogue and collaboration between statisticians and users of statistics in producing timely statistics that inform policy has been illustrated time and again in the field of gender statistics. An exceptional example of this is the active role played by the Self-Employed Women's Association of India (SEWA) over the course of more than 20 years. SEWA has worked with national research organizations, government commissions and the national statistical system to develop statistics on the working poor women in the informal economy that it represents. In doing so, SEWA furthered not only the development of statistics on these women workers but also the improvement of labour force data in India.

Since its beginning in the 1970's SEWA has made the development of statistics on informal workers a priority. It began to develop these statistics with research institutions and then gradually with the official statistical system. In the last 10 years, SEWA collaborated closely with the National Sample Survey Organization (NSSO) in the planning and design of the 1999-2000 and the 2004-5 Survey of Employment and Unemployment. This was the first official survey in India that included questions that provided for the identification of the informal economy in both urban and rural areas. In addition, the survey allowed for the classification of home-based workers, both self-employed and industrial outworkers (called home-workers), and of street vendors.

SEWA is a member of the Independent Group on Home-based Workers in India. Organized in 2007, the Independent Group has brought together statisticians, researchers and advocates to address: 1) concepts and definitions of home-based workers and their categories for data collection purposes; 2) a plan for tabulation and analysis of data from various official sources; and 3) identification of data needs and recommendations for filling the gaps.[a]

The collaboration of statisticians and the various data-user groups in India to improve statistics on informal workers has been very fruitful. With national labour force surveys showing over 90 percent of the labour force in informal employment, there is now greater recognition of these workers and their situation, and new programmes have been developed to improve the livelihood of women and men in informal employment. In addition, steps are being taken to further develop data on these workers in India. As a result, the statistical services of the Government of India have been leaders worldwide in the development of statistics on informal employment. This includes responsibility for the standing expert group of the United Nations Statistical Commission on informal sector statistics, known as the Delhi Group.

a   Report of the Independent Group on Home-based Workers (New Delhi, India, 2008), *http://www.unifem. org.in/PDF/IG%20HBW%20 Report.pdf.*

---

occupation groups associated with the sector, namely "skilled agricultural and fishery workers" and "elementary occupations".[11] This is the case in Eastern Africa, South-Eastern Asia, Southern Asia and the CIS in Asia, and to some extent in Northern Africa, Southern Africa, Central America and South America (table 4.8).

In the other regions of the world, the difference between the sexes is more distinct. In these regions, certain types of occupations are taken up by a significant proportion of women while others are taken up by a significant proportion of men. For women, the occupation group "service workers and shop and market sales workers" is the biggest source of employment in 7 out of the 12

sub-regions where agricultural and elementary occupations are not the top two occupation groups and the second biggest in 4 sub-regions. In these 11 sub-regions, service and sales engage at least 18 per cent of all employed women. A slightly smaller proportion of women works as "technicians and associate professionals" (in all four sub-regions of Europe and in Northern Africa) or as clerks (Eastern Asia, the Caribbean and the more developed regions outside Europe). For men in all sub-regions (excluding those where agricultural and elementary occupations make up the two biggest groups), "craft and related trade workers" is an important occupation group. This group employs the largest proportion of men in the more developed regions, the Caribbean and South America – 20 per cent or more – and the second largest proportion of men in the remaining sub-regions.

Over the years women have entered various traditionally male-dominated occupations. However, they are still rarely employed in jobs with

11 Elementary occupations consist of tasks connected with street or door-to-door sales or services, cleaning, property watching and caretaking, delivering goods and messages or carrying luggage, as well as agricultural, fishery, mining, construction, manufacturing and transport labourers (International Standard Classification of Occupations (ISCO-88) major group 9).

Table 4.8

Two largest occupation groups by region and sex, 2004–2008 (*latest available*)

	Two largest occupation groups (and their percentage share of total employment)	
	Women	Men
Africa		
Northern Africa (3)	Agric (41), Tech (13)	Agric (26), Craft (17)
Southern Africa (3)	Elem (29), Svce&Sales (18)	Elem (24), Craft (18)
Eastern Africa (5)	Agric (51), Elem (20)	Agric (53), Elem (15)
Asia		
Eastern Asia (4)	Svce&Sales (22), Clerk (20)	Svce&Sales (14), Craft (14)
South-Eastern Asia (8)	Elem (24), Agric (20)	Agric (24), Elem (20)
Southern Asia (5)	Agric (47), Elem (15)	Agric (34), Elem (17)
Western Asia (12)	Svce&Sales (21), Prof (18)	Svce&Sales (18), Craft (15)
CIS in Asia (4)	Agric (30), Elem (20)	Agric (32), Craft (14)
Latin America and the Caribbean		
Caribbean (7)	Svce&Sales (24), Clerk (23)	Craft (22), Elem (16)
Central America (6)	Svce&Sales (27), Elem (25)	Elem (25), Craft (17)
South America (9)	Elem (26), Svce&Sales (23)	Craft (20), Elem (19)
More developed regions		
Eastern Europe (9)	Svce&Sales (19), Tech (18)	Craft (24), Oper (18)
Northern Europe (9)	Svce&Sales (25), Tech (21)	Craft (23), Prof (14)
Southern Europe (9)	Svce&Sales (20), Tech (16)	Craft (22), Oper (13)
Western Europe (6)	Tech (21), Svce&Sales (20)	Craft (21), Tech (16)
Other more developed regions (3)	Clerk (21), Svce&Sales (20)	Craft (19), Prof (15)

Source: Computed by the United Nations Statistics Division based on data from ILO, LABORSTA table 2C (accessed in January 2010). Note: Unweighted averages; the numbers in brackets indicate the number of countries averaged. Agric=Skilled agricultural and fishery workers; Tech=Technicians and associate professionals; Craft=Craft and related trade workers; Elem=Elementary occupations; Svce&Sales =Service workers and shop and market sales workers; Clerk=Clerks; Oper=Plant and machine operators and assemblers; Prof=Professionals. The average for Eastern Asia does not include China. Western Asia excludes Armenia, Azerbaijan and Georgia; CIS in Asia includes the aforementioned countries plus Kazakhstan, Kyrgyzstan, Tajikistan, Turkmenistan and Uzbekistan.

status, power and authority and in traditionally male blue-collar occupations. Relative to their overall share of total employment, women are significantly underrepresented among "legislators, senior officials and managers", "craft and related trade workers" and "plant and machine operators and assemblers", and heavily overrepresented among "clerks", "professionals", and "service workers and shop and market sales workers" (figure 4.6).

However, to more fully understand the depth of occupational segregation, it is important to analyse each of the occupation groups in more detail. Major groups encompass a large number of occupations that are a mixture of male-dominated, female-dominated and neutral ones. For example, the group "professionals" includes both heavily male-dominated occupations (such as architects, engineers and related professionals) and heavily female-dominated occupations (such as pre-primary, primary and secondary education teachers). It has been observed that traditionally women are found in occupations with caring and nurturing functions or in jobs requiring household-related or low-level skills. Stereotypes, education and vocational training, the structure of the labour market and discrimination at entry and in work are among the causes often cited for gender segregation of occupations.[12]

The extent to which women and men are found in different occupations, referred to as horizontal job segregation, has been the subject of extensive research in the last few decades. One such study, based on detailed occupational data from the International Labour Office (ILO) SEGREGAT database, showed Thailand and the United States of America to have the lowest occupational segregation of the 15 countries analysed.[13]

Few women are in positions of authority and decision-making

In all regions, the proportion of women among legislators, senior officials and managers is much less than their overall proportion in the employed population. The proportion female in this occupation group ranges from a low of 10 per cent in Northern Africa to 40 per cent in the Caribbean. It is between 30 and 40 per cent in all sub-regions of Latin America and the Caribbean

12 See discussion in Anker and others, 2003.
13 Anker and others, 2003.

Figure 4.6

Women's share of employment in eight occupation groups relative to their share of total employment, 2004–2008 (*latest available*)

(a) Four occupation groups in which women are overrepresented

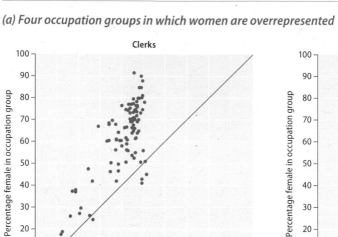

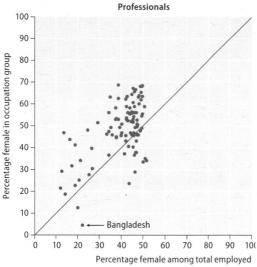

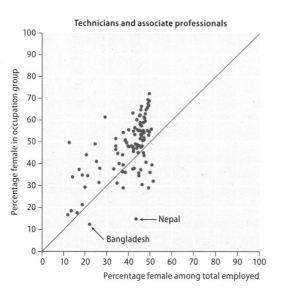

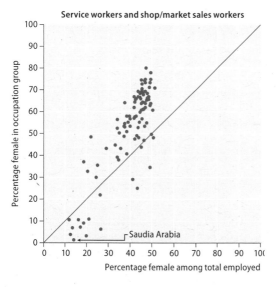

Note: Women are also overrepresented in elementary occupations but to a lesser degree than the above four occupation groups.

and the more developed regions, but less than 30 per cent in Northern and Eastern Africa and Asia (figure 4.7). Studies based on detailed occupations within this group show that women are even rarer in occupations with the highest degree of power and influence (i.e., chief directors and chief executives), and that this phenomenon is true across all regions, all cultures and all levels of economic and social development.[14] For example, in 14 countries out of the European Union

group of 27, there is no woman CEO in the top 50 publicly quoted companies.[15] (See also Chapter 5 – Power and decision-making)

Vertical job segregation (the situation where women and men are employed at different levels, grades or positions within the same occupation) exists in almost all occupations, with women often at the lower end of the spectrum.[16] In the teaching profession, for example, women consti-

14 Anker, 2005. See also Chapter 5 – Power and decision-making.

15 Bettio and Verashchagina, 2009.

16 United Nations, 2000

(b) Four occupation groups in which women are underrepresented

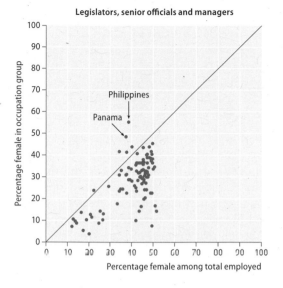

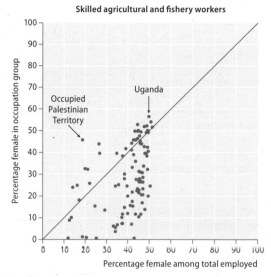

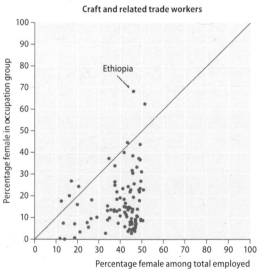

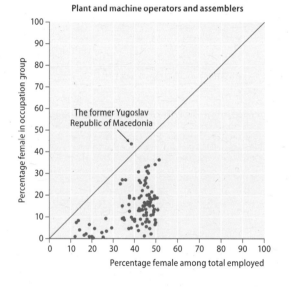

Source: Computed by the United Nations Statistics Division based on data from ILO, LABORSTA table 2C (accessed in January 2010).

Note: Each point represents one country. If the proportion female in an occupation group is the same as the overall proportion of women among the total employed, the point will lie on the diagonal line. A point above and to the left of the diagonal line indicates that women are overrepresented in the occupation group relative to their overall share of total employment, while a point below and to the right of the diagonal line indicates that women are underrepresented in the occupation group relative to their overall share of total employment.

tute a high proportion of primary school teachers but a much lower proportion of university teaching staff (see Chapter 3 – Education).

5. Part-time work

The steady rise in women's employment in the last few decades is primarily due to the creation and growth of a part-time female work force, at least in developed economies.[17] For example, part-time work has been the source of the Dutch "employment miracle" – three quarters of the two million new jobs since 1983 have been part-time, the majority of them going to women.[18]

Part-time work facilitates the gradual entry of young persons into and the exit of older persons out of the labour market.[19] For example, women and men may take part-time jobs during their transition from full-time studies into the labour force or during the transition out of full-time employment into retirement. Part-time work also offers a solution for women and men trying to balance working life and family responsibilities. However, even when part-time work options are available to both women and men, they are taken up mostly by women because of stereotypical assumptions about women's roles as caregivers and the lower earnings of women. (See also section C. Reconciliation of work and family life.)

17 Hakim, 2004, chapter 3; ILO, 2007.

18 Cousins and Tang, 2003.

19 United Nations, 2000; ILO, 2007.

Figure 4.7

Women's share of legislators, senior officials and managers and of total employed, by region, 2004–2008 (*latest available*)

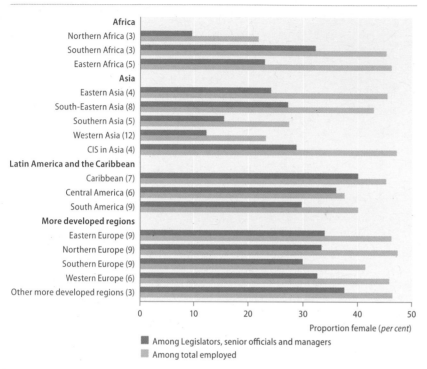

Proportion female (*per cent*)

■ Among Legislators, senior officials and managers
■ Among total employed

Source: Computed by the United Nations Statistics Division based on data from ILO, LABORSTA table 2C (accessed in January 2010).

Note: Unweighted averages; the numbers in brackets indicate the number of countries averaged. The average for Eastern Asia does not include China. Western Asia excludes Armenia, Azerbaijan and Georgia; CIS in Asia includes the aforementioned countries plus Kazakhstan, Kyrgyzstan, Tajikistan, Turkmenistan and Uzbekistan.

Part-time employment is increasing for both women and men

The costs of part-time employment can be great. Part-time employment is associated with lower income – with a long-term impact on pensions – and does not carry the same social benefits as full-time employment. Career advancement of part-time workers, who are predominantly women, is often jeopardized because the image persists that they are not serious about their jobs and careers. The types of part-time jobs available and the conditions of work are also a concern. Thus, although part-time work may be a solution for women reconciling work with family responsibilities, it reinforces the male breadwinner model, relegating women to a secondary role in the labour market.[20]

At present the part-time work force is increasing in many countries around the world, not just for women but also for men. Between 1990 and 2007, out of 35 countries with available data,

20 ILO, 2004b.

part-time employment (defined here as employment of less than 30 hours per week) was seen to have increased for women in 21 countries and for men in 26. Particularly high increases during the period were observed for both women and men in Germany, Honduras and the Bolivarian Republic of Venezuela (table 4.9), as well as for women in Ireland and Italy and for men in the Republic of Korea and Spain.[21]

There were only a few significant declines in part-time employment during the same period, all confined to Northern Europe and the Caribbean. The proportion of women working part-time decreased in Denmark, Iceland, Norway and Sweden (by 5 percentage points or more) although that for men increased slightly. In the Bahamas and Trinidad and Tobago, declines of 4 and 5 percentage points, respectively, were registered for both women and men.

Part-time employment is particularly prevalent among women in Northern and Western Europe

In 2007, 60 per cent of employed women in the Netherlands were working part-time, the most by far in the world.[22] Part-time employment among women is also common in several Northern and Western European countries, exceeding 35 per cent in Germany, Ireland, Switzerland and the United Kingdom. In some of these countries, this reflects the lack of paid parental leave and affordable childcare services. Outside Europe, a part-time rate of 35 per cent or more was recorded for women in Argentina, Australia, Honduras and New Zealand. Most countries in Latin America (but not the Caribbean) also have significant proportions of part-time workers (at least 20 per cent) among women. Part-time employment of women is not as common in the United States of America and the countries of Eastern Europe (table 4.9).

Everywhere, part-time employment is much more common among women than among men, with the prevalence rate for women exceeding twice that for men in about three quarters of the coun-

21 These are cases where the proportions employed part-time either increased by more than 10 percentage points or more than doubled between 1990 and 2007 (between 1990 and 2003 in the case of Honduras and Venezuela (Bolivarian Republic of)).

22 In the Netherlands, part-time jobs are highly protected and regulated. There is legislation providing all workers with a general right to change their working hours. In the United Kingdom, parents with a child younger than 6 years old have a right to request flexible work arrangements, which could be reduced hours of work.

Table 4.9

Proportion of employed people working part-time by sex, 1990 and 2007

| | Percentage of employed persons working part-time (less than 30 hours per week) | | | | | |
| | Women | | | Men | | |
	1990	2007	Difference	1990	2007	Difference
Asia						
Republic of Korea	7	13	6	3	6	3
Turkey	19	19	0	5	5	-1
Latin America and the Caribbean						
Argentina	..	43	..	..	19	..
Bahamas	16	12	-4	14	10	-4
Bolivia (Plurinational State of)	..	31	..	..	17	..
Costa Rica	21	25	5	7	10	3
Dominican Republic	..	23	..	..	12	..
Ecuador	18	23	6	7	12	5
El Salvador	20	20	0	11	15	4
Honduras	25	35	11	7	16	9
Mexico	19	28	9	8	8	1
Nicaragua	17	20	4	11	10	-1
Panama	15	22	7	11	16	5
Paraguay	16	25	9	8	14	5
Trinidad and Tobago	14	10	-5	12	7	-5
Venezuela (Bolivarian Rep. of)	10	32	22	2	15	13
Eastern Europe						
Czech Republic	6	6	0	2	2	0
Hungary	..	4	..	..	2	..
Poland	..	15	..	..	6	..
Slovakia	4	4	0	1	1	0
Rest of Europe						
Austria	..	32	..	..	5	..
Belgium	29	33	4	4	6	2
Denmark	30	24	-6	10	12	2
Finland	11	16	5	5	8	3
France	23	23	1	5	5	1
Germany	25	39	14	2	8	6
Greece	12	14	2	4	4	0
Iceland	40	25	-14	8	8	1
Ireland	21	36	14	4	8	3
Italy	18	30	12	4	5	1
Luxembourg	19	29	10	2	2	0
Netherlands	53	60	8	13	16	3
Norway	40	32	-8	7	11	4
Portugal	13	14	2	4	6	2
Spain	12	21	9	1	4	2
Sweden	25	20	-5	5	10	4
Switzerland	43	46	3	7	9	2
United Kingdom	40	39	-1	5	10	5
Other more developed regions						
Australia	..	39	..	..	12	..
Canada	27	26	-1	9	11	2
Japan	..	33	..	..	9	..
New Zealand	35	35	0	8	11	3
United States of America	20	18	-2	9	8	-1

Source: ILO, Key Indicators of the Labour Market, 5th edition, table 5 (accessed in July 2009).

Note: For Latin America and the Caribbean, figures shown refer to 1990 and 2003. The cut-off for part-time work in the Bahamas and Trinidad and Tobago is 32 hours per week. Due to rounding, the numbers in the difference column may not coincide exactly with the difference between the figures for the two years.

tries. Part-time employment rates among men ranged from 1 to 19 per cent in 2007. Out of the 35 countries with available data, the 10 countries with the highest proportions of men working part-time include seven from Latin America (Argentina, Bolivia (Plurinational State of), El Salvador, Honduras, Panama, Paraguay and Venezuela (Bolivarian Republic of)) and three from the more developed regions (Australia, Denmark and the Netherlands). In those countries, more than 12 per cent of employed men are part-time workers.

6. Gender pay gap

The gender pay gap reflects inequalities that affect mainly women, notably horizontal and vertical segregation of the labour market, traditions and stereotypes that influence the choice of education, professions and career paths, and the difficulty of balancing work and private life that often leads to part-time work and career breaks for women.[23]

A simple indicator is used in this section to examine trends in gender pay gap – the ratio of women's average earnings to men's average earnings, expressed per 100. A ratio of 100 indicates that there is no gender pay gap: women are paid the same as men. A ratio below 100 indicates that women earn less than men and a ratio above 100 that they earn more than men – in other words, the closer the ratio is to 100, the smaller the gap.

The gender pay gap is closing slowly in some countries but not in others

---

The analysis of trends in gender pay gap is limited to the manufacturing sector since wage statistics for this sector are more widely available than those for other industrial sectors. Furthermore, manufacturing is one of the industries where the gender pay gap is high. It should be noted that statistics of average wages from which the gender pay gap is derived cover only the "formal" sector of the economy. They do not shed light on earnings from self-employment or informal sector activities. Also, a simple indicator based on statistics of average earnings without controlling for occupation, qualifications, job grade or hours actually worked has been cited as causing misleading comparisons. Nevertheless, this "gross" measure reflects the realities of gender inequalities in the labour market, where higher proportions of women than men work part-time and are in the lower rungs of the occupation ladder (see the previous two sections).

In some countries, there was a narrowing of the gender pay gap in manufacturing between 1990 and 2008. As reported earnings can for various reasons fluctuate considerably from year to year (see box 4.7), only sizeable changes in that period are highlighted. From the available data, presented in table 4.10, Japan, Mexico and Paraguay appear to have significantly reduced the gender pay gap (a decrease of at least 20 percentage points) in the manufacturing sector. Japan and Mexico were both coming from notably large gender gaps in the past. Two other countries with large gender gaps in 1990, Cyprus and the Republic of Korea, did not make significant progress. For the remaining countries, the evidence points to the gender pay gap closing slightly in most countries but remaining unchanged in others. This is consistent with recent reports by the ILO that the wage gap has been stable or is closing only very slowly.[24]

Box 4.7

Comparability issues in statistics of average earnings

Average reported earnings can fluctuate considerably from year to year. Depending on the source, earnings may be reported as average earnings per hour, per day, per week or per month. Workers covered also vary, from wage earners (i.e., manual or production workers) to salaried employees (i.e., non-manual workers) to all employees (i.e., wage earners plus salaried workers). Some countries limit the data to full-time employees or report data in terms of full-time equivalent employees. These variations have a bearing on the results. For example, based on a comparison made by the Statistics Division of the United Nations of multiple earnings types reported by the same country for the same year, it was found that the gender pay gap is generally greater for salaried employees than wage earners. Also, the gender pay gap tends to be higher for average earnings reported on a per month basis, compared to those reported on a per hour basis. With women on average working fewer hours than men, the difference in their earnings would be greater the longer the time period covered. Thus, trends and cross-country differences should be interpreted with caution.

---

23 European Commission, 2007.

24 ILO, 2008a; ILO, 2009c.

Table 4.10

Ratio of female to male earnings
in manufacturing, 1990–1992 and 2006–2008
(*latest available in each interval*)

	Female/male ratio of average earnings per month in manufacturing (*per cent*)	
	1990–1992	2006–2008
Africa		
Egypt[a, b]	68	66
Asia		
China, Hong Kong SAR[b, c]	69	60[d]
Cyprus[a, b]	58	56
Jordan	57	69
Republic of Korea	50	57
Singapore	55	65
Sri Lanka[b, e]	88	77
Thailand[f]	64	75
Latin America and the Caribbean		
Costa Rica	74	81[g]
Mexico	50	72
Paraguay	66	86
Europe		
Czech Republic	68	65[b]
Denmark[g]	85	87[h]
France[b, g]	79	85
Hungary[i]	70	73
Ireland[b, g]	69	80
Latvia	84	81
Luxembourg[b, g]	62	73
Netherlands	74[a]	83
Sweden[b, g]	89	91
Switzerland	71	77
United Kingdom[i]	61	75
Other more developed regions		
Australia[g, i]	82	90
Japan[h]	41	61
New Zealand[g, i]	75	81

Source: Computed by the United Nations Statistics Division based on data from ILO, LABORSTA tables 5A and 5B (accessed in October 2009).

Notes

a Earnings per week.

b Wage earners.

c Wage rates per day.

d Including outworkers.

e Earnings per day.

f Wage rates per month.

g Earnings per hour.

h Data are for the private sector only.

i Full-time or full-time equivalent employees.

A gender pay gap persists everywhere

While constraints in both data and methods make it difficult to present a comprehensive global analysis of gender pay gaps, the ILO recognizes that women's wages represent between 70 and 90 per cent of men's wages in a majority of countries.[25] For Europe, where data are more comparable and available than for other regions, recent estimates of the gender pay gap for 30 countries vary from 15 per cent[26] to 25 per cent.[27] Statistics from countries in the European Union show that the pay gap increases with age, level of educational attainment and years of service; for example, it exceeds 30 per cent in the 50–59 age group compared to only 7 per cent for those under 30.[28]

There are also significant variations in the gender pay gap from one occupation to another. This is illustrated for six countries in figure 4.8. In the Republic of Korea, there are no jobs that pay women more than men; on average, women earn between 46 and 90 per cent of what men earn, depending on their occupation. Averaged over all occupations, women in the Republic of Korea earn 68 per cent of what men earn.

In Brazil and the United Kingdom there are a few occupations in which women earn more than men: 5 out of 31 occupations in the former and 8 out of 116 in the latter. In most occupations in these two countries, women earn from 60 to 100 per cent of what men earn. Considering all occupations, the average earnings ratio is 81 in Brazil and 85 in the United Kingdom. In Australia, Russian Federation and Thailand, the earnings ratios for the various occupations vary widely, exceeding 125 for some occupations and even reaching as high as 150 in two cases, but also dipping well below 50 for one or two occupations in the Russian Federation and Thailand. Compared to the first three countries, the latter three have a relatively better gender balance in earnings: some occupations pay women more while others pay men more. Across all occupations, the average earnings ratio in Australia is 88, in the Russian Federation 89 and in Thailand 92. Although smaller than for the other countries, these gender pay gaps are still significant.

25 ILO, 2008a.

26 Based on official statistics and reported in European Commission, 2007; the same estimate, based on publicly available data of gross hourly earnings for 30 European countries, is reported in International Trade Union Confederation, 2008.

27 Based on a 2002 survey that covered only employees in the private sector, cited in Plantenga and Remery, 2006.

28 European Commission, 2007.

Box 4.8

Concept of work within the framework of the System of National Accounts

The production boundary as defined in the System of National Accounts (SNA)[a] includes (1) the production of goods and services actually destined for the market, whether for sale or barter; (2) all goods and services provided free to individual households or collectively to the community by government units or non-profit institutions serving households; and (3) the production of goods for own use, in particular:

a) The production of agricultural goods by households for own consumption;

b) The production of other goods for own final use by households such as the construction of dwellings and the production of foodstuffs and clothing; and

c) Own-account production of housing services for own final consumption by owner occupiers.

However, the SNA production boundary excludes all production of services for own final consumption within households; i.e., domestic and personal services produced and consumed by members of the same household.

Within the SNA framework, work may fall either within or outside the production boundary. Work that falls within the SNA production boundary is considered "economic" in labour force statistics, and persons engaged in such activities are recorded as being economically active. In the statistics of time use presented in the current chapter, such work is referred to as "paid work" (even if some may actually be unpaid, such as work falling within the SNA production boundary performed by contributing family workers). Work that falls outside the SNA production boundary is considered "non-economic" in labour force statistics. In this chapter such work is referred to as "unpaid work" and consists mainly of (a) domestic work and (b) community or volunteer work. Domestic work includes food preparation, dish washing, cleaning and upkeep of dwelling, laundry, ironing, handicraft, gardening, caring for pets, construction and repairs, shopping, installation, servicing and repair of personal and household goods, childcare, care of sick, elderly or disabled household members, etc. Community/ volunteer work includes volunteer services for organizations, unpaid community work, informal help to other households, etc.

a For more detail on the SNA, see European Commission and others, 2009.

The six countries vary greatly in the occupations that have high or low gender pay gaps. For countries as diverse as these, commonalities are difficult to find. For example, only two occupations (electronic equipment assembler and sewing-machine operator) are common to three countries in having a wage ratio exceeding 100, and an additional 12 occupations[29] if the wage ratio cut-off is reduced to 90. On the other hand, it is not unusual for an occupation to have gender wage gaps in opposite directions in different countries. For example, first-level women education teachers in Brazil earned only 49 per cent of what their men colleagues earned, but in the Russian Federation they earned 121 per cent of what men earned; female journalists earned 57 per cent of what men journalists earned in Thailand, but 111 per cent of what men earned in the Russian Federation.

The gender pay gap tends to be wider in the highest-paid occupations, at least in Australia, Brazil, Republic of Korea and the United Kingdom, where the highest-paying two or three occupations have wage ratios of 75 or lower. In contrast, in the Russian Federation and Thailand the wage ratios for the highest-paying occupations are closer to 100 (figure 4.8).

C. Reconciliation of work and family life

1. Sharing of domestic work

Women are the primary caretakers of the family

In spite of the changes that have occurred in women's participation in the labour market discussed above, women continue to bear most of the responsibilities for the home: caring for children and other dependent household members, preparing meals and doing other housework. This work, while productive, is outside the boundary of the System of National Accounts (SNA) and therefore not counted as economic activity (see box 4.8). Those who carry the burden of work for the home – mainly women – enter the labour market from a highly disadvantaged position, as the time they spend on domestic work restricts their access to full and productive employment and also leaves them with less time for education and training, leisure, self-care and social and political activities.[30]

29 Post office counter clerk, computer programmer, mathematics teacher (second and third levels), teacher in languages and literature (second and third levels), technical education teacher (second level), education teacher (first level), dentist (general), professional nurse (general), physiotherapist, medical X-ray technician, book-keeper and hotel receptionist.

30 Addati and Cassirer, 2008; Razavi and Staab, 2008.

Figure 4.8
Average female/male earnings ratios in various occupations, six countries, 2006–2007

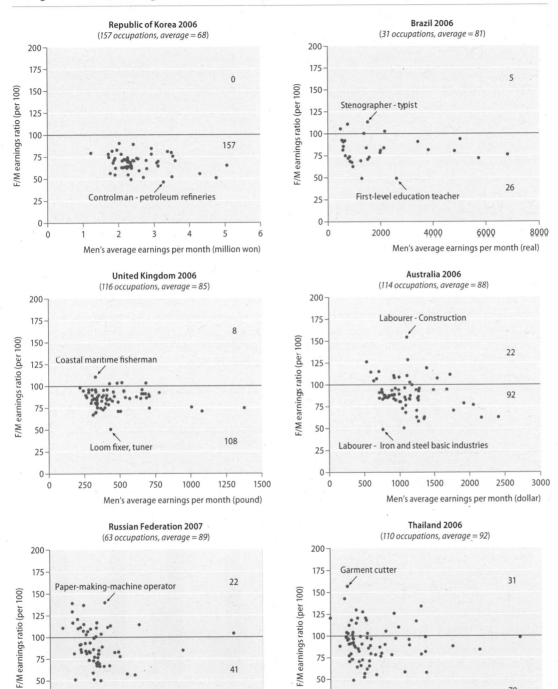

Source: Computed by the United Nations Statistics Division based on data from ILO, LABORSTA table O1 (accessed in October 2009).

Note: The total number of occupations is shown in brackets below the country name, together with the unweighted average of female/male (F/M) earnings ratio. The number on the upper part of each graph refers to the number of occupations where the F/M earnings ratio exceeds 100; the number on the lower part of the graph refers to the number of occupations where the ratio is below 100.

In general, women's increased participation in paid employment has not been accompanied by an increase in men's participation in unpaid domestic work (comprised mainly of housework and caring for dependent household members). Time use statistics (see box 4.9 on interpreting the statistics) show that in all regions, women dedicate much more time to domestic work than men do (figure 4.9). In the more developed regions, women spend an average of almost five hours a day on domestic work, whereas men spend on average less than two and a half hours a day on this, or half the amount of time spent by women. In some countries – for example, Italy, Japan, Portugal, Spain and the former Yugoslav Republic of Macedonia – the difference is even greater, with women spending three- to four-fold the amount of time spent by men on domestic work.

Although still very far from equitable, the sharing of domestic tasks between the sexes is more favourable in the more developed regions compared to other regions. Men perform far less domestic work in Asia. For example, in the Occupied Palestinian Territory, Pakistan and Turkey, the time men spend on domestic work is not even a fifth of what women spend (see Statistical Annex).

Evidence from Latin America and Africa is weaker, as there are data for only a few countries. Nevertheless, from the available data it is apparent that in both of these regions, women spend far more than twice the time men spend on unpaid domestic work (figure 4.9).

Cultural conceptions of women's and men's roles no doubt play an important part in the unequal sharing of domestic work between the sexes. Change may be slow, but a trend towards a more equitable division of household work is evident in many European countries. In the Nordic countries and the United States of America, where time use studies over a number of years allow long-term comparisons, findings indicate that the number of hours spent by the average woman on household work has decreased while that spent by the average man has increased. In Norway, for example, the time women use for household work per day declined by about two hours in the 30 years between 1971 and 2000, whereas for men it increased by about half an hour, due mainly to more men taking part in household work than before.[31] In the United States of America, women's and men's hours spent in housework moved towards convergence over the 30-year period from 1965 to 1995, primarily due to the steep decline in women's hours but also due to an increase in men's hours.[32] Recent results[33] indicate a continuation of the trend, although the convergence has been much slower since 1985.

Box 4.9

Interpreting statistics of time spent on activities

Data from time use surveys may be summarized and presented as either *participant averages* or *population averages*. In the participant average, the total time spent by all individuals who performed an activity is divided by the number of persons who performed it (participants). In the population average, the total time is divided by the total relevant population (or a sub-group thereof) regardless of whether people performed the activity or not. In this chapter, all statistics presented on time spent in various activities are population averages. Population averages can be used to compare groups and assess changes over time. Differences between groups or over time may be due to a difference (or change) in proportions participating in the specific activity or a difference (or change) in the amount of time spent by participants, or both.

When time spent is expressed as an average per day, it is an average over seven days of the week, weekdays and weekends not differentiated. Thus, for paid work, a five-day work week averaging seven hours per day would show up as an average of five hours of paid work per day (35 hours divided by 7 days).

Finally, statistics presented refer to the "main activity". Any "secondary activity" performed simultaneously with the main activity is not reflected in the average times shown. It should be noted that limiting analysis to the main activity results in a downward bias on the actual time spent on many activities, especially those that are often secondary to other activities. One such activity is childcare, a considerable portion of which is recorded as secondary activity (for example, parents may be looking after their children while cooking or cleaning the house).

Figure 4.9

Time spent on domestic work by region and sex, 1999–2008 (*latest available*)

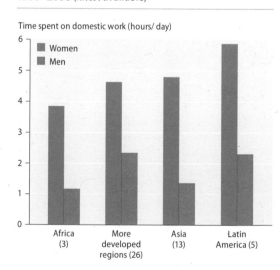

Time spent on domestic work (hours/ day)

Source: Computed by the United Nations Statistics Division based on country-level data from Statistics Sweden, UNECE, UNECLAC and national statistical offices (as of December 2009).
Note: Unweighted averages; the numbers in brackets indicate the number of countries averaged.

---

31 Based on time use of women and men aged 16–74 years. Statistics Norway, 2002.

32 Bianchi, 2000.

33 United States Bureau of Labor Statistics, 2009.

Figure 4.10

Time spent on major household tasks by sex, 1999–2008 (*latest available*)

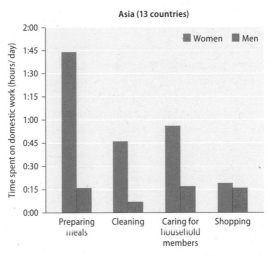

Asia (13 countries)

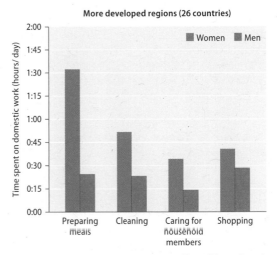

More developed regions (26 countries)

Source: Computed by the United Nations Statistics Division based on country-level data from Statistics Sweden, UNECE and national statistical offices (as of December 2009).
Note: Unweighted averages.

Of the various unpaid domestic tasks, the preparation of meals takes by far the most of women's time – on average an hour and 45 minutes per day in Asian countries and an hour and a half among countries in the more developed regions (figure 4.10). In contrast, men spend on average 15 minutes a day on this activity in Asian countries and 25 minutes in countries in the more developed regions. A large discrepancy also occurs in household cleaning tasks. In Asian countries, women spend 45 minutes per day to men's 6 minutes. The ratio is not as great in countries in the more developed regions, where women devote on average 50 minutes a day to cleaning to men's 23 minutes. In developing countries where there is less access to technologies that would reduce the time needed for meal preparation and house cleaning, these tasks can be particularly arduous.

Actively caring[34] for children and sick, elderly or disabled household members is a time-consuming task, especially in the less developed regions where public services for such care are few.[35] In Asia, caring takes up a large amount of women's time (55 minutes per day). While this work is done predominantly by women, men are seen to share relatively more (16 minutes) than in either

cooking or cleaning. In Europe, due in part to lower fertility rates and consequently fewer children to look after and in part to some availability of public or private care services, the average time spent on care of children and other household members is lower, about 35 minutes for women and 15 minutes for men. Shopping is an activity where men come closer to women in terms of time devoted. Doing repairs around the house as well as taking care of the dwelling premises are activities where men tend to spend more time than women.

2. Combining family responsibilities with employment

Women work longer hours than men when unpaid work is factored in

As shown earlier, women spend more time than men on domestic work, on average roughly twice as much or more (figure 4.9). Many women are also employed, although they tend to spend less time in paid work than men (figure 4.11). Nevertheless, the total work burden – considering both paid and unpaid work[36] – is higher for women

---

34 Time spent caring for children and for sick, elderly or disabled household members relates only to time where no other activity is carried out, or where it is the main activity. Time spent cleaning the house, for example, while looking after children is not considered here.

35 Antonopoulus and Hirway, 2010, p. 17.

36 Unpaid work refers productive work that is outside the boundary of the System of National Accounts and comprises (a) domestic work (housework, caring for children and other household members such as the sick, elderly, disabled, etc.); and (b) unpaid help to other households and community and volunteer services. In most countries, the second category contributes only a small portion towards the total time spent on unpaid work.

Figure 4.11

Time spent on paid and unpaid work by region and sex, 1999–2008 (*latest available*)

Time spent on work (hours/ day)

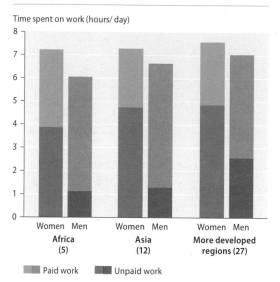

Africa (5)   Asia (12)   More developed regions (27)

Women   Men   Women   Men   Women   Men

■ Paid work   ■ Unpaid work

Source: Computed by the United Nations Statistics Division based on country-level data from Statistics Sweden, UNECE and national statistical offices (as of December 2009).
Note: Unweighted averages; the numbers in brackets indicate the number of countries averaged.

Balancing paid work with family responsibilities is particularly difficult for women who are employed full-time. In many countries, employed women spend an inordinate amount of time on this "double burden", as they typically continue to assume most of the responsibility for domestic work. Employed men spend less time on paid and domestic work combined. In 9 out of 15 European countries with data, women employed full-time work about an hour more per day than men when both paid and domestic work are considered (figure 4.12). In only six out of the 15 countries do men's total number of hours worked approach that of women. In these countries (all in Northern or Western Europe) women enjoy the shortest hours of work, about seven to eight hours per day, and men only slightly less. Norway and Sweden stand out as countries where men spend more than two hours on domestic work per day and end up with a total work day that is as long as that of women.

than men in all regions. From the available data, it is apparent that on average women work at least half an hour longer than men each day in Africa, Asia and the more developed regions.

**Balancing work and family
is particularly challenging for employed
parents with young children**

Balancing the dual demands of family and employment is particularly difficult for couples with young children. One solution to the challenge of the "double burden" in this situation is for one member of the couple to work part-time or not be in employment at all – in most instances the woman. This is evident from an examination of the economic activity status of couples with young children (table 4.11). In nine out of the 12 countries studied, the majority of couples with young children end up with the man in full-time employment and the woman either working part-time or not employed at all. In Austria, Germany, the Netherlands and Switzerland, less than 20 per cent of couples with young children both worked full-time and in another five countries, just 30–40 per cent of couples did. Other data show that in Australia, among couples with children under 15, the most common arrangement was for both parents to work, although in three fifths of families where both parents were employed, one worked full-time and the other worked part-time. In 95 per cent of those cases, it was the mother who was working part-time.[37]

However, the scenario where only one member of the couple works full-time is not always a feasible

Table 4.11

Distribution of couples with young children by activity status, for 12 European countries, 2006

	Percentage distribution of couples aged 25–49 years with children less than 6 years old, by activity status, 2006			
	Both woman and man working full-time	Woman working part-time, man working full-time	Woman not working, man working full-time	Other combinations of activity status
Netherlands	7	49	31	13
Switzerland	8	45	38	10
Germany	13	31	43	14
Austria	19	38	32	11
Italy	31	20	42	8
Hungary	32	3	52	13
Belgium	35	33	20	12
Sweden	36	38	10	17
Spain	38	16	38	8
Finland	53	9	30	9
Romania	59	3	20	18
Portugal	69	5	21	6

Source: L'Office fédéral de la statistique de Suisse, Modèles d'activité dans les couples, partage des taches et garde des enfants (2009).
Note: Arranged in ascending order of "Both woman and man working full-time". Due to rounding, row totals might not equal 100. For Germany and Sweden, data refer to 2005.

37 Australia Bureau of Statistics, 2009.

or practicable option. Many couples with young children find themselves working full-time. In Finland, Portugal and Romania, for example, more than half of all couples with children below six years old both work full-time (table 4.11).

Some countries and organizations help employed parents reconcile work and family life by instituting shorter work hours and family-friendly working arrangements such as flexible hours, part-time work, job-sharing and work from home (including telecommuting). Such measures, however, are often not available or adequate. Faced with the lack of collective measures and support for balancing paid work and family responsibilities, many families who can afford to do so turn to hiring private childcare, health providers to care for sick family members or domestic workers to free up time for paid work. For the poor, however, the need to resolve work-family conflict often requires difficult trade-offs between employment and family responsibilities in terms of quality of employment and/or quality of care.[38] Thus, while the decision about employment may be a lifestyle choice for some,[39] full-time work may represent the only viable choice for women faced with the financial needs of their family.

3. Maternity and paternity leave and related benefits

Maternity leave and related benefits

Maternity protection for employed women is an essential element in equality of opportunity, enabling women to successfully combine their productive and reproductive roles. Essentially, maternity protection has two aims: to preserve the health of (and the special relationship between) the mother and her newborn; and to provide a measure of job security. The latter aim includes access to jobs by women of childbearing age, maintenance of wages and benefits during maternity, and prevention of dismissal during pregnancy, maternity leave and a period of time after return to work.

**Maternity leave is widely recognized
but still inadequate in many countries**

The current international standard for the duration of maternity leave as provided for in the Maternity Protection Convention 2000

Figure 4.12

Time spent on paid work and domestic work by persons employed full-time, by sex, for 15 European countries, 1999–2005 *(latest available)*

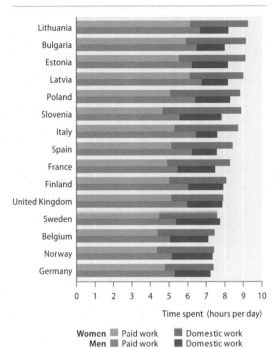

Time spent (hours per day)

| Women | Paid work | Domestic work |
| Men | Paid work | Domestic work |

Source: Statistics Sweden, Harmonized European Time Use Survey online database (accessed in December 2009).

(No. 183)[40] is 14 weeks. This is an increase from the standard of 12 weeks specified in the previous Convention.[41]

Many countries in the less developed regions have not caught up to the new standard. In 2009, as many as 141 out of 167 countries, or 85 per cent, have durations of maternity leave that meet the 12-week standard stipulated in the earlier ILO Convention. However, only half of countries worldwide – specifically 85 countries – meet the new international standard of 14 weeks. The regions farthest from achieving the new standard are Asia-Pacific and Latin America and the Caribbean, where only 30 per cent and 24 per cent of countries, respectively, provide maternity leave of 14 weeks or more. In Africa, 46 per cent of countries provide the recommended coverage while in the more developed regions, 95 per cent do (figure 4.13). (For maternity leave information by country, see Statistical Annex.)

---

38 ILO, 2009b.

39 Hakim, 2004; ILO, 2009c.

40 Adopted by the International Labour Conference in June 2000. The Maternity Protection Recommendation 2000 (No. 191) that accompanies the Convention proposes 18 weeks of maternity leave.

41 Maternity Protection Convention (Revised) (No. 103), adopted in 1952.

Figure 4.13

Distribution of countries by legislated length of maternity leave, by region, 2009

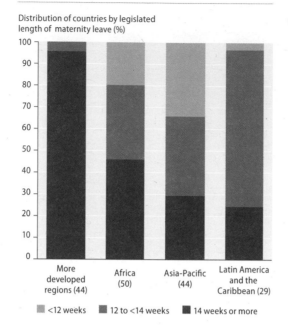

Distribution of countries by legislated
length of maternity leave (%)

More developed regions (44) · Africa (50) · Asia-Pacific (44) · Latin America and the Caribbean (29)

☐ <12 weeks   ▨ 12 to <14 weeks   ■ 14 weeks or more

Source: Computed by the United Nations Statistics Division based on data from United Nations, Statistics and Indicators on Women and Men, table 5g – Maternity leave benefits (accessed in February 2010).
Note: The numbers in brackets indicate the number of countries with data.

The right to cash benefits during maternity leave is essential for maternity protection, and the vast majority of countries provide these benefits to a greater or lesser extent. Worldwide, only five countries[42] have not legislated for paid maternity leave

across the workforce.[43] Without paid benefits, or where paid benefits are insufficient, a woman may be pressured to return to work sooner than her health or that of her infant permits.

The new ILO Convention stipulates that cash benefits during maternity leave be paid at the rate of at least two thirds of the woman's previous or insured earnings for a minimum period of 14 weeks. Currently only 73 countries (44 per cent) meet this standard, more than half of them (37 countries) in the more developed regions. Overall in these regions, 84 per cent of countries provide 14 weeks or more of cash benefit at the rate of at least two thirds the woman's average earnings. In comparison, only 36 per cent of the countries in Africa, 25 per cent in Asia-Pacific and 24 per cent in Latin America and the Caribbean are able to meet this standard (figure 4.14).

In certain cases women may not be eligible for cash benefits at all or may have reduced benefits. For example, eligibility or the amounts payable in some countries depend on the woman's length of employment, length of contribution into the insurance scheme, type of contract, or whether employed by government or by a private employer. In others, the benefits may be subject to a ceiling or are reduced after a given number of weeks. (For details by country, see Statistical Annex.)

The gap between law and practice is a problem confronting many women. Maternity continues to be a source of discrimination in employment and access to employment. Even with maternity legislation, many pregnant women still lose their jobs, and complaints of maternity-related dismissals are common in the courts.[44]

Where the funding of maternity benefits comes from presents an important source of discrimination against women. Payment through social insurance or public funds may reduce discrimination against women of childbearing age in the labour market, as employers are freed from bearing the direct costs of maternity. At present, however, many countries (26 per cent) continue to stipulate that payment during maternity leave be covered by the employer with no public or social security provision.[45] This is the case in many countries in Africa and Asia, and is particularly prevalent in the Arab States (see Statistical Annex).

Figure 4.14

Proportion of countries that meet the international standard for cash benefits during maternity leave, by region, 2009

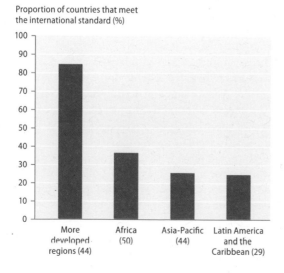

Proportion of countries that meet
the international standard (%)

More developed regions (44) · Africa (50) · Asia-Pacific (44) · Latin America and the Caribbean (29)

Source: Computed by the United Nations Statistics Division based on data from United Nations, Statistics and Indicators on Women and Men, table 5g – Maternity leave benefits (accessed in February 2010).
Note: The numbers in brackets indicate the number of countries with data. The international standard is cash benefits paid at the rate of at least two thirds of the woman's previous or insured earnings, for a minimum period of 14 weeks.

42 Australia, Lesotho, Papua New Guinea, Swaziland and the United States of America.

43 Oun and Trujillo, 2005.
44 ILO, 2009a.
45 Oun and Trujillo, 2005.

The right to continue breastfeeding upon return to work is important for both the health of the mother and especially that of her child. At present, more than 90 countries provide legislation for nursing breaks of at least an hour a day. In most countries the duration is one hour in total, and the most frequent provision is until the child reaches the age of one year.[46]

Maternity protection continues to be unavailable to many groups of women such as domestic workers, those working in small enterprises, those with less than one year with the employer, agricultural workers, casual workers, as well as part-time, temporary, sub-contract and home-based workers. In many developing countries, these groups constitute a large majority of the female labour force but do not receive the protection available to women in formal full-time employment. A new provision of the Maternity Protection Convention 2000 expands the scope of coverage to include women employed in such atypical forms of work.

Paternity leave

Paternity leave is becoming more common

Paternity leave is a short period of leave taken by a father around the time of the birth of his child. Although there is no international standard for this, paternity leave provisions are becoming more common around the world,[47] perhaps an indication of the increased awareness of men's parenting roles and their need to reconcile work and family life. Paternity leave benefits, when available, vary considerably in duration and compensation. Compared to maternity leave, they are much shorter and more often unpaid. Paid leave provisions other than paternity leave may also be used by a father at the time of the birth of his child. Some examples are shown in table 4.12.

Another option to further help working parents care for children is parental leave,[48] a relatively long-term leave offered mainly in countries in the more developed regions that is available to either parent to enable them to take care of an infant or young child over a period of time, usually following the maternity or paternity leave period. The duration, cash benefits, age of the child at which

Table 4.12

Examples of paid paternity leave and other paid leave provisions that may be used by fathers at the time of the birth of their child, 2005

Paid leave provision	
Africa	
Algeria	3 days paid paternity leave
Cameroon	Up to 10 days paid leave for family events concerning the worker's home
Côte d'Ivoire	Up to 10 days paid leave for family events concerning the worker's home
South Africa	3 days paid family responsibility leave
Asia	
Indonesia	2 days paid leave when wife gives birth
Philippines	7 days paid paternity leave for married workers
Latin America	
Argentina	2 days paid paternity leave
Brazil	7 days paid paternity leave
Chile	1 day paid paternity leave
Paraguay	2 days paid paternity leave
More developed regions	
Belgium	3 days paid paternity leave
Finland	14 days paid paternity leave
Romania	5 days paid paternity leave
Sweden	10 days paid paternity leave

Source: ILO, Examples of leave provisions for fathers (2005).

the right to such leave lapses, and transferability of leave vary widely across countries.

Because parental leave is available to either parent, it encourages the sharing of family responsibilities, recognizing that both mothers and fathers are responsible for raising their children. However, women are usually the ones who take parental leave once maternity leave is exhausted, and men's take-up rates are very low. Some countries have introduced a paternity quota that can only be taken by the father and is lost if he does not use it. This is the case, for example, in Norway and Sweden.[49]

D. Child labour

1. Child employment and child labour

The magnitude of child employment and child labour

In recent years, national and international attention paid to the measurement of child labour has led to many new surveys on the topic and to the addition of questions on child labour in national

---

46 ILO, 2004c.

47 ILO, 2009a.

48 Not to be confused with maternity or paternity leave.

49 Oun and Trujillo, 2005.

Box 4.10
Definition of child labour

The term child labour refers to the engagement of children in prohibited work and, more generally, in types of work to be eliminated as socially and morally undesirable, as guided by national legislation and international conventions.[a] Child labour may be measured in terms of the engagement of children in productive activities either on the basis of the general production boundary, or on the basis of the System of National Accounts (SNA) production boundary.

When measured in terms of the SNA production boundary, children in child labour encompass all persons aged 5 to 17 years who, during a specified time period, were engaged in one or more of the following categories of activities:

a) Worst forms of child labour, which include:

   i) Hazardous work – employment in industries and occupations designated as hazardous, or working for long hours and/or at night in tasks and duties that by themselves may or may not be hazardous for children;

   ii) Worst forms of child labour other than hazardous work – consists of all forms of slavery or practices similar to slavery, such as the sale and trafficking of children, debt bondage and serfdom, as well as forced or compulsory labour, including forced or compulsory recruitment of children for use in armed conflict; the use, procuring or offering of a child for prostitution, for the production of pornography or for pornographic performances; the use, procuring or offering of a child for illicit activities, in particular for the production and trafficking of drugs;

b) Employment below the minimum age, as specified in national legislation – includes any work that is carried out by a child who is below the minimum age specified for the kind of work performed.

If national policies and circumstances determine that the measurement of productive activities by children use the general production boundary, child labour will include the following additional category:

c) Hazardous unpaid household services – unpaid household services performed in the child's own household for long hours, in an unhealthy environment, involving unsafe equipment or heavy loads, etc.

Source: ILO, 2009d, pp. 56–66.
a Specifically the ILO Minimum Age Convention, 1973 (Convention No. 138) and the Worst Forms of Child Labour Convention, 1999 (No. 182) as well as their respective supplementing recommendations (Nos. 146 and 190).

household surveys. However, child labour is still a relatively new topic in national data collection activities. Establishing reliable data on many of the worst forms of child labour – such as forced labour, involvement in armed conflict, commercial sexual exploitation and human trafficking – remains a challenge. Household surveys are ill suited to capture these worst forms of child labour; standardized statistical concepts and definitions are not fully developed and measurement methods are at an experimental stage.[50] Thus, the 2004 global estimates of child labour do not include the category "worst forms of child labour other than hazardous labour". Furthermore, since the global estimates used the framework of the SNA production boundary, the category "hazardous unpaid household services" was also not included. (See box 4.10 for the definition of child labour)

Globally, many children are engaged in employment and in child labour

[50] Hagemann and others, 2006; and ILO, 2009d, pp. 56-66.

The latest global estimates of child labour refer to the year 2004. They indicate that 317 million children (149 million girls and 168 million boys) aged 5–17 were employed (i.e., were in the labour force) worldwide. More than half of all employed children were considered to be engaged in child labour: specifically, 218 million (101 million girls and 117 million boys). Furthermore, more than half of these child labourers (53 million girls and 73 million boys) were engaged in hazardous work (table 4.13).

The global estimates indicate that boys outnumber girls slightly among both the total numbers employed and those engaged in child labour and that they outnumber girls substantially in engagement in hazardous work. These estimates of employment, however, do not reflect the totality of work that children perform, as the definition of employment does not include household chores. From a gender perspective, this omission distorts the overall picture of children's total work burden since housework is disproportionately

Table 4.13
Global estimates of child employment, child labour and children in hazardous labour, by sex, 2004

	Total		Girls		Boys	
	Number (*millions*)	As a percentage of the population aged 5–17	Number (*millions*)	As a percentage of the population aged 5–17	Number (*millions*)	As a percentage of the population aged 5–17
Population aged 5–17	1 566.3		762.3		804.0	
Of which in employment	317.4	20	149.0	20	168.4	21
Of which in child labour	217.7	14	100.5	13	117.2	15
Of which in hazardous labour	126.3	8	53.0	7	73.3	9

Source: Hagemann and others, *Global Child Labour Trends 2000–2004* (2006).

done by girls in most societies (see next section). In addition, girls comprise a large proportion of those working in the forms of child labour that the global estimates have not included (the worst forms of child labour other than hazardous work and "hazardous unpaid household services").[51]

Economic sector of employment of girls and boys

Most employed children work in agriculture but girls in Latin America are mostly in services

When they are employed, children work predominantly in the agricultural sector. In sub-Saharan Africa, where agriculture is the predominant sector, at least three quarters of employed girls and boys work in this area (figure 4.15). The corresponding proportions are lower in Asia and still lower in Latin America. In all regions boys were more likely than girls to be in agriculture. Girls, on the other hand, were more likely than boys to be employed in services, and the phenomenon is particularly striking in Latin America. In the eight Latin American countries with available data, on average half of all employed girls were in the services sector. Girls' employment in services involves mostly two activities: child domestic work (CDW)[52] and wholesale and retail trade, most of the latter performed within the informal sector of the economy.[53] Collecting fuel wood

and fetching water for the household, which are economic activities within the SNA production boundary, are also more likely to be performed by girls than boys.[54]

Studies by ILO-IPEC (International Programme on the Elimination of Child Labour) confirm that CDW is pervasive in Africa, Asia and Latin America.[55] In three[56] out of eight countries for which prevalence rates can be derived, more than 10 per cent of employed girls aged 5–14 were engaged in CDW; and for girls aged 15–17, the proportions exceeded 10 per cent in seven[57] of the eight countries and exceeded 20 per cent in three of them. The proportion in CDW among boys was 2 per cent or lower, except for Mali where it was 9 per cent for boys aged 5–14 and 6 per cent for boys aged 15–17. According to the ILO, more girls under age 16 are engaged in domestic service than in any other category of child labour. However, the low recognition of domestic labour as a form of economic activity and of CDW as a form of child labour, coupled with its hidden nature, has led to difficulty in obtaining reliable figures on the extent of this phenomenon. In many environments some elements of CDW – long working days, working with toxic chemicals, carrying heavy loads, handling dangerous items such as knives, axes, irons and hot pans – are such that it would be considered hazardous work.[58]

---

51 Blanco, 2009.

52 Child domestic work (CDW) is considered an economic activity under the SNA production boundary and should not be confused with household chores. The former is performed outside the child's own household for an employer, while the latter is performed in the child's own household.

53 Blanco, 2009.

---

54 See Chapter 7– Environment.

55 Blanco, 2009.

56 Colombia, Mali and Senegal.

57 Colombia, Ecuador, El Salvador, Guatemala, Mali, Senegal and the Philippines. The proportion exceeded 20 per cent in El Salvador, Mali and the Philippines.

58 ILO-IPEC, undated.

Figure 4.15
Sectoral distribution of children's employment, by sex and region, 1999–2003 (*latest available*)

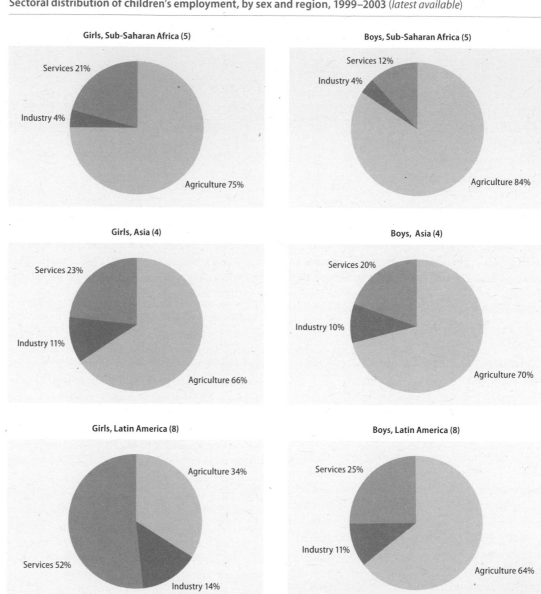

Source: Computed by the United Nations Statistics Division based on data from ILO-IPEC, Child labour data country briefs: data from SIMPOC surveys (2009).
Note: Unweighted averages; the numbers in brackets indicate the number of countries averaged. Data refer to children aged 5–14.

2. Unpaid housework

Girls are more likely than boys to do unpaid housework

Like their adult counterparts, girls are more likely than boys to perform unpaid work within their own household. In many regions, girls start to take on a large amount of household chores at a young age (5 to 14), including care-giving, cooking and cleaning. Boys also participate in household chores but not as much. The extent of girls' and boys' participation varies considerably across countries,

but the proportions in the less developed regions and the transition countries of Eastern and Southern Europe range roughly from 40–90 per cent for girls aged 5–14 and from 15–90 per cent for boys of the same age (figure 4.16). In virtually all countries, girls' participation in household chores exceeds that of boys. On average, the proportion of girls aged 5–14 involved in household chores is about 10 percentage points more than the corresponding proportion for boys.

Older girls are even more likely than boys to be engaged in household chores. At ages 15–17, an average 90 per cent of girls and 67 per cent of

Figure 4.16

Proportion of children aged 5–14 engaged in household chores, by region and sex, 1999–2006 (*latest available*)

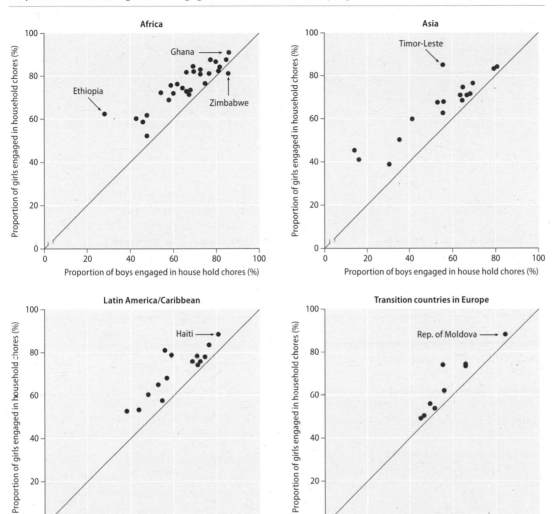

Source: Compiled by the United Nations Statistics Division from ILO, UNICEF and World Bank, Understanding Children's Work (UCW) Country Reports (accessed in June 2009).

Note: Each point represents one country. Points above and left of the diagonal line represent countries where higher proportions of girls than boys are engaged in household chores.

boys are engaged in housework, a difference of 23 percentage points.[59]

The total burden of work is higher for girls, especially older girls

Girls generally work longer hours than boys, regardless of the type of work activity. Data from 16 sample countries from the less developed regions and transition economies indicate that girls aged 5–14 work about three hours longer per week than boys, whether they are engaged in housework exclusively (no employment) or engaged in both employment and housework.

For children aged 5–14 whose work is limited to employment (no housework), boys work longer in some countries while girls work longer in others. Children's burden of work is highest when they are engaged in both employment and housework, consuming on average 32 hours per week of girls' time and 29 of boys'. The time spent by children in employment exclusively is much shorter and that by children working on housework only is shortest (figure 4.17).

Older children aged 15–17, having attained the legal age of employment,[60] spent more time than younger children in every working category. Girls

---

59 Based on 16 sample countries from different regions of the world, in Blanco, 2009.

60 The legal age of employment is 14 or 15 in most countries and 16 in others.

Figure 4.17

Time spent by children on work, by type of work engaged in, by sex and age group, 1999–2006
(*latest available*)

Average number of hours
worked per week

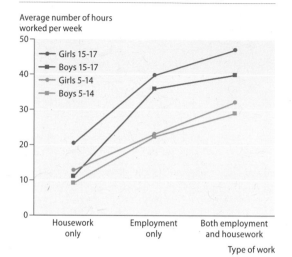

Source: Prepared by the United Nations Statistics Division from Blanco, Assessing the gender gap: Evidence from SIMPOC surveys, tables 4 and 5 (2009).

spent on average 47 hours per week and boys 40 hours if they were employed and at the same time helping with housework. Many girls and boys aged 15–17 find themselves in this situation – on average 29 and 28 per cent, respectively. For this group, as well as for those in employment only, the significant amount of time spent on work reduces their time for study, leisure and other activities essential to child social and human

Figure 4.18

School attendance rate of children aged 5–14 by amount of time spent on household chores, by sex, 1999–2006

School attendance rate (%)

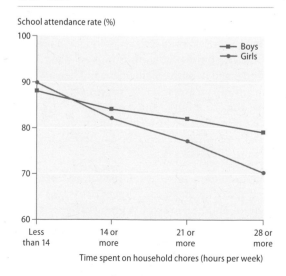

Source: ILO, Gender equality at the heart of decent work (2009), p. 62.

development. The same holds for the 14 per cent of younger children (aged 5–14) who find themselves similarly burdened with both employment and household chores.

3. Children's work and education

Long hours of work affect children's school attendance, especially girls'

Child labour constitutes a major hindrance to the education of girls and boys. It affects children's ability to participate fully in education. Analysis based on survey data for 23 countries shows that school attendance declines as the number of hours spent on household chores increases, and that the decline is steeper for girls compared to boys.[61] On average, 90 per cent of girls who spend less than 14 hours on housework attend school, but only 70 per cent of those who spend 28 hours or more per week on household chores do so (figure 4.18). For boys the difference is smaller, about 10 percentage points. The lower school attendance rate of girls compared to that of boys among the group that performed 28 or more hours of housework may be explained in part by the higher proportion of girls, compared to boys, who work much longer than 28 hours.

A similar inverse relationship is evident between school attendance and hours spent on employment, with an even stronger effect than seen for girls engaged in household chores. In this case the impact on school attendance was the same for girls and boys.[62]

The effect of excessive work on children's education extends beyond school attendance. For example, research from Latin America and the Caribbean suggests that classroom performance of working children are among the poorest, and that performance declined with the hours worked.[63] The longer hours worked by girls, whether in employment, housework or both, translate to missed opportunities and an increased risk of ending up without the basic tools to escape marginalization and poverty.

61 ILO, 2009a.
62 See Blanco, 2009.
63 Guarcello and others, 2006.

Chapter 5
Power and decision-making

Key findings

- Becoming the Head of State or Head of Government remains elusive for women, with only 14 women in the world currently holding either position.
- In just 23 countries do women comprise a critical mass – over 30 per cent – in the lower or single house of their national parliament.
- Worldwide on average only one in six cabinet ministers is a woman.
- Women are highly underrepresented in decision-making positions at local government levels.
- In the private sector, women continue to be severely underrepresented in the top decision-making positions.
- Only 13 of the 500 largest corporations in the world have a female Chief Executive Officer.

Introduction

The Universal Declaration of Human Rights recognises the right of every individual to take part in the government of her or his country.[1] Equal access to power, decision-making and leadership at all levels is a necessary condition for the proper functioning of democracy. Ensuring women's freedom to participate in politics, both as voters and as representatives, has been central to international, regional and national efforts aimed at more inclusive and democratic governance. These freedoms and rights are not limited to politics but extend to participation and leadership in public life, the private sector and civil society in general.

The Convention on the Elimination of All Forms of Discrimination against Women commits States Parties to act appropriately to ensure that women and men have equal rights in regards to voting, participation in the formulation of government policies, participation in non-governmental organizations and representation of their governments at the international level.[2]

The Beijing Declaration and Platform for Action states that the empowerment and autonomy of women and the improvement of women's social, economic and political status are essential for the achievement of transparent and accountable government that works for the benefit of both women and men. It recognizes that women's empowerment and full participation on an equal basis with men in all spheres of life, including participation in the decision-making process and access to power, are fundamental to the achievement of equality, development and peace. In addition to setting out government commitments, the Platform for Action urges a range of actors to take measures in support of women's participation in all levels of power and decision-making.[3] These include political parties, the private sector, trade unions, national, regional and sub-regional bodies, employers' organizations, research and academic institutions and non-governmental organizations.[4]

This chapter provides an assessment of the current situation as well as recent trends in the participation of women and men in positions of power and decision-making across the world. Four main areas are covered: politics and governance, the judiciary, civil service and the private sector.

Identification of trends and cross-country comparisons are limited by the lack of data at the inter-

---

1 United Nations, 1946. Article 21.
2 United Nations, 1979. Articles 7 and 8.

3 United Nations, 1995.
4 Ibid., section G, paragraphs 190-195.

national and national levels. Statistical agencies in many countries do not routinely collect and disseminate data on women in power and decision-making, and few international or regional organizations compile those statistics. The most readily available information on decision-making is the number and proportion of women in national parliaments and key elected positions, collected under the auspices of the Inter-Parliamentary Union and monitored within the framework of the Millennium Development Goals (MDGs).

The European Commission's database on women and men in decision-making gives a comprehensive regional picture of women and men in top positions.[5] The United Nations Economic Commission for Europe's (UNECE) Gender Statistics Database and the United Nations Development Fund's (UNIFEM) biennial *Progress of the World's Women* provided additional statistics on some of the topics covered in the chapter.

Data at the international level are especially lacking on women's access to high-level decision-making positions in local government and in the private sector. The statistics and analysis on some of these topics are based in large part on sources available from private or non-governmental organizations. The presentation and analysis on these topics are therefore relatively limited.

A. Politics and governance

Public governance is one of the arenas where inequality between men and women is highly visible. Limited female participation in structures of governance where key policy decisions are made and resource allocations decided often has a negative impact on women's political, economic and social opportunities.

1. Representation in national parliament

Although women make up about half of the electorate and have attained the right to vote and hold office in almost all countries of the world, they continue to be underrepresented as members of national parliaments. The importance of women's political empowerment has been recognized within the framework of the MDGs, with one of

the indicators for monitoring Goal 3 (promote gender equality and empower women) being the proportion of seats held by women in lower or single houses of national parliaments.

Levels and trends

Improvement in the representation
of women in national parliaments worldwide
has been steady but slow

There has been a slow and steady improvement in the representation of women in national parliaments worldwide. At the time the Beijing Platform for Action was adopted in 1995, women accounted for on average 10 per cent of members of the lower or single houses of national parliaments. This figure had increased to 17 per cent by April 2009 (table 5.1).

All regions have showed progress in improving gender balance in national parliaments since 1995. In all sub-regions of Africa and in 4 out of 5 sub-regions in Asia, the average proportion of women in the lower or single houses of parliament doubled or more than doubled. Most of these sub-regions have had less than 10 per cent female members of parliament in 1995 but have achieved double-digit figures by 2009. The exception is Western Asia, where women's representation has improved from a very low average (4 per cent) in 1995 to the current 9 per cent. Southern Asia has had a particularly notable improvement, helped no doubt by a positive intervention by several governments through such legislation as the implementation of candidate quotas and reserved seats (see also sub-section on the use of gender quotas). Four out of nine countries in Southern Asia have introduced quotas to boost female representation at the level of the national parliament (Afghanistan, Bangladesh, Nepal and Pakistan).[6]

Elsewhere, all sub-regions within Latin America and the Caribbean and the more developed regions have also experienced steady gains since 1995. In comparison, Eastern Asia and Oceania (excluding Australia and New Zealand) have seen very little increase in their share of women members of parliament. The latter stands out for its continued low share of female parliamentarians.

Following recent improvements, the proportion of women parliamentarians in the lower or sin-

---

5 European Commission, 2010. The database covers decision-making in politics, public administration, judiciary, and business and finance for the 27 European Union member States as well as Croatia, Iceland, Norway, Serbia, the former Yugoslav Republic of Macedonia and Turkey.

6 International IDEA and others, 2010.

gle house of parliament averaged 15 per cent or better in most sub-regions in 2009 (table 5.1). Western Europe had the highest female representation, averaging 29 per cent. In Southern Africa, South-Eastern Asia, South America and the more developed regions outside Europe women's representation averaged at least 20 per cent. However, average female representation was still below 15 per cent in Northern Africa (10 per cent), Eastern and Western Asia (14 and 9 per cent, respectively) and Oceania[7] (3 per cent).

At the country level, progress in women's representation is apparent from the count of countries wherein women comprise a critical mass[8] – at least 30 per cent – of parliamentarians. In 2009, women attained this mass in the lower or single house of parliament in only 23 countries (see Statistical Annex) – still a small number but a considerable increase over the five countries that had achieved this level in 1995.[9]

The 23 countries with at least 30 per cent women parliamentarians include nine from Western Europe and seven from sub-Saharan Africa (see Statistical Annex). The highest proportion in the world was registered by Rwanda in its 2008 elections. The first country ever to have achieved a gender balance in national parliament, Rwanda's achievement (56 per cent) is a marked increase over the 17 per cent representation of women in 1995,[10] and can be attributed partly to focused and coordinated efforts to address the issue of gender balance during post-conflict reconstruction, and might also be associated with the fact that the majority of survivors of the preceding conflict were women. In fact, a number of post-conflict countries rank high with regard to women's participation in both lower and upper chambers of legislative bodies (see Statistical Annex).

A few countries are close to attaining gender parity in parliamenty representation. In addition to Rwanda, seven countries currently have at least 40 per cent female representation in parliament:

7 Excluding Australia and New Zealand.

8 According to a classic theory of minority behaviour, women who are successful in a man's world absorb the dominant culture to such an extent that they tend to dissociate themselves from other women, to underrate their own success and to perceive any discrimination they meet as a result of their own shortcomings. It takes a minority of a certain minimum size, 30–35 per cent, to be able to influence the culture of groups and to facilitate alliances between group members (United Nations Division for the Advancement of Women, 1992).

9 Inter-Parliamentary Union, 2006a.

10 Inter-Parliamentary Union, 2009a.

Table 5.1

Proportion of parliamentary seats in lower or single chamber occupied by women, by region, 1995, 1999 and 2009

	Proportion women (per cent)		
	1995	1999	2009
World	10	11	17
Africa			
Northern Africa	4	3	10
Southern Africa	12	14	24
Eastern, Middle and Western Africa	8	9	16
Asia			
Central Asia	8	8	19
Eastern Asia	12	13	11
South-Eastern Asia	9	12	20
Southern Asia	5	5	16
Western Asia	4	5	9
Latin America and the Caribbean			
Caribbean	13	13	17
Central America	10	13	19
South America	9	13	20
Oceania	2	4	3
More developed regions			
Eastern Europe	9	10	17
Western Europe	20	23	29
Other more developed regions	12	18	22

Source: Computed by the United Nations Statistics Division based on data from Inter-Parliamentary Union, *Women in National Parliaments* (2009a).
Note: Unweighted averages.

Argentina, Cuba, Finland, Iceland, Netherlands, South Africa and Sweden.

Elsewhere, the countries that lead their sub-region in terms of women's representation in parliament include Tunisia in Northern Africa with 23 per cent, Kyrgyzstan in Central Asia with 26 per cent, China in Eastern Asia with 21 per cent, Timor-

Box 5.1

The first-ever success of women candidates in a Kuwait election

Four women members of parliament are among 21 newcomers to the 50-seat Kuwaiti National Assembly, following the polls of May 2009. This development stems from the country's shift towards merit and political competency from an association with tribal ties and expediency. That all four hold PhDs, have a formidable reputation for professionalism and now represent 54% of eligible voters points to a radical shift in opinion across Kuwait's society.

Source: *The Economist*, 2009.

Leste in South-Eastern Asia with 29 per cent, Nepal in Southern Asia with 33 per cent, Iraq in Western Asia with 26 per cent, Costa Rica in Central America with 37 per cent and Belarus in Eastern Europe with 32 per cent.

At the opposite end, in 2009 six countries still had no women in their lower or single chamber of parliament.[11] In addition, as many as 40 countries or areas had less than 10 per cent female representation (see Statistical Annex).

Presiding officers

Women rarely hold the top positions in national parliaments, as shown by the small number of women serving as presiding officers. In 2009 only 21 out of 176 lower or single chambers of parliaments in the world[12] and 10 out of 73 upper chambers were presided by a woman. (table 5.2)

The highest concentration of female presiding officers was found in the more developed regions, where

Table 5.2

Countries with a woman presiding over parliament, by region, 2009

Lower or single house	Upper house
Africa	
Gambia	Gabon
Ghana	Swaziland
Lesotho	Zimbabwe
Rwanda	
Asia	
India	
Pakistan	
Turkmenistan	
Uzbekistan	
Latin America and the Caribbean	
Saint Lucia	Bahamas
Venezuela (Bolivarian Republic of)	Belize
	Grenada
	Saint Lucia
More developed regions	
Albania	Bosnia and Herzegovina
Austria	Netherlands
Bulgaria	United Kingdom
Estonia	
Hungary	
Iceland	
Netherlands	
Romania	
Serbia	
Switzerland	
United States of America	

Source: Inter-Parliamentary Union, *Women speakers of national parliaments* (2009b).

11 Belize, Federated States of Micronesia, Oman, Qatar, Saudi Arabia and Solomon Islands.

12 Countries or areas with population size lower than 100,000 are excluded from the counts.

a total of 14 women presided over the single, lower or upper chamber of parliament. Seven women held this position in the parliaments of Africa (all sub-Saharan), four in Asia (two in Southern Asia and two in Central Asia) and six in Latin America and the Caribbean (of which 4 in the Caribbean).

Candidacy and election

> **In most countries in Africa, Asia and Oceania, women comprised less than 20 per cent of candidates in the last elections for the lower or single house of parliament**

The limited data (available for 65 countries) on women and men electoral candidates illustrate that the low proportion of women electoral candidates is directly correlated to women's limited representation in their parliaments. The proportion of female candidates for lower or single house of parliament tended to be low in countries within the less developed regions, being predominantly in the range of zero to 30 per cent in the last elections (table 5.3). Women in countries within the more developed regions fared better, comprising in most cases 20 to 45 per cent of the candidates. In only four countries – Belgium, Costa Rica, Iceland and Rwanda – were candidates distributed roughly evenly by sex.

Available data in Africa display a low proportion of female candidates for the lower or single house of parliament – lower than 20 per cent, with the exception of Burundi and Rwanda. The proportion is under 10 per cent in 3 of the 4 countries with available data in Oceania; this low proportion of female electoral candidates in the region parallels the limited representation of women in their parliaments as seen in the earlier section.

In all 14 Asian countries for which data are available (the majority of which are Western Asian countries), women comprised less than 30 per cent of candidates in the last election for the lower or single house. In Latin America and the Caribbean the five countries with available data show a wider spread of the proportion of female candidates, from a low of 3 per cent in Belize to a high of 51 per cent in Costa Rica. For the more developed regions, the proportion of women candidates ranged from 12 per cent in Japan to 49 per cent in Belgium and tended to cluster within the range of 20 to 45 per cent.

The low proportion of women in parliaments is related not just to the lower proportion of female candidates but also the lower election rate of women compared to men. For the 65 countries

Table 5.3

Countries by proportion of female candidates for the lower or single house of parliament, by region, 2003–2008 (*latest election year*)

0–9%	10–19%	20–29%	30–45%	46–53%
Africa				
Central African Rep. (2005) Ghana (2008)	Benin (2003) Cameroon (2007) Dem. Republic of the Congo (2006) Djibouti (2003) Ethiopia (2005) Kenya (2007) Mauritius (2005) Zambia (2006) Zimbabwe (2008)	Burundi (2005)		Rwanda (2003)
Asia				
Bahrain (2006) Iran (Islamic Republic of) (2008) Nepal (2008) Oman (2007) Yemen (2003)	Kuwait (2008) Syrian Arab Republic (2007) Tajikistan (2005) Turkey (2007) United Arab Emirates (2006)	Armenia (2007) Cyprus (2006) Jordan (2007) Lao People's Dem. Republic (2006)		
Latin America and the Caribbean				
Belize (2008)		Trinidad and Tobago (2007)	Paraguay (2003) Peru (2006)	Costa Rica (2006)
Oceania				
Samoa (2006) Solomon Islands (2006) Vanuatu (2008)	Tonga (2008)			
More developed regions				
	Hungary (2006) Ireland (2007) Japan (2005) Malta (2003) Ukraine (2006)	Australia (2007) Belarus (2008) Canada (2006) Croatia (2003) Czech Rep. (2006) Estonia (2007) Germany (2005) Latvia (2006) New Zealand (2008) Poland (2007) Slovakia (2006) United Kingdom (2005)	Bosnia and Herzegovina (2006) Denmark (2005) Finland (2007) France (2007) Netherlands (2003) Portugal (2005) Serbia (2008) Sweden (2006) Switzerland (2003) The former Yugoslav Republic of Macedonia (2008)	Belgium (2007) Iceland (2007)

Source: Compiled by the United Nations Statistics Division from Inter-Parliamentary Union, *Women in Parliament: The year in perspective* (2003, 2005, 2006, 2007 and 2008).

with available data, female candidates for the lower or single house of parliament have, on average, a lower likelihood than male candidates of winning a seat, a likelihood that amounts to 0.87 that of men[13] (figure 5.1). Variations across regions under-

lie this global ratio. Regionally, the average likelihood of women candidates winning a seat in the lower or single house of parliament is higher than that of men candidates only in Africa – by a factor of 1.17. In Asia and the more developed regions, women's likelihood of getting elected is 0.85 that of men. The regions where women candidates are most disadvantaged compared to men candidates in terms of the probability of getting elected are Latin America and the Caribbean and Oceania.

13 The likelihood of a female candidate winning a seat (also called female election rate) refers to the proportion of female candidates that were successfully elected; and the likelihood of a male candidate winning a seat, to the proportion of male candidates that were successfully elected. The female/male ratio of the likelihoods is an indication of how successful female candidates were in getting elected compared to male candidates. A ratio of one means that female and male candidates generally had the same likelihood of winning a seat; a ratio lower than one means that female candidates in general had a

lower likelihood of winning a seat than male candidates; while a ratio higher than one means that female candidates in general had a higher likelihood of winning than male candidates.

At the country level, Nepal stands out as having a much higher election rate for women compared to men: a success rate of 54 per cent against 10 per cent for men (see Statistical Annex). Belarus also had a much higher election rate for women, showing a female/male election rate ratio of greater than 2. A further 22 countries also had the same or higher female election rates than men, with female/male ratios ranging from 1 to 1.9 in the latest parliamentary elections between 2003 and 2008. In contrast, women's election rates were lower than men's in 36 countries, displaying female/male ratios ranging from 0.98 to as low as 0.23; and five countries had a ratio of zero, signifying the extreme case where no female candidates were successfully elected. Those five countries are Belize, Kuwait[14], Oman, Solomon Islands and Tonga.

The use of gender quotas

In many countries electoral gender quotas (see box 5.2) are considered to be an effective measure to improve gender balance in parliament. Generally, quotas for women require that women constitute a certain number or percentage of a body, such as a candidate list or a parliamentary assembly. Today quota systems aim at ensuring that women constitute at least 30 or 40 per cent, or even a true gender balance of 50 per cent, as opposed to only a few tokens.[15]

Many countries in the world implement gender quotas to offset obstacles that women have faced in

the electoral process. At present, at least 90 countries apply an electoral gender quota of some kind for the lower or single chamber of their national parliaments. Of these countries, 16 have reserved seats for women in the lower or single chamber of parliament, 33 have legislated candidate quotas and 54 have voluntary political party quotas (table 5.4). Reserved seats for women are found only in Africa (11 countries) and Asia (5 countries) and are particularly concentrated in Eastern Africa and Southern Asia (see box 5.3 for list of countries with legislated reserved seats). Legislated candidate quotas and voluntary political party quotas are the more common types of quota found in Latin America and in Eastern and Western Europe.

Eighteen of the 23 countries with a 30 per cent or better representation of women in the lower or single house of parliament implement some kind of gender quota

---

Gender quotas are shown to have helped increase the representation of women in parliament. Eighteen out of the 23 countries with at least 30 per cent representation of women in their lower or sin-

Figure 5.1
Average ratio of female election rate to male election rate for candidates to the lower or single house of parliament, by region, 2003–2008
(latest available election)

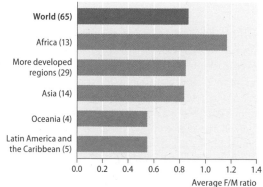

Source: Computed by the United Nations Statistics Division based on data from Inter-Parliamentary Union, *Women in Parliament: The year in perspective* (2003, 2005, 2006, 2007 and 2008).
Note: Unweighted averages; the numbers in brackets indicate the number of countries with available data.

[14] Kuwait has since successfully elected four women to its National Assembly (see box 5.1).

[15] International IDEA and others, 2010.

Box 5.2
Types of electoral quota for women

An electoral quota for women may be mandated in the constitution, stipulated in the national legislation of the country or formulated in a political party statute. Typically, three types of electoral quota are distinguished, the first two being legislated quotas (constitutional and/or legislative) and the third one voluntary, thus:

- Reserved seats – reserves a number of seats for women in a legislative assembly
- Legislated candidate quotas – reserves a number of places on electoral lists for female candidates
- Voluntary political party quota – rules or targets voluntarily adopted by political parties to include a certain percentage of women as election candidates. This does not include quotas for internal party structures.

One country may have several quota types.

Source: International IDEA and others, Quota Project: Global database of quotas for women (2010).

gle house have implemented some kind of gender quota for national parliaments, either legislated or voluntary. Furthermore, in 2009, women comprised on average 21 per cent of parliamentarians in countries that used gender quotas, compared to an average of 13 per cent in countries that did not have such measures.[16]

The introduction of gender quotas, however, is not without controversy. While quotas compensate for actual barriers that prevent women from their fair share of the political seats, it has been argued that they contradict the principles of equal opportunity since women are given preference over men.[17] It has also been observed that quotas are hard to apply in single winner systems, where each party nominates a single candidate per district. Furthermore, the re-election of parliament members restricts the rate of member turnover at each election, which makes gender quotas difficult to comply with. Analysis by the European Commission shows that around two thirds of members of parliament are re-elected at each election, leaving limited opportunities for new leaders and hence limited opportunities for progress towards gender balance.[18]

2. Heads of State or Government

Very few women get to the top position of power within their government. A glance at the number of female Heads of State or Government reveals that these positions remain elusive for women. Only seven out of 150 elected Heads of State in

Table 5.4

Number of countries with a gender quota for lower or single house of parliament, by type of quota and region, 2009

	Any type of quota	Reserved seats	Legislated candidate quotas	Voluntary political party quotas
World	90	16	33	54
Africa	24	11	3	12
Northern Africa	4	1	0	3
Eastern Africa	11	9	0	3
Middle Africa	2	0	1	1
Southern Africa	2	0	0	2
Western Africa	5	1	2	3
Asia	18	5	8	6
Central Asia	2	1	1	0
Eastern Asia	1	0	1	1
South-Eastern Asia	4	0	2	2
Southern Asia	5	3	1	1
Western Asia	6	1	3	2
Latin America and the Caribbean	18	0	13	12
Caribbean	1	0	1	1
Central America	7	0	4	5
South America	10	0	8	6
Oceania	0	0	0	0
More developed regions	30	0	9	24
Eastern Europe	12	0	5	8
Western Europe	16	0	4	14
Other more developed regions	2	0	0	2

Source: Computed by the United Nations Statistics Division based on data from International IDEA and others, Global database of quotas for women (accessed in June 2010).

the world are women, and only 11 of 192 governments are headed by women (table 5.5). Notable developments in both developing and developed countries include the election of female Heads of State or Government in Iceland in 2009, in Haiti and the Republic of Moldova in 2008, Argentina, India and Ukraine in 2007, Chile in 2006 and Germany and Liberia in 2005. Thus, the number of female Heads of State or Government in 2009 totalled 14, compared to 12 in 1995.[19]

3. Ministers

> **Worldwide, on average only one in six cabinet members is a woman**

Women continue to be underrepresented in cabinet appointments in all regions of the world. Globally, the average share of women among ministers was only 17 per cent in 2008 (figure 5.2). Although low,

Box 5.3

Countries that mandate reserved seats for women in the lower or single chamber of parliament through the Constitution or electoral law

- Eastern Africa (9): Burundi, Djibouti, Eritrea, Kenya, Rwanda, Somalia, Sudan, Uganda, United Republic of Tanzania.
- Other Africa (2): Egypt, Niger.
- Southern Asia (3): Afghanistan, Bangladesh, Pakistan.
- Other Asia (2): Kyrgyzstan, Jordan.

Source: International IDEA and others, Quota Project: Global database of quotas for women (accessed in June 2010).

---

16 Inter-Parliamentary Union, 2009c.

17 International IDEA and others, 2010.

18 European Commission, 2009.

19 Inter-Parliamentary Union, 2006d.

Table 5.5

Countries with a woman Head of State or Government, by region, as of April 2009

Head of State	Head of Government
Africa	
Liberia	Liberia
	Mozambique
Asia	
India	Bangladesh
Philippines	Philippines
Latin America and the Caribbean	
Argentina	Argentina
Chile	Chile
	Haiti
More developed regions	
Finland	Germany
Ireland	Iceland
	Republic of Moldova
	Ukraine

Source: Compiled by the United Nations Statistics Division from country reports.

it is a significant improvement from the average of 8 per cent in 1998. In all regions and sub-regions, the share of women is significantly higher compared to 10 years ago, with the recent proportions more than double those of 1998 in most sub-regions. The four sub-regions with the highest proportions of women ministers in 2008 (Western Europe, Southern Africa, South America and Central America) all

showed improvements of greater than 15 percentage points compared to 1998.

Western Europe and Southern Africa led the way in women's representation with an average of 33 and 30 per cent, respectively, of cabinet appointments being a woman. Elsewhere women's representation in the cabinet exceeded 20 per cent in all sub-regions of Latin America and the Caribbean and in the more developed regions outside Europe. The average share in Eastern, Middle and Western Africa coincided with the global average (17 per cent). Eastern Europe, Northern Africa, Oceania and all five sub-regions of Asia lagged behind in women's representation among ministers.

At the country level, progress is shown by the increase in the number of countries where women held at least 20 per cent of ministerial positions: 63 countries in 2008 (see Statistical Annex) compared to only 13 in 1998.[20] Worldwide, women's share of ministerial positions in countries ranged from zero to 58 per cent in 2008. Countries with the highest proportions of female ministers include six from Western Europe (three of them Nordic countries), three from Latin America and the Caribbean and one from Africa (table 5.6).

Progress, however, bypassed some countries. In 2008 there was no female minister at all in nine countries[21] (see Statistical Annex). This number is slightly lower than the 14 countries in 1998.[22]

Figure 5.2

Share of women among ministers, by region, 1998 and 2008

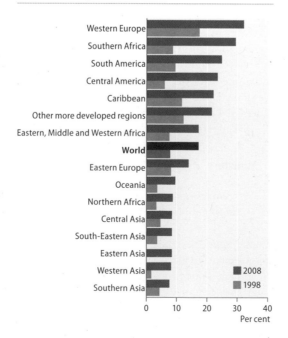

Source: Computed by the United Nations Statistics Division based on data from United Nations, *The World's Women 2000: Trends and Statistics* (2000); and Inter-Parliamentary Union and United Nations Division for the Advancement of Women, *Women in Politics: 2008* (2008).

Note: Unweighted averages. No data for Eastern Asia 1998.

Table 5.6

Countries with highest proportion of women ministers, 2008

Country	Percentage of women ministers
Finland	58
Norway	56
Grenada	50
Sweden	48
France	47
South Africa	45
Spain	44
Switzerland	43
Chile	41
El Salvador	39

Source: Inter-Parliamentary Union and United Nations Division for the Advancement of Women, *Women in Politics: 2008* (2008).

20 United Nations, 2000.

21 Bhutan, Bosnia and Herzegovina, Democratic People's Republic of Korea, Libyan Arab Jamahiriya, Myanmar, Romania, Saudi Arabia, Singapore and Solomon Islands.

22 United Nations, 2000.

Worldwide four countries, all in Asia, had no woman in their cabinet in both 1998 and 2008: Bhutan, Myanmar, Saudi Arabia and Singapore.

In general, women aspiring to careers in politics still encounter difficulties, suggesting that the democratic principles of parity and equality continue to be hampered by structural and attitudinal barriers, including discrimination and gender stereotypes that disadvantage women in many regions.

4. Local governments

Most countries have elected bodies at sub-national levels, some with state or provincial governments and most with local councils. Local governments are closest to their constituents and have the capacity to provide them with such social services as public transportation, drinking water, sanitation and the planning of cities. For the same reasons as in national government, gender balance is important in local government; however, like national government, local governments worldwide suffer from a low representation of women.

Women are a small percentage of councillors in local government

---

Similar to the situation in national parliaments, local governments in all world regions are far from achieving gender balance within decision-making positions. Regional averages for the proportion of women among elected councillors ranged from a low of 8 per cent in Northern Africa to a high of 30 per cent in sub-Saharan Africa (figure 5.3). In other parts of the world, the sub-regions in Latin America and in the more developed regions registered averages in the range of 24 to 29 per cent, while South-Eastern, Southern and Western Asia all showed averages below 20 per cent.

Of the 83 countries of the world with available data for 2003–2008, only four had more women than men councillors: Belarus, Costa Rica, Republic of Moldova and Ukraine.[23] In contrast, women are a very small minority (less than 5 per cent) among councillors in eight countries: Azerbaijan, Egypt, Estonia, Iran (Islamic Republic of), Morocco, Lebanon, Sri Lanka and Turkey.[24]

A number of countries have applied constitutional or legislative gender quotas to hasten progress towards more equitable representation at the local

---

23 UNECE Gender Statistics Database (2009) and national reports.

24 Ibid.

Figure 5.3

Share of women among councillors, by region, 2003–2008 (*latest available*)

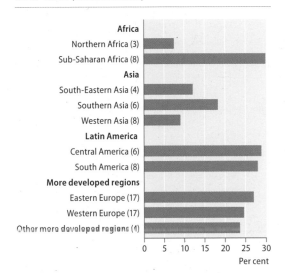

Source: Computed by the United Nations Statistics Division based on data from United Cities and Local Governments (2009) and national sources.

Note: Unweighted averages; the numbers in brackets indicate the number of countries with available data.

level of government. For example, India's constitutional amendments in 1993 to strengthen local governance included the reservation of one third of seats in local governing councils for women; this quota was increased to 50 per cent in 2009. Similarly, Pakistan's Devolution of Power Plan in 2000 reserved 33 per cent of seats for women at all sub-national levels.[25] This has played a part in the higher proportions of women in the local councils of India and Pakistan (38 and 25 per cent, respectively) compared to other countries in Southern Asia.

Women comprise no more than a fifth of all mayors in 73 out of 77 countries or areas

---

The proportion of women in top leadership positions in local government is much more limited than in local councils. In none of the sub-regions with available data[26] did the average proportion of women mayors exceed 10 per cent except in the more developed regions outside Europe, which registered an average of 14 per cent (figure 5.4). This proportion is much lower than the average of 24 per cent for councillors in the same sub-region (figure 5.3).

Women mayors in the countries of Eastern and Western Europe accounted for, on average, 10 per

---

25 UN Millennium Project, 2005, p. 105.

26 United Cities and Local Governments (UCLG) collected and published data on women and men councillors and mayors for 2003. The data presented here come from the UCLG's dataset and, in addition, include data extracted from the UNECE Gender Statistics Database and several national sources (see Statistical Annex).

Figure 5.4

Share of women among mayors, by region, 2003–2008 (*latest available*)

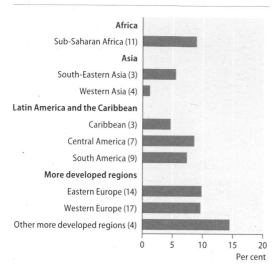

Source: Computed by the United Nations Statistics Division based on data from United Cities and Local Governments (2009) and national sources.

Note: Unweighted averages; the numbers in brackets indicate the number of countries with available data.

cent of all mayors; again, this is a much lower proportion than women's 25 per cent or higher average representation in local councils. In the 11 countries with available data in sub-Saharan Africa, on average only 9 per cent of mayors were women. For South-Eastern Asia and for the three sub-regions of Latin America and the Caribbean, the figures range from 5 to 9 per cent. The four countries with available data in Western Asia had the lowest average proportion of women (1 per cent) at the mayoral level.

Out of the 77 countries or areas with available data, the ones with the highest proportion of women mayors include Latvia (25 per cent), Mauritius (40 per cent), New Zealand (26 per cent) and Serbia (26 per cent). The low proportion of women among mayors is evident worldwide; other than the above-mentioned four countries, the averages were below 20 per cent in all countries or areas with available data, and three (Bangladesh, Mayotte and Trinidad and Tobago) had no female mayor (see Statistical Annex).

Mayoral positions are in the same class, so to speak, as heads of State or Government and presiding officers of parliament, being positions that are hardest for women to attain. For women, the difficulty of attaining the top executive position may be related in part to the stereotypical perception that women lack the leadership qualities necessitated by the job. Women are relatively more successful in landing positions as members of a legislative or governing body. For example, the five Nordic countries may boast relatively high representation

of women among members of parliament and local councils (the percentage of women in these bodies range from 26 to 47 per cent in all five countries). In contrast, only one of the five countries had a woman head of State (Finland) or head of Government (Iceland), and only one had a woman presiding over its parliament (Iceland). With respect to mayors, the proportion of women among mayors in the five countries range from only 9 to 17 per cent (see Statistical Annex).

The difficulties of combining family life, work life and politics remain a severe obstacle to women seeking political office. Among the political challenges that women face, the prevalence of the "masculine model" of political life and lack of party support feature prominently.[27] In particular, the barriers to the political participation of women at the local level may be related to lack of community support, lack of family co-responsibility within households to release women from unpaid household work, little recognition and legitimacy allocated to their contribution within public power spheres, and the lack of economic resources to pursue a candidature.[28]

B. The judiciary

1. National courts

The judiciary is still predominantly male except in Eastern Europe. In 11 of the 12 countries with available data in that sub-region, female judges in general outnumbered male judges, with 64 per cent of all judges in the average country being female (table 5.7). The situation is not as positive for women judges in the Supreme Court, the apex of judicial power within the national judiciary. As with other areas already examined in earlier sections and in other chapters, so it is with the judiciary: the further up the judicial hierarchy, the smaller the representation of women. Thus, in the supreme courts in the Eastern European sub-region, women outnumbered men in only four countries. Notable, however, is that in two of these (Bulgaria and Romania), women in the Supreme Court outnumbered men to an even greater degree than they did in all courts combined, occupying 78 and 75 per cent, respectively, of the Supreme Court seats.

In Western Europe and Western Asia, the proportion of women in all courts was below 50 per

27 International IDEA, 2005.

28 Instituto Nacional de las Mujeres Mexico, 2006.

cent. The same pattern of lower female presence in the supreme courts compared to all courts is observed, with two exceptions: Ireland and Sweden, where the share of women judges is higher in the Supreme Court than in all courts combined (table 5.7)

In other regions of the world, two countries stand out as having a large presence of women in the Supreme Court: Honduras where one of two judges in the Supreme Court was a woman, and the Philippines where women accounted for one third of Supreme Court judges. At the other end of the spectrum, all judges in the supreme courts of India and Pakistan were male.[29]

2. International courts

Women are also underrepresented in international and regional courts, with only four of 12 such courts having 30 per cent or more women judges. The highest share is seen in the International Criminal Court (ICC), where seven of 18 judges (39 per cent) were women (table 5.8). This high representation of women was achieved because the Rome Statute, the governing document of the ICC, calls for a fair representation of female and male judges.[30] In contrast, the International Tribunal for the Law of the Sea was composed entirely of male judges, while in the International Court of Justice only 7 per cent of the judges were women.

C. Civil service

Women's representation in decision-making positions in the civil service is among the concerns raised in the Beijing Platform for Action. The limited information available to assess levels and trends pose challenges to addressing gender disparities in these areas.

1. Senior administrators

Available data indicate that women are underrepresented among high-ranking government administrators with decision-making power. In 33 countries (EU-27 plus 6 other countries) monitored by the European Commission, for example, women occupied on average only 25 per cent of the highest level non-political administrative positions and 33 per cent of second-level administrative positions

---

29 UNIFEM, 2009.

30 United Nations, 1998.

Table 5.7

Share of women among Supreme Court judges and all judges, by region, 2003–2009 (latest available)

Country	Supreme Court judges (per cent)	All judges (per cent)
Western Asia (4)	**9**	**33**
Armenia	—	21
Cyprus	8	38
Georgia	11	46
Turkey	17	28
Eastern Europe (12)	**41**	**64**
Bosnia and Herzegovina	25	68
Bulgaria	78	66
Croatia	47	65
Czech Republic	25	62
Estonia	16	63
Hungary	61	72
Latvia	57	71
Lithuania	19	54
Poland	26	64
Republic of Moldova	33	33
Romania	75	71
Slovenia	34	75
Western Europe (6)	**19**	**33**
Iceland	22	30
Ireland	25	22
Italy	13	38
Portugal	2	49
Sweden	44	38
United Kingdom	8	20

Sources: Compiled by United Nations Statistics Division from UNECE, Gender statistics database (2009); European Commission, Database on women and men in decision-making (2008); UNIFEM, Progress of the World's Women 2008/2009 (2009); and national reports.

Table 5.8

Share of women among judges in international and regional courts, 2006

0–9%	10–19%	20–29%	30–39%
International Court of Justice (7%)	European Court of Justice (17%)	European Court of Human Rights (27%)	International Criminal Court (39%)
International Tribunal for the Law of the Sea (0%)	Caribbean Court of Justice (14%)	Andean Court of Justice (25%)	Court of First Instance (36%)
	Inter-American Court of Human Rights (14%)		International Criminal Tribunal for Rwanda (33%)
	International Criminal Tribunal for the former Yugoslavia (11%)		Special Court of Sierra Leone (30%)

Source: UNIFEM, Progress of the World's Women 2008/2009 (2009), p. 79.

Figure 5.5

Number and list of countries or areas where the national statistical office (NSO) is headed by a woman, by region, 2010

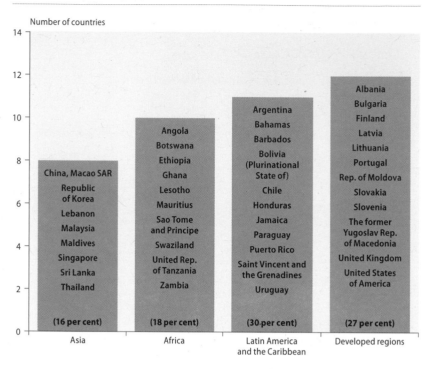

Source: United Nations Statistics Division, Contacts database (accessed in January 2010).
Note: The percentage in brackets refer to the proportion of countries or areas in the region that have a woman as chief statistician.

in government ministries.[31] High-ranking female administrators were more likely to occupy the high-level posts in socio-cultural ministries (education, welfare, health, etc.) as opposed to ministries associated with the basic government functions (foreign affairs, interior, defence, justice, etc.). Women occupied 33 per cent of the highest-level positions in socio-cultural ministries compared to only 22 per cent in the ministries with basic functions.

Out of 190 national statistical offices worldwide, 41 are headed by women

---

A specific high-ranking administrative position in a country is that of chief statistician, the person in charge of the government entity responsible for producing official statistics. Worldwide, 41 of 190 national statistical offices (22 per cent) have a woman as chief statistician.[32] Female heads are more common in Latin America and the Caribbean and in the more developed regions compared

31 European Commission, 2010.

32 Data on chief statisticians come from the contacts database maintained by the United Nations Statistics Division.

to Africa and Asia. In the former two regions, women account for 30 and 27 per cent, respectively, of chief statisticians, as opposed to 18 and 16 per cent, respectively, in Africa and Asia (figure 5.5). There are two regions where all chief statisticians are male: Northern Africa and Oceania.

A very important high-ranking position in government is the Governor of the central bank, the entity responsible for overseeing the monetary system for the country. Available data from Europe shows that no woman has attained this position (box 5.4).

2. Women and men in the United Nations

Article 8 of the Convention on the Elimination of Discrimination against Women requires States to ensure that women have equal opportunities to represent their governments at the international level and to participate in the work of international organizations. The Beijing Platform for Action called on the United Nations to implement employment policies in order to achieve overall gender equality at the professional level and above by 2000, and a target was set for women to hold 50 per cent of managerial and decision-making positions in the United Nations by 2000; this target, however, has been met only in the case of junior professionals.

Between 1998 and 2009, there was an increase in the proportion of women at every level of the professional and higher categories of staff in the United Nations Secretariat. Progress was more marked (greater than 10 percentage point increase) in the highest decision-making and managerial positions, namely those at the under-secretary-general and assistant secretary-general levels – positions where women were extremely underrepresented in 1998 (figure 5.6). The two director categories (D-2 and D-1), which also involve managerial decision-mak-

Box 5.4

Central banks are male dominated in the European Union

In 2009, the central banks of all 27 European Union Member States are led by a male governor and their boards have on average five men for every woman.

Source: European Commission, Database on women and men in decision-making (2010).

ing, showed increases of five percentage points in the 11-year interval. The senior and mid-level professionals (P-5, P-4 and P-3) registered the smallest gains (2 to 4 percentage points), while the junior professional level (P-2) improved by 6 percentage points. Apart from the junior professionals which were 45 per cent female in 1998 and are now 51 per cent, no other category achieved the 50 per cent target envisioned in 1995.

The current situation of women in the United Nations Secretariat, where the proportion of women at each level of the hierarchy is lower than that in the next level down, echoes the trend in national governments. The deficit of women at the most senior levels persists, with women comprising only between 20 and 30 per cent of directors, assistant secretaries-general and under-secretaries-general.

D. The private sector

Women around the world have gradually gained more opportunities to participate in and contribute to the development of society. However, despite some advances toward gender equality in the private sector, the gaps in the corporate sphere remain enormous.

1. Corporate boards

Evidence suggests that corporate boards with more female members have greater participation of members in decision-making and better board governance.[33] Specifically women are less likely to have attendance problems than men. Furthermore, the greater the proportion of women on the board, the better are the attendance levels of male directors and the more equity-based is the pay for directors. In addition, companies where at least three women serve as board members show stronger than average results in financial performance; this association holds across industries.[34]

Although women directors are now present on most boards of directors of large companies, their number remains low compared to men. For example, in the United States of America in 2009, while 89 per cent of the Standard and Poor 500 companies[35] had at least one woman director on

Figure 5.6

Proportion of women in the professional and higher-level positions in the United Nations Secretariat, 1998 and 2009

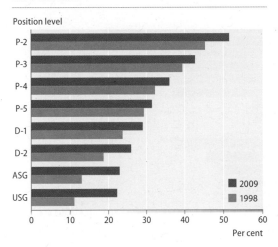

Source: United Nations Office of the Special Adviser on Gender Issues and Advancement of Women, *The Status of Women in the United Nations System and in the United Nations Secretariat, as of 30 June 2009 (Secretariat), as of 30 December 2008 (United Nations System).*

their board, women comprised on average only 16 per cent of board directors.[36] Companies with a female Chief Executive Officer (CEO) were more likely to have a greater number of women on their board of directors:[37] 32 per cent, compared to 15 per cent in companies with a male CEO.[38]

The low proportion of women in the boards of large companies is also evident in Europe. In 2009 women directors comprised on average 12 per cent of directors on the board of the top publicly traded companies in 33 countries (EU-27 plus 6 others).[39] The proportion of women directors on corporate boards was highest by far in Norway (42 per cent). This proportion exceeded 20 per cent in only two other countries: Finland (24 per cent) and Sweden (27 per cent).

Some countries have implemented proactive policies to boost female participation at the board level of private companies, particularly in Scandinavia. In Norway, for example, legislation passed in 2002 requires state-owned companies to have at

33 Adams and Ferreira, 2008.

34 Joy and others, 2007.

35 Large publicly held companies included in the Standard and Poor 500 index; all 500 companies trade on either of the two largest American stock market companies: the NYSE

Euronext and the NASDAQ OMX. The average board size for the Standard and Poor 500 companies was 11 in 2009.

36 Spencer Stuart, 2009.

37 The higher proportion of female directors in companies with a female CEO is in part due to the fact that the CEO is often a member of the board of directors and would thus count towards the total number of women directors in those companies. At the same time, a large female presence in the company's board may be a factor in the ascendance of a female CEO.

38 Spencer Stuart, 2009.

39 European Commission. 2010. Based on the largest publicly listed companies compiled from the primary blue-chip index of the stock exchange(s) in each country.

Figure 5.7

Proportion of women among directors and chief executives of enterprises or organizations, 2000

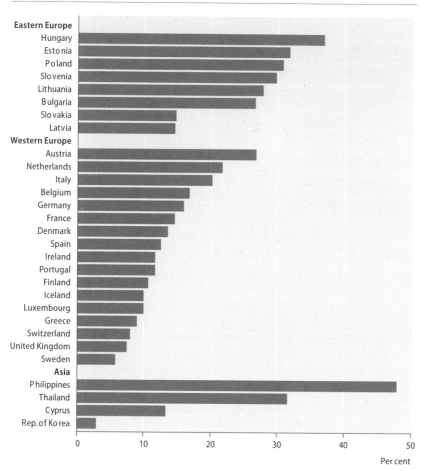

Source: Computed by the United Nations Statistics Division based on data from ILO, Labour Statistics database (LABORSTA), Employment by sex and detailed occupational groups (SEGREGAT), ISCO-88 code 121 (accessed in June 2009).

least 40 per cent representation of each sex on their boards. Another law was passed in 2006 requiring the private sector to comply with the same rule.[40] These government measures contributed to raising female board membership to 42 per cent by 2009 from only a quarter in 2005.[41]

Spain is another country which mandated a quota to raise the number of women on boards.[42] The gains, however, have been modest since the legislation was put in place in 2007: the proportion of women increased from 6 per cent in 2007 to only 10 per cent in 2009.

40 Norway, Ministry of Children, Equality and Social Inclusion, 2010.

41 European Commission, 2008 and 2010.

42 Ibid.

2. Chief executives

Women corporate leaders have a potential to influence the way employees live and work by promoting fairer management practices, a better balance between work and family life and fewer gender disparities in the workplace. However, as in leadership and decision-making positions in the government (see sections A to C above), women chief executives are not common in the private sector.

Figure 5.7 presents the proportion of female directors and chief executives for 25 countries in Europe and 4 in Asia. The analysis is based on detailed occupation data by sex from 2000 and focuses on occupations variably listed as director, chief executive, president, managing director or other similar position at the head of an enterprise or organization. The available data show that the proportion of directors and chief executives who are women varies widely among countries even within the same region, ranging from 15 to 37 per cent in Eastern Europe, from 6 to 27 per cent in Western Europe and, for the 4 countries in Asia, from 3 to 48 per cent. In most of the Eastern European countries (6 out of 8), women comprised more than 25 per cent of directors and chief executives. In comparison, this was the case in only one (Austria) of 17 Western European countries with available data; the large majority of countries in this region had proportions below 20 per cent. In Asia, the Philippines and Thailand both had comparatively high proportions of women among directors and chief executives, with 48 and 32 per cent, respectively; while the Republic of Korea registered the lowest proportion among all the countries, with 3 per cent.

Only 13 of the 500 largest corporations in the world had a female CEO in 2009

The glass ceiling appears to be most impenetrable in the largest corporations, which are still essentially male domains. Of the 500 largest corporations in the world[43], only 13 had a female CEO in 2009,[44] a proportion amounting to less than 3 per cent. In 33 countries in Europe (EU-27 plus 6 others), the same pattern emerges of a very low proportion of women in the top position of

43 The Fortune Global 500, which is a ranking of the top 500 corporations worldwide as measured by revenue. The list of companies is compiled annually by Fortune magazine.

44 Fortune, 2009.

the highest decision-making body in the largest companies, namely the chairman of the board. In 16 of the 33 countries, the chairman of the board of all the top publicly traded companies[45] in 2009 was male; and in only three countries (Bulgaria, Slovakia and Norway) were women at the helm of at least 10 per cent of the country's top companies as chairman of the board.[46] For the European countries, the average proportion of women serving as chairman of the board of top companies was 3 per cent.

In sum, women are still severely underrepresented in the highest decision-making positions within the private sector, at least in the more developed regions. The situation is unlikely to be more encouraging in the less developed regions, although there is not enough data to confirm or refute this. Compared to the underrepresentation of women in top leadership and decision-making positions in the government, judiciary and civil service (see sections A to C), the situation in the private sector is even more severe.

---

45 The number of top publicly traded companies considered range from 9 in Iceland to 50 in the United Kingdom.

46 European Commission, 2010.

Chapter 6
Violence against women

Key findings

- Violence against women is a universal phenomenon.
- Women are subjected to different forms of violence – physical, sexual, psychological and economic – both within and outside their homes.
- Rates of women experiencing physical violence at least once in their lifetime vary from several per cent to over 59 per cent depending on where they live.
- Current statistical measurements of violence against women provide a limited source of information, and statistical definitions and classifications require more work and harmonization at the international level.
- Female genital mutilation – the most harmful mass perpetuation of violence against women – shows a slight decline.
- In many regions of the world longstanding customs put considerable pressure on women to accept abuse.

Introduction

Violence against women is an obstacle to the achievement of the objectives of equality, development and peace. It both violates and impairs or nullifies the enjoyment by women of their human rights and fundamental freedoms. In all societies, to a greater or lesser degree, women and girls are subjected to physical, sexual and psychological abuse that cuts across lines of income, class and culture. The low social and economic status of women can be both a cause and a consequence of this violence.[1]

Violence against women throughout their life cycle is a manifestation of the historically unequal power relations between women and men. It is perpetuated by traditional and customary practices that accord women lower status in the family, workplace, community and society, and it is exacerbated by social pressures. These include the shame surrounding and hence difficulty of denouncing certain acts against women; women's lack of access to legal information, aid or protection; a dearth of laws that effectively prohibit violence against women; inadequate efforts on the part of public

authorities to promote awareness of and enforce existing laws; and the absence of educational and other means to address the causes and consequences of violence. Images in the media of violence against women – especially those that depict rape, sexual slavery or the use of women and girls as sex objects, including pornography – are factors contributing to the continued prevalence of such violence, adversely influencing the community at large, in particular children and young people.[2]

The Beijing Platform for Action requested all governments and the United Nations, among others, to promote research, collect data and compile statistics relating to the prevalence of different forms of violence against women (especially domestic violence) and to encourage research into their causes, nature, seriousness and consequences as well as the effectiveness of measures implemented to prevent and redress violence against women.[3] An elaboration of the situation with regard to statistics on violence against women was presented in the previous issue of *The World's Women*.[4]

1 United Nations, 2005.

2 Ibid.
3 Ibid.
4 United Nations, 2006a.

The United Nations has recently significantly stepped up activities aimed at combating violence against women. The United Nations Secretary-General's 2006 study on violence against women[5] elaborates on the context and causes of this violence and on its forms, consequences and costs. The study dedicates a separate chapter to issues related to data collection and the gaps and challenges in the different sources of data used for quantification, with an emphasis on types of violence and ethical and safety issues related to population-based surveys used as sources. Furthermore, the study points to the fact that the development and use of common indicators on violence against women is critical for a full and comprehensive overview of this phenomenon.

The General Assembly adopted four resolutions[6] in the period 2006–2009 on intensification of efforts to eliminate all forms of violence against women, thus emphasizing countries' concern about the issue. It also built on the Secretary-General's call for developing global indicators, requesting in its resolution 61/142 of December 2006 that such undertaking take place as a matter of urgency to assist governments in assessing the scope, prevalence and incidence of violence against women.

Simultaneously the United Nations is undertaking work on defining and identifying the different forms this violence takes in order to enable accurate assessment and quantification. This is best reflected in the Secretary-General's Campaign UNiTE to End Violence against Women. The overall objective is to raise public awareness and increase political will and resources. One of the five key outcomes as benchmarks for the campaign to be achieved in all countries by 2015 is the "establishment of data collection and analysis systems on the prevalence of various forms of violence against women and girls".[7] Three outputs are listed under this benchmark: (1) All countries have undertaken a dedicated population-based survey or module on violence against women and girls; (2) All countries have integrated data collection on violence against women and girls in their administrative and routine reporting systems, including for health, police and justice; and (3) All countries, the international community and other actors commit to ensuring the gender disaggregation of existing data, where possible.

This chapter focuses on relevant methodological issues and sources of statistics that influence the availability of accurate, robust and comparable data on violence against women. It also describes the work on global statistical indicators for measuring such violence. The interim set of these global indicators is then used to present data on violence against women compiled from national and international surveys. The final sections of the chapter look at statistics on female genital mutilation and at the attitudes of women towards the violence inflicted on them.

A. Statistical methodology

1. Development of global statistical indicators

Comparability of statistics on violence against women is one of the major requirements for providing an accurate quantification of this phenomenon across time, nations, regions and the world. Violence experienced by women takes many different forms, and it is necessary to classify them into sets of indicators to create a common statistical instrument that should be applied in data collection exercises.

The work on global statistical indicators is mandated by the General Assembly.[8] The United Nations Statistical Commission, in response, established the Friends of the Chair group to identify and list statistical indicators on violence against women.[9] Since population-based surveys and administrative records are the source of statistics measuring this violence, the indicators are differentiated on that basis. For surveys, the list of indicators consists of:

i. Total and age-specific rate of women subjected to physical violence in the last 12 months by severity of violence, relationship to the perpetrator and frequency

ii. Total and age-specific rate of women subjected to physical violence during lifetime by severity of violence, relationship to the perpetrator and frequency

iii. Total and age-specific rate of women subjected to sexual violence in the last 12 months by severity of violence, relationship to the perpetrator and frequency

---

5 United Nations, 2006b.

6 General Assembly resolutions 61/143 of 2006, 62/133 of 2007, 63/155 of 2008 and 64/137 of 2009.

7 United Nations, 2009a.

8 United Nations General Assembly, 2006.

9 For the composition and proceedings of the group, visit: *http://unstats.un.org/unsd/demographic/meetings/vaw/default.htm.*

iv. Total and age-specific rate of women subjected to sexual violence during lifetime by severity of violence, relationship to the perpetrator and frequency

v. Total and age-specific rate of ever-partnered women subjected to sexual and/or physical violence by current or former intimate partner in the last 12 months by frequency

vi. Total and age-specific rate of ever-partnered women subjected to sexual and/or physical violence by current or former intimate partner during lifetime by frequency

vii. Total and age-specific rate of women subjected to psychological violence in the past 12 months by intimate partner

viii. Total and age-specific rate of women subjected to economic violence in the past 12 months by intimate partner

ix. Total and age-specific rate of women subjected to female genital mutilation

Statistics on the following indicators should be drawn from administrative records:

i. Femicide and spousal homicide by personal characteristics of the victim and the perpetrator

ii. Forced marriage

iii. Trafficking of women

The work on identifying and listing statistical indicators for measuring violence against women is on-going and will result in the development of guidelines[10] for producing statistics that will allow for international statistical standards. All national statistical authorities will be urged to apply them in order to ensure the availability of accurate and regular information on the issue.

2. Administrative records as a source of statistics on violence against women

Police and court statistics represent a potential source of statistics on violence against women. A detailed elaboration of the use of these sources is provided in the previous issue of *The World's Women*.[11] The value of police statistics for measuring violence against women is currently limited as this is often not reported to the authorities, especially in cases of domestic violence. However, for crimes such as femicide police statistics could provide use-

ful statistics, provided that data on the victim – as well as data on the perpetrator, if available – are disaggregated by age and other personal characteristics. The adaptation of crime statistics in general to produce data on violence against women is part of the work on developing and adopting international statistical standards for measuring such violence.[12]

The health sector is another source of statistics on various forms of violence, as are records kept by non-governmental organizations involved with the protection of abused and battered women. It should be noted, however, that statistics from these sources are scarce and lack full reliability. This is because information on the occurrences and consequences of violence is usually collected on a voluntary basis since recording incidents and reporting on victims of violence is often not mandatory for health-care and other systems.

3. Surveys as a source of statistics on violence against women

In principle, population-based stand-alone surveys are the instruments of choice for collecting statistics on violence against women.[13] Where there are resource problems, however, a well-designed module within a general or other purpose survey would be an appropriate tool as well. In both cases they need to comply with strict protocols of confidentiality and security for the interviewees.[14]

Specialized, stand-alone statistical surveys provide the possibility of examining in detail the characteristics of the woman, the perpetrator and their relationship, the number of occurrences of violence and all the other pertinent information. These surveys require careful preparation, sampling design and training of the interviewers, and they raise a whole set of ethical concerns in terms of ensuring confidentiality of data and the protection of respondents.[15]

Gender violence in general and violence against women in particular is recognized as a global phenomenon. The roots of such violence, however, are many and varied, which poses serious challenges to developing monitoring instruments.

---

10 Expected to be issued in 2011.

11 United Nations, 2006a.

12 See the report of the meeting of the Friends of the Chair of the United Nations Statistical Commission on Statistical Indicators for Measuring Violence against Women at: *http:// unstats.un.org/unsd/demographic/meetings/vaw/default*.htm.

13 United Nations, 2009b.

14 Ibid.

15 United Nations Statistics Division, 2009.

Researchers point to the fact that interpersonal behaviours must be understood within the wider contexts of power and inequality.[16] Thus one of the major issues in designing and conducting statistical surveys on violence against women is ensuring the cooperation of respondent victims, primarily in overcoming the societal barriers to disclosing intimate partner violence.

Even when surveys are conducted, their results are often difficult to compare as a consequence of the lack of international statistical standards and also due to the nature of the phenomenon. Surveys use different approaches and sample design; they define the acts of violence in different ways; and they differ in their coverage in terms of perpetrator – intimate partner(s) versus all men, for example.

Another issue is that the level of severity of violence experienced by women is often difficult to properly assess. While certain forms of physical violence by themselves might not be interpreted as severe, inflicting them repeatedly often causes significant harm to the victim. On the other hand, occasional or even a one-time occurrence of violence may result in serious injury. Most statistical surveys attempting to grasp the severity of violence apply a classification of different physical violent acts that hurt the victim and further qualifying these as either "moderate" or "severe" violence. However, another – more subjective – approach is also applied in some surveys and essentially solicits the victim's assessment of the severity of the violence.

The results of different national and international surveys are not completely comparable also due to yet another of their components: phrasing and sequence of questions. The framing and wording of the questions may have adverse effects on the willingness of the respondent to cooperate and, due to the fact that questions have to be sensitive to national circumstances, the statistics produced from these surveys do not always describe the same phenomenon. The sequence of the questions is also often different among different surveys; some ask questions regarding violence suffered from an intimate partner first and then turn to violence committed by other perpetrators, while other surveys[17] start with experience of physical violence irrespective of the perpetrator.

---

16 Merry, 2009.
17 International Violence against Women Surveys (IVAWS), for example, as presented in Johnson and others, 2008.

Differences between surveys also arise as a consequence of the choice of data collection method. Whether telephone or face-to-face interviews were used can affect the willingness and the readiness of the respondents to discuss sensitive topics such as violent acts.

All of these issues highlight the need to develop, adopt and implement international statistical standards in this field to ensure sub-national, national, regional and international comparability. The statistics and their description that follow need to be interpreted keeping in mind the characteristics of violence against women surveys that have just been discussed.

B. Prevalence and incidence of violence against women

In the past 15 years, a number of countries have conducted statistical surveys in an attempt to provide data on violence against women. In preparing this issue of *The World's Women* the United Nations Statistics Division undertook the compilation of data collected by these surveys (to the extent possible) based on the set of indicators listed above – i.e., the percentage of women subjected to physical and sexual violence in their lifetime and in the 12 months prior to data collection. While every effort was made to incorporate as many surveys as possible, the results from some surveys could not be included due either to the timing of the release of the results or the unavailability of data for some other reason. The complete list of surveys is presented in the Statistical Annex.

As noted in the first section, there are significant differences in the methodologies applied in the surveys and so the results might not be directly comparable. Major statistics for indicators as elaborated above are presented here as an approximation of the prevalence of violence against women in countries that conducted surveys on this issue and for which data were available.

1. Physical violence against women

Overall physical violence

Physical violence against women during their lifetime is expressed as a percentage of women, out of the total number of women, that experienced this at least once in their lifetime (usually after age 15). As already noted, data are usually collected on the physical violence women suffered both during their whole lifetime and in the past 12 months prior to the data collection. Physical violence consists of acts aimed at hurting the victim and include, but are not limited, to pushing, grabbing, twisting the arm, pulling the hair, slapping, kicking, biting or hitting with the fist or an object, to trying to strangle or suffocate, burning or scalding on purpose and attacking with some sort of weapon, a gun or knife. The proportion of women who were victimized by physical violence (irrespective of the perpetrator) at least once in their lifetime and in the past 12 months is presented in figure 6.1.

Women are exposed to physical violence throughout their lifetime

The proportion of women exposed to physical violence in their lifetime ranges from 12 per cent in China, Hong Kong SAR and 13 per cent in Azerbaijan to about a half or more in Australia and Mozambique (48 per cent), the Czech Republic (51 per cent) and Zambia (59 per cent). As for the violence experienced in the 12 months preceding the survey, the proportion of women is, as expected, lower. Still, over one-tenth of women report recent abuse in Costa Rica, the Republic of Moldova, the Czech Republic and Mozambique. In interpreting these results it is necessary to take into account the different methodologies used in these surveys and the fact that definitions of violence and collection methods were not identical (see the discussion earlier in this chapter). For example, the rate for India refers only to ever-married women, not the total number of women. Nevertheless, all statistics clearly point to the fact that a significant share of women was physically abused at least once in their lifetime, whether by their intimate partners or some other men.

Intimate partner physical violence

Violence that women suffer from their intimate partners carries particularly serious and potentially long-lasting consequences, as it tends to be repetitive and accompanied by psychological and sexual violence as well. This form of violence is especially in the focus of statistical surveys on violence against women.

Intimate partners physically abuse women

Statistics indicate that there are significant differences in the prevalence of intimate partner physi-

Figure 6.1

Proportion of women experiencing physical violence (irrespective of the perpetrator) at least once in their lifetime and in the last 12 months, 1995–2006 *(latest available)*

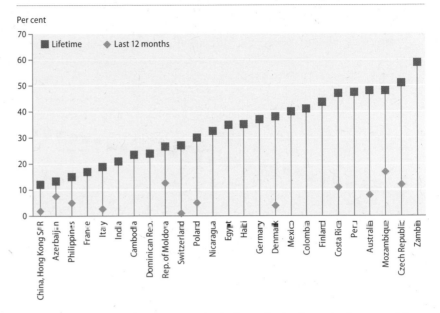

Source: Compiled by the United Nations Statistics Division from national and international surveys on violence against women.

Note: Statistics on physical violence against women in the last 12 months were not available for all the countries. Data for India and Cambodia refer to ever-partnered women. Data for Finland refer to at least one form of violence or threat.

cal violence around the world. According to data from national and international statistical surveys presented in graph 6.2, the percentage of ever-partnered or ever-married women that suffered physical violence perpetrated by a current or former intimate partner at least once in their lifetime ranges from 6 per cent in China, Hong Kong SAR and 7 per cent in Canada (data refer to spousal assaults only), to over 48 per cent in Zambia, Peru–city[18], Ethiopia–province and Peru–province. These available statistics do not point to any particular pattern of these prevalence rates in terms of geographical distribution of countries/areas or their level of development. However, it needs to be pointed out that violence against women surveys were not conducted in many countries of the world, thus making identification of regional or developmental trends considerably difficult.

The proportion of women subjected to physical violence by their intimate partners in the last 12

18 In a number of countries covered in this chapter, surveys on violence against women were conducted separately in a city and in a province in an attempt to distinguish between urban and rural areas. In all such cases the annotation indicates whether the data and findings refer to the city or the province of the country.

Figure 6.2

Proportion of women experiencing intimate partner physical violence at least once in their lifetime and in the last 12 months, 1995–2006 (*latest available*)

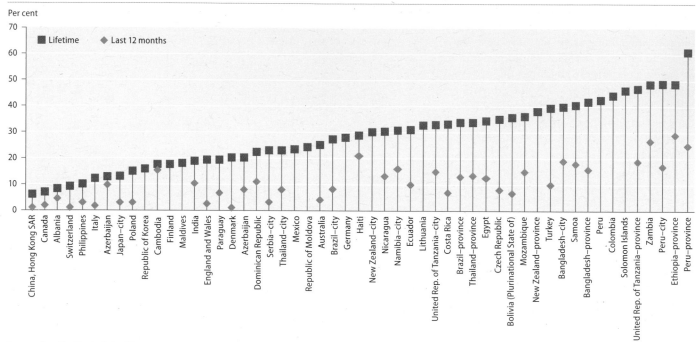

Source: Compiled by the United Nations Statistics Division from national and international surveys on violence against women.
Note: Statistics on intimate partner physical violence against women in the last 12 months were not available for all the countries. Data for India and Cambodia refer to ever-partnered women. Data for Finland refer to at least one form of violence or threat. Data for Canada refer to spousal assaults only. Data for the Plurinational State of Bolivia refer to hits by partner's hand only; not included are showings, hits with hard objects and attempted strangulation.

Figure 6.3

Proportion of women experiencing intimate partner physical violence at least once in their lifetime by severity, 2000–2008 (*latest available*)

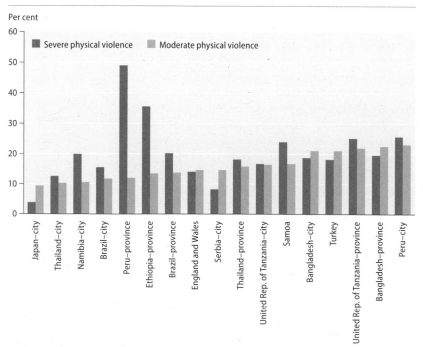

Source: Compiled by the United Nations Statistics Division from national and international surveys on violence against women.

months was 3 per cent or less in China, Hong Kong SAR, Canada (data refer to spousal assaults only), Switzerland, the Philippines, Poland, England and Wales and Denmark. While expressing these results as percentages allows for easier comparison, it is also important to look at the absolute values in order to fully understand the magnitude of this phenomenon. For example, the total number of women falling within the scope of this survey in Poland in 2004 was around 17.8 million while the total rate of women who were physically victimized was just over 3 per cent. This indicates that physical violence affected almost 534 thousand individual women in 2003 – in the 12 months prior to the survey – or 1,463 women on any given day.

> **Women are subjected to both moderate and severe physical violence from their intimate partners, with the preponderance of one or the other varying by country**

Whether the violence experienced by women from their intimate partners in their lifetime is moderate or severe varies across the countries with avail-

Figure 6.4

Age-specific rates of women subjected to physical violence by their intimate partners in the last 12 months prior to data collection, 2000–2002 (*latest available*)

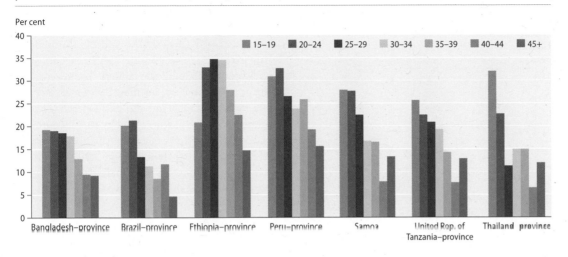

Source: Garcia Moreno and others, *WHO Multi-country Study on Domestic Health and Domestic Violence against Women* (2005).

able statistics, as presented in figure 6.3. There are countries where severe violence was experienced by many more women than those experiencing moderate physical violence – for example, almost 50 per cent of women in Peru-province experienced severe violence compared to around 12 per cent of women victimized by moderate violence. This difference was also significant in Ethiopia-province and the United Republic of Tanzania-province. On the other hand, significantly more women were subjected to moderate rather than severe physical violence during their lifetime in Bangladesh (both province and city) and Turkey, for example.

Young women are more exposed to intimate partner physical violence

Young women are more likely to be exposed to violence than older women. Standard (five-year interval) age-specific rates of women subjected to physical violence in the last 12 months consistently showed that women in younger age groups have been victimized in greater numbers (figure 6.4). This is particularly the case for the first two five-year intervals – i.e., women from 15–24 years of age. For example, one third of all women of that age were subjected to physical violence in Peru-province, as were around a fifth in both Bangladesh–province and Brazil–province. The situation was not the same in all countries, however – for example, women aged 25–34 in Ethiopia–province were proportionately more exposed to violence than those aged 15–24.

2. Sexual violence against women

Although not as frequent as physical violence, sexual violence has consequences that usually severely affect the victim for a prolonged period of time and often last a lifetime. The term "sexual violence", broadly interpreted, may include aggressive and abusive behaviours of different intensity and consequences, from unwanted touching to forced intercourse and rape.

Many women are sexually molested in their lifetimes

The percentage of women experiencing sexual violence at least once in their lifetime ranges from around 4 per cent in Azerbaijan, 5 per cent in France and 6 per cent in the Philippines, to a quarter or more women in Switzerland (25 per cent), Denmark (28 per cent), Australia (34 per cent), the Czech Republic (35 per cent), Costa Rica (41 per cent) and Mexico (44 per cent), as presented in figure 6.5.

Intimate partners often sexually assault women

As is the case with physical violence, sexual violence experienced by women in intimate partnerships carry a heavy toll on the victim and the partnership. In societies with traditional gender roles and attitudes toward marriage and divorce, it may be more difficult to leave a partner even if violent and women continue to endure ongoing abuse. [19]

---

19 Holly Johnson and others, 2008.

Figure 6.5

Proportion of women experiencing sexual violence (irrespective of the perpetrator) at least once in their lifetime and in the last 12 months, 2002–2006 (*latest available*)

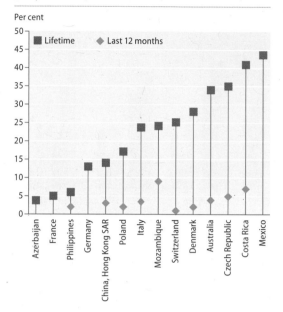

Per cent

Source: Compiled by the United Nations Statistics Division from national and international surveys on violence against women.
Note: Statistics on sexual violence against women in the last 12 months were not available for all the countries.

Figure 6.6 displays the percentage of ever-partnered women that were subjected to sexual violence committed by their intimate partner at least once in their lifetime and in the last 12 months

prior to the survey. This percentage varies considerably among countries or areas that collected these statistics. For example, while the lifetime experience of sexual violence in intimate partnership was reported by around 3 per cent of women in Albania, Azerbaijan, Switzerland and the Philippines, this percentage was considerably higher in quite a few countries in all the regions. The recent – in the past 12 months – intimate partner sexual violence was extremely low (up to 2 per cent of total number of ever-partnered women) in a number of countries or areas, such as Albania, Australia, Azerbaijan, China, Hong Kong SAR, the Czech Republic, Denmark, Italy, Japan–city, the Philippines, Poland, Serbia–city and Switzerland.

3. Femicide

Femicide is the name given to the gender-based murder of women, implying that women are targeted and murdered solely on the basis of gender inequalities in contemporary societies.

Out of different modalities of femicide *intimate femicide* – i.e., the killing of the woman by her male intimate partner – appears to be predominant. For example, over half of all the women murdered in South Africa in 1999 were killed by an intimate partner (husband, common-law husband, boy-

Figure 6.6.

Proportion of women experiencing intimate partner sexual violence at least once in their lifetime and in the last 12 months, 2000–2006 (*latest available*)

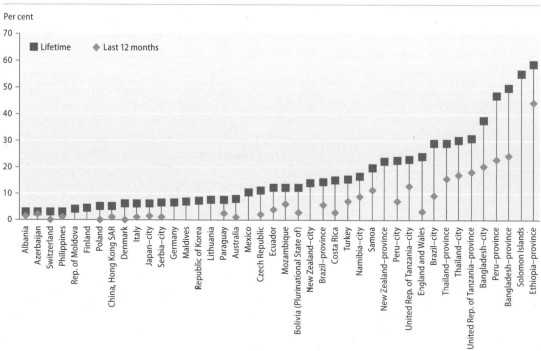

Per cent

Source: Compiled by the United Nations Statistics Division from national and international surveys on violence against women.
Note: Statistics on intimate partner sexual violence against women in the last 12 months were not available for all the countries.

friend), resulting in one intimate femicide every six hours.[20] Other forms of femicide include "honour killings", dowry deaths (bride burning), targeting women in civil conflicts and so forth.

However, internationally uniform statistical definitions of femicide are still in the making and different sources that could lead to reliable data on this phenomenon (police statistics, mortuary statistics and so forth) require adjustments in order to properly quantify and describe these occurrences, as well as to allow a more accurate assessment at regional and global levels.

In conclusion, while the percentage of women exposed to and experiencing physical and sexual violence (including femicide) varies among countries and regions in the world, statistics clearly and unambiguously document the existence of this phenomenon and give an idea of its extent and frequency. It is of crucial importance to establish violence against women surveys as regular statistical exercises within all national statistical systems, thus ensuring regular and accurate monitoring.

C. Female genital mutilation

The term "female genital mutilation" (FGM, also called "female genital cutting" and "female genital mutilation/cutting") refers to all procedures involving partial or total removal of the external female genitalia or other injury to the female genital organs for non-medical reasons.[21] Female genital mutilation has been reported to occur in all parts of the world.[22] It is recognized internationally as a violation of the human rights of girls and women and constitutes an extreme form of discrimination against women.[23]

The World Health Organization (WHO) groups female genital mutilation into four types:

a) Clitoridectomy: partial or total removal of the clitoris (a small, sensitive and erectile part of the female genitals) and, in very rare cases, only the prepuce (the fold of skin surrounding the clitoris).

b) Excision: partial or total removal of the clitoris and the labia minora, with or without excision of the labia majora (the labia are "the lips" that surround the vagina).

c) Infibulation: narrowing of the vaginal opening through the creation of a covering seal. The seal is formed by cutting and repositioning the inner, or outer, labia, with or without removal of the clitoris.

d) Other: all other harmful procedures to the female genitalia for non-medical purposes, e.g. pricking, piercing, incising, scraping and cauterizing the genital area.[24]

Female genital mutilation is always traumatic. Apart from excruciating pain, immediate complications can include shock, urine retention, ulceration of the genitals and injury to the adjacent tissue. Other outcomes can include septicaemia (blood poisoning), infertility and obstructed labour. Haemorrhaging and infection can lead to death.[25]

Female genital mutilation continues to be widely performed but appears to be declining slightly

Statistics on the prevalence of female genital mutilation among women come from population surveys focusing on demographic phenomena and health. Figure 6.7 presents these statistics for countries where such data was collected through two surveys at different points in time in recent years. In several countries the percentage of women aged 15–49 that were subjected to female genital mutilation is extremely high, and it even approaches 100 per cent in Guinea, Egypt and Eritrea. Another three countries where more than half the women have undergone these procedures are Burkina Faso, Ethiopia and Mali. Statistics indicate a downward trend in the percentage of women subjected to female genital mutilation in most of the countries presented here. For example, in Mali, 92 per cent of women aged 15–49 had undergone the procedure in 2001, but by 2006 this figure had dropped to around 86 per cent. Similar decreases were recorded in Benin, Central African Republic, Côte d'Ivoire, Ethiopia, Ghana, Guinea, Egypt, Eritrea, Kenya, Nigeria and the United Republic of Tanzania. An increase was recorded in two countries: Burkina Faso, where the share of women aged 15–49 that were cut increased from 72 per cent in 1998 to 77 per cent in 2003, and Yemen, where this figure was around 23 per cent in 1997 only to reach 38 per cent in 2003. Chad was the only country out of those with available statistics where the share

---

20 Mathews, 2009.
21 OHCHR, UNAIDS, UNDP, UNECA, UNESCO, UNFPA, UNHCR, UNICEF, UNIFEM, WHO, 2008.
22 Ibid.
23 WHO, 2010.

24 WHO, 2010.
25 UNICEF, 2005.

Figure 6.7

Women aged 15–49 subjected to female genital mutilation, two points in time

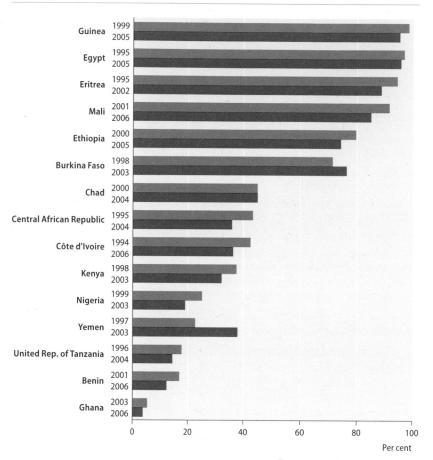

Sources: Population Reference Bureau, *Female Genital Mutilation/Cutting: Data and Trends* (2008); and UNICEF, *Female Genital Mutilation/Cutting: A Statistical Exploration* (2005).

is almost identical in both age groups – 15–29 and 30–49 years of age. When the ratio exceeds the value of 1 it indicates that prevalence among women in the younger age group is lower than in the older group. Conversely, ratio values below 1 indicate that prevalence is higher in younger than in older women.

The figure indicates that in the majority of countries for which data were available the value of the ratio exceeds 1, thus showing that female genital mutilation is being performed less on younger generations of women and girls. In Kenya the ratio reached 1.7 as around 43 per cent of women aged 30–49 were subjected to the practice compared to only 26 per cent of women aged 15–29. Similar occurrences were noted in Benin, Central African Republic, Ghana and Nigeria and to a smaller extent in Burkina Faso, Cameroon, Chad, Côte d'Ivoire, Eritrea, Ethiopia and Senegal. There were no differences in prevalence in younger and older women in Egypt, Guinea, Mali and Mauritania, and in Niger there were actually proportionally more younger women undergoing these procedures than older ones. It should be emphasized, however, that the overall prevalence rate in Niger is relatively low – just around 5 per cent of all women aged 15–49.

There are many factors that influence the practice of subjecting women to genital mutilation, including education, place of residence (urban/rural), religion, ethnicity and household wealth. Establishing a relationship between a women's genital mutilation status and her educational level can often be difficult, however, as mutilation usually takes place before education is completed and often even before it commences. Findings do show though that prevalence levels are generally lower among women with higher education, indicating that circumcised girls are also likely to grow up with lower levels of educational attainment.[27] Mothers' level of educational attainment, moreover, appears to be a significant determinant of the genital mutilation status of their daughters. It is generally observed that women with higher education are less likely to have their daughters subjected to genital mutilation than women with lower or no formal education.[28]

of women subjected to genital mutilation did not change – in both 2000 and 2004 it was recorded at around 45 per cent.

Female genital mutilation is more prevalent in older women

Findings that female genital mutilation appears to be less prevalent in young women as compared to older generations of women further substantiates the positive developments in quite a few countries. Figure 6.8 presents the ratio of two age-group values of FGM prevalence[26]. A ratio closer to the value of 1 indicates that prevalence

---

26 In producing the ratio of female genital mutilation, the first step is to compute the unweighted average of percentage of women subjected to female genital mutilation for three age groups: 15–19, 20–24 and 25–29. The second step is to compute the unweighted average of percentage of women subjected to female genital mutilation for the remaining four age

groups: 30–34, 35–39, 40–44 and 45–49. In the last step, the older group average is divided by the younger group average.
27 UNICEF, 2005.
28 Ibid.

D. Women's attitudes towards wife-beating

Wife-beating is a clear expression of male dominance; it is both a cause and consequence of women's serious disadvantage and unequal position compared to men. Indicators related to perceptions of wife-beating aim to test women's attitudes towards gender roles and gender equality.[29] In many regions of the world, women are still expected to endure being beaten based on ingrained social conditioning about the status of a wife. The strength and weight of traditions is such that many women even find it justifiable to be physically punished in certain circumstances.

The series of Demographic and Health Surveys conducted in countries and regions all over the world included questions regarding women's attitudes towards violence they suffered or were expected to suffer as a consequence of their acts and behaviours. Specifically, questions asked whether a husband was justified in hitting or beating his wife if she (1) burnt the food, (2) argued with him, (3) refused to have sex with him (4) went out without telling him, and (5) neglected the children.

Women continue to accept wife-beating

In 33 countries for which statistics are available, the percentage of women that found it appropriate to be hit or beaten for one of these acts varies considerably.

Around 29 per cent of women agreed that being hit or beaten for arguing with the husband was justifiable, 25 per cent for refusing to have sex with the husband and 21 per cent for burning the food. Figure 6.9 illustrates that, for example, 74 per cent of women in Mali would accept physical punishment for refusing to have sex with the husband, 62 per cent in the case of arguing with him and 33 per cent for burning the food. In the majority of countries arguing with the husband is the most accepted reason for being hit or beaten out of the three justifications mentioned above, according to the percentage of women that find it appropriate, as per figure 6.9.

However, a higher percentage – around 41 per cent of all women in these countries on average – found it appropriate to be physically punished for neglecting children and around 36 per cent

---

29 Ibid.

Figure 6.8

Ratio of FGM prevalence for 30–49 years old to FGM prevalence for 15-29 years old, 1998–2004 (*latest available*)

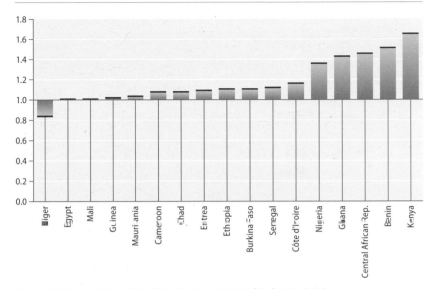

Source: UNICEF, *Female Genital Mutilation/Cutting: A Statistical Exploration* (2005).

for going out without telling the husband. In terms of neglecting the children, the percentage varied from around 7 per cent and 9 per cent in Dominican Republic and Nicaragua, respectively, to around 70 per cent in Ethiopia, Guinea, Mali and Uganda, as presented in figure 6.9.

Statistics show that, in general, the majority of women considered neglecting children a more serious "offence", although more women in a few countries – such as in Eritrea, Guinea, Haiti, Mali, Nigeria, Senegal and Zambia – considered going out without telling the husband to be more "punishable".

It has to be emphasized that not all women in these societies and countries have the same level of acceptance of physical punishment. Education certainly plays a crucial role in rejecting these "entitlements to violence" bestowed on husbands. For example, in Benin, while 51 per cent of interviewed women with no education found it appropriate to be hit or beaten for venturing outside without telling the husband, the percentage of women with the same opinion who had a primary education was 39 per cent and this dropped to 20 per cent in the case of women with secondary or higher education. Another example, in Rwanda in 2000, shows that 46 per cent of women with no education found it appropriate to being physically punished for venturing outside without telling the husband, as opposed

Figure 6.9

Proportion of women justifying wife-beating for: 1) burning the food, 2) arguing with the husband, 3) refusing to have sex, 4) going out without telling husband, and 5) neglecting children, 1999–2005 (*latest available*)

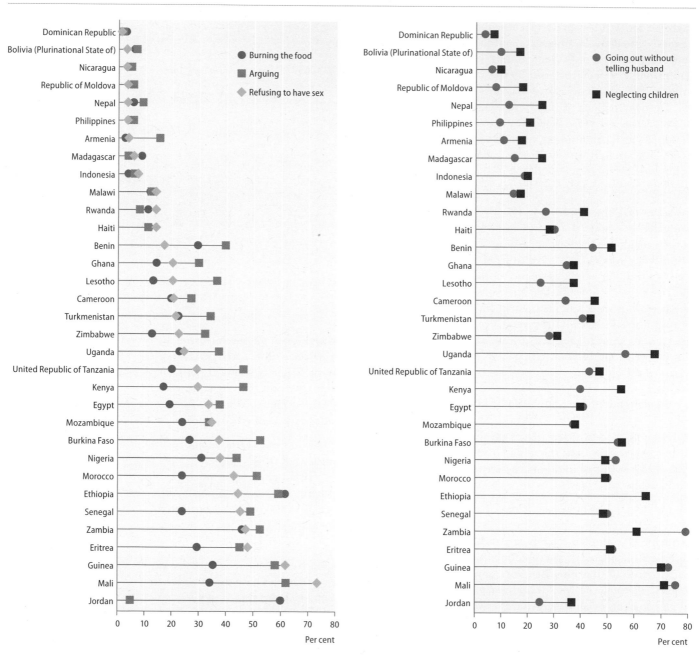

Source: Macro International, MEASURE DHS STATcompiler (2009).

to 36 per cent of women with primary education and only 17 per cent of women with secondary or higher education.[30]

In conclusion, attitudes of women in regard to the violence to which they are exposed in their marriages and other intimate relationships is still

largely based on concepts and constructs that heavily favour inequity and dominance of men in quite a few regions of the world. Statistics document that the impact of these misconceptions varies significantly among regions and societies; yet, it is clear that, even if the numbers of women under their influence is small, they still persist almost everywhere.

30 Macro International Inc, 2009.

Trafficking in women

Trafficking in women is a serious issue that has been addressed at the international level by the Protocol to Prevent, Suppress and Punish Trafficking in Persons, Especially Women and Children (Palermo Protocol), which supplements the United Nations Convention against Transnational Organized Crime. In its most recent resolution on this topic – resolution 63/156 of 30 January 2009 – the United Nations General Assembly expressed serious concern regarding an increasing number of women and girls being trafficked from some less developed countries and countries with economies in transition to more developed countries as well as within and between regions and States.

The ILO has estimated that more than 43 per cent of people trafficked across borders are used for forced commercial sexual exploitation, of whom 98 per cent are women and girls.[a] However, accurate statistics on the volume and patterns of trafficking of women are very hard to come by and, while a wealth of individual evidence and testimonies exists, it is generally not possible to generate reliable data on this topic. This calls for further research into the most appropriate statistical measurements to meet this challenge.

a See ILO, Forced labour statistics (2005).

Chapter 7
Environment

Key findings

- More than half of rural households and about a quarter of urban households in sub-Saharan Africa lack easy access to sources of drinking water, and most of the burden of water collection falls on women.
- The majority of households in sub-Saharan Africa and in Southern and South-Eastern Asia use solid fuels for cooking on open fires or traditional stoves with no chimney or hood, disproportionately affecting the health of women.
- Fewer women than men participate in high-level decision-making related to the environment.

Introduction

Women and the environment is one of the 12 critical areas of concern for achieving gender equality identified by the Beijing Platform for Action in 1995.[1] The Platform for Action recognizes that environmental conditions have a different impact on the lives of women and men due to existing gender inequality. In particular, lack of access to clean water and energy, environmental degradation and natural disasters disproportionately affect women in terms of health, unremunerated work and well-being. Furthermore, the Platform for Action stresses that women's role in sustainable development is hampered by unequal access to land, financial resources and agricultural information and technologies; unequal access to formal training in professional natural resources management; and limited involvement in policy formulation and decision-making in natural resources and environment management. All these barriers continue to exist 15 years after the Platform for Action was endorsed by governments.

There are also concerns that climate change may deepen environment-related gender inequality, particularly in the less developed regions.[2] The rise in temperature, the increasing risk of heat waves, droughts and floods, and the more frequent and more intense storms and tropical cyclones that are all part of climate change are expected to have an overall negative impact on agricultural livelihoods, availability of food and human health and survival.[3] Women are considered among the most vulnerable groups, as they tend to be more dependent on the natural resources threatened by climate change and have fewer assets to cope with the change.[4]

This chapter examines several environmental aspects with gender-differentiated impacts. The first part of the chapter looks at access to water and firewood, while the second part discusses the effects on health of environmental factors such as indoor smoke from solid fuels, unsafe water and sanitation, and natural disasters. Awareness of environmental problems and the participation of women and men in preserving the environment, particularly in high-level decision-making, are addressed in the last part of the chapter.

The choice of issues examined in this chapter was constrained by availability of data. More statistical information on links between gender and the environment is needed in several areas. Time use data are largely missing in countries from the less developed regions, where poor infrastructure and housing conditions, as well as natural hazards, result in increased work burdens. Data

---

1 United Nations, 1995.
2 See, for example, UNDP, 2009; Commission on the Status of Women, 2008; Masika, 2002.
3 IPCC, 2007.
4 UN Women Watch, 2009.

on trends and on smaller areas than the national level, needed to assess changes in women's and men's work burdens as a consequence of droughts, floods, deforestation or desertification, for example, are rarely available. Sex-disaggregated data on the effects of natural hazards on other human dimensions, such as education, health, food and economic security are also difficult to obtain.

Monitoring the impacts of climate change on the lives of women and men is particularly challenging. On the one hand, the gendered effects may not be easily detectable at the level of larger geographical units – region, country or even urban/rural area – where the traditional systems of social statistics have been focused; hence, monitoring may need to take into account smaller areas that are particularly prone to climate change manifestations. On the other hand, separating the effect of climate change on women and men's lives from other environmental and socio-economic factors is difficult. Non-climate factors such as demographic pressure or over-exploitation of resources also increase the risk of environmental degradation and have an effect on access to natural resources and on human health and survival.

Finally, data to assess the capability of women and men to protect local natural resources are not available. There is little information on access to environment-related practical knowledge, including access to modern agricultural information and techniques in the less developed regions. Sex-disaggregated data on participation in the management of local natural resources such as water, forests or biodiversity are also lacking.

A. Access to water and firewood

Investment in infrastructure to reduce women's and girls' time burdens in water and firewood collection has been identified by the Millennium Development Goal (MDG) Task Force on Education and Gender Equality as one of seven strategic priorities to achieve gender equality, "empower women and alter the historical legacy of female disadvantage".[5] This is particularly important in the context of declining supplies of water and firewood linked to desertification, deforestation and climate change, especially in some parts of Africa and Asia.[6] For example, between 1990 and 2005 the total forest area in the world declined at an

estimated rate of 8.4 million hectares annually.[7] More than half of this loss, 4.3 million hectares annually, was in sub-Saharan Africa, the region with the highest household dependency on firewood for cooking. Also, increasing frequency and intensity of droughts was noted in some parts of Africa and in many parts of Asia.[8] By 2020, between 75 and 250 million people in Africa are projected to be exposed to increased water stress due to climate change, and by 2050, freshwater availability is projected to decrease in Central, Southern, Eastern and South-Eastern Asia.[9]

1. Access to sources of drinking water

Lack of access to drinking water on the premises or within a short distance continues to affect the lives of women and men in the less developed regions. In sub-Saharan Africa, only 54 per cent of households are within 15 minutes from a source of drinking water (table 7.1). The proportion of such households is considerably higher in Asia (84 per cent), Latin America and the Caribbean (90 per cent) and Eastern Europe (97 per cent). Within sub-Saharan Africa, easy access to drinking water is particularly low in Eastern Africa (46 per cent of households on average). Less than a quarter of households in Burundi and Uganda and less than a third in Eritrea, Malawi, Rwanda and Somalia have access to water within 15 minutes.

> More than half of rural households and about a quarter of urban households in sub-Saharan Africa lack access to drinking water on the premises or within a short distance

The proportion of households within a short distance from a water source is lower in rural areas than in urban areas in all regions (table 7.1). The urban-rural gap is the largest in sub-Saharan Africa where 42 per cent of rural households have easy access to sources of drinking water, compared to 74 per cent of urban households. In rural areas of some sub-Saharan African countries only a minority of households can benefit from easy access to drinking water. The proportion of rural households within 15 minutes from a source of drinking water is as low as 8 per cent in Eritrea, 15 per cent in Somalia and in Uganda and 25 per cent or less in Burkina Faso, Burundi, Democratic Republic of the Congo and Mozambique.

---

5 UN Millennium Project, 2005, p. 3.
6 UNEP, 2005; IPCC, 2007.

7 FAO, 2005.
8 IPCC, 2007.
9 Ibid.

Women are more often responsible for water collection than men are

When water is not available on the premises, women are more often responsible for water collection than men are. In 38 of the 48 countries with available data, the percentage of households where an adult woman (15 years or over) is the person responsible for water collection is much larger than the percentage of households where an adult man is the person responsible. This is the case in both rural and urban areas in the majority of sub-Saharan African countries and in rural areas of some Asian countries. On average, an adult woman is the person usually carrying home the water in 63 per cent of rural households and 29 per cent of urban households in sub-Saharan Africa (figure 7.1). In comparison, an adult man has this responsibility in 11 per cent of rural households and 10 per cent of urban households. In rural areas in Asia, women are the ones fetching the water in 30 per cent of households and men in 13 per cent. In contrast, in rural and urban areas in Latin America and the Caribbean the burden falls more often on men.

Girls under 15 years are also more likely than boys of the same age to be in charge of water collection (figure 7.1). In sub-Saharan Africa, the usual person collecting water in rural areas is a girl in 7 per cent of households and a boy in 3 per cent of households. In Cameroon, Ghana, Sierra Leone and Uganda, a girl is the main person to collect water in more than 10 per cent of rural households. In urban areas of sub-Saharan Africa, girls and boys are the predominant water collectors in

4 and 3 per cent of households, respectively. In rural areas in Asia, girls and boys from 2 per cent of households are the usual persons collecting the water. It must be noted that the percentages shown refer to the situation where a child is the main person collecting water; the proportion of households where children are involved to some degree in water collection is undoubtedly much higher.

Table 7.1

Households within 15 minutes from a source of drinking water by region and urban/rural areas, 2000–2008 (*latest available*)

	Households within 15 minutes from a source of drinking water (%)		
	Total	**Urban**	**Rural**
Sub-Saharan Africa (40)	**54**	**74**	**42**
Eastern Africa (15)	46	71	33
Middle Africa (6)	51	69	37
Southern Africa (4)	66	89	49
Western Africa (15)	60	75	50
Asia (24)	**84**	**93**	**78**
Central Asia (5)	82	93	72
South Eastern Asia (6)	80	95	86
Southern Asia (4)	83	90	80
Western Asia (8)	88	97	79
Latin America and the Caribbean (13)	**90**	**94**	**83**
Caribbean (5)	85	90	74
Central America (4)	91	95	87
South America (4)	94	97	88
Eastern Europe (7)	**97**	**98**	**95**

Source: Computed by the United Nations Statistics Division based on data from Macro International, Demographic and Health Survey (DHS) reports (2009a); Macro International, Demographic and Health Survey (DHS) STATcompiler (2009b); UNICEF, Multiple Indicator Cluster Survey (MICS) reports (2009).
Note: Unweighted averages; the numbers in brackets indicate the number of countries averaged. The averages calculated for Asia cover countries from the four sub-regions presented in the table and Mongolia (Eastern Asia).

Figure 7.1

Distribution of households by person responsible for water collection, by region and urban/rural areas, 2005–2007 (*latest available*)

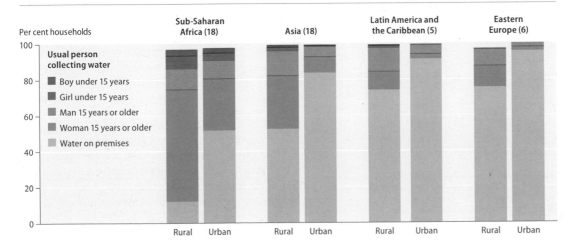

Source: Computed by the United Nations Statistics Division based on data from Macro International, Demographic and Health Survey (DHS) reports (2009a) and UNICEF, Multiple Indicator Cluster Survey (MICS) reports (2009).
Note: Unweighted averages; the numbers in brackets indicate the number of countries averaged. The difference up to 100 per cent is made up by the share of households where a person from outside the household would collect the water or missing information.

Women in rural sub-Saharan Africa expend the most time to bring water home

Women in rural sub-Saharan Africa are the most burdened not only because they are usually the ones in charge of water collection but also because more time is needed in that region to bring the water home (table 7.2). The time needed to go to

Table 7.2

Average time (*in minutes*) **needed to collect water per trip to the source of drinking water by region and rural/urban areas, 2005–2007** (*latest available*)

	Sub-Saharan Africa (13)	Asia (13)	Latin America and the Caribbean (4)	Eastern Europe (7)
National level	34	21	17	15
Urban areas	25	17	19	20
Rural areas	36	23	17	13

Source: Computed by the United Nations Statistics Division based on data from Macro International, Demographic and Health Survey (DHS) reports (2009a) and UNICEF, Multiple Indicator Cluster Survey (MICS) reports (2009).

Note: Unweighted averages; the numbers in brackets indicate the number of countries averaged. Time needed to collect water is measured as the time spent in one trip to go to the source of drinking water, get water and return home.

the source of drinking water, get water and return home is on average 36 minutes in rural areas, compared to 25 minutes in urban areas. However, in rural areas of some countries in the region, the time burden is much greater. For example, one

Table 7.3

Women and men engaged in water collection and average time burden

	Year	Percentage collecting water		Average time burden in population (*minutes per day*)		
		Women	Men	Women	Men	Gender gap
Sub-Saharan Africa						
Benin	1998	73	19	45	12	33
Ghana	1998/99	60	38	41	33	8
Madagascar	2001	44	16	27	9	18
Malawi	2004/05	..	..	54	6	48
South Africa	2000	13	7	8	3	5
Asia						
Lao People's Dem. Rep.	2002/03	..	..	12	6	6
Pakistan	2007	3	1	3	0	3
Central America						
Nicaragua	1998	30	29	38	23	15

Sources: Compiled by the United Nations Statistics Division from World Bank, *Gender, Time Use, and Poverty in Sub-Saharan Africa* (2006) and time use survey reports from national statistical offices of Lao People's Democratic Republic, Nicaragua, Pakistan and South Africa.

Note: Average time burden in population is calculated taking into account those involved in water collection as well as those not involved. Data may not be strictly comparable across countries as the methods involved for data collection may differ.

trip back and forth to the water source takes on average one hour and 22 minutes in rural areas in Somalia and one hour and 11 minutes in rural areas in Mauritania. More than one trip per day may be needed to cover all the household needs and this limits the amount of time that women can spend on other activities, whether income-earning, educational or leisure.

The data presented above, only recently made available through DHS and MICS surveys for a large number of countries from the less developed regions, provide an overview of the role of women in water collection. Still, they offer only a crude measure of women's burden in this area. When available, further information from time use surveys can show the proportion of women and men actually involved in water collection, how much time they spend doing this activity, as well as how the gender-specific time burden is associated with other factors such as age, employment or economic status. However, limited data on time use are available. So far only a small number of countries from the less developed regions – where drinking water on premises is most lacking – have implemented time use surveys and, although disseminated results have been disaggregated by sex, other demographic or socio-economic factors have not been systematically considered.

Nevertheless, time use data for eight countries from the less developed regions confirm that larger proportions of women are involved in water collection and that the average time burden is greater for women than for men (table 7.3). In Benin, for example, 73 per cent of women collect water, compared to only 19 per cent of men. The average woman spends 45 minutes every day on this task, 33 minutes more than a man does. In Madagascar, 44 per cent of women collect water, compared to 16 per cent of men, and spend 18 minutes longer. The average woman in Malawi takes almost an hour a day to collect water, more than three quarters of an hour longer than a man does. The gender gap is lower in countries where low proportions of women and men need to collect water, such as in Pakistan and South Africa.

In rural areas the work burden of water collection is greater than in urban areas and so is the gender gap. For example, to collect water, an average woman from Benin spends about one hour a day if she lives in a village and about a quarter of an hour a day if she lives in a city or town.[10] This is

10 World Bank, 2006.

46 minutes more per day than a man in a village and 10 minutes more per day than a man in a city. In Guinea, women spend on average almost half an hour a day to bring water home in rural areas and 10 minutes a day in urban areas.[11] The daily time burden is greater for women than for men by 22 minutes in rural areas and by 7 minutes in urban areas.

2. Access to firewood

In the less developed regions, a large proportion of households still use firewood for cooking and heating. On average, 66 per cent of households in sub-Saharan Africa, 55 per cent of households in Southern and South-Eastern Asia and 31 per cent of households in Latin America rely on firewood for cooking.[12] The dependency on firewood is particularly high in some African and Asian countries. In sub-Saharan Africa, over 90 per cent of households in Central African Republic, Malawi, Rwanda and Sierra Leone are dependent on firewood. In Asia, more than 75 per cent of households in Cambodia, the Lao People's Democratic Republic and Nepal depend on firewood.

In communities from poor areas affected by deforestation or where nearby forests are protected, women and men may need to take longer and longer trips to collect firewood. For example, in Uganda, as a result of deforestation, the average distance to collect firewood – travelled usually by women and children – increased between 1992 and 2000 from 0.06 km to 0.9 km at the country level.[13] In some villages in India, women used to spend one to two hours per trip to gather firewood in the early 1990s prior to forest protection policies being put in place, but about three to five hours afterwards.[14]

Very few countries have available statistics on how many women and men collect firewood for their household needs and how much time they spend on this work. In addition, even when time use data on firewood collection are available, information is lacking on the purposes for which women and men collect wood – for example, for household needs (cooking and heating), to sell (and gain

income) or as an input for income-earning activities (for example, a bakery or brick kiln). Men, for example, may be more likely than women to collect wood for selling purposes.[15]

Available time use data (table 7.4) show that in some countries women spend more time than men collecting firewood, while in others men spend more time. In Benin, Ghana, Malawi and the Lao People's Democratic Republic, for example, women are more burdened. In Benin, 22 per cent of women collect firewood compared to only 5 per cent of men, and the average time burden is 16 minutes per day for women and 4 minutes for men. By contrast, in Madagascar and Nicaragua, men are more burdened. In Nicaragua, for instance, 34 per cent of men take care of firewood collection compared to 9 per cent of women, and the average time burden is 39 minutes per day for men and 8 minutes for women.

B. Environmental factors with an impact on women's health

Lack of access to clean water and energy has a major impact on women's and men's health. In 2004 almost 2 million deaths were attributable to unsafe water, sanitation and hygiene, and 2 mil-

Table 7.4

Women and men engaged in firewood collection and average time burden

	Year	Percentage collecting firewood		Average time burden in population (*minutes per day*)	
		Women	Men	Women	Men
Africa					
Benin	1998	22	5	16	4
Ghana	1998/99	35	16	37	30
Madagascar	2001	10	15	7	13
Malawi	2004/05	..	..	19	3
Morocco	1997/98	3	..	3	..
South Africa	2000	5	2	5	3
Asia					
Lao People's Dem. Rep.	2002/03	..	..	18	6
Pakistan	2007	4	2	3	2
Central America					
Nicaragua	1998	9	34	8	39

Sources: Compiled by the United Nations Statistics Division from World Bank, *Gender, Time Use, and Poverty in Sub-Saharan Africa* (2006) and time use survey reports from national statistical offices of Lao People's Democratic Republic, Nicaragua, Pakistan and South Africa.

Note: Average time burden in population is calculated taking into account those involved in firewood collection as well as those not involved. Data may not be strictly comparable across countries as the methods involved for data collection may differ.

11 Ibid.

12 Unweighted averages computed by the United Nations Statistics Division based on data from Macro International, 2009a and 2009b; UNICEF, 2009.

13 Uganda Ministry of Finance, Planning and Economic Development, 2003.

14 Agarwal, 2001.

15 Jackson, 1993.

Box 7.1

Estimating the mortality attributable to environmental risk factors

The World Health Organization (WHO) estimates mortality and burden of disease caused by health risk factors. Although the number of such factors is countless, WHO focuses on selected risk factors "which have global spread, for which data are available to estimate population exposures and health outcomes, and for which the means to reduce them are known" (WHO, 2009, p. v). Among the risk factors assessed, six were environment-related: indoor smoke from solid fuels; unsafe water, sanitation and hygiene; urban air pollution; occupational risks; lead exposure; and climate change. Altogether, the six environmental factors accounted for 6.3 million deaths in 2004, about 11 per cent of total number of deaths in that year.

Mortality attributable to a risk factor is estimated by WHO based on three types of information: (a) the proportion of population exposed to the risk factor by level of exposure; (b) the relative risk of specific disease for each exposure level; and (c) the total number of deaths. For example, the number of deaths attributable to indoor smoke is estimated based on (a) data on proportion of population using solid fuels (biomass and coal) for cooking, adjusted by a ventilation factor; (b) information on relative risks of lower respiratory infections, chronic obstructive pulmonary disease and lung cancer, obtained from epidemiological studies; and (c) data on total number of deaths.

Methodologically, the idea is to estimate the proportional reduction in death that would occur if exposure to a selected risk factor were reduced to zero. The fraction of deaths attributed to a selected risk factor is estimated by WHO based on an analysis where the observed level of death under the current distribution of exposure by age, sex and region is compared to the expected level of death if an alternative exposure distribution that would lead to the lowest level of death had applied. In the case of indoor smoke from solid fuels, for example, the alternative exposure distribution is zero.

Sources: WHO, *Global Health Risks: Mortality and Burden of Disease Attributable to Selected Major Risks* (2009) and Ezzati and others, *Comparative Quantification of Health Risks: Global and Regional Burden of Diseases Attributable to Selected Major Risk Factors* (2004).

---

lion more were attributable to indoor smoke from solid fuels.[16] The two factors combined accounted for almost two thirds of all deaths attributable to environmental risks (see box 7.1).

1. Access to improved water and sanitation

Of the almost 2 million deaths in 2004 attributed to unsafe water, sanitation and hygiene[17], 48 per cent were female deaths and 52 per cent were male deaths. Women and men living in the less developed regions were most vulnerable. Almost 8 per cent of the total number of deaths in sub-Saharan Africa and almost 5 per cent in Southern Asia and in Oceania (excluding Australia and New Zealand) were due to unsafe water, sanitation and hygiene, compared to less than 0.1 per cent in the more developed regions.[18]

---

16 WHO, 2009.

17 The estimated number of deaths reflects mainly the disease burden of infectious diarrhoea and a small additional contribution related to schistosomiasis, trachoma, ascariasis, trichuriasis and hookworm disease. Although it is recognized that unsafe water, sanitation and hygiene are important determinants in a number of additional diseases such as malaria, yellow fever, dengue, hepatitis A, hepatitis E, typhoid fever or others, they were not included in the above estimate (Prüss-Üstün and others, 2004).

18 WHO, 2009.

> There have been improvements in access to safe water and sanitation, but some regions are still lagging behind

Although access to improved drinking water and sanitation is increasing at the world level, some regions are still lagging behind. It is estimated that in 2008, 87 per cent of the world's population used an improved drinking water source, an increase of 10 percentage points from 1990.[19] All regions of the world gained in access to improved drinking water over the period except for Oceania (excluding Australia and New Zealand), which remained at about the same level of 50 per cent of the population. In sub-Saharan Africa, 60 per cent of the population in 2008 had access to improved drinking water, an increase of 11 percentage points since 1990.

In 2008, 61 per cent of the world's population used improved sanitation facilities, an increase of 7 percentage points since 1990.[20] The regions with lowest access to improved sanitation facilities remained sub-Saharan Africa (31 per cent) and Southern Asia (36 per cent), although improvements were seen in both regions (3 and 11 percent-

---

19 WHO and UNICEF Joint Monitoring Programme for Water Supply and Sanitation, 2010.

20 Ibid.

age points respectively). Although declining, open defecation is still substantial in the two regions, resulting in considerable health risks for women and men. In 2008, 44 per cent of the population in Southern Asia was still practicing open defecation (a decline of 22 percentage points since 1990) and 27 per cent in sub-Saharan Africa (a decline of 9 percentage points from 1990). At the world level, 17 per cent of the population was estimated as practicing open defecation in 2008, a decline of 8 percentage points since 1990.

2. Use of solid fuels for cooking and indoor smoke pollution

There are increased health risks for people exposed to smoke from solid fuels, especially women

Almost 2 million deaths a year were attributable to indoor smoke from solid fuel in 2004. More than 1 million (55 per cent) were female deaths and less than 900,000 (45 per cent) were male deaths.[21] Women and men living in the less developed regions were most vulnerable. Almost 6 per cent of the total number of deaths in Eastern Asia and almost 5 per cent in Southern Asia and sub-Saharan Africa were due to indoor smoke from solid fuels, compared to less than 0.2 per cent in the more developed regions.[22]

Strong evidence suggests that women and men exposed to smoke from solid fuels have an increased risk of developing acute lower respiratory infections, chronic obstructive pulmonary disease and lung cancer (table 7.5). A WHO meta-analysis of epidemiological studies reviewing the impact of exposure to indoor air pollution on health[23] concluded that women over 30 years who were exposed to solid fuel smoke are on average about three times more likely to develop chronic obstructive pulmonary disease than women who had not been exposed. In comparison, the risk for men exposed to solid fuel smoke increases less than twice. Also, women exposed to coal smoke are 1.9 times more likely to develop lung cancer than women not exposed, and exposed men are 1.5 times more likely to develop lung cancer than men not exposed. Small children, often carried on their mothers' backs during cooking or when being taken care of indoors, are 2.3 times more likely to develop acute lower respiratory

Table 7.5

Relative risks for health outcomes from exposure to solid fuel smoke

Strength of evidence	Health outcome	Sex and age group	Relative risk
Strong evidence			
	Acute lower respiratory infection	Children < 5	2.3
	Chronic obstructive pulmonary disease	Women ≥ 30	3.2
	Lung cancer (from exposure to coal smoke)	Women ≥ 30	1.9
Strong evidence for specific groups only			
	Chronic obstructive pulmonary disease	Men ≥ 30	1.8
	Lung cancer (from exposure to coal smoke)	Men ≥ 30	1.5
Limited evidence			
	Lung cancer (from exposure to biomass smoke)	Women ≥ 30	1.5
	Asthma	Children 5–14	1.6
	Asthma	All ≥ 15	1.2
	Cataracts	All ≥ 15	1.3
	Tuberculosis	All ≥ 15	1.5

Source: Desai and others, Indoor smoke from solid fuels: assessing the environmental burden of disease at national and local levels (2004).

Note: Relative risk is defined as the probability of the health outcome in the population exposed to smoke from solid fuels relative to the probability of the health outcome in the population not exposed to smoke from solid fuels. For confidence interval values of the relative risk of health outcomes shown, see Desai and others (2004).

infection (a disease with a high risk of mortality in developing countries) when exposed to solid fuel smoke compared to children not exposed.

Three factors are mainly responsible for varying levels of exposure to indoor smoke for women and men across countries[24] and, consequently, for varying levels of relative health risks. The first is the type of fuel used for cooking. The level of indoor smoke pollution varies from practically none when electricity is used, to medium for gas and liquid fuels such as kerosene and liquid petroleum gas, to a high level when solid fuels are used. Among the solid fuels, biomass fuels – such as animal dung, crop residues and wood – produce the highest levels of pollutants, followed by coal and charcoal. When burnt, solid fuels emit substantial amounts of pollutants with health-damaging potential, including particulate matter, carbon monoxide, nitrogen oxide, sulphur oxide and benzene.

The second factor is related to ventilation. The concentration of pollutants is lower when the cooking takes place outdoors and/or when improved stoves with a chimney or hood are utilized instead of an open fire or a stove with no chimney or hood. The third factor is the different amount of time spent indoors and near the fire by women and men. Compared to men, women spend more time indoors and more time near the fire while cook-

---

21 WHO, 2009.

22 Ibid.

23 Desai and others, 2004.

24 WHO, 2006.

ing, and are therefore more exposed to high-intensity pollution episodes. Statistics for these three main determinants of exposure to indoor smoke are presented in the following sections.

Use of solid fuels for cooking

Several regions of the world still rely heavily on solid fuels for cooking

---

Sub-Saharan Africa, Southern Asia and South-Eastern Asia are the regions that still rely heavily on solid fuels for cooking. This is the case for, on average, more than 80 per cent of households in sub-Saharan Africa (table 7.6). In 21 of the 38 countries with available data in that region, over 90 per cent of households cook with solid fuels. A similar situation is seen for some countries in Southern and South-Eastern Asia. Solid fuels are used by more than two thirds of households in India, Mongolia, Pakistan and Viet Nam; more than 80 per cent in Nepal; and more than 90 per cent in Bangladesh, Cambodia and the Lao People's Democratic Republic. The lowest use of solid fuels for cooking is found in Northern Africa and in the more developed regions other than Eastern Europe, with the percentage of households relying on solid fuels for cooking close to zero.[25]

Table 7.6

Households using solid fuels for cooking by region and urban/rural areas, 2005–2007 (*latest available*)

	Households using solid fuels for cooking (%)		
	Total	Urban	Rural
Sub-Saharan Africa (38)	82	66	95
Eastern Africa (14)	85	68	97
Middle Africa (6)	73	57	94
Southern Africa (3)	58	12	83
Western Africa (15)	89	78	96
Asia (22)	43	22	56
Central Asia (5)	21	5	34
South-Eastern Asia (5)	69	44	80
Southern Asia (4)	78	38	93
Western Asia (7)	16	3	27
Latin America and the Caribbean (10)	33	17	56
Eastern Europe (8)	29	13	47

Source: Computed by the United Nations Statistics Division based on data from Macro International, Demographic and Health Survey (DHS) reports (2009a) and UNICEF, Multiple Indicator Cluster Survey (MICS) reports (2009).
Note: Unweighted averages; the numbers in brackets indicate the number of countries averaged. The averages calculated for Asia cover countries from the four sub-regions presented in the table and Mongolia (Eastern Asia).

25 Desai and others, 2004.

Overall, households in rural areas are more likely to use solid fuels than those in urban areas (table 7.6), although urban-rural disparities are larger in some countries than in others. In sub-Saharan Africa, Southern Asia and South-Eastern Asia, the overwhelming majority of rural households use solid fuels for cooking. The urban areas in some countries from those regions also have high proportions of households that do so. For example, in the United Republic of Tanzania, 99 per cent of rural households and 87 per cent of urban households use solid fuels. In the Gambia, the corresponding proportions are 97 per cent and 84 per cent, respectively. In the Lao People's Democratic Republic, all rural households and 91 per cent of urban households use solid fuels for cooking. In some other countries, however, urban-rural disparities are large. In Namibia, for example, 90 per cent of rural households use solid fuels for cooking, but only 16 per cent of urban households do. In Nepal, 92 per cent of rural households and 39 per cent of urban households use solid fuels.

Ventilation factors: outdoor cooking and type of stoves

In countries where households rely on solid fuels for cooking, cooking usually takes place indoors rather than outdoors.[26] For example, in Ethiopia, 95 per cent of households use solid fuels for cooking, but only 6 per cent have the cooking area outdoors. In Nepal, 83 per cent of households use solid fuels for cooking, but only 5 per cent cook outdoors. On the other hand, Liberia, where 99 per cent of households use solid fuels for cooking, has one of the highest percentages of households cooking outdoors (57 per cent).

Only a small proportion of households using solid fuels in sub-Saharan Africa and Southern and South-Eastern Asia have improved stoves that would reduce the exposure to indoor smoke

---

The use of improved stoves as opposed to an open fire/stove with no chimney or hood varies among regions (figure 7.2) In countries in sub-Saharan Africa and Southern and South-Eastern Asia, only a small proportion of households using solid fuels have improved stoves that would reduce the exposure to indoor smoke. For

26 Data compiled by the United Nations Statistics Division from Macro International, 2009a and UNICEF, 2009.

example, in Ethiopia, out of the 95 per cent of households using solid fuels for cooking, only 3 per cent have improved stoves. Similarly, in Nepal, out of the 83 per cent of households using solid fuels, only 5 per cent have improved stoves. On the other hand, in Guinea-Bissau, more than half of the 98 per cent of households using solid fuels for cooking have improved stoves. In countries in Eastern Europe and Central and Western Asia, although significant proportions of households use solid fuels for cooking, the exposure to indoor smoke is reduced through the utilization of improved stoves.

More people living in rural than in urban areas are exposed to indoor smoke from solid fuels

Women and men living in rural areas are more exposed to indoor smoke than people living in urban areas, not only because they are more likely to use solid fuels for cooking but also because they are more likely to use open fires or traditional stoves with no chimney or hood (figure 7.3). In countries such as Burundi, India, Nepal, Viet Nam and Zimbabwe, people living in cities have considerably better access to cleaner fuels and improved stoves compared to people living in rural areas. However, in some other countries the percentage of households with high potential exposure to indoor smoke from solid fuels is almost as high in urban as it is in rural areas. In Lao People's Democratic Republic, Malawi, Sierra Leone, Somalia and Togo over 80 per cent of households from urban areas and over 85 per cent of households from rural areas use solid fuels for cooking on open fires or traditional stoves with no chimney.

The type of stove used for cooking and the place of cooking (indoors or outdoors) have a considerable impact on health outcomes. A study in central Kenya showed a big reduction in acute respiratory infection (ARI) and acute lower respiratory infection (ALRI) rates when a switch was made from an open fire indoors to certain types of stoves inside and when the place of cooking was moved from indoors to outdoors[27] (table 7.7). Women benefited more than men from changing the type of stove than by changing the cooking place from indoors to outdoors, due to the fact that they spend more time close to the fire while cooking and are therefore more

27 Ezzati and Kammen, 2002.

Figure 7.2

Households using solid fuels for cooking by type of stove, 2005–2007 (*latest available*)

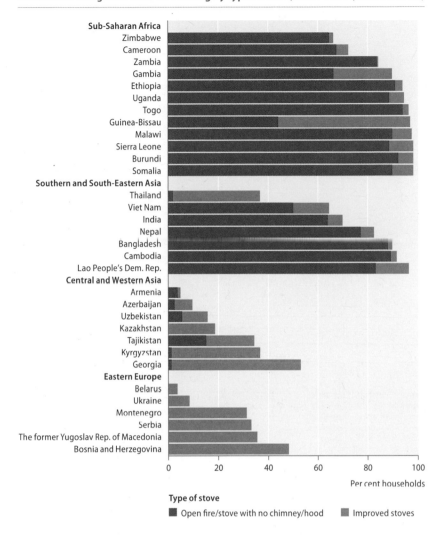

Source: Compiled by the United Nations Statistics Division from Macro International, Demographic and Health Survey (DHS) reports (2009a) and UNICEF, Multiple Indicator Cluster Survey (MICS) reports (2009).

exposed to high-intensity pollution episodes both indoors and outdoors. Men benefited from changes in the stove and cooking area, since they are more likely to be affected by the smoke trapped indoors during the hours of sleep than by the pollution emissions during cooking time. For example, switching indoors from an open fire to a ceramic woodstove reduced the ARI and ALRI rates for women by 14 per cent and 15 per cent respectively, while for men it was by 2 and 10 per cent respectively. On the other hand, having the cooking area outdoors as opposed to inside reduced the ARI and ALRI rates for women by 15 and 17 per cent respectively, and for men by 50 and 38 per cent respectively.

Figure 7.3

Households using solid fuels on open fire or stove with no chimney or hood, by urban/rural areas – selected countries with the highest values, 2005–2007 *(latest available)*

■ Urban
■ Rural

Source: Compiled by the United Nations Statistics Division from Macro International, Demographic and Health Survey (DHS) reports (2009a) and UNICEF, Multiple Indicator Cluster Survey (MICS) reports (2009).

Time spent cooking and near a fire

Women are more exposed than men to smoke from cooking with solid fuels

Because they spend more time than men cooking (as shown in Chapter 4 – Work), women are more exposed to smoke from cooking with solid fuels, especially when using open fires or a stove without a chimney or hood. For example, in the Lao People's Democratic Republic, where 84 per cent of households use solid fuels in an open fire or stove with no chimney or hood, a woman on average spends 54 minutes a day cooking, while a man spends only 6 minutes. In Benin, 93 per cent of households use solid fuels for cooking, and women spend on average one hour and 15 minutes a day cooking compared to men's 6 minutes.

In central Kenya, adult women, girls aged 5–14 and children less than 5 years spend more time indoors and more time near a fire compared to adult men and 5–14-year-old boys[28] (figure 7.4). For example, a woman aged 15–49 spends more than five hours a day near a fire, compared to less than an hour for a man in the same age group. A girl (5–14 years old) spends more than three hours a day close to a fire, while a boy spends less than two hours. Similarly, in Bangladesh (in 2004), an adult woman (20–60 years old) spends almost four hours a day in the cooking area while an adult man spends less than a quarter of an hour.[29] A teenage girl (13–19 years old) spends almost two and a half hours per day in the cooking area, while a teenage boy spends less than 20 minutes. Children under 5 years old of both sexes spend about an hour a day in the cooking area.

3. Natural disasters and their impact on number of female and male deaths

The lives of thousands of women and men are lost worldwide every year as a result of natural disasters. Between 2000 and 2008, an average of 5,600 deaths per year occurred due to floods, 3,500 due to storms/tropical cyclones and 1,700 due to extreme temperature.[30] These averages do not include the number of deaths caused by extreme temperature in 2003, when the Euro-

Table 7.7

Reduction in acute respiratory infections and acute lower respiratory infections for women and men aged 15–49 by switching the cooking from indoor open fires to different indoor and outdoor stoves, Central Kenya, Laikipia District, Mpala Ranch, 1999

	Disease rate (%)	Disease reduction (%) by switching to...			
	Open fire inside	Ceramic woodstove inside	Charcoal stove inside	Open fire outside	Ceramic woodstove outside
Acute respiratory infection					
Female	7	14	68	15	37
Male	4	2	62	50	58
Acute lower respiratory infection					
Female	2	15	65	17	43
Male	1	10	45	38	42

Source: Ezzati and Kammen, Evaluating the health benefits of transitions in household energy technologies in Kenya (2002).
Note: Disease rate was calculated as the percentage of weekly examinations (in a two-year period) during which a person was diagnosed with acute respiratory infection or acute lower respiratory infection.

28 Ibid.

29 Dasgupta and others, 2006.

30 Computed by the United Nations Statistics Division based on data from the Centre for Research on the Epidemiology of Disasters (CRED) and Universite Catholique de Louvain, Emergency Events Database EM-DAT, 2009.

pean heat wave struck, or the number of deaths caused by storms in 2008, when Cyclone Nargis hit Myanmar. Those extreme weather events drove the number of casualties exceptionally high. The number of deaths due to extreme temperature in 2003 climbed to about 75,000, and the number due to storms in 2008 escalated to over 142,000. It is predicted that climate change will further increase the number of human deaths from heat waves, floods, storms and droughts, as these extreme weather events will increase in frequency and intensity.[31]

In this context, as one of the agreed conclusions on the mitigation of natural disasters during its forty-sixth session, in 2002, the Commission on the Status of Women urged governments and relevant international agencies to develop national gender-sensitive indicators and analyse gender differences with regard to disaster occurrence and associated losses and risks as well as vulnerability reduction.[32] Yet, systematic collection and compilation of statistics on gender and natural disasters are lacking at the international level. In general, the availability and reliability of data on disaster occurrence and its effect on people is affected by constraints of time, funding and complexity of situation, as well as by the lack of standardized definitions and methodological tools of data collection.[33] However, some data on victims of natural disasters disaggregated by sex are available for a small number of countries and for certain weather events. Such cases, presented in the following paragraphs, suggest that mortality differences by sex may vary from one country to another and by type of hazard.

Recent information on the impact of the tsunami in December 2004 suggests that women and girls may be more vulnerable to some natural disasters as a result of less access to information and life skills development and culturally constrained mobility of women outside of their homes.[34] Many more women than men died in several locations particularly hit by the tsunami.[35] In Indonesia, in four villages from North Aceh district, female deaths accounted for 77 per cent of total deaths. In India, female deaths represented 73 per cent of the total deaths in Cuddalore and 56 per cent in Nagapattinam district of Tamil Nadu.

31 IPCC, 2007; Confalonieri and others, 2007.
32 Commission on the Status of Women, 2002.
33 Tschoegl and others, 2006; Guha-Sapir and Below, 2002.
34 Oxfam International, 2005.
35 Ibid.

Figure 7.4

Time spent indoors and near fire by age group and sex in central Kenya, Laikipia District, Mpala Ranch, 1999

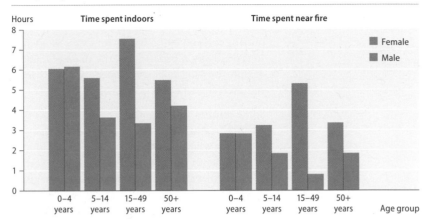

Source: Ezzati and Kammen, Evaluating the health benefits of transitions in household energy technologies in Kenya (2002).
Note: The results are averages among different days, and the time calculated refers to the interval between 6:30 a.m. and 8:30 p.m.

The census conducted in Sri Lanka in the areas affected by the tsunami revealed that women were the majority of casualties.[36] Out of the more than 13,000 dead and missing persons, 65 per cent were women. The share of females in the total number of deaths was highest in the age group 19–29 years (figure 7.5), 79 per cent, suggesting a combination of increased vulnerability of women staying home with children at the time of the sea-level rise and the more fortunate situation of some of the young men who were far away from the coastline, fishing at sea or out in the agricultural fields.[37]

Figure 7.5

Distribution of deaths due to the 2004 tsunami in Sri Lanka by sex within age category

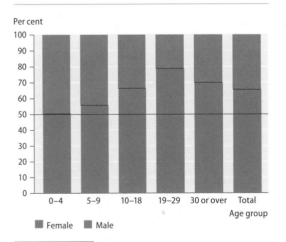

Source: Computed by the United Nations Statistics Division based on data from Sri Lanka Department of Census and Statistics, Sri Lanka Census on the Persons and Buildings affected by the Tsunami 2004 (2005).

36 Sri Lanka Department of Census and Statistics, 2005.
37 Oxfam International, 2005.

Similarly, the Post-Nargis Joint Assessment in Myanmar concluded that women were overrepresented among the people who died or went missing during the May 2008 cyclone. Out of the over 85,000 people dead and 53,000 people still missing in June 2008, 61 per cent were women.[38] In the villages most affected, the share of females dead or missing in the age category 18–60 years was even higher at 68 per cent.

Some studies indicate that the excess mortality due to the 2003 summer heat wave in Europe was higher for women and older persons. For example, the number of excess deaths estimated for women in Portugal was more than twice the number estimated for men,[39] while mortality in France was 70 per cent higher than expected for women and 40 per cent higher than expected for men.[40] Higher excess mortality for older persons and women was also reported in three cities in Italy (table 7.8).[41] For example, compared to values recorded in previous years, the number of deaths during the heat wave in Rome was higher than expected by 26 per cent for persons aged 75–84, and by 38 per cent for persons over 85 years. The number of female deaths was higher than expected by 27 per cent and the number of male deaths by 10 per cent. It is not yet clear how much of the sex difference is due to the fact that women are overrepresented among

older persons and how much is due to other factors (see Chapter 1 – Population and families for more information on sex distribution at older ages).

While the extreme cases of the 2004 tsunami, the 2008 cyclone in Myanmar and the 2003 summer heat wave in Europe underline the vulnerability of women, natural hazards in other regions of the world caused larger shares of male deaths, thus suggesting that gender differences may vary by type of hazard and across regions. For example, in Nicaragua and El Salvador, men represented 54 per cent and 57 per cent respectively of those killed by the 1998 hurricane Mitch.[42] Also, a study on male-female flood death ratios in Australia showed that out of the 1,513 fatalities reported by sex between 1930 and 1996, 81 per cent were male.[43] Over the period studied, the male-female death rate ratio fluctuated between 10:1 and 1:1, and although it declined overall, it continued to disfavour men, suggesting that men were more inclined to risk-taking or more involved in activities that would put them at risk.

Similar findings to those from Australia are found in statistics from the United States of America on natural hazards. More than 60 per cent of the total deaths due to natural hazards in 2000–2008 were male (figure 7.6). Among different types of

Table 7.8

Excess mortality by age group and by sex in Rome, Milan and Turin during 2003 summer heat wave

	Rome		Milan		Turin	
	Number of deaths	%	Number of deaths	%	Number of deaths	%
Age category						
0–64	-58	-6	-35	-9	21	7
65–74	51	5	-23	-5	58	16
75–84	397	26	305	43	213	40
85+	554	38	312	40	285	50
Sex						
Male	246	10	141	12	215	25
Female	698	27	418	33	362	40
Total	944	19	559	23	577	33

Source: Michelozzi and others, Heat waves in Italy (2005).
Note: Expected daily mortality was computed as the mean daily value from a specific reference period: 1995–2002 for Rome and Milan and 1998–2002 for Turin. Daily excess mortality was calculated as the difference between the number of deaths observed on a given day and the smoothed daily average for the previous years. Negative figures are shown when daily mortality observed was lower than expected.

Figure 7.6

Average share of female and male deaths in total deaths due to natural hazards for selected types of hazard, United States of America, 2000–2008

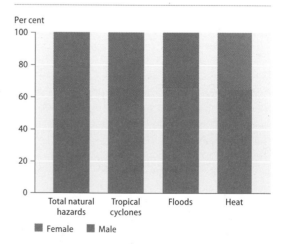

Source: Computed by the United Nations Statistics Division based on data from United States National Weather Service, Natural hazard statistics (2009).
Note: Natural hazards included for the total are cold, heat, flood, lightning, tornado, tropical cyclone, wind and winter storms.

38 Myanmar Government, Association of Southeast Asian Nations and the United Nations, 2008.

39 Nogueira and others, 2005.

40 Pirard and others, 2005.

41 Michelozzi and others, 2005.

42 Delaney and Shrader, 2000.

43 Coates, 1999.

natural hazards, floods and heat were associated with a larger share of males in total deaths (65 per cent for each type), compared to tropical cyclones/hurricanes (54 per cent).

C. Involvement of women and men in preserving the environment

1. Awareness of environmental problems

As reflected in the fourth assessment of the Intergovernmental Panel on Climate Change (IPCC), the vast majority of scientists agree that emissions of greenhouse gases due to human activity, of which carbon dioxide and methane are the most significant, are already causing climate change.[44] In addition, carbon dioxide emissions are continuing to rise, highlighting the urgent need to address the issue.[45] The level of global carbon dioxide emissions reached 29 billion metric tons in 2006, 31 per cent above the 1990 level. Countries from the more developed regions still have the highest emissions per capita, about 12 metric tons of carbon dioxide per person per year, compared to about three metric tons per person per year in the less developed regions. Loss of environmental resources are also an increasing concern. According to the 2009 MDG report, only 12 per cent of terrestrial and marine areas were under some form of protection in 2008, the number of species threatened with extinction continued to grow and the stress on water resources was severe.[46]

Large proportions of women and men around the world recognize that the global environmental problems are very serious

---

Across the world, environmental problems are now recognized to be very serious by large proportions of women and men. In most of the countries with available internationally comparable data[47] more than half of the people are concerned with regard to three global environmental issues: global warming or the greenhouse effect; loss of plant or animal species; and water pollution (table 7.9). Among these issues, the pollution of rivers, lakes and oceans was considered as very serious by the largest proportions of women and men, reaching

---

[44] IPCC, 2007.

[45] United Nations, 2009.

[46] Ibid.

[47] Forty-four countries covered by national representative sample surveys conducted within the fifth round of the World Values Survey (2009).

Table 7.9

Proportion of persons considering as very serious three major environmental issues at the global level, by region and sex, 2005–2007 (*latest available*)

	Global warming or the greenhouse effect		Loss of plant or animal species or biodiversity		Pollution of rivers, lakes and oceans	
	Women (%)	Men (%)	Women (%)	Men (%)	Women (%)	Men (%)
Africa (9)	57	57	55	56	67	67
Asia (12)	52	55	46	50	54	56
Latin America and the Caribbean (6)	71	73	74	74	83	83
Eastern Europe (7)	60	59	56	55	72	71
Western Europe and other developed countries (10)	65	57	56	50	72	65

Source: Computed by the United Nations Statistics Division based on data from World Values Survey, Fifth wave of the World Values Survey. Online data analysis (2009).

Note: Unweighted averages; the numbers in brackets indicate the number of countries averaged. Women and men surveyed were asked how serious ("very serious", "somewhat serious", "not very serious" or "not serious at all") they considered the environmental problems listed in the table to be in the world as a whole. Only percentages for those who answered "very serious" are shown in the table.

about 90 per cent in countries such as Argentina, Egypt and Trinidad and Tobago. In only a few countries – Malaysia, Thailand and Zambia – was the proportion of women and men who defined the three environmental issues as very serious only about a third or less.[48]

In most of the countries from the less developed regions, there are no significant differences by sex in the perception of the environmental problems as being very serious. By contrast, higher proportions of women than men define the environmental problems as very serious in most of the countries with available data from the more developed regions except Eastern Europe. These are Australia, Finland, Germany, Japan, Sweden, Switzerland and the United States of America. For example, in Sweden, 83 per cent of women and 66 per cent of men thought that the pollution of rivers, lakes and oceans was very serious. In Finland the corresponding proportions of concerned women and men were 68 per cent and 55 per cent, respectively. In the United States of America, 51 per cent of women and 40 per cent of men considered the loss of plant or animal species or biodiversity to be very serious. In Australia, 69 per cent of women and 58 per cent of men considered as very serious global warming or the greenhouse effect.[49]

---

[48] World Values Survey, 2009.

[49] Ibid.

Table 7.10

Share of women in national coordinating bodies for the implementation of the United Nations Convention to Combat Desertification, 2002–2006 (*latest available*)

0–9%	10–19%	20–29%	30–39%	40–49%	50–59%
Africa					
Angola Benin Chad Mali	Côte d'Ivoire Djibouti Eritrea Guinea Guinea-Bissau Kenya	Algeria Burkina Faso Congo Mauritania Namibia Niger	Botswana Cape Verde Central African Rep. Comoros Gabon Madagascar South Africa Uganda Zambia Zimbabwe	Swaziland	Lesotho
Asia					
Sri Lanka Thailand	Indonesia Lebanon Turkmenistan Viet Nam	China Iran (Islamic Republic of)			
Latin America and the Caribbean					
	Costa Rica Saint Vincent and the Grenadines	Paraguay Peru	Panama	Brazil	Argentina Cuba
Oceania					
		Fiji		Samoa	

Source: Compiled by the United Nations Statistics Division from UNCCD, National reports on the implementation of the United Nations Convention to Combat Desertification (2009).

Although large proportions of women and men recognize that environmental problems in the world are very serious, public awareness of environmental issues at national or more local levels is still lacking, as indicated by some countries during the review conducted for the forty-ninth session of the Commission on the Status of Women.[50] As emphasized by other countries, there is also a lack of awareness about the harmful effects of environmental change and degradation on women.[51]

2. Participation in environmental decision-making

Women are underrepresented in environmental decision-making

Involvement of women in environmental decision-making at all levels is a key step in ensuring that women's issues and gender perspectives on the environment are included in policy-making

---

50 United Nations, 2004.

51 Ibid.

from local to national and global level.[52] However, as presented in Chapter 5 – Power and decision-making, women still hold a minority of decision-making positions in most public and private institutions. Consistent with these findings, women participate less than men in high-level decision-making related to environmental issues in many countries. For example, a survey on gender mainstreaming among 17 environment ministries conducted in 2006 showed that women made up 41 per cent of the entire staff of the ministries but only 27 per cent of managerial positions.[53]

The underrepresentation of women in environmental decision-making is also illustrated by the low share of women in national coordinating bodies for the implementation of the United Nations Convention to Combat Desertification[54]. The share of women in the Convention coordinating bodies varied greatly among the countries with available data, ranging from 0 per cent in Chad to over 50 per cent in Argentina, Cuba and Lesotho (table 7.10). Women were less than 30 per cent of the members in more than half of the African countries and in all the Asian countries with available data.

Women's involvement in high-level decision-making related to the environment continues to be hampered by limited access to formal training. As shown in Chapter 3 – Education, science and agriculture are two of the tertiary fields of education where women are underrepresented in most countries. Further disaggregated data within the field of study, available for a few countries, also illustrate the point. For example, women represented only 18 per cent of college graduates in environmental protection in Croatia in 2006;[55] 27 per cent of college graduates in environment science in Nigeria in 2005;[56] and 25 per cent of students enrolled for the higher diploma and certificate in water at the Kenya Water Institute between 2000 and 2004.[57]

Analysis of the role of women and men in protecting the environment at more local levels of decision-making – at community level, in local

---

52 United Nations, 1995.

53 UNEP, 2007.

54 This is one of the few major conventions on natural resource issues that explicitly addresses the participation of women in environmental decision-making.

55 Croatia Central Bureau of Statistics, 2008.

56 Nigeria National Bureau of Statistics, 2005.

57 UNESCO World Water Assessment Programme, 2005.

non-governmental or grass-roots organizations – and through day-to-day activities is hampered by a lack of sex-disaggregated data, particularly in the less developed regions. In some instances, such data are available only for women, thus limiting the gender analysis. Some information on women's and men's behaviour in the area of environmental protection is available, but mainly for countries from the more developed regions. For example, a review covering Western Euro-pean countries, Australia and the United States of America showed that women tend to be more environmentally friendly with regard to recy-cling; choice of public transport for commuting; choice of smaller, less polluting and more efficient cars; and choice of organic food.[58] These gender-specific choices are connected to some extent with the specific household and social roles of women and men. Nevertheless, such information can be used in maximizing policy effectiveness.[59]

---

[58] OECD, 2008
[59] UNEP, 2005.

Chapter 8
Poverty

Key findings

- Households of lone mothers with young children are more likely to be poor than households of lone fathers with young children.
- Women are more likely to be poor than men when living in one-person households in many countries from both the more developed and the less developed regions.
- Women are overrepresented among the older poor in the more developed regions.
- Existing statutory and customary laws limit women's access to land and other types of property in most countries in Africa and about half the countries in Asia.
- Fewer women than men have cash income in the less developed regions, and a significant proportion of married women have no say in how their cash earnings are spent.
- Married women from the less developed regions do not fully participate in intrahousehold decision-making on spending, particularly in African countries and in poorer households.

Introduction

Poverty is a multi-dimensional phenomenon. The Beijing Platform for Action recognized that "poverty has various manifestations, including lack of income and productive resources sufficient to ensure sustainable livelihoods; hunger and malnutrition; ill health; limited or lack of access to education and other basic services; increased morbidity and mortality from illness; homelessness and inadequate housing; unsafe environments; and social discrimination and exclusion. It is also characterized by a lack of participation in decision-making and in civil, social and cultural life".[1] Thus, while the economic dimension remains central, other factors such as lack of opportunities, vulnerabilities and social exclusion are recognized as important in defining poverty.[2] The use of a broad concept of poverty is considered essential for integrating gender into countries' poverty reduction strategies as well as for monitoring, from a gender perspective, progress towards achieving the first Millennium Development Goal (MDG) of eradicating extreme poverty and hunger.[3]

This chapter considers the available statistics on poverty from a gender perspective. The first part is based on a traditional concept of poverty, as measured by consumption or income at household level. Poverty data are presented disaggregated as far as possible by sex, by sex of the head of household and by household type. The review shows that simple disaggregation of poverty by sex results in small gender gaps; however, the gender gap may be underestimated by not taking into account intrahousehold inequality. Furthermore, when female- and male-headed households are examined, consistent gender differences appear only when these are further disaggregated – for example, female or male one-person households and households of female or male lone parents with children. The second part of the chapter looks at statistics at individual level. Women's poverty is seen through aspects of control over household resources as reflected by property ownership, cash income and participation in intrahousehold decision-making on spending.

---

1 United Nations, 1995a, para. 47. This characterization of poverty was first stated in the Copenhagen Programme of Action of the World Summit for Social Development (United Nations, 1995b, Annex II, para. 19).

2 United Nations, 2009.

3 World Bank, 2003.

Other individual-level statistics that may be considered under a broad concept of poverty are covered in other chapters of this report. Time use data are reviewed in Chapter 1 – Population and families and Chapter 4 – Work. Women's vulnerable employment is also presented in the latter. Statistics on human capabilities such as nutrition and good health, on the one hand, and education, on the other, are covered in Chapter 2 – Health and Chapter 3 – Education, respectively.

The conclusions of this chapter are limited by the lack of comparable household-level poverty statistics across countries and regions. First, data are not available for countries in all regions. Data disaggregated by sex of the household members, by sex of the head of household and by type of household are not regularly produced by all countries, and they are not systematically compiled at global level. However, such data are estimated or compiled by regional agencies in Europe and Latin America and the Caribbean, and consequently data on poverty incidence disaggregated by sex for almost all countries in those regions are presented in the chapter. Data are also available disaggregated by sex of the head of household and type of household in Latin America and the Caribbean, and by type of household in Europe. In contrast, poverty data compiled for this report cover only a small number of countries in Africa and Asia and none of the countries in Oceania. In addition, data on other monetary measures of poverty such as the poverty gap and severity of poverty are seldom available disaggregated by sex, by type of

household and by sex of the head of household, especially in the less developed regions.

Second, poverty data used in the chapter are not comparable from one region to another and across countries, with the exception of those for countries in Latin America and the Caribbean. Cross-country comparison is hampered by the use of different poverty lines, differences in the measurement of income or consumption aggregates, and various practices in adjusting for differences in age and sex composition of households. All these issues may have further consequences, not yet fully understood, for the assessment of gender differences in poverty. The choice of a certain poverty line, for example, may influence the extent of the gender gap in poverty (see, for example, box 8.4).

A. Household-level poverty

1. Poverty data disaggregated by sex

In 2005, 1.4 billion people from developing countries were living below the international poverty line of $1.25 a day, 0.4 billion less than in 1990.[4] While the share of people living on less than $1.25 a day decreased from 42 per cent in 1990 to 25 per cent in 2005, regions did not benefit proportionally from this substantial decline. The greatest reduction was estimated for East Asia and Pacific[5] – the only region consistently on track to meet the MDG target of halving the 1990 poverty rates by 2015 – where the number of people living on less than $1.25 a day decreased during this period by almost 0.6 billion while the poverty rate fell from 55 per cent to 17 per cent. Much of the decline was contributed by China. At the other extreme, sub-Saharan Africa lagged behind the other regions in poverty reduction: the poverty rate decreased by only 7 percentage points, from 58 per cent in 1990 to 51 per cent in 2005, while the number of poor increased by 91 million due to population increase.

Simple disaggregation of poverty by sex without taking into account intrahousehold inequality results in small but probably underestimated gender gaps

---

While estimates of poverty rates and the number of poor are available, based either on international

---

[4] World Bank, 2009.

[5] Weighted regional aggregates based on the World Bank regions as calculated by the World Bank (2009).

Box 8.1
Poverty line and poverty rate

The new international extreme poverty line set by the World Bank in 2008 is $1.25 a day in 2005 PPP (purchasing power parity) terms, and it represents the mean of the national poverty lines used in the poorest 15 countries ranked by per capita consumption. The revision of the international poverty line and corresponding estimated poverty data reflects new data on PPPs compiled in the 2005 round of the International Comparison Program.

A poverty line may be internationally defined in a comparable manner, as is the $1.25 a day line, or nationally specific. It may refer to an absolute or to a relative standard. An absolute poverty line usually reflects a minimum cost necessary to cover basic caloric and non-caloric needs, without reference to social context or norms. A relative poverty line is defined relative to the average or median income or consumption in a particular society.

The poverty rate (or poverty incidence or headcount index) is the share of population living in households with income or consumption expenditure below the poverty line.

Box 8.2
Working poor

Working poor or in-work poor are defined as those individuals who are employed but nevertheless live in households whose total income is below the poverty line. The proportion of people in employment living below the poverty line is one of the four MDG indicators used to monitor progress toward achieving "full and productive employment and decent work for all, including women and young people", within MDG 1 of eradicating extreme poverty and hunger.

The International Labour Organization (ILO) regularly publishes global and regional estimates of the working poor based on a macroeconomic estimation model; however, data produced are not sex-disaggregated. A new effort to provide estimates of the working poor is currently being undertaken by ILO and the World Bank, this time based on household surveys. The pilot exercise used data from nationally representative surveys in eight countries from the less developed regions: Benin (2003), Bhutan (2003), Burundi (1998), Congo (2005), Democratic Republic of the Congo (2005), Kenya (2005), Mali (2006) and Niger (2005). Poverty rates were calculated based on the international poverty line of $1.25 per day and were disaggregated by sex. The results show that in some of the countries the poverty rates for employed women over 15 years are higher than the corresponding rates for employed men. The largest differences by sex are observed for Congo (7 percentage points), followed by Mali (5 percentage points) and the Democratic Republic of the Congo (5 percentage points).

EUROSTAT regularly disseminates sex- and age-disaggregated data on the proportion of the employed population living below the national poverty line for European countries. Analysis of such data shows that in-work poor owe their status not only to labour market conditions – for example, unemployment, unstable jobs or low wages – but also to household circumstances. For example, lone parents (where women represent a majority) or sole earners with children are more vulnerable. However, in general, women in European countries have a comparable or lower risk of in-work poverty than men, even if women are more likely to occupy unstable and lower paid jobs. The lower risk for women may be related to the fact that they are often second earners in the household. In 2008, in-work poverty rates for women were lower than for men by more than 3 percentage points in Greece, Italy, Malta, Romania and Spain. Only in Estonia was the in-work poverty rate for women slightly higher than for men, by 3 percentage points.

Sources: United Nations, Official list of MDG Indicators (2008a); International Labour Office, Key Indicators of the Labour Market, 6th edition, Chapter 1, section B (2010); Bardone and Guio, In-work poverty: new commonly agreed indicators at the EU level (2005); EUROSTAT, Living Conditions and Social Protection database online (2010).

or national poverty lines, the gender dimension of poverty is not as easily captured through statistics. Poverty is traditionally measured based on income or expenditure aggregated at household level, and the number of poor is calculated as the number of people living in poor households. Inequality within the household in satisfying individual basic needs is not taken into account, mainly because it is difficult to know how household income is spent or consumed on an individual basis within the household or how expenditures are distributed to each household member. If in the same household women consume or spend less than what they need to function properly physically and socially, while men consume what they need or more, those women and men in the household are still considered to have the same poverty status, either poor or non-poor, depending on the average consumption estimated at the household level. Therefore if the total number of poor is disaggregated by sex (i.e., the sex of the household members), the results are not going to reflect possible gender inequality within the households but merely the distribution of population by sex in poor households.

However, even assuming the same consumption level for women and men living in the same household, some differences in poverty counts for women as compared to men might appear.[6] In some types of households where the share of women is higher, the earnings per capita tend to be lower because women's participation in the labour market and their earnings are lower than men's (see Chapter 4 – Work). In addition, the ratio of women to men increases with age (see Chapter 1 – Population and families), and the presence of non-earning older persons in extended households depresses the household income per capita. Households with an overrepresentation of women might therefore be more likely to be found below the poverty line, potentially leading to sex differences in poverty rates.

Data on poverty rates by sex and share of women among people living in poor households are available for some countries, as presented in figure 8.1

---

6 For a presentation of the factors associated with differential poverty counts for women and men, see Case and Deaton, 2002.

Figure 8.1
Poverty rates by sex, 1999–2008 (*latest available*)

Source: Compiled by the United Nations Statistics Division from EUROSTAT, Living Conditions and Social Protection database online (2009); CEDLAS and The World Bank, Socio-Economic Database for Latin America and the Caribbean (SEDLAC) (2009); national statistical offices (as of October 2009); and International Labour Office, Key Indicators of the Labour Market, 6th edition, Chapter 1, section B (2010).

Note: No comparison of poverty rates can be made between the regions as they are based on different poverty lines. Cross-country comparison is only possible within Latin America and the Caribbean, where the same absolute poverty line of $2.50 a day was applied. For European countries a relative poverty line of 60 per cent of the national median equivalized income is used in each of the countries (equivalized income is household income adjusted for differences in age and sex composition of households). Poverty rates for six African countries – Benin, Congo, Democratic Republic of the Congo, Kenya, Mali and Niger – are based on the same poverty line of $1.25 a day and are therefore comparable; however, poverty rates for the other three – Burkina Faso, Côte d'Ivoire and Morocco – are country-specific.

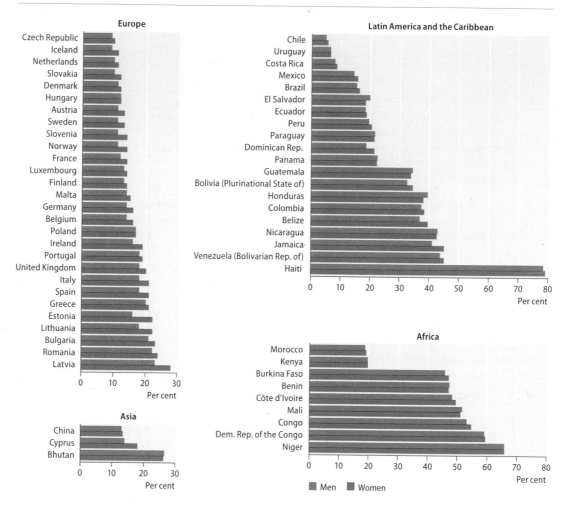

and table 8.1. However, it is important to keep in mind when considering these statistics the points made above that the outcome of a simple disaggregation of poverty counts by sex does not account for any potential intrahousehold gender inequality and is heavily influenced by country-specific living arrangements and ageing factors. First, in societies where women have less access to goods and services than men in the same household, the simple disaggregation of poverty counts by sex will lead to underestimated gender gaps in poverty, because additional poor women might be found in some non-poor households. Second, the gender gap in poverty may appear larger in some countries with higher proportions of households with overrepresentation of women (for example, households of lone mothers with young children and female one-person households, particularly one-person households of older women). The analysis of poverty for those specific types of households is thus

a necessary further step in understanding some of the links between gender and poverty.

The simple disaggregation of poverty counts by sex available for 60 countries shows that in the majority of countries women and men have similar poverty rates, while in a small number of countries, mostly located in Europe, women have higher poverty rates than men (figure 8.1). In 8 of the 28 European countries with available data women have poverty rates higher by 3 percentage points or more. The largest differences are observed in the Baltic countries: 22 per cent of women are poor compared to 16 per cent of men in Estonia (a difference of 6 percentage points); 28 per cent of women compared to 23 per cent of men in Latvia; and 22 per cent of women compared to 18 per cent of men in Lithuania. In Latin America and the Caribbean, women have higher poverty rates by 3 percentage points or more in 3 of the 20 countries

Table 8.1
Countries by share of women in total persons living in poor households, 1999–2008 (*latest available*)

Below 50 per cent			50–54 per cent				55–61 per cent	
Africa	Asia	Latin America and the Caribbean	Africa	Asia	Latin America and the Caribbean	More developed regions	Asia	More developed regions
Benin	China	Panama	Burkina Faso	Bhutan	Belize	Belgium	Cyprus	Austria
Mali	Philippines	Paraguay	Cameroon		Bolivia (Plurinational State of)	Denmark	Armenia	Bulgaria
			Cape Verde		Brazil	Finland		Czech Republic
			Congo		Chile	France		Estonia
			Dem. Republic of the Congo		Colombia	Germany		Iceland
			Guinea		Costa Rica	Greece		Italy
			Kenya		Dominican Republic	Hungary		Latvia
			Niger		Ecuador	Ireland		Lithuania
					El Salvador	Luxembourg		Norway
					Guatemala	Malta		Slovakia
					Haiti	Netherlands		Slovenia
					Honduras	Poland		United States of America
					Jamaica	Portugal		
					Mexico	Romania		
					Nicaragua	Serbia		
					Peru	Spain		
					Uruguay	Sweden		
					Venezuela (Bolivarian Republic of)	United Kingdom		

Source: Compiled by the United Nations Statistics Division from EUROSTAT, Living Conditions and Social Protection database online (2009); CEDLAS and The World Bank, Socio-Economic Database for Latin America and the Caribbean (SEDLAC) (2009); national statistical offices (as of October 2009); and International Labour Office, Key Indicators of the Labour Market, 6th edition, Chapter 1, section B (2010).
Note: Poverty measured based on different poverty lines; for details, see note below figure 8.1.

with available data: Belize, Dominican Republic and Jamaica. In Jamaica, the country with the largest sex difference, 45 per cent of women are poor compared to 41 per cent of men.

Based on data available for 65 countries, the share of women in total persons living in poor households varies from 46 per cent in the Philippines and 48 per cent in China to 61 per cent in Estonia, with the share in most of the countries between 50 and 54 per cent (table 8.1). In Europe the share of women among the total poor ranges from 51 per cent in Poland to 61 per cent in Estonia. In Latin America and the Caribbean, women's share ranges from less than 50 per cent in Panama and Paraguay to 54 per cent in Chile and Mexico. In the 10 countries with available data in Africa, women's share is between 48 and 53 per cent.

2. Female- and male-headed households

Higher incidence of poverty may be associated with female-headed households or with male-headed households depending on the country-specific context

Poverty data disaggregated by sex of the head of household, available for 41 countries or areas in Africa, Asia and Latin America and the Caribbean, show that disparities in poverty for female- and male-headed households are country specific (see figures 8.2 and 8.3). In some countries or areas, female-headed households are more likely to be poor, while in others male-headed households are more likely to be poor. For example, only in 4 of the 16 countries in Africa with available data – Burundi, Malawi, Sao Tome and Principe and Zambia – were the poverty rates for female-headed households higher compared to male-headed households (figure 8.2). The largest difference, of 8 percentage points, is observed in Malawi, where 59 per cent of people living in female-headed households are poor compared to 51 per cent of those living in male-headed households. In the other countries or areas with available data in the region, male-headed households had similar or higher poverty rates than female-headed households. In Burkina Faso, Ghana, Niger and Nigeria (all in Western Africa) the poverty rates for male-headed households were higher than those for female-headed households by more than 8 percentage points. For example, 44 per cent of people living in female-headed households in Nigeria were poor compared to 58 per cent of people living in male-headed households. In Asia, female-headed households had higher poverty rates than male-headed households in Armenia and the

Figure 8.2

Poverty rate by sex of the head of household, 2000–2008 (*latest available*)

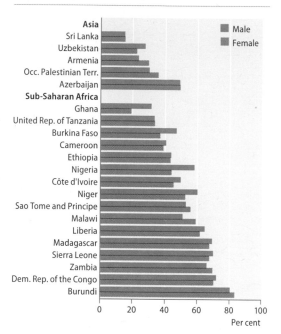

Per cent

Source: Compiled by the United Nations Statistics Division from national statistical offices (as of October 2009).

Note: Data are based on country-specific poverty lines and therefore not comparable from one country to another.

Occupied Palestinian Territory but lower poverty rates in Uzbekistan.

In Latin America and the Caribbean, slightly more countries have higher poverty rates for female-headed households compared to male-headed households (figure 8.3). Greater poverty rates for female-headed households, by more than 5 percentage points, were observed in Colombia, the Dominican Republic, Jamaica and the Bolivarian Republic of Venezuela. On the other hand, higher poverty rates for male-headed households, by more than 5 percentage points, were observed in El Salvador, Guatemala, Honduras, Nicaragua and Peru.

Consistent with the above-mentioned findings, an earlier review of more than 60 Poverty Assessments carried out by the World Bank showed that "while there is evidence that in some countries female-headed households have a higher incidence of poverty than male-headed households, it is impossible to generalize".[7] The review also acknowledged the importance of examining different types of female- and male-headed households further disaggregated by urban and rural areas, with or without children, *de jure* and *de facto*. Data disaggregated by those characteristics would enable the identification of clearer gender patterns, yet such data have not been systematically produced and disseminated.

7 Lampietti and Stalker, 2000, p. 25.

The difficulty in generalizing about poverty disparities between "female-headed households" and "male-headed households" is likely to be linked not only to contextual differences in women's and men's status but also to the combination of various types of households that may be included under these labels and the definitions used to define the headship (see box 8.3). As shown in the next section of this chapter, when the analysis is focused on more homogeneous categories of female- and male-headed households, a pattern of higher poverty rates associated with female-headed households becomes apparent. The types of households analysed are female and male lone-parent households on the one hand, and female and male one-person households on the other.

Lone-parent households

Households of lone mothers with children in Latin America and the Caribbean have higher poverty rates than those of lone fathers with children

Households of lone mothers with children have consistently higher poverty rates than those of lone fathers with children in Latin America and the Caribbean, as revealed by poverty data disaggregated by type of household and sex of the head of household (figure 8.3). In 16 of the 20 countries with available data in the region, the poverty rates for households of lone mothers with children are higher than they are for households of lone fathers with children by more than 5 percentage points. In the remaining four countries – El Salvador, Honduras, Nicaragua and Panama – the poverty rates for the two types of households are similar. By comparison, households of couples with or without children in the same region that are headed by women tend to have lower or similar poverty rates compared to those headed by men (figure 8.3). For example, in the Plurinational State of Bolivia, households of couples with or without children have a poverty rate of 18 per cent when headed by women, considerably less than the 36 per cent poverty rate when headed by men; in contrast, households of lone mothers with children have a poverty rate of 34 per cent, higher than the 17 per cent poverty rate for lone fathers with children. In Colombia, households of couples with or without children have comparable poverty rates when headed by women or men, 34 per cent and 36 per cent respectively; however, lone mothers with children

Figure 8.3

Poverty rate by type of household and sex of the head of household, Latin America and the Caribbean, 1999–2008 (*latest available*)

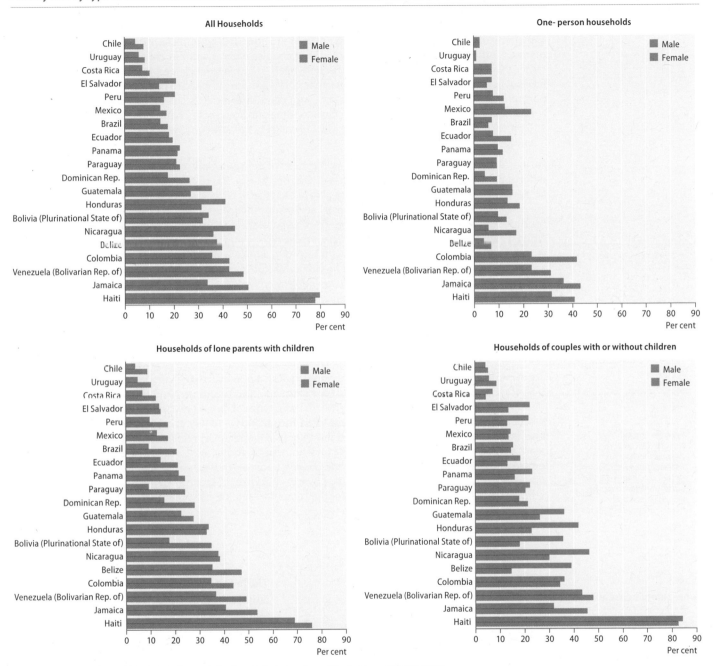

Source: CEDLAS and The World Bank, Socio-Economic Database for Latin America and the Caribbean (SEDLAC) (2009).
Note: Poverty rates are based on $2.50 a day poverty line.

have a higher poverty rate than lone fathers with children, 44 per cent compared to 35 per cent.

Although households of couples with or without children headed by women in general fare better in Latin America and the Caribbean, it must be noted that their proportion in total households is relatively low, ranging from 1 per cent in Guate-

mala to 12 per cent in Jamaica, with an exceptionally high value of 20 per cent for Haiti.[8] Households of lone mothers with children are not only more often found in poverty but are also more frequent. Their proportion in total households varies from 15 per cent in Belize to 28 per cent in Haiti.

8 CEDLAS and The World Bank, 2009.

Box 8.3
Female-headed households: a heterogeneous category

Female-headed households cover a broad range of situations from one-person households, households of lone mothers with children and households of couples with or without children where the woman rather than the man is reported as the household head. They may include *de jure* female-headed households, where women do not have a male partner, or *de facto* female-headed households, where the male partner is temporarily absent and may or may not contribute remittances to the household's welfare. Similarly, male-headed households may include one-person households, households of lone fathers with children or households of couples with or without children. In some countries, the male head may also be a polygamist rather than a monogamist.

Furthermore, the criteria used in identifying the head of the household may not always be clear. The traditional notion of head of household assumes that one person has primary authority and responsibility for household affairs and is, in the majority of cases, its chief economic support. However, where spouses are considered equal in household authority and responsibility and may share economic support, the concept of head of household is no longer considered valid. Even in the many countries where the traditional concept is still relevant, it is important to recognize that the procedures followed in applying it may distort the true picture, particularly with regard to female heads of households. The most common assumption that can skew the facts is that no woman can be the head of any household that also contains an adult male. The United Nation's *Principles and Recommendations for Population and Housing Censuses* advises the use of a household reference person in identifying and listing the members of a household. Countries may choose to use the term they deem most appropriate to identify this person – household reference person, head of household or householder – as long as the person so identified is used solely to determine relationships between household members. It is also recommended that the criteria for choosing that person are specified.

Use of different criteria in defining the household headship may lead to the identification of different sets of households with different poverty rates. For example, a study based on the 1997 LSMS (Living Standard Measurement Study) data for Panama identified three types of female-headed households: the first set was identified based on self-reporting of the head; the second was defined as "potential" female-headed, if no working-age male was present; and the third was identified as female-headed using a "working head" definition, with more than half of the total household labour hours worked contributed by a single female member. The study showed that the overlap between these three sets of households was low, around 40 to 60 per cent. The corresponding poverty rates were different: 29 per cent for the self-declared female-headed households; 23 per cent for the "potential" female-headed households; and 21 per cent for the households headed by a "working female".

Sources: United Nations, *Principles and Recommendations for Population and Housing Censuses* (2008b); Fuwa, The poverty and heterogeneity among female-headed households revisited (2000).

Table 8. 2
Lone-parent households below the national poverty line by sex of parent

	Year	Poor lone mothers with children (%)	Poor lone fathers with children (%)
Eastern Europe			
Albania	1998	27	17
Republic of Moldova	2007	23	12
Other more developed regions			
Canada	2003	38	13
France	2007	35	16
United States of America	2008	37	18

Source: Compiled by the United Nations Statistics Division from national statistical offices (as of October 2009).
Notes: Poverty rates are based on country-specific poverty lines and therefore not comparable from one country to another. Poverty rates for France and the Republic of Moldova are calculated as percentage of population living in lone-parent households that are below the poverty line, while for the other countries the poverty rates are calculated as percentage of lone-parent households that are below the poverty line. Poverty rates for Canada are based on income after taxes.

The proportion of households of lone fathers with children varies from 3 per cent in Belize and Guatemala to 9 per cent in Haiti and Jamaica.

Lone mothers with children are more likely to be poor in other parts of the world as well (table 8.2). In Albania, for example, 27 per cent of lone mothers with children are poor, compared to 17 per cent of lone fathers with children. In the United States of America, 37 per cent of lone mothers with children are poor compared to 18 per cent of lone fathers with children.

One-person households

One-person households are not a dominant type of living arrangements, although their frequency is not negligible. In Latin America and the Caribbean the share of households formed by women living alone in the total number of households varies from 1 per cent in Nicaragua to 13 per cent in Uruguay. Similarly, the share of households of men living alone varies from 3 per cent in Guatemala and Nicaragua to 15 per cent in Jamaica.[9] In Europe, the proportion of female one-person households ranges from 4 per cent in Bulgaria, Ireland, Malta and Spain to 12 per cent in Denmark, while the proportion of male one-person households varies from 2 per cent in Bulgaria, Portugal and Slovakia to 11 per cent in Denmark.[10]

Poverty rates are higher for women than for men when living in one-person households

---

Women are more often poor than men when living in one-person households. This is true for the majority of countries in Latin America and the Caribbean, for example (figure 8.3). The difference in poverty rate between women and men is highest in Colombia, followed by Mexico and Nicaragua. When living in one-person households, 42 per cent of women and 23 per cent of men are poor in Colombia, 23 per cent of women and 12 per cent of men in Mexico and 17 per cent of women and 6 per cent of men in Nicaragua.

In most European countries as well, women living in one-person households have higher poverty rates than men (figure 8.4). The difference is substantial in some countries. In Bulgaria, 54 per cent of women in this type of household are poor compared to 28 per cent of men, while in Spain this is the case for 40 per cent of women compared to 21 per cent of men. By contrast, men in one-person households have much higher poverty rates than women in such households in two European countries: Hungary (12 per cent of women and 23 per cent of men) and Poland (18 and 26 per cent, respectively).

Women are overrepresented among the older poor in European countries

---

The higher poverty risk for women than men living in one-person households can be partly explained by the economic status of older women, as older persons constitute a large segment of population in this type of living arrangement. Women are overrepresented among the older poor in European

---

9 CEDLAS and The World Bank, 2009.
10 EUROSTAT, 2009.

Figure 8.4

Poverty rate for women and men living in one-person households, Europe, 2007–2008 (*latest available*)

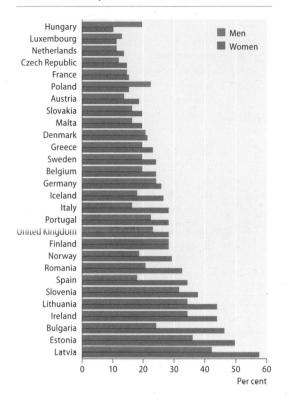

Source: EUROSTAT, Living Conditions and Social Protection database online (2009).
Note: Poverty is measured based on relative poverty lines defined as 60 per cent of the national median equivalized income; cross-country comparisons should be made with caution.

countries both because they tend to live longer and because they have higher poverty rates than men. As shown in figure 8.5, the share of women among the poor under 65 years of age fluctuates around 50 per cent and is relatively close to the share of women in the total population under 65 years. By comparison, the share of women in the total population over 65 years is considerably higher than 50 per cent in most of the countries, while the share of women among the poor over 65 years is even higher. The overrepresentation of women among the older poor is striking in several cases, such as in Czech Republic, Hungary, Lithuania, Norway, Slovakia, Slovenia and Sweden. For example, women in Czech Republic are 57 per cent of the total older population but 88 per cent of the older poor. Similarly, women in Norway represent 57 per cent of the total older population but 82 per cent of the older poor. By contrast, in some European countries such as France, Latvia, Luxembourg, Malta and Portugal, a more balanced distribution of the older poor by sex is observed, matching relatively closely the distribution in the total older population.

In the absence of data, it is not clear to what extent older women from the less developed regions have

Figure 8.5

Share of women in population and in total poor, below and above 65 years, Europe, 2007–2008 *(latest available)*

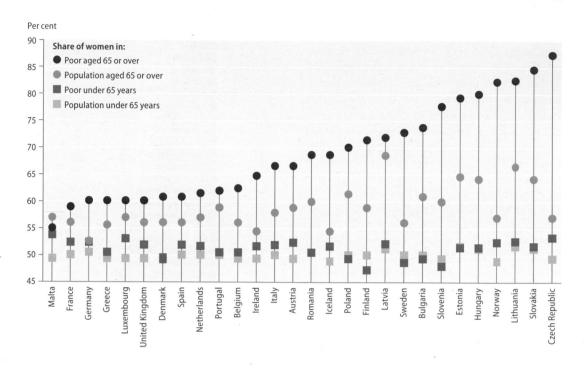

Per cent

Share of women in:
- ● Poor aged 65 or over
- ● Population aged 65 or over
- ■ Poor under 65 years
- ■ Population under 65 years

Source: EUROSTAT, Living Conditions and Social Protection database online (2009).
Note: Poverty is measured based on national poverty lines defined as 60 per cent of the national median equivalized income; cross-country comparisons should be made with caution.

higher poverty rates than older men. Compared to the more developed regions, older women and men in the less developed regions are less likely to live in one-person households. The proportion of women over 60 years living in one-person households is 32 per cent in the more developed regions, compared to 10 per cent in the less developed regions, while for men it is 13 per cent in the more developed regions, compared to 6 per cent in the less developed regions.[11] Furthermore, women may not become a more vulnerable group with age in contexts where the elderly are expected to receive support from their children or relatives.[12]

B. Individual access to and control over resources

1. Inequality in intrahousehold allocation of resources

According to some analysts, the focus on poverty rates for female-headed households "avoids the more important and more difficult area of intrahousehold poverty"[13] or what has also been

termed secondary poverty for women. As shown in the first part of the chapter, household-based measures of poverty can give an indication of the overall economic status of women relative to men when applied to certain types of households – for instance, when adult women and men live separately in one-person households or in households of lone parents with children. However, the most common type of household is one where an adult woman lives with an adult man, with or without other persons. The concerns are that within such households women may have a subordinated status relative to men, that they may have less decision-making power on intrahousehold allocation of resources, and that ultimately fewer resources may be allocated to them.

Yet, it is difficult to measure intrahousehold inequality using consumption as an indicator of individual welfare, as traditionally used at household level. When collecting data on individual consumption, only part of the goods – for example, adult clothing, alcohol or tobacco – can be assigned to specific members of the household. It is less easy to measure how much of the food or household common goods (such as housing, water supply or sanitation) is consumed or used by each individual household member. In addition, when different patterns of consumption are

---

11 United Nations, 2010.

12 Chant, 2007.

13 Jackson, 1996, p.493.

Box 8.4

In some European countries, the poverty risk for women living in one-person households may be higher or lower than for men depending on the poverty line chosen

The choice of poverty line may influence the gender gap in poverty for persons living in one-person households, as shown by the use of three poverty lines for European countries (see figure below). Women have higher poverty rates than men in most of the countries in the region for the upper poverty line (60 per cent of the median equivalized income). However, in some of those countries, the poverty rates for women are lower than for men for the lowest poverty line (40 per cent of the median equivalized income). In Estonia, Lithuania, Slovakia or Slovenia, if the upper poverty line is chosen to estimate poverty, women will appear as more likely to be poor than men. However, if the lowest poverty line is chosen, men will appear as more likely to be poor than women. For example, in Lithuania, the poverty rate for the upper poverty line is 11 percentage points higher for women than for men. By comparison, the poverty rate for the lowest poverty line is 13 percentage points lower for women than for men.

Female-male difference in poverty rate for one-person households for three poverty lines, Europe, 2007–2008 (*latest available*)

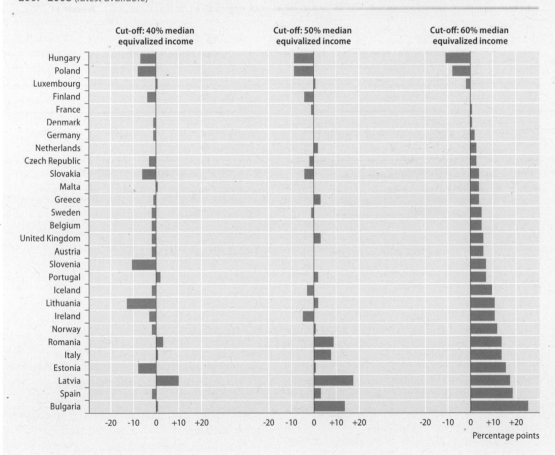

Source: Computed by the United Nations Statistics Division based on data from EUROSTAT, Living Conditions and Social Protection database online (2009).

Note: Poverty is measured based on national poverty lines defined as 40, 50 and 60 per cent respectively of the national median equivalized income; cross-country comparisons should be made with caution.

observed it is not always clear if they are related to different individual levels of need (for example, women may require a lower caloric intake than men), to different preferences or to unequal distribution of resources. Attempts to infer gender bias in consumption based on aggregate household-level expenditures on certain types of goods and household composition[14] have been made, but they have had little success so far.[15]

---

14 Usually such analysis examines whether an additional girl in the household has the same effect as an additional boy on the aggregate household-level consumption of certain types of adult goods such as tobacco and alcohol.

15 See, for example, Deaton, 1989; and Fuwa and others, 2006.

Figure 8.6

Married women and men aged 15–49 who were employed and earned cash income in the last 12 months, 2003–2008 (*latest available*)

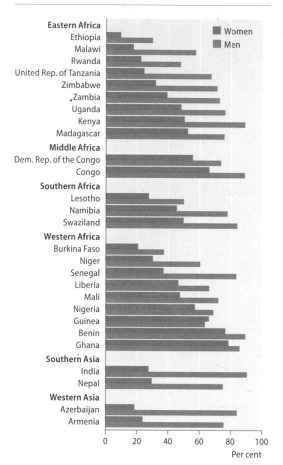

Source: Macro International, Demographic and Health Survey (DHS) database (2009).
Note: Data refer to currently married/in union women and men who earned cash income only or cash and in-kind income at any time in the last 12 months.

The use of non-consumption indicators has been more successful in illustrating gender inequality in the allocation of resources within the household.[16] As noted earlier, poverty is increasingly seen not only in terms of the adequacy of economic resources to avoid deprivation but also in broader terms of the actual level of deprivation. It thus covers a wide range of aspects, from basic needs in terms of food, shelter, clothing and sanitation, to elements of capability to function in society such as good health and education.[17] Various chapters in this report illustrate the overall inequality between women and men on several dimensions as shaped by different gender roles and expectations in reproductive and productive areas. For example, as shown in Chapter 3 – Education, in some countries the level of enrolment is lower for girls than for boys and this may be due to lower returns expected from investing in girls' education. Moreover, the subordinate status of women in the household has been argued with reference to time use and violence against women.[18] Women work longer hours than men and they may have fewer chances in the formal labour market because the domestic tasks are not equally distributed in the household (see Chapter 4 – Work), and significant proportions of women are victims of domestic violence (see Chapter 6 – Violence against women).

Non-consumption indicators can further underline the gendered experience of poverty. Women experience more disadvantages when they live in poor households. For example, in countries such as Pakistan and Yemen, girls and boys from the wealthiest quintile have relatively similar net school attendance rates in primary education, but in the poorest quintile the net school attendance of girls is lower than that of boys by 17 and 25 percentage points respectively.[19] In households with poor access to clean water and energy, women bear most of the resulting work burden and harmful health effects (see Chapter 7 – Environment).

2. Economic autonomy of women

Women's individual control over resources is considered important not only because of the fairness of equal access to resources, but also because of the resulting economic autonomy of women and their increased bargaining power within the household and how these may translate into more egalitarian intrahousehold relations.

Access to cash income

A small proportion of women have cash income in the less developed regions

More women than men work in vulnerable employment with low or no cash returns, and they spend more of their time on unpaid domestic tasks (see Chapter 4 – Work). This gender division of labour increases women's economic dependency on men. When men with higher earnings or a pension are not around any more because of divorce, migration or death, women as lone mothers and older women living alone have a higher risk of poverty.

16 Marcoux, 1998.
17 See for example, Kabeer, 1994; Sen, 1999; United Nations, 1995b; United Nations, 2009.
18 Jackson, 1996.
19 UNESCO, 2010.

Women's access to cash income is systematically low in the less developed regions (figure 8.6). The proportion of women who were employed and earned cash income in the last 12 months is particularly low in some Asian countries, in both the Southern and Western sub-regions, and the gender differences are very high. For example, only 27 per cent of married women aged 15–49 in India were employed and earned cash income in the last 12 months, compared to 90 per cent of married men of the same age. In Azerbaijan, 19 per cent of married women earned cash compared to 84 per cent of married men. Within sub-Saharan Africa, the proportion of women with cash income is lower in countries from Eastern Africa. The gender gap is large in Eastern and Southern Africa, but less pronounced in Western Africa. For example, 18 per cent of married women 15–49 years old in Malawi had cash income compared to 57 per cent of married men of the same age. By contrast, 79 per cent of married women and 86 per cent of married men in Ghana had cash income.

Ownership of land and other property

Women are disadvantaged with respect to inheritance and property rights

---

In most countries in Africa and about half the countries in Asia women are disadvantaged by statutory and customary laws in their access to land ownership and other types of property (table 8.3). Elements of gender inequality with regard to inheritance rights were identified in 45 out of the 48 African countries reviewed and in 25 out of the 42 Asian ones. With regard to entitlements to ownership of land, gender inequality was identified in 43 African countries and 21 Asian countries. Better conditions were observed for Latin America and the Caribbean and for Eastern Europe.

While their availability is limited, individual-level data on property ownership point to gender inequality in the less developed regions

---

Data on property ownership are usually recorded at the household level in both censuses and household surveys. However, where data are collected at individual level and disseminated disaggregated by sex of the owner, gender inequality becomes apparent. Women own land, houses or livestock

Table 8.3

Number of countries with gender inequality with regard to inheritance rights and entitlements to ownership of land and other property, by region

	Number of countries with gender inequality related to		
	Inheritance rights	Right to acquire and own land	Right to own property other than land
Africa (48)	45	43	35
Northern Africa (5)	5	3	1
Sub-Saharan Africa (43)	40	40	34
Eastern Africa (15)	13	13	12
Middle Africa (8)	7	8	8
Southern Africa (5)	5	5	4
Western Africa (15)	15	14	10
Asia (42)	25	21	19
Central Asia (5)	2	2	2
Eastern Asia (4)	0	1	0
South-Eastern Asia (10)	4	2	1
Southern Asia (8)	7	7	7
Western Asia (15)	12	9	9
Latin America and the Caribbean (22)	2	5	2
Caribbean (6)	2	1	1
Central America (6)	0	3	0
South America (10)	0	1	1
Oceania (2)	0	2	2
Eastern Europe (9)	2	2	1

Source: Computed by the United Nations Statistics Division based on data from OECD, Gender, Institutions and Development Database online (as of December 2009).

Note: The numbers in brackets indicate the number of countries reviewed. The quality of women's ownership rights was graded from 0 meaning "no restrictions" to 1 signifying complete discrimination against women. Variations between 0 and 1 may indicate the extent of restrictions or the size of the group of women for which the restrictions may apply. Countries presented in the table are those with partial (graded 0.5) or complete (graded 1) discrimination against women on the issue considered.

less often than men, as shown by statistics available for Nepal, the Occupied Palestinian Territory, Peru and Viet Nam.

For example, in South-Eastern Asia the 2006 Survey on the Family in Viet Nam[20] revealed that only a small proportion of house and land titles are in the hands of women in that country (figure 8.7). In urban areas 21 per cent of the house and residential titles are in the name of women, 61 per cent are in the name of men and 18 per cent are joint titles. In rural areas, 8 per cent of the farm and forest land titles are in the name of women, 87 per cent are in the name of men and 5 per cent are joint titles.

In Nepal, only in a small proportion of households do women own the house or a share of it,

---

20 Viet Nam Ministry of Culture, Sports and Tourism and others, 2008.

Figure 8.7

Distribution of property titles by sex of the owner and urban/ rural areas, Viet Nam, 2006

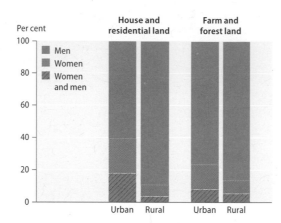

Source: Viet Nam Ministry of Culture, Sports and Tourism and others, *Results of Nation-wide Survey on the Family in Viet Nam 2006: Key Findings* (2008).

some land or livestock, as shown by the 2001 population census.[21] While 88 per cent of households own their house, only in 6 per cent does a woman have partial or full ownership of the house. Similarly, women own some of the land in only 11 per cent of the households and some livestock in only 7 per cent.

A survey conducted in the Occupied Palestinian Territory in 1999 showed that 52 per cent of men owned a house/real estate or a share of it, compared to only 8 per cent of women.[22] Also, 24 per cent of men owned some land, compared to only 5 per cent of women. Among women entitled to inherit property, only 20 per cent obtained their complete share of inheritance and an additional 12 per cent obtained just a part of their share.

Although both inheritance and state programmes of land distribution and titling are becoming more egalitarian in Latin America, the gender asset gap is still significant and it is due to four factors: male preference in inheritance; male privilege in marriage; male bias in both community and state programmes of land distribution; and male bias in the land market.[23] In Peru, looking at the distribution of ownership of titled land parcels reveals that women represent 13 per cent of landowners, with an additional 13 per cent joint ownership.[24]

While these case studies point to gender inequality in land ownership, data on individual ownership of land have yet to be systematically collected.

According to the Food and Agriculture Organization of the United Nations (FAO), the focus in previous rounds of agricultural censuses has been on the "agricultural holder", defined as the "person who makes the major decisions regarding resource use, and exercises management control over the agricultural holding operation".[25] Such a definition does not allow for multiple decision makers (for example, a couple) or more than one owner of the land. The situation of distinct areas owned and managed separately by the wife and husband – relevant for some African countries, for example – cannot be accounted for either. The World Programme for the Census of Agriculture 2010 recognizes that "the agricultural holder concept is often difficult to apply because of a gender bias in reporting of data", and for the 2010 census round "the concept of agricultural holder has been modified to recognize that the agricultural holder could be a group of persons – for example, a husband and wife".[26]

3. Participation in intrahousehold decision-making on spending

A significant proportion of married women in the less developed regions have no say on how their own cash earnings are spent

Women's lower control over household resources is further indicated by their limited participation in intrahousehold decision-making on spending. The proportion of married women aged 15–49 not involved in decision-making on how their own earnings are spent is particularly high in some countries in sub-Saharan Africa and in Asia (figure 8.8 and Statistical Annex). In sub-Saharan Africa, the proportion of women with no say in how their own cash income is spent is greatest in Malawi (34 per cent) followed by Democratic Republic of the Congo (28 per cent), Liberia (23 per cent), Rwanda (22 per cent) and United Republic of Tanzania and Zambia (21 per cent). In Asia, higher proportions were observed in India (18 per cent), Nepal (14 per cent), Bangladesh (13 per cent) and Turkey (11 per cent).

This lack of decision-making power is more often associated with the poorest wealth quintiles (figure 8.9). Large disparities between the poorest and wealthiest quintiles are observed for Democratic

---

21 Nepal Central Bureau of Statistics, 2003.

22 Palestinian Central Bureau of Statistics, 2002.

23 Deere and Leon, 2003.

24 Ibid.

25 FAO, 2005, para. 3.36.

26 FAO, 2005, para. 2.29.

Republic of the Congo, Lesotho, Liberia, Malawi, United Republic of Tanzania and Zambia (in Africa) and for Turkey (in Asia). For example, 21 per cent of the married women who earn cash income in the United Republic of Tanzania, on average, have no say in how their money is spent. However, this proportion is reduced to 10 per cent for women in the wealthiest quintile and expands to 44 per cent for women in the poorest quintile. Similarly, 11 per cent of married women in Turkey who earn cash income have no decision-making power on how their money is spent. The proportion is reduced to 2 per cent for women in the wealthiest quintile but goes up to 28 per cent for women in the poorest quintile.

Married women in the less developed regions do not fully participate in decision-making on household purchases, particularly in poorer households

---

Lack of participation in decision-making is also observed with regards to expenditures on major household purchases and, to a lesser extent, on daily household needs (which are more likely to fall within the traditional areas of decision-making for women). The percentage of married women participating in intrahousehold decision-making is particularly low in Africa, followed by Asia (table 8.4). On average, only 60 per cent of married women in sub-Saharan Africa can decide by themselves or together with their husbands on daily purchases for household needs, and even fewer than that, 46 per cent, on major purchases. Within the region the variation is substantial. Less than a quarter of married women have a say in purchases for daily household needs in Niger and Senegal, while more than three quarters have a say in Ethiopia, Ghana, Lesotho, Liberia, Madagascar, Namibia, Swaziland, Zambia and Zimbabwe. The pattern of variation is similar for decisions on major household purchases: less than a quarter of married women have a say in Burkina Faso, Malawi, Mali, Niger, Nigeria and Senegal, while three quarters or more have a say in Liberia, Madagascar, Namibia and Zimbabwe (see Statistical Annex).

Within Asia, women from countries in South-Eastern Asia – Cambodia, Indonesia and the Philippines – have more decision-making power within the household with regard to household purchases than women from countries in Southern Asia – Bangladesh, India and Nepal (see Statistical Annex). The proportion of women usually making decisions by themselves or with their

Figure 8.8

Proportion of married women aged 15–49 not participating in the decision on how their own earned money is spent, 2003–2008 (*latest available*)

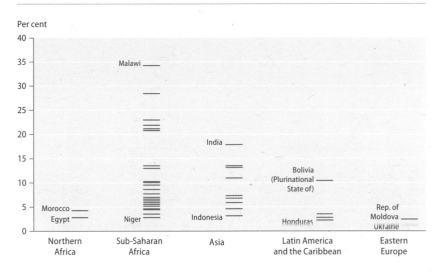

Source: Macro International, Demographic and Health Survey (DHS) database (2009).
Note: Each line represents one country. Currently married/in union women who earned cash income in the last 12 months were asked "Who usually decides how the money you earn will be used: mainly you, mainly your husband/partner, or you and your husband/partner jointly?". The graph shows the proportion of women who answered "husband/partner alone", "mainly husband/partner" or "somebody else". Excluded were the answers where the woman indicated that she decided "alone", "mainly alone", "jointly with husband", "jointly with somebody else" and non-answers.

Figure 8.9

Married women aged 15–49 not participating in the decision of how own earned money is spent, for poorest and wealthiest quintiles, 2003–2008 (*latest available*), **selected countries with highest percentages of non-participation**

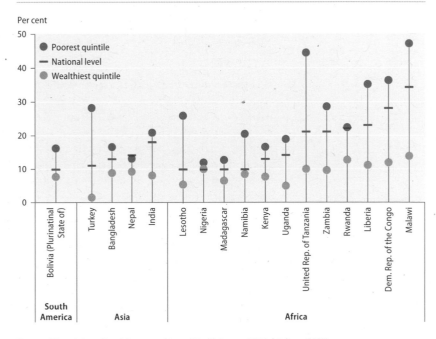

Source: Macro International, Demographic and Health Survey (DHS) database (2009).
Note: Data refer to women who are currently married or in union.

Table 8. 4

Married women aged 15–49 usually making decisions, by themselves or with their husbands, on purchases for daily household needs and major purchases, by region, 2003–2008 (*latest available*)

	Proportion of women (%) making decisions on	
	Purchases for daily household needs	Major purchases
Africa (25)	61	47
Sub-Saharan Africa (23)	60	46
Asia (9)	73	66
Latin America and the Caribbean (5)	82	71

Source: Computed by the United Nations Statistics Division based on data from Macro International, Demographic and Health Survey (DHS) database (2009).
Note: Unweighted averages; the numbers in brackets indicate the number of countries averaged. Currently married/in union women were asked "Who usually makes decisions about purchases for daily household needs?" and "Who usually makes decisions about major household purchases?" The averages above are calculated based on the proportions of women who answered "themselves" or "jointly with their husbands/partners".

tions of women participating in decision-making are over 85 per cent in the South-Eastern Asian countries and around 60 per cent in the Southern Asian countries.

Women in the poorest quintiles participate less in intrahousehold decision-making on purchases for daily household needs (figure 8.10). Disparities of more than 20 percentage points between the poorest and wealthiest quintiles are observed for Cameroon, Morocco, Namibia, Nigeria, the United Republic of Tanzania and Zambia (in Africa) and for Honduras and Peru (in Latin America). For example, 66 per cent of married women in the wealthiest quintile in Morocco usually make decisions by themselves or jointly with their husbands with regard to purchases for daily household needs. The proportion is reduced to 32 per cent for women in the poorest quintile. In Honduras, most of the married women from the wealthiest quintile, 91 per cent, are usually part of decisions on daily household needs, compared to 59 per cent of women from the poorest quintile. The participation is almost universal in both wealthiest and poorest quintiles in countries such

husbands on major household purchases is over 75 per cent in the South-Eastern Asian countries mentioned while only slightly over 50 per cent in the Southern Asian countries. With regard to purchases for daily household needs, the propor-

Figure 8.10

Married women aged 15–49 usually making decisions, by themselves or jointly with their husbands, on purchases for household daily needs, in the poorest and wealthiest quintiles, 2003–2008 (*latest available*)

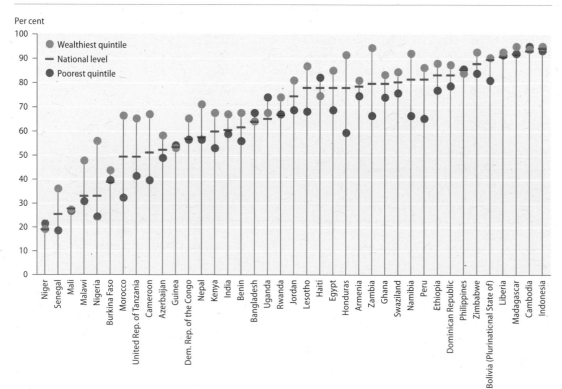

Source: Macro International, Demographic and Health Survey (DHS) database (2009).
Note: Data refer to women who are currently married or in union.

as Cambodia, Indonesia, Liberia and Madagascar. By contrast, women's participation is low in both wealthiest and poorest quintiles in Burkina Faso, Mali and Niger.

In summary, individual-level data presented in the second part of this chapter indicate that there is substantial gender inequality within the household in the less developed regions, particularly in poorer households. Women do not fully participate in intrahousehold decision-making on spending, and female and male members of the household do not always have equal access to household resources. Fewer women have cash income and they own land or other property less often than men. This lower access to resources increases women's economic dependency on men and make them more vulnerable to various economic and environmental shocks.

Statistical Annex

List of tables

Table 1.A
Population

Country or area	Population (in thousands) 1950 Women	Men	1980 Women	Men	2010 Women	Men	Number of men per 100 women 2010	Share of population age 60 and above, 2010 (%) Women	Men	Total fertility rate (births per women) 1950–1955	1980–1985	2005–2010	Singulate mean age at marriage Year	Women	Men
Africa															
Algeria	4 288	4 465	9 371	9 440	17 540	17 882	102	4	3	7.3	6.5	2.4	2002	29.5	33.0
Angola	2 113	2 034	3 992	3 862	9 631	9 362	97	2	2	7.0	7.2	5.8	..	..	..
Benin	1 095	955	1 837	1 723	4 560	4 651	102	3	2	5.7	7.0	5.5	2006	20.5	25.3
Botswana	213	200	504	481	988	989	100	4	3	6.5	6.0	2.9	2001	26.5	30.9
Burkina Faso	1 940	2 141	3 467	3 395	8 149	8 138	100	2	1	6.1	7.1	5.9	2003	19.4	26.1
Burundi	1 200	1 176	2 113	1 987	4 310	4 170	96	3	2	6.8	6.8	4.7	2002	22.7	26.1
Cameroon	2 277	2 189	4 580	4 500	9 978	9 981	100	3	3	5.7	6.4	4.7	2004	20.2	..
Cape Verde	80	66	157	133	267	245	92	4	2	6.6	6.1	2.8	2000	24.6	28.8
Central African Republic	673	654	1 154	1 115	2 292	2 214	97	4	3	5.5	6.0	4.8	1995	19.4	24.4
Chad	1 230	1 199	2 339	2 269	5 786	5 720	99	3	2	6.1	6.8	6.2	2004	18.3	24.5
Comoros	79	78	165	164	344	347	101	3	2	6.0	7.1	4.0	1996	23.6	28.5
Congo	411	397	913	902	1 882	1 877	100	3	2	5.7	6.0	4.4	2005	21.9	25.8
Côte d'Ivoire	1 235	1 270	4 038	4 382	10 595	10 976	104	3	3	6.8	7.3	4.6	1999	21.9	28.0
Democratic Republic of the Congo	6 477	5 707	13 882	13 288	34 208	33 620	98	3	2	6.0	6.7	6.1	2007	20.8	25.2
Djibouti	31	31	171	169	440	439	100	3	3	7.8	6.6	3.9	2002	27.7	30.8
Egypt	10 817	10 697	22 170	22 263	41 998	42 477	101	4	4	6.4	5.5	2.9	2005	23.0	..
Equatorial Guinea	115	111	113	107	349	344	98	3	2	5.5	5.8	5.4	..	..	..
Eritrea	576	565	1 253	1 216	2 653	2 571	97	3	2	7.0	6.5	4.7	2002	20.6	..
Ethiopia	9 303	9 131	17 844	17 565	42 694	42 281	99	3	3	7.2	6.9	5.4	2005	20.9	25.7
Gabon	240	229	346	335	751	750	100	4	3	4.0	5.2	3.4	2000	22.1	26.2
Gambia	133	126	312	304	882	868	98	3	2	5.4	6.3	5.1	1993	19.6	28.4
Ghana	2 463	2 518	5 458	5 568	12 000	12 333	103	3	3	6.4	6.3	4.3	2003	22.4	26.6
Guinea	1 313	1 306	2 304	2 324	5 110	5 214	102	3	2	6.5	6.9	5.5	2005	19.3	26.3
Guinea-Bissau	262	256	423	413	831	816	98	3	3	7.4	5.7	5.7	2006	19.9	..
Kenya	3 012	3 065	8 163	8 098	20 432	20 431	100	2	2	7.5	7.2	5.0	2003	21.4	26.2
Lesotho	390	344	698	598	1 099	985	90	5	3	5.8	5.5	3.4	2004	22.5	27.3
Liberia	416	408	969	941	2 063	2 039	99	3	2	6.2	6.6	5.1	2007	22.1	25.3
Libyan Arab Jamahiriya	498	531	1 426	1 637	3 165	3 381	107	4	4	6.9	7.2	2.7	1995	29.2	32.0
Madagascar	1 984	2 100	4 272	4 332	10 116	10 031	99	3	2	7.3	6.1	4.8	2004	19.8	24.1
Malawi	1 491	1 389	3 207	3 008	7 890	7 802	99	3	2	6.8	7.5	5.6	2004	19.0	23.6
Mali	2 082	2 186	3 584	3 599	6 743	6 580	98	2	2	6.2	6.6	5.5	2006	17.8	24.0
Mauritania	331	320	760	766	1 659	1 707	103	3	2	6.3	6.3	4.5	2001	21.8	29.4
Mauritius	248	246	490	476	655	642	98	8	5	6.3	2.5	1.8	2000	22.6	28.5
Mayotte	7	8	27	28	99	100	100	3	3	8.0	6.5	3.2	..	..	..
Morocco	4 472	4 481	9 781	9 786	16 484	15 897	96	5	4	7.2	5.4	2.4	2004	26.4	31.2
Mozambique	3 294	3 149	6 202	5 936	12 006	11 399	95	3	2	6.6	6.4	5.1	2003	18.7	..
Namibia	244	241	519	494	1 121	1 091	97	4	3	6.0	6.2	3.4	2007	28.3	30.2
Niger	1 306	1 155	2 970	2 952	7 931	7 961	100	2	2	6.9	8.1	7.1	2006	17.6	25.1
Nigeria	18 693	17 987	37 508	37 015	78 916	79 343	101	3	2	6.5	6.9	5.3	2003	20.9	28.0

Table 1.A
Population (*continued*)

Country or area	Population (*in thousands*)						Number of men per 100 women 2010	Share of population age 60 and above, 2010 (%)		Total fertility rate (*births per women*)			Singulate mean age at marriage		
	1950		1980		2010					1950–1955	1980–1985	2005–2010			
	Women	Men	Women	Men	Women	Men	2010	Women	Men				Year	Women	Men
Africa (*continued*)															
Réunion	129	119	259	248	429	408	95	8	5	5.7	2.9	2.4	1999	30.5	32.8
Rwanda	1 093	1 069	2 705	2 492	5 296	4 981	94	2	2	7.8	8.3	5.4	2005	23.7	26.5
Sao Tome and Principe	27	33	48	47	83	82	98	3	3	6.2	6.2	3.9	1991	17.8	23.1
Senegal	1 207	1 209	2 787	2 849	6 486	6 375	98	2	2	6.0	7.3	5.0	2005	21.2	..
Sierra Leone	992	952	1 675	1 586	2 992	2 844	95	2	2	5.5	5.7	5.2	2004	20.7	27.5
Somalia	1 140	1 124	3 254	3 180	4 717	4 642	98	3	2	7.3	6.7	6.4	..	..	..
South Africa	6 868	6 816	14 613	14 463	25 590	24 903	97	5	3	6.5	4.6	2.6	2003	28.0	30.6
Sudan	4 608	4 582	10 228	10 281	21 442	21 750	101	3	3	6.7	6.3	4.2	1993	22.7	29.1
Swaziland	140	133	317	286	613	588	96	3	2	6.7	6.5	3.6	2006	26.0	30.0
Togo	674	655	1 411	1 374	3 423	3 357	98	3	3	6.3	7.1	4.3	1998	21.3	27.0
Tunisia	1 771	1 759	3 185	3 272	5 158	5 216	101	6	5	6.9	4.9	1.9	1994	26.6	30.3
Uganda	2 586	2 572	6 357	6 298	16 864	16 932	100	2	2	6.9	7.1	6.4	2006	20.4	..
United Republic of Tanzania	3 918	3 731	9 450	9 212	22 574	22 466	100	3	2	6.7	6.6	5.6	2004	20.0	25.1
Western Sahara	7	7	69	81	250	280	112	2	2	6.6	5.6	2.7	..	..	..
Zambia	1 175	1 165	2 904	2 871	6 641	6 616	100	3	2	6.8	7.0	5.9	2002	20.5	24.8
Zimbabwe	1 377	1 370	3 661	3 621	6 526	6 118	94	4	3	6.8	6.7	3.5	2006	20.8	..
Asia															
Afghanistan	3 932	4 220	6 709	7 237	14 038	15 079	107	2	2	7.7	7.8	6.6	..	..	..
Armenia	711	642	1 587	1 509	1 650	1 440	87	11	7	4.5	2.4	1.7	2001	23.0	27.2
Azerbaijan	1 533	1 363	3 161	3 000	4 563	4 371	96	6	4	5.5	3.0	2.2	2006	23.1	26.7
Bahrain	53	62	145	202	344	463	134	2	2	7.0	4.6	2.3	2001	25.9	29.8
Bangladesh	20 191	23 404	43 869	46 528	81 292	83 134	102	3	3	6.7	5.9	2.4	2004	18.7	..
Bhutan	82	86	204	219	335	373	111	4	4	6.7	6.5	2.7	2005	21.8	25.4
Brunei Darussalam	23	25	90	103	197	210	106	3	3	7.0	3.8	2.1	1991	25.1	27.3
Cambodia	2 173	2 173	3 623	3 124	7 679	7 374	96	4	2	6.3	6.6	3.0	2004	22.8	24.6
China	261 847	283 104	475 493	505 435	651 304	702 843	108	7	7	6.1	2.6	1.8	2000	23.3	25.1
China, Hong Kong SAR	960	1 014	2 414	2 625	3 721	3 348	90	12	10	4.4	1.8	1.0	2006	30.3	32.8
China, Macao SAR	90	100	124	128	287	261	91	7	7	5.0	2.5	1.0	2001	27.9	29.5
Cyprus	250	244	306	305	451	429	95	12	10	3.7	2.4	1.5	2001	25.2	28.7
Democratic People's Republic of Korea	5 284	4 453	8 849	8 390	12 139	11 852	98	9	6	2.7	2.9	1.9	..	..	..
Georgia	1 898	1 629	2 692	2 381	2 236	1 983	89	14	9	3.0	2.3	1.6	..	..	..
India	178 748	193 108	332 121	360 517	587 266	627 198	107	4	4	5.9	4.5	2.8	2005	20.2	..
Indonesia	38 880	38 271	73 110	73 472	116 455	116 062	100	5	4	5.5	4.1	2.2	2005	23.4	27.0
Iran (Islamic Republic of)	8 327	8 586	19 212	20 118	36 924	38 154	103	4	4	7.0	6.6	1.8	2006	23.5	26.4
Iraq	2 867	2 852	6 877	7 147	15 557	15 909	102	3	2	7.3	6.4	4.1	2007	22.8	..
Israel	611	647	1 883	1 881	3 670	3 615	98	10	7	4.2	3.1	2.8	2006	25.8	28.7
Jordan	227	245	1 074	1 152	3 155	3 317	105	3	3	7.4	6.8	3.1	2004	25.4	28.6
Kazakhstan	3 459	3 244	7 733	7 186	8 257	7 497	91	8	4	4.4	3.0	2.3	1999	23.4	26.1

Table 1.A
Population (*continued*)

Country or area	Population (*in thousands*)						Number of men per 100 women	Share of population age 60 and above, 2010 (%)		Total fertility rate (*births per women*)			Singulate mean age at marriage		
	1950		1980		2010		2010			1950–1955	1980–1985	2005–2010	Year	Women	Men
	Women	Men	Women	Men	Women	Men	2010	Women	Men						
Asia (*continued*)															
Kuwait	62	90	587	788	1 239	1 811	146	2	3	7.2	4.9	2.2	1995	27.0	28.5
Kyrgyzstan	911	829	1 868	1 759	2 811	2 739	97	5	3	4.5	4.1	2.6	1999	21.9	25.0
Lao People's Democratic Republic	845	821	1 629	1 608	3 223	3 213	100	3	3	6.1	6.3	3.5	2005	21.7	24.7
Lebanon	717	726	1 405	1 380	2 172	2 083	96	6	5	5.7	3.9	1.9	2004	27.4	31.4
Malaysia	2 966	3 144	6 835	6 929	13 744	14 170	103	4	4	6.8	4.2	2.6	2000	25.1	28.6
Maldives	38	44	75	83	155	158	102	3	3	7.0	6.8	2.1	2006	23.0	26.4
Mongolia	389	373	830	834	1 366	1 336	98	4	3	6.0	5.7	2.0	2000	23.7	25.7
Myanmar	8 651	8 507	16 970	16 591	25 839	24 657	95	5	4	6.0	4.6	2.3	1991	24.5	26.4
Nepal	3 845	4 281	7 335	7 722	15 028	14 824	99	4	3	6.2	5.7	2.9	2006	19.4	22.4
Occupied Palestinian Territory	483	521	714	762	2 165	2 244	104	3	2	7.4	7.0	5.1	2004	22.4	..
Oman	225	232	562	625	1 269	1 636	129	2	3	7.2	7.2	3.1	2003	24.8	28.1
Pakistan	18 339	22 838	39 179	43 430	89 638	95 115	106	3	3	6.6	6.6	4.0	2007	23.1	..
Philippines	10 053	9 943	23 858	24 254	46 467	47 149	101	4	3	7.3	5.0	3.1	2003	23.2	26.1
Qatar	12	13	83	146	371	1 138	307	1	2	7.0	5.5	2.4	2004	25.8	27.6
Republic of Korea	9 643	9 568	18 703	18 756	24 485	24 016	98	10	7	5.1	2.2	1.2	2005	28.8	32.0
Saudi Arabia	1 577	1 625	4 416	5 188	11 891	14 355	121	2	3	7.2	7.0	3.2	2007	24.6	27.2
Singapore	493	529	1 182	1 232	2 408	2 429	101	10	8	6.4	1.7	1.3	2005	26.9	30.1
Sri Lanka	3 741	4 499	7 378	7 682	10 368	10 042	97	8	6	5.8	3.2	2.3	2001	23.8	27.6
Syrian Arab Republic	1 699	1 837	4 453	4 518	11 142	11 363	102	3	2	7.3	7.2	3.3	2001	25.4	29.3
Tajikistan	790	741	1 998	1 955	3 583	3 492	97	3	2	6.0	5.5	3.5	2000	21.3	24.1
Thailand	10 270	10 337	23 593	23 671	34 639	33 501	97	7	6	6.3	2.9	1.8	2000	24.1	27.4
Timor-Leste	214	219	285	296	575	596	104	3	2	6.4	5.4	6.5	2004	22.8	27.0
Turkey	10 762	10 722	22 840	23 321	37 689	38 016	101	5	4	6.9	4.0	2.1	2003	23.4	..
Turkmenistan	617	594	1 455	1 406	2 626	2 550	97	4	3	6.0	4.8	2.5	2000	23.4	..
United Arab Emirates	34	35	314	701	1 550	3 157	204	1	1	7.0	5.2	1.9	1995	24.4	26.6
Uzbekistan	3 257	3 057	8 108	7 844	13 979	13 815	99	4	3	6.0	4.7	2.3	1996	20.6	..
Viet Nam	13 757	13 610	27 444	25 874	45 018	44 011	98	6	4	5.7	4.5	2.1	2007	23.3	26.6
Yemen	2 137	2 179	4 201	4 181	11 994	12 262	102	2	2	8.2	8.7	5.3	2004	22.2	25.4
Latin America and the Caribbean															
Argentina	8 323	8 827	14 252	13 901	20 719	19 947	96	10	7	3.2	3.2	2.3	2001	24.6	26.9
Aruba	20	18	31	30	56	51	92	9	7	5.7	2.4	1.7	2000	26.8	29.9
Bahamas	42	37	106	104	177	169	96	7	5	4.1	3.2	2.0	2000	27.4	29.9
Barbados	114	97	130	119	132	125	94	11	7	4.7	1.9	1.5	1990	31.8	34.3
Belize	35	34	71	73	155	158	102	4	3	6.7	5.4	2.9	2000	21.0	23.7
Bolivia (Plurinational State of)	1 360	1 353	2 715	2 641	5 028	5 003	99	4	4	6.8	5.3	3.5	2003	22.6	24.5
Brazil	27 199	26 776	60 942	60 676	99 224	96 199	97	7	5	6.2	3.8	1.9	2000	23.1	26.2
Chile	3 069	3 012	5 666	5 515	8 661	8 474	98	9	7	5.0	2.7	1.9	2002	24.6	27.7

Table 1.A
Population (*continued*)

Country or area	Population (*in thousands*)						Number of men per 100 women	Share of population age 60 and above, 2010 (%)		Total fertility rate (*births per women*)			Singulate mean age at marriage		
	1950		1980		2010		2010			1950–1955	1980–1985	2005–2010	Year		
	Women	Men	Women	Men	Women	Men		Women	Men					Women	Men
Latin America and the Caribbean (*continued*)															
Colombia	6 027	5 973	13 501	13 390	23 515	22 785	97	5	4	6.8	3.7	2.5	2005	23.1	26.5
Costa Rica	473	493	1 151	1 197	2 284	2 356	103	6	5	6.7	3.5	2.0	2007	24.1	27.6
Cuba	2 863	3 057	4 858	4 977	5 588	5 616	100	11	9	4.2	1.8	1.5	2002	21.1	25.3
Dominican Republic	1 191	1 236	2 925	3 001	5 090	5 135	101	5	5	7.6	4.2	2.7	2002	21.9	26.1
Ecuador	1 704	1 684	3 960	4 005	6 877	6 898	100	6	5	6.7	4.7	2.6	2001	21.5	24.6
El Salvador	1 114	1 085	2 370	2 293	3 276	2 918	89	7	5	6.3	4.8	2.3	2007	22.5	25.5
French Guiana	12	13	33	35	116	115	100	4	3	5.0	3.6	3.3	1999	31.7	34.2
Grenada	42	35	46	43	52	52	100	7	5	5.8	4.2	2.3	1991	31.0	34.4
Guadeloupe	109	101	167	160	243	224	92	12	10	5.6	2.6	2.1	1999	31.6	34.2
Guatemala	1 557	1 589	3 469	3 547	7 370	7 007	95	4	3	7.0	6.1	4.2	1999	20.4	..
Guyana	217	206	392	384	370	391	106	5	5	6.7	3.3	2.3	2002	19.6	26.5
Haiti	1 649	1 572	2 891	2 800	5 155	5 033	98	4	3	6.3	6.2	3.5	2006	22.2	27.5
Honduras	739	748	1 809	1 825	3 809	3 806	100	4	3	7.5	6.0	3.3	2005	21.3	..
Jamaica	720	682	1 081	1 052	1 394	1 336	96	7	6	4.2	3.6	2.4	2001	33.2	34.8
Martinique	116	106	168	158	216	190	88	14	10	5.7	2.1	1.9	1999	33.3	35.6
Mexico	13 946	13 795	34 542	34 330	56 179	54 466	97	6	5	6.7	4.3	2.2	2000	22.7	25.0
Netherlands Antilles	58	54	90	84	108	93	86	10	7	5.7	2.4	2.0	2001	30.2	32.6
Nicaragua	651	644	1 622	1 628	2 941	2 881	98	4	3	7.2	5.9	2.8	2005	20.6	24.4
Panama	419	441	959	991	1 740	1 768	102	6	5	5.7	3.5	2.6	2000	21.9	25.8
Paraguay	748	725	1 586	1 613	3 200	3 260	102	5	4	6.5	5.2	3.1	2002	22.7	26.8
Peru	3 790	3 842	8 606	8 723	14 715	14 782	100	5	5	6.9	4.7	2.6	2004	24.7	..
Puerto Rico	1 104	1 114	1 640	1 557	2 081	1 917	92	13	10	5.0	2.5	1.8	2000	24.1	26.2
Saint Lucia	42	41	60	58	89	85	96	6	5	6.0	4.2	2.0	2001	22.8	27.7
Saint Vincent and the Grenadines	35	32	52	49	54	55	102	6	5	7.3	3.6	2.1	2002	21.2	27.8
Suriname	108	107	181	185	262	263	100	6	5	6.6	3.7	2.4	..	..	..
Trinidad and Tobago	319	317	541	541	691	653	94	7	5	5.3	3.2	1.6	1990	26.8	29.8
United States Virgin Islands	14	13	51	47	58	52	90	13	10	5.6	3.7	2.1	1990	27.5	30.1
Uruguay	1 106	1 132	1 486	1 430	1 745	1 628	93	13	9	2.7	2.6	2.1	1996	23.3	25.6
Venezuela (Bolivarian Republic of)	2 514	2 579	7 456	7 641	14 468	14 576	101	5	5	6.5	4.0	2.5	2001	22.7	26.0
Oceania															
Fiji	138	151	313	321	421	433	103	5	4	6.6	3.8	2.8	1996	22.9	26.1
French Polynesia	30	31	72	79	133	139	104	5	5	6.0	3.8	2.2	2007	33.1	35.5
Guam	19	40	51	56	88	91	103	6	6	5.5	3.1	2.5	1990	24.4	26.8
Micronesia (Federated States of)	16	16	36	37	54	57	104	4	3	7.2	6.0	3.6	1994	24.3	26.5
New Caledonia	31	34	69	73	127	127	100	7	6	5.0	3.3	2.1	1996	30.4	32.5
Papua New Guinea	851	947	1 498	1 701	3 388	3 500	103	2	2	6.2	5.5	4.1	1996	20.8	..
Samoa	40	42	76	79	86	93	109	5	3	5.0	4.9	4.0	2001	24.3	28.6

Table 1.A
Population (*continued*)

Country or area	Population (*in thousands*)						Number of men per 100 women	Share of population age 60 and above, 2010 (%)		Total fertility rate (*births per women*)			Singulate mean age at marriage		
	1950		1980		2010		2010								
	Women	Men	Women	Men	Women	Men	2010	Women	Men	1950–1955	1980–1985	2005–2010	Year	Women	Men
Oceania (*continued*)															
Solomon Islands	40	49	110	119	258	277	107	3	3	6.4	6.4	3.9	..	..	..
Tonga	23	24	48	49	51	53	103	5	4	7.3	5.5	4.0	1996	25.5	28.0
Vanuatu	23	25	55	62	120	125	104	3	3	7.6	5.4	4.0	..	..	..
More developed regions															
Albania	603	612	1 293	1 379	1 606	1 563	97	9	7	5.6	3.4	1.9	2001	23.3	27.3
Australia	4 075	4 144	7 357	7 338	10 817	10 695	99	13	11	3.2	1.9	1.8	2006	29.7	31.6
Austria	3 716	3 220	3 982	3 567	4 294	4 093	95	16	11	2.1	1.6	1.4	2001	26.6	29.5
Belarus	4 321	3 424	5 173	4 485	5 132	4 456	87	14	7	2.6	2.1	1.3	1999	22.8	25.4
Belgium	4 376	4 252	5 026	4 802	5 458	5 240	96	16	12	2.3	1.6	1.8	2006	29.8	32.2
Bosnia and Herzegovina	1 377	1 285	1 987	1 926	1 951	1 809	93	12	9	4.8	2.0	1.2	..	..	..
Bulgaria	3 627	3 624	4 446	4 415	3 875	3 622	93	17	12	2.5	2.0	1.4	2001	24.2	27.5
Canada	6 768	6 969	12 305	12 211	17 103	16 787	98	13	11	3.6	1.6	1.6	2006	26.6	28.6
Channel Islands	53	49	67	62	77	73	96	15	12	2.1	1.4	1.4	..	..	..
Croatia	2 016	1 834	2 258	2 118	2 285	2 125	93	17	11	2.8	2.0	1.4	2001	26.2	29.8
Czech Republic	4 588	4 337	5 300	4 984	5 296	5 115	97	15	10	2.7	2.0	1.4	2007	28.9	31.2
Denmark	2 153	2 118	2 594	2 529	2 763	2 718	98	15	12	2.6	1.4	1.8	2008	30.8	32.7
Estonia	631	470	792	681	722	618	86	18	9	2.1	2.1	1.6	2000	24.5	26.7
Finland	2 093	1 916	2 469	2 311	2 725	2 621	96	17	12	3.0	1.7	1.8	2007	30.5	32.2
France	21 723	20 109	27 623	26 327	32 175	30 461	95	17	12	2.7	1.9	1.9	2006	31.6	33.4
Germany	36 883	31 493	41 032	37 257	41 801	40 255	96	18	13	2.2	1.5	1.3	2006	31.0	33.7
Greece	3 879	3 687	4 909	4 733	5 638	5 545	98	16	13	2.3	2.0	1.4	2001	26.9	31.3
Hungary	4 848	4 490	5 520	5 188	5 239	4 734	90	16	10	2.7	1.8	1.4	2007	29.7	32.0
Iceland	72	71	113	115	160	169	106	11	9	3.7	2.2	2.1	2007	27.6	29.7
Ireland	1 458	1 511	1 691	1 710	2 290	2 299	100	10	8	3.4	2.9	2.0	2006	31.4	32.4
Italy	23 795	22 571	29 018	27 289	30 846	29 252	95	19	14	2.4	1.5	1.4	2006	30.0	33.3
Japan	42 199	40 625	59 344	57 450	65 161	61 834	95	21	16	3.0	1.8	1.3	2005	29.4	31.1
Latvia	1 106	843	1 356	1 156	1 207	1 033	86	18	9	2.0	2.0	1.4	2008	28.8	31.2
Lithuania	1 409	1 158	1 807	1 607	1 731	1 525	88	17	9	2.7	2.0	1.3	2008	27.1	29.7
Luxembourg	148	148	186	178	248	244	99	13	10	2.0	1.5	1.7	2001	27.8	30.6
Malta	158	154	166	158	206	204	99	14	11	4.1	2.0	1.3	..	..	..
Montenegro	209	190	290	286	318	308	97	11	9	3.2	2.2	1.6	2003	29.3	34.5
Netherlands	5 073	5 041	7 128	7 021	8 394	8 259	98	15	11	3.1	1.5	1.7	2008	31.2	33.6
New Zealand	949	959	1 582	1 565	2 177	2 126	98	12	10	3.7	2.0	2.0	2006	25.6	27.0
Norway	1 647	1 618	2 061	2 025	2 440	2 415	99	14	11	2.6	1.7	1.9	2007	31.9	34.0
Poland	12 994	11 830	18 242	17 332	19 700	18 338	93	14	9	3.6	2.3	1.3	2002	25.3	28.0
Portugal	4 362	4 043	5 065	4 701	5 535	5 197	94	16	12	3.0	2.0	1.4	2001	25.6	28.3
Republic of Moldova	1 248	1 093	2 114	1 896	1 878	1 698	90	11	7	3.5	2.6	1.5	2005	21.9	25.4
Romania	8 444	7 867	11 248	10 954	10 893	10 297	95	14	10	2.9	2.3	1.3	2008	26.0	29.2
Russian Federation	58 624	44 078	74 768	63 888	75 547	64 820	86	14	7	2.9	2.0	1.4	2002	23.6	26.3

Table 1.A
Population (*continued*)

Country or area	Population (*in thousands*) 1950 Women	1950 Men	1980 Women	1980 Men	2010 Women	2010 Men	Number of men per 100 women 2010	Share of population age 60 and above, 2010 (%) Women	Men	Total fertility rate (*births per women*) 1950–1955	1980–1985	2005–2010	Singulate mean age at marriage Year	Women	Men
More developed regions (*continued*)															
Serbia	3 462	3 270	4 513	4 434	4 979	4 877	98	13	10	3.2	2.3	1.6	2002	25.9	29.8
Slovakia	1 782	1 681	2 531	2 446	2 787	2 625	94	13	8	3.5	2.3	1.3	2006	27.6	30.1
Slovenia	769	704	947	885	1 036	989	96	16	10	2.8	1.9	1.4	2006	31.2	33.4
Spain	14 483	13 526	19 121	18 406	22 956	22 360	97	16	12	2.6	1.9	1.4	2001	29.3	31.6
Sweden	3 521	3 493	4 193	4 118	4 679	4 614	99	17	13	2.2	1.6	1.9	2006	32.2	34.3
Switzerland	2 431	2 261	3 245	3 074	3 887	3 707	95	16	12	2.3	1.5	1.5	2007	29.4	32.2
The former Yugoslav Republic of Macedonia	613	616	886	909	1 023	1 020	100	11	8	5.3	2.3	1.4	1994	22.9	26.7
Ukraine	21 289	16 009	27 179	22 865	24 489	20 944	86	16	8	2.8	2.0	1.3	2007	23.1	25.9
United Kingdom	26 041	24 575	28 912	27 402	31 512	30 388	96	16	12	2.2	1.8	1.8	2001	26.3	28.1
United States of America	78 983	78 830	117 017	112 452	160 847	156 794	97	13	9	3.4	1.8	2.1	2000	26.0	27.8

Sources

Population: United Nations, *World Population Prospects: The 2008 Revision*, New York, 2009.

Number of men per 100 women: Computed by the United Nations Statistics Division based on data from United Nations, *World Population Prospects: The 2008 Revision*, New York, 2009.

Share of population age 60 and above: Computed by the United Nations Statistics Division based on data from United Nations, *World Population Prospects: The 2008 Revision*, New York, 2009.

Total fertility rate: United Nations, *World Population Prospects: The 2008 Revision, New York*, 2009.

Singulate mean age at marriage: United Nations, World Marriage Data 2008, *http://www.un.org/esa/population/publications/WMD2008/Main.html* (accessed in December 2009).

Definitions

Population: Estimated de facto population in a country or area as of 1 July of the year indicated.

Share of population age 60 and above: Percentage of the population in the country or area aged 60 and above, calculated separately for each sex.

Total fertility rate: The number of children that a woman would have over her child-bearing period if she experienced the age-specific fertility rates of the given period.

Singulate mean age at marriage: Average number of years lived prior to first marriage by a hypothetical cohort, if they marry before age 50. Data shown refer to the latest year available in the period 1990 to 2008.

Note

.. Data not available or not reported separately.

Table 2.A
Health

Country or area	Life expectancy at birth, 2005–2010 (*years*)		Under 5 mortality, 2005–2010 (*per thousand live births*)		Pregnant women who received prenatal care, 2000–2008[a] (%)	Deliveries attended by skilled attendant, 2000–2007[a] (%)	Maternal mortality ratio, 2005 (per 100,000 live births)	Contraceptive prevalence, 2000–2008[a] (%)	People living with HIV, 2007	
	Women	Men	Girls	Boys					Estimated number (thousands)	Women among adults (%)
Africa										
Algeria	74	71	31	35	89	95	180	61	21	29
Angola	49	45	189	220	80	47	1 400	6	190	58
Benin	62	60	118	123	88	78	840	17	64	58
Botswana	55	55	47	60	97	94	380	44	300	57
Burkina Faso	54	52	154	160	85	54	700	17	130	47
Burundi	52	49	155	177	92	34	1 100	20	110	48
Cameroon	52	50	136	151	82	63	1 000	29	540	56
Cape Verde	74	68	23	38	98	78	210	61	..	..
Central African Republic	48	45	163	196	69	53	980	19	160	57
Chad	50	47	201	220	39	14	1 500	3	200	55
Comoros	67	63	54	71	75	62	400	26	—	..
Congo	55	53	122	135	86	83	740	44	79	54
Côte d'Ivoire	59	56	117	129	85	57	810	13	480	52
Democratic Republic of the Congo	49	46	187	209	85	74	1 100	21	..	..
Djibouti	57	54	116	134	92	61	650	18	16	54
Egypt	72	68	39	42	74	79	130	60	9	28
Equatorial Guinea	51	49	160	177	86	65	680	10	11	54
Eritrea	62	57	71	78	70	28	450	8	38	55
Ethiopia	56	54	124	138	28	6	720	15	980	54
Gabon	62	59	75	85	94	86	520	33	49	55
Gambia	57	54	109	123	98	57	690	18	8	55
Ghana	57	56	115	119	92	50	560	24	260	58
Guinea	60	56	138	157	82	38	910	9	87	55
Guinea-Bissau	49	46	186	207	78	39	1 100	10	16	54
Kenya	55	54	95	112	88	42	560	39	..	..
Lesotho	46	44	96	112	90	55	960	37	270	56
Liberia	59	57	136	144	79	46	1 200	11	35	54
Libyan Arab Jamahiriya	77	72	19	20	..	..	97	..	..	..
Madagascar	62	59	95	105	80	51	510	27	14	24
Malawi	54	52	117	125	92	54	1 100	41	930	53
Mali	49	48	188	193	70	49	970	8	100	56
Mauritania	59	55	112	128	75	61	820	9	14	28
Mauritius	76	69	15	20	..	98	15	76	13	29
Mayotte	80	72	8	10	..	..	..	..	..	..
Morocco	73	69	29	43	98	63	240	63	21	28
Mozambique	49	47	144	162	85	48	520	17	1 500	54
Namibia	62	60	45	58	95	81	210	55	200	55
Niger	52	50	173	171	46	33	1 800	11	60	28
Nigeria	48	47	184	190	58	35	1 100	15	2 600	54

Table 2.A
Health (continued)

Country or area	Life expectancy at birth, 2005–2010 (years)		Under 5 mortality, 2005–2010 (per thousand live births)		Pregnant women who received prenatal care, 2000–2008[a] (%)	Deliveries attended by skilled attendant, 2000–2007[a] (%)	Maternal mortality ratio, 2005 (per 100,000 live births)	Contraceptive prevalence, 2000–2008[a] (%)	People living with HIV, 2007	
	Women	Men	Girls	Boys					Estimated number (thousands)	Women among adults (%)
Africa (continued)										
Réunion	81	72	8	10	..	..	..	..	..	..
Rwanda	52	48	143	167	96	52	1 300	36	150	52
Sao Tome and Principe	67	64	90	99	97	81	..	29	..	..
Senegal	57	54	114	125	87	52	980	12	67	57
Sierra Leone	49	46	136	160	81	43	2 100	8	55	55
Somalia	51	48	174	186	26	33	1 400	15	24	28
South Africa	53	50	64	79	92	92	400	60	5 700	56
Sudan	60	56	104	117	64	49	450	8	320	53
Swaziland	45	46	92	111	85	69	390	50	190	53
Togo	64	61	91	105	84	62	510	17	130	53
Tunisia	76	72	21	24	92	90	100	60	4	27
Uganda	53	52	116	129	94	42	550	24	940	51
United Republic of Tanzania	56	55	100	112	78	43	950	26	1 400	54
Western Sahara	68	64	50	62	..	..	..	..	..	..
Zambia	46	45	152	169	94	47	830	41	1 100	51
Zimbabwe	44	43	88	100	95	69	880	60	1 300	52
Asia										
Afghanistan	44	44	238	233	16	14	1 800	19	..	..
Armenia	77	70	25	29	93	98	76	53	2	..
Azerbaijan	72	68	52	54	77	88	82	51	8	17
Bahrain	77	74	13	13	..	..	32	..	<1	..
Bangladesh	67	65	56	58	51	18	570	56	12	17
Bhutan	68	64	59	69	88	56	440	31	—	..
Brunei Darussalam	80	75	6	7	..	..	13	..	..	..
Cambodia	63	59	85	92	69	44	540	40	75	27
China	75	71	35	25	90	98	45	87	700	29
China, Hong Kong SAR	85	79	4	5	..	..	..	84	..	..
China, Macao SAR	83	79	5	6	..	..	..	..	..	..
Cyprus	82	77	6	7	..	100	10	..	—	..
Democratic People's Republic of Korea	69	65	63	63	..	97	370	69	..	..
Georgia	75	68	33	39	94	98	66	47	3	..
India	65	62	86	77	74	47	450	56	2 400	37
Indonesia	73	69	27	37	93	73	420	61	270	20
Iran (Islamic Republic of)	73	70	35	33	..	97	140	73	86	28
Iraq	72	63	38	43	84	89	300	50	..	..
Israel	83	79	5	6	..	..	4	..	5	57
Jordan	74	71	19	24	99	99	62	57	<1	..
Kazakhstan	71	59	26	34	100	100	140	51	12	28

Table 2.A
Health (*continued*)

Country or area	Life expectancy at birth, 2005–2010 (*years*)		Under 5 mortality, 2005–2010 (*per thousand live births*)		Pregnant women who received prenatal care, 2000–2008[a] (%)	Deliveries attended by skilled attendant, 2000–2007[a] (%)	Maternal mortality ratio, 2005 (per 100,000 live births)	Contraceptive prevalence, 2000–2008[a] (%)	People living with HIV, 2007	
	Women	Men	Girls	Boys					Estimated number (thousands)	Women among adults (%)
Asia (*continued*)										
Kuwait	80	76	9	11	..	..	4	..	<1	..
Kyrgyzstan	72	64	42	49	97	98	150	48	4	26
Lao People's Democratic Republic	66	63	61	68	35	20	660	32	5	24
Lebanon	74	70	21	31	96	..	150	58	3	..
Malaysia	77	72	10	12	79	98	62	..	80	26
Maldives	73	70	20	31	81	84	120	39	..	..
Mongolia	70	63	40	49	99	99	46	66	<1	..
Myanmar	63	59	102	120	76	57	380	37	240	42
Nepal	67	66	55	52	77	19	830	48	70	24
Occupied Palestinian Territory	75	72	18	23	99	99	..	50	..	..
Oman	77	74	13	14	100	98	64	..	..	..
Pakistan	67	66	94	85	61	39	320	30	96	28
Philippines	74	70	21	32	88	60	230	51	8	27
Qatar	77	75	10	10	..	..	12	..	..	..
Republic of Korea	83	76	6	6	..	..	14	80	13	28
Saudi Arabia	75	71	17	26	..	..	18	24	..	..
Singapore	83	78	4	4	..	..	14	..	4	29
Sri Lanka	78	70	18	21	99	99	58	68	4	37
Syrian Arab Republic	76	72	16	21	84	93	130	58	..	..
Tajikistan	69	64	74	83	77	83	170	38	10	21
Thailand	72	66	8	13	98	97	110	81	610	41
Timor-Leste	62	60	91	92	61	18	380	10	..	..
Turkey	74	69	27	36	81	83	44	71	<2	..
Turkmenistan	69	61	56	72	99	100	130	62	—	..
United Arab Emirates	79	77	12	10	..	..	37	..	..	..
Uzbekistan	71	65	53	63	99	100	24	65	16	29
Viet Nam	76	72	20	27	91	88	150	79	290	26
Yemen	64	61	73	84	94	36	430	28	..	..
Latin America and the Caribbean										
Argentina	79	72	14	17	99	99	77	65	..	..
Aruba	77	72	14	22	..	..	..	..	..	..
Bahamas	76	71	12	14	98	99	16	..	6	26
Barbados	80	74	10	12	100	100	16	55	2	..
Belize	78	74	19	23	94	96	52	34	4	56
Bolivia (Plurinational State of)	68	63	56	65	77	66	290	61	8	27
Brazil	76	69	25	33	97	..	110	..	730	33
Chile	82	76	8	10	..	100	16	64	31	28
Colombia	77	69	22	30	94	96	130	78	170	28

Table 2.A
Health (continued)

Country or area	Life expectancy at birth, 2005–2010 (years)		Under 5 mortality, 2005–2010 (per thousand live births)		Pregnant women who received prenatal care, 2000–2008[a] (%)	Deliveries attended by skilled attendant, 2000–2007[a] (%)	Maternal mortality ratio, 2005 (per 100,000 live births)	Contraceptive prevalence, 2000–2008[a] (%)	People living with HIV, 2007	
	Women	Men	Girls	Boys					Estimated number (thousands)	Women among adults (%)
Latin America and the Caribbean (continued)										
Costa Rica	81	76	10	13	92	99	30	..	10	28
Cuba	81	77	6	9	100	100	45	73	6	29
Dominican Republic	75	70	29	37	99	99	150	73	62	48
Ecuador	78	72	22	29	84	..	210	73	26	27
El Salvador	76	67	23	29	86	92	170	73	35	28
French Guiana	80	73	10	20	..	..	..	..	..	..
Grenada	77	74	15	16	100	100	..	54	..	..
Guadeloupe	82	76	8	10	..	..	..	..	..	..
Guatemala	74	67	34	45	84	41	290	43	59	25
Guyana	70	64	47	66	81	83	470	34	13	55
Haiti	63	59	80	90	85	26	670	32	120	48
Honduras	75	70	35	44	92	67	280	65	28	26
Jamaica	75	68	28	28	91	97	170	69	27	28
Martinique	82	77	8	8	..	..	..	..	..	..
Mexico	79	74	18	22	..	93	60	71	200	29
Netherlands Antilles	79	73	12	16	..	..	..	..	..	..
Nicaragua	76	70	22	29	90	74	170	72	8	27
Panama	78	73	20	27	..	91	130	..	20	28
Paraguay	74	70	32	44	94	77	150	79	21	28
Peru	76	71	27	38	91	71	240	71	76	28
Puerto Rico	83	75	8	9	..	..	..	84	..	..
Saint Lucia	76	72	14	18	99	100	..	..	..	..
Saint Vincent and the Grenadines	74	69	22	33	..	100	..	..	..	..
Suriname	73	65	26	35	90	90	72	42	7	28
Trinidad and Tobago	73	66	28	37	96	98	45	43	14	55
United States Virgin Islands	82	76	10	10	..	..	..	78	..	..
Uruguay	80	73	15	18	97	..	20	77	10	28
Venezuela (Bolivarian Republic of)	77	71	19	24	94	95	57	..	..	..
Oceania										
Fiji	71	67	24	25	..	99	210	44	..	..
French Polynesia	77	72	10	10	..	..	..	..	..	..
Guam	78	73	10	11	..	..	..	..	..	..
Micronesia (Federated States of)	69	68	43	41	..	88	..	..	..	..
New Caledonia	80	73	8	9	..	..	..	..	..	..
Papua New Guinea	63	59	68	70	..	41	470	..	54	39
Samoa	75	69	25	28	..	..	..	..	..	..
Solomon Islands	67	65	57	56	..	..	220	7	..	..

Table 2.A
Health. (continued)

Country or area	Life expectancy at birth, 2005–2010 (years)		Under 5 mortality, 2005–2010 (per thousand live births)		Pregnant women who received prenatal care, 2000–2008[a] (%)	Deliveries attended by skilled attendant, 2000–2007[a] (%)	Maternal mortality ratio, 2005 (per 100,000 live births)	Contraceptive prevalence, 2000–2008[a] (%)	People living with HIV, 2007	
	Women	Men	Girls	Boys					Estimated number (thousands)	Women among adults (%)
Oceania (continued)										
Tonga	75	69	26	26	..	95	..	33	..	..
Vanuatu	72	68	29	39	..	..	..	28	..	..
More developed regions										
Albania	80	73	17	18	97	100	92	60	..	..
Australia	84	79	5	6	..	..	4	71	18	7
Austria	83	77	5	6	..	..	4	..	10	30
Belarus	75	63	9	14	99	100	18	73	13	30
Belgium	83	77	5	6	..	..	8	75	15	27
Bosnia and Herzegovina	78	72	12	17	99	100	3	36	—	..
Bulgaria	77	70	13	17	..	99	11	..	..	..
Canada	83	78	6	6	..	98	7	74	73	27
Channel Islands	81	77	6	6	..	..	..	..	..	..
Croatia	80	73	7	8	..	100	7	..	—	..
Czech Republic	80	73	4	5	..	100	4	..	1	..
Denmark	81	76	6	6	..	..	3	..	5	23
Estonia	78	68	8	11	..	100	25	..	10	24
Finland	83	76	4	5	..	..	7	..	2	..
France	85	78	4	5	..	..	8	82	140	27
Germany	82	77	5	5	..	..	4	..	53	28
Greece	81	77	4	5	..	..	3	76	11	27
Hungary	77	69	8	9	..	100	6	..	3	..
Iceland	83	80	4	4	..	..	4	..	—	..
Ireland	82	78	6	6	..	100	1	75	5	27
Italy	84	78	4	5	..	..	3	..	150	27
Japan	86	79	4	5	..	..	6	54	10	24
Latvia	77	67	10	12	..	100	10	..	10	27
Lithuania	78	66	9	14	..	100	11	..	2	..
Luxembourg	82	77	6	6	..	100	12	..	..	..
Malta	81	78	7	7	..	..	8	..	—	..
Republic of Moldova	72	65	21	26	98	100	22	68	9	30
Montenegro	76	72	9	11	97	100	..	39	..	..
Netherlands	82	78	5	6	..	..	6	67	18	27
New Zealand	82	78	5	6	..	..	9	..	1	..
Norway	83	78	4	5	..	..	7	..	3	..
Poland	80	71	7	9	..	100	8	..	20	29
Portugal	82	75	5	6	..	100	11	67	34	28
Romania	76	69	15	20	94	98	24	70	15	47
Russian Federation	73	60	14	18	..	100	28	..	940	26
Serbia	76	72	13	15	98	99	..	41	6	28
Slovakia	79	71	8	9	..	100	6	..	—	..

Table 2.A
Health (continued)

Country or area	Life expectancy at birth, 2005–2010 (years)		Under 5 mortality, 2005–2010 (per thousand live births)		Pregnant women who received prenatal care, 2000–2008[a] (%)	Deliveries attended by skilled attendant, 2000–2007[a] (%)	Maternal mortality ratio, 2005 (per 100,000 live births)	Contraceptive prevalence, 2000–2008[a] (%)	People living with HIV, 2007	
	Women	Men	Girls	Boys					Estimated number (thousands)	Women among adults (%)
More developed regions (continued)										
Slovenia	82	75	4	5	..	100	6	..	—	..
Spain	84	78	5	5	..	..	4	66	140	20
Sweden	83	79	4	4	..	..	3	..	6	47
Switzerland	84	79	5	6	..	..	5	..	25	37
The former Yugoslav Republic of Macedonia	77	72	16	17	94	99	10	14	—	..
Ukraine	74	63	13	18	99	99	18	67	440	43
United Kingdom	82	77	6	6	..	..	8	82	77	29
United States of America	81	77	8	7	..	..	11	73	1 200	19

Sources

Life expectancy at birth: United Nations, World Population Prospects: 2008 Revision, New York, 2009.

Under 5 mortality: United Nations, World Population Prospects: 2008 Revision, New York, 2009.

Pregnant women who received prenatal care: United Nations, MDG Database, *http://mdgs.un.org/unsd/mdg/Data.aspx* (accessed August 2009).

Deliveries attended by skilled attendant: United Nations, MDG Database, *http://mdgs.un.org/unsd/mdg/Data.aspx* (accessed August 2009).

Maternal mortality ratio: WHO, Maternal Mortality in 2005: Estimates prepared by WHO, UNICEF, UNFPA and the World Bank, Geneva, 2007.

Contraceptive prevalence: United Nations, World Contraceptive Use 2009, Wall chart, New York, 2009

People living with HIV/AIDS: UNAIDS (The Joint United Nations Programme on HIV/AIDS), 2008 Report on the Global AIDS Epidemic, Geneva, 2008.

Definitions

Life expectancy: The average number of years a newborn infant can expect to live if prevailing patterns of age-specific mortality rates at the time of her (or his) birth were to stay the same throughout her (his) life.

Under 5 mortality: The probability of dying between birth and exact age 5, expressed as deaths per 1,000 live births.

Pregnant women who received at least once prenatal care: Women aged 15-49 who received antenatal care provided by skilled health personnel (doctors, nurses, or midwives) at least once during pregnancy, as a percentage of women age 15-49 years with a live birth in a given time period.

Deliveries attended by skilled attendant: Percentage of deliveries attended by personnel trained to give the necessary care, supervision and advice to women during pregnancy, labour and the post-partum period; to conduct deliveries on their own; and to care for newborns, such as doctors, nurses or midwives. Traditional birth attendants, even if they receive a short training course, are not included.

Maternal mortality ratio: The annual number of female deaths from any cause related to or aggravated by pregnancy or its management (excluding accidental or incidental causes) during pregnancy and childbirth or within 42 days of termination of pregnancy, irrespective of the duration and site of the pregnancy, for a specified year (expressed per 100,000 live births).

Contraceptive prevalence: Percentage of married or in union women aged 15-49 years using, or whose partners are using, any form of contraception. A union involves a man and a woman regularly cohabiting in a marriage-like relationship.

People living with HIV: The estimated number of adults and children alive with HIV infection, regardless of whether they have developed symptoms of AIDS. Estimates are for the end of 2007.

Notes

.. Data not available or not reported separately.

— Magnitude nil or less than half of unit employed.

a Data refer to the latest year available in the given interval.

Table 3.A
Education: Literacy and primary education

| | Literacy | | | | | Primary education | | | | | | |
| | Adult literacy rate, 2005–2008[a] (%) | | Youth literacy rate, 2005–2008[a] (%) | | Women's share among adult illiterate population, 2005–2008[a] (%) | Primary net enrolment rate, 2000–2007[a] (%) | | Survival rate to final grade of primary, 2000–2007[a] (%) | | Primary level repeaters, 2000–2007[a] (%) | | Girls' share among out-of-primary-school children, 2005–2008[a] (%) |
Country or area	Women	Men	Young women	Young men		Girls	Boys	Girls	Boys	Girls	Boys	
Africa												
Algeria	64	81	89	94	66	95	96	95	89	8	14	59
Angola	57[b]	83[b]	65[b]	81[b]	72[b]	..	..	..	..	..	..	..
Benin	28[b]	54[b]	42[b]	64[b]	61[b]	73	87	63	67	8	8	71
Botswana	84[b]	83[b]	96[b]	94[b]	50[b]	85	83	78	71	4[b]	6[b]	45
Burkina Faso	22	37	33	47	56	47	57	71	68	12	12	54
Burundi	60[b]	72[b]	75[b]	77[b]	61[b]	80	82	61	56	32	32	53
Cameroon	68[b]	84[b]	84[b]	88[b]	67[b]	..	..	58[b]	60[b]	20	20	..
Cape Verde	79[b]	90[b]	99[b]	97[b]	70[b]	84	85	92	86	10	15	52
Central African Republic	41[b]	69[b]	56[b]	72[b]	67[b]	45	63	35	43	27[b]	27[b]	60
Chad	22[b]	44[b]	37[b]	54[b]	59[b]	49[b]	71[b]	25	33	23[b]	21[b]	..
Comoros	68[b]	79[b]	84[b]	86[b]	61[b]	50[c]	60[c]	74[b]	69[b]	26[b]	28[b]	..
Congo	..	..	78	87	..	52[b]	56[b]	55	55	21[b]	21[b]	52[b]
Côte d'Ivoire	44[b]	64[b]	60[b]	72[b]	59[b]	49[c]	61[c]	66	83	21	22	..
Democratic Republic of the Congo	56[b]	78[b]	62[b]	69[b]	67[b]	32[d]	34[d]	..	..	16	16	..
Djibouti	..	..	..	..	..	37	43	..	..	9	9	52
Egypt	58	75	82	88	63	94[b]	98[b]	96[b]	94[b]	2	4	96[b]
Equatorial Guinea	89[b]	97[b]	98[b]	98[b]	78[b]	83	91	31[b]	34[b]	23	25	52
Eritrea	55[b]	77[b]	84[b]	91[b]	68[b]	38	44	61	59	14	15	52
Ethiopia	23[b]	50[b]	39[b]	62[b]	61[b]	68	74	59	57	5	7	55
Gabon	83[b]	91[b]	96[b]	98[b]	65[b]	88[b]	88[b]	57[b]	54[b]	34[b]	35[b]	..
Gambia	34[b]	57[b]	58[b]	70[b]	61[b]	73	69	66[b]	62[b]	6	6	45
Ghana	59[b]	72[b]	78[b]	81[b]	59[b]	71	73	65	55	6	6	48
Guinea	26[b]	50[b]	51[b]	67[b]	59[b]	69	79	72	82	10	9	60
Guinea-Bissau	37[b]	66[b]	62[b]	78[b]	66[b]	37[b]	53[b]	..	..	24[b]	24[b]	..
Kenya	83[b]	90[b]	93[b]	92[b]	64[b]	86	86	71[b]	74[b]	6[b]	6[b]	50
Lesotho	95[b]	83[b]	98[b]	86[b]	26[b]	74	71	71	53	18	24	47
Liberia	53[b]	63[b]	80[b]	70[b]	57[b]	39	40	..	..	6	6	51
Libyan Arab Jamahiriya	81[b]	95[b]	100[b]	100[b]	77[b]	..	..	..	..	..	..	..
Madagascar	65[b]	77[b]	68[b]	73[b]	60[b]	99	98	43	42	18	20	16
Malawi	66[b]	80[b]	85[b]	87[b]	64[b]	90	84	35	37	20	21	37
Mali	18	35	31	47	57	56	70	70	75	17[b]	17[b]	59
Mauritania	50[b]	64[b]	63[b]	71[b]	58[b]	83	78	55	54	3	3	42
Mauritius	85[b]	90[b]	97[b]	95[b]	62[b]	96	95	98	98	3	4	43
Morocco	44[b]	69[b]	68[b]	85[b]	66[b]	86	91	76	79	10	14	60
Mozambique	40[b]	70[b]	62[b]	78[b]	69[b]	73	79	41	48	6	6	56
Namibia	88[b]	89[b]	95[b]	91[b]	53[b]	89	84	87[b]	87[b]	14[b]	19[b]	38

Table 3.A
Education: Literacy and primary education (*continued*)

Country or area	Literacy					Primary education						
	Adult literacy rate, 2005–2008[a] (%)		Youth literacy rate, 2005–2008[a] (%)		Women's share among adult illiterate population, 2005–2008[a] (%)	Primary net enrolment rate, 2000–2007[a] (%)		Survival rate to final grade of primary, 2000–2007[a] (%)		Primary level repeaters, 2000–2007[a] (%)		Girls' share among out-of-primary-school children, 2005–2008[a] (%)
	Women	Men	Young women	Young men		Girls	Boys	Girls	Boys	Girls	Boys	
Africa (*continued*)												
Niger	15	43	23	52	61	38	51	67	72	5	5	55
Nigeria	49[b]	72[b]	65[b]	78[b]	65[b]	60[b]	68[b]	75[b]	75[b]	3[b]	3[b]	55[b]
Rwanda	66[b]	75[b]	77[b]	77[b]	60[b]	95	92	32	30	15[b]	15[b]	40
Sao Tome and Principe	83[b]	94[b]	96[b]	95[b]	73[b]	98	97	71	77	24	27	..
Senegal	33	52	45	58	59	72	72	53	54	10[b]	11[b]	50
Sierra Leone	29[b]	52[b]	46[b]	66[b]	62[b]	..	..	..	..	10	10	..
South Africa	88[b]	90[b]	98[b]	96[b]	66[b]	86[b]	86[b]	79	75	8[b]	8[b]	44[b]
Sudan	60[b]	79[b]	82[b]	89[b]	55[b]	37[b]	45[b]	60	64	3	3	..
Swaziland	86[b]	87[b]	95[b]	92[b]	55[b]	88	86	76	71	15	21	47
Togo	54[b]	77[b]	80[b]	87[b]	67[b]	72	82	39	49	24	23	63
Tunisia	71	86	96	98	68	95	95	94	94	6	9	40
Uganda	67[b]	82[b]	86[b]	89[b]	66[b]	96	93	25[b]	26[b]	13[b]	13[b]	36
United Republic of Tanzania	66[b]	79[b]	76[b]	79[b]	62[b]	97	98	85[b]	81[b]	4	4	65
Zambia	61[b]	81[b]	68[b]	82[b]	67[b]	94	94	67	83	6	7	44
Zimbabwe	89[b]	94[b]	99[b]	98[b]	69[b]	88	87	63[b]	62[b]	..	..	47
Asia												
Afghanistan	..	..	..	..	..	..	..	..	..	14	18	..
Armenia	99[b]	100[b]	100[b]	100[b]	71[b]	87	84	97	98	—	—	35
Azerbaijan	99	100	100	100	81	95[c]	96[c]	100	98	—	—	55[c]
Bahrain	89[b]	92[b]	100[b]	100[b]	46[b]	98	98	97	100	2	3	25
Bangladesh	50[b]	60[b]	76[b]	73[b]	55[b]	90[b]	83[b]	58	52	11	11	33[b]
Bhutan	39	65	68	80	60	79	79	88	81	6	8	45
Brunei Darussalam	93[b]	97[b]	100[b]	100[b]	65[b]	93	93	99	97	1	3	47
Cambodia	71	85	86	89	68	87	91	56	53	10	13	58
China	91[b]	97[b]	99[b]	99[b]	73[b]	..	..	..	..	—	—	..
China, Hong Kong SAR	..	..	..	..	..	89[b]	93[b]	100	99	1	1	..
China, Macao SAR	91	96	100	100	75	91	94	..	..	4	7	62
Cyprus	97[b]	99[b]	100[b]	100[b]	78[b]	99[c]	99[c]	100	100	—	—	50
Democratic People's Republic of Korea	100	100	100	100	71	..	..	..	..	..	..	..
Georgia	100[b]	100[b]	100[b]	100[b]	64[b]	92	95	89	83	—[b]	—[b]	60
India	51	75	74	88	65	87	90	65	66	3	3	65
Indonesia	89	95	96	97	70	93	97	81[b]	78[b]	3	4	..
Iran (Islamic Republic of)	77	87	96	97	63	100	91	87	88	1[b]	3[b]	..
Iraq	69[b]	86[b]	80[b]	85[b]	69[b]	82[b]	95[b]	61[b]	78[b]	7[b]	9[b]	78[b]
Israel	..	..	..	..	..	98	97	99	100	1	2	39

Table 3.A
Education: Literacy and primary education (*continued*)

Country or area	Literacy					Primary education						
	Adult literacy rate, 2005–2008[a] (%)		Youth literacy rate, 2005–2008[a] (%)		Women's share among adult illiterate population, 2005–2008[a] (%)	Primary net enrolment rate, 2000–2007[a] (%)		Survival rate to final grade of primary, 2000–2007[a] (%)		Primary level repeaters, 2000–2007[a] (%)		Girls' share among out-of-primary-school children, 2005–2008[a] (%)
	Women	Men	Young women	Young men		Girls	Boys	Girls	Boys	Girls	Boys	
Asia (*continued*)												
Jordan	89	95	99	99	70	89	88	95	96	1	1	44
Kazakhstan	100[b]	100[b]	100[b]	100[b]	74[b]	90	90	100	99	—	—	25
Kuwait	93	95	99	98	46	87	89	99	100	1	1	58
Kyrgyzstan	99[b]	100[b]	100[b]	100[b]	66[b]	84	85	97	96	—	—	49
Lao People's Democratic Republic	63	82	79	89	69	84	88	61	62	16	18	57
Lebanon	86	93	99	98	69	82	83	93	86	8	11	50
Malaysia	90[b]	94[b]	99[b]	98[b]	64[b]	97	98	90	89	..	..	52
Maldives	98	98	99	99	49	97	96	..	..	4	6	36
Mongolia	98[b]	97[b]	97[b]	93[b]	41[b]	89	88	83	86	—	1	21
Myanmar	89[b]	95[b]	95[b]	96[b]	69[b]	..	..	72	68	—	1	..
Nepal	45[h]	71[h]	75[h]	86[h]	67[b]	74	78	66[b]	57[b]	20[b]	21[b]	53
Occupied Palestinian Territory	91	97	99	99	76	73	73	99	99	1	1	48
Oman	81	90	98	98	57	74	72	98	97	2	1	47
Pakistan	40	67	59	79	63	57[b]	73[b]	72	68	5	6	60[b]
Philippines	94[b]	93[b]	96[b]	94[b]	48[b]	92	90	78	69	2	3	43
Qatar	90	94	99	99	29	93	93	89	89	1	1	42
Republic of Korea	..	..	..	..	..	93	100	97	97	—	—	..
Saudi Arabia	80[b]	90[b]	96[b]	98[b]	59[b]	84[c]	85[c]	..	..	3[c]	3[c]	51[c]
Singapore	92[b]	97[b]	100[b]	100[b]	76[b]	..	..	..	..	—[c]	—[c]	..
Sri Lanka	89	92	99	97	60	100[b]	99[b]	94[b]	93[b]	1[b]	1[b]	..
Syrian Arab Republic	77[b]	90[b]	93[b]	96[b]	69[b]	92	97	96	95	6	8	..
Tajikistan	100[b]	100[b]	100[b]	100[b]	73[b]	95	99	97[b]	100[b]	—[b]	—[b]	86
Thailand	92	96	98	98	67	94	94	..	..	6	12	43
Timor-Leste	..	..	..	..	..	67[b]	70[b]	..	..	14	15	50
Turkey	81	96	94	99	83	91	94	93	95	3[b]	3[b]	59
Turkmenistan	99[b]	100[b]	100[b]	100[b]	71[b]	..	..	..	..	..	..	..
United Arab Emirates	91	89	97	94	24	90	91	100	100	2	2	60
Uzbekistan	99[b]	100[b]	100[b]	100[b]	69[b]	90	92	99	99	—	—	59
Viet Nam	90[b]	95[b]	96[b]	97[b]	68[b]	91[b]	96[b]	86[b]	87[b]	2[b]	3[b]	..
Yemen	43[b]	79[b]	70[b]	95[b]	73[b]	65	85	57	61	4	5	70
Latin America and the Caribbean												
Argentina	98[b]	98[b]	99[b]	99[b]	51[b]	98	99	96	93	5	8	..
Aruba	98[b]	98[b]	99[b]	99[b]	55[b]	100	100	97	94	8	9	..
Bahamas	..	..	..	..	..	92	89	84	79	..	..	41
Barbados	..	..	..	..	..	97	96	99	96	..	..	43
Belize	..	..	..	..	..	98	96	86	82	8	11	..

Table 3.A
Education: Literacy and primary education (*continued*)

Country or area	Literacy					Primary education						
	Adult literacy rate, 2005–2008[a] (%)		Youth literacy rate, 2005–2008[a] (%)		Women's share among adult illiterate population, 2005–2008[a] (%)	Primary net enrolment rate, 2000–2007[a] (%)		Survival rate to final grade of primary, 2000–2007[a] (%)		Primary level repeaters, 2000–2007[a] (%)		Girls' share among out-of-primary-school children, 2005–2008[a] (%)
	Women	Men	Young women	Young men		Girls	Boys	Girls	Boys	Girls	Boys	
Latin America and the Caribbean (*continued*)												
Bolivia (Plurinational State of)	86	96	99	100	79	94	93	80	81	2	3	45
Brazil	90	90	99	97	50	95	93	84[b]	76[b]	20[b]	20[b]	49
Chile	99	99	99	99	49	94	95	98	98	2	3	53
Colombia	93	93	98	98	51	87	87	92	85	3	4	47
Costa Rica	96[b]	96[b]	99[b]	98[b]	46[b]	..	..	86	82	6	9	..
Cuba	100[b]	100[b]	100[b]	100[b]	50[b]	98	98	97	97	—	1	58
Dominican Republic	88	88	97	95	50	83	82	65	58	4	7	46
Ecuador	82	87	96	95	59	97	96	82	79	1	2	..
El Salvador	81	87	96	95	63	92	92	71	67	5	8	45
Grenada	..	..	..	..	..	75	77	..	..	2	3	53
Guatemala	69[b]	80[b]	84[b]	89[b]	63[b]	93	97	62	63	11	13	76
Guyana	..	..	..	..	..	..	..	56[b]	62[b]	1	2	..
Honduras	83	84	95	93	51	94	93	85	77	7	7	43
Jamaica	91[b]	81[b]	98[b]	92[b]	34[b]	87	86	91	84	2	3	46
Mexico	91	95	98	98	63	97	98	94	91	3	5	..
Netherlands Antilles	96[b]	96[b]	98[b]	98[b]	55[b]	..	..	91[b,d]	78[b,d]	10[b]	16[b]	..
Nicaragua	78	78	89	85	51	96	95	48	40	8	10	39
Panama	93[b]	94[b]	96[b]	97[b]	55[b]	98	99	89	88	4	7	63
Paraguay	93	96	99	99	60	95	94	86	82	4	6	46
Peru	85	95	97	98	75	97	95	90	90	8	8	..
Saint Lucia	..	..	..	..	..	97	98	97	95	2	3	50
Saint Vincent and the Grenadines	..	..	..	..	..	88	94	..	..	3	5	60
Suriname	88[b]	93[b]	95[b]	96[b]	63[b]	95	93	72	63	13	18	41
Trinidad and Tobago	98[b]	99[b]	100[b]	100[b]	68[b]	93	94	87[c]	80[c]	2	4	58
Uruguay	98	98	99	99	44	97	97	95	92	6	8	47
Venezuela (Bolivarian Republic of)	95	95	99	98	52	92	92	100	95	4	6	46
Oceania												
Fiji	..	..	..	..	.	91	91	82[b]	80[b]	2[b]	3[b]	47
Papua New Guinea	56[b]	64[b]	69[b]	65[b]	55[b]	..	..	..	..	..	..	..
Samoa	99[b]	99[b]	100[b]	99[b]	58[b]	91[b]	90[b]	94[c,d]	91[c,d]	1	2	..
Solomon Islands	69[d]	84[d]	80[d]	90[d]	64[d]	61	62	..	..	..	..	48
Tonga	99	99	100	99	47	94	97	92	90	4	6	..
Vanuatu	80[b]	83[b]	94[b]	94[b]	54[b]	86	88	71[d]	67[d]	10[b]	12[b]	51
More developed regions												
Albania	99[b]	99[b]	100[b]	99[b]	66[b]	93	94	91	89	2	3	..

Table 3.A
Education: Literacy and primary education (*continued*)

	Literacy					Primary education						
	Adult literacy rate, 2005–2008[a] (%)		Youth literacy rate, 2005–2008[a] (%)		Women's share among adult illiterate population, 2005–2008[a] (%)	Primary net enrolment rate, 2000–2007[a] (%)		Survival rate to final grade of primary, 2000–2007[a] (%)		Primary level repeaters, 2000–2007[a] (%)		Girls' share among out-of-primary-school children, 2005–2008[a] (%)
Country or area	Women	Men	Young women	Young men		Girls	Boys	Girls	Boys	Girls	Boys	
More developed regions (*continued*)												
Australia	..	..	..	..	..	97	97	..	..	..	..	43
Austria	..	..	..	..	..	98[b]	97[b]	99	97	1	1	38[b]
Belarus	100[b]	100[b]	100[b]	100[b]	64[b]	88[b]	90[b]	100	99	—	—	42
Belgium	..	..	..	..	..	98	98	95	92	3	3	..
Bosnia and Herzegovina	96[b]	99[b]	99[b]	100[b]	88[b]	..	..	..	..	—	1	..
Bulgaria	98[b]	99[b]	97[b]	97[b]	62[b]	94	95	94	94	2	3	51
Canada	..	..	..	..	..	100[b]	99[b]	..	..	..	..	..
Croatia	98[b]	100[b]	100[b]	100[b]	81[b]	90	91	100	100	—	—	5
Czech Republic	..	..	..	..	..	94[b]	91[b]	99	98	—	1	40[b]
Denmark	..	..	..	..	..	96	95	92	92	..	..	39
Estonia	100[b]	100[b]	100[b]	100[b]	55[b]	94	95	97	96	1	3	46
Finland	..	..	..	..	..	96	96	100	100	—	1	47
France	..	..	..	..	..	99	98	97[b,d]	98[b,d]	4[b]	4[b]	32
Germany	..	..	..	..	..	98[b]	98[b]	99	98	1	1	..
Greece	96[b]	98[b]	99[b]	99[b]	70[b]	100	100	98	98	1	1	50
Hungary	99[b]	99[b]	99[b]	98[b]	58[b]	86	87	98	98	2	2	48
Iceland	..	..	..	..	..	97	97	100	98	..	..	50
Ireland	..	..	..	..	..	96	96	..	..	1	1	43
Italy	99[b]	99[b]	100[b]	100[b]	64[b]	98	99	100	99	—	—	73
Latvia	100[b]	100[b]	100[b]	100[b]	55[b]	92[b]	89[b]	98	98	2	4	38[b]
Lithuania	100[b]	100[b]	100[b]	100[b]	54[b]	90	91	98	98	1	1	48
Luxembourg	..	..	..	..	..	98	97	92	88	3	5	25
Malta	94	91	99	97	43	91	92	100	99	2	3	50
Netherlands	..	..	..	..	..	98	99	98[b]	99[b]	..	..	69
New Zealand	..	..	..	..	..	99	99	..	..	..	..	24
Norway	..	..	..	..	..	99	99	99	100	..	..	48
Poland	99[b]	100[b]	100[b]	100[b]	72[b]	96	95	..	..	—	1	45
Portugal	93[b]	97[b]	100[b]	100[b]	69[b]	98	99	..	..	7[b]	13[b]	69
Republic of Moldova	98[b]	99[b]	100[b]	99[b]	71[b]	87[c]	88[c]	96	96	—	—	51[c]
Romania	97[b]	98[b]	98[b]	97[b]	66[b]	94	94	95	95	1	2	46
Russian Federation	99[b]	100[b]	100[b]	100[b]	71[b]	..	..	..	..	1[b]	1[b]	..
Serbia	96[b]	99[b]	99[b]	99[b]	81[b]	95[c]	95[c]	..	..	..	..	47[c]
Slovakia	..	..	..	..	..	92[b]	92[b]	98	98	2	3	47[b]
Slovenia	100[b]	100[b]	100[b]	100[b]	52[b]	96	96	99	98	—	1	50
Spain	97	98	100	100	67	100	100	100	100	2	3	80
Sweden	..	..	..	..	..	94	94	100	100	..	..	51
Switzerland	..	..	..	..	..	89	89	..	..	1	2	48

Table 3.A

Education: Literacy and primary education (*continued*)

Country or area	Literacy					Primary education						
	Adult literacy rate, 2005–2008[a] (%)		Youth literacy rate, 2005–2008[a] (%)		Women's share among adult illiterate population, 2005–2008[a] (%)	Primary net enrolment rate, 2000–2007[a] (%)		Survival rate to final grade of primary, 2000–2007[a] (%)		Primary level repeaters, 2000–2007[a] (%)		Girls' share among out-of-primary-school children, 2005–2008[a] (%)
	Women	Men	Young women	Young men		Girls	Boys	Girls	Boys	Girls	Boys	
More developed regions (*continued*)												
The former Yugoslav Republic of Macedonia	95[b]	99[b]	99[b]	99[b]	77[b]	89	89	99	98	—	—	46
Ukraine	100[b]	100[b]	100[b]	100[b]	71[b]	89[c]	89[c]	99[c]	97[c]	—[c]	—[c]	49[c]
United Kingdom	..	..	..	..	..	98	97	..	..	..	..	37
United States of America	..	..	..	..	..	93	92	87	100	..	..	43

Sources

Adult literacy rate: UNESCO Institute for Statistics, UIS Data Centre, *http://www.uis.unesco.org* (accessed in December 2009).

Youth literacy rate: UNESCO Institute for Statistics, UIS Data Centre, *http://www.uis.unesco.org* (accessed in December 2009).

Women's share among adult illiterate population: UNESCO Institute for Statistics, UIS Data Centre, *http://www.uis.unesco.org* (accessed in December 2009).

Primary net enrolment rate: UNESCO Institute for Statistics, correspondence in June 2009.

Survival rate to final grade of primary: UNESCO Institute for Statistics, correspondence in June 2009.

Primary level repeaters: UNESCO Institute for Statistics, correspondence in June 2009.

Girls' share among out-of-primary-school children: UNESCO, *EFA Global Monitoring Report 2010: Reaching the marginalized*, Paris, 2010.

Definitions

Adult literacy rate: Percentage of the population aged 15 years and over who can read and write with understanding a simple statement related to their daily life.

Youth literacy rate: Percentage of the population aged 15 to 24 years who can read and write with understanding a simple statement related to their daily life.

Women's share among adult illiterate population: Percentage of women among the adult population aged 15 years and over who cannot read and write with understanding a simple statement related to her (his) daily life.

Primary net enrolment rate: The number of children of official primary school age who are enrolled in primary education as a percentage of the total number of children of official primary school age.

Survival rate to final grade of primary: Percentage of a cohort of students enrolled in the first grade of the primary level of education in a given school year who are expected to reach the last grade of primary school, regardless of repetition.

Primary level repeaters: Proportion of students from a cohort enrolled in primary school in a given school year who study in the same grade in the following school year.

Girls' share among out-of-primary-school children: Percentage of girls among children of official primary school age who are not enrolled in either primary or secondary school.

Notes

..   Data not available or not reported separately.

—   Magnitude nil or less than 0.5 per cent.

a   Data refer to the latest year available in the given interval.

b   UIS estimation.

c   National estimation.

d   Data refer to year 1999.

Table 3.B
Education: Secondary and tertiary education, teaching staff and researchers

| Country or area | Secondary education | | | Tertiary education | | | Women's share among teaching staff, 2000–2007[a] (%) | | | Women's share among researchers, 2000–2007[a] (%) |
| | Secondary net enrolment rate, 2000–2007[a] (%) | | Girls' share of enrolment in secondary TVET, 2000–2007[a] (%) | Tertiary gross enrolment ratio, 2000–2007[a] (%) | | Women's share in total tertiary enrolment, 2000–2007[a] (%) | | | | |
	Girls	Boys		Women	Men		Primary	Secondary	Tertiary	
Africa										
Algeria	68[b]	65[b]	39[b]	28	20	57	53	49[b]	35[b]	35
Angola	..	..	42[b]	..	..	40[c]	..	30[b]	20[b]	..
Benin	11[b]	23[b]	43[b]	..	..	20[b]	17	12[b]	9[b]	..
Botswana	60[b]	52[b]	38	5	5	50	78	54[b]	37	31
Burkina Faso	10	14	49	2	3	31	31	17	9	13
Burundi	..	..	44	1	3	32	53	24	14[b]	..
Cameroon	..	..	39	6	8	44	43	26[b]	14[b]	19
Cape Verde	65	57	43	10	8	55	67	39	39	52
Central African Republic	..	..	..	..	..	22	13[b]	..	9	41
Chad	5[b]	16[b]	46	..	..	13[b]	13	5[b]	3[b]	..
Comoros	..	..	7[b]	2[b]	3[b]	43[b]	33[b]	13[b]	15[b]	..
Congo	..	..	51[b]	1[b]	6[b]	16[b]	44	14[b]	5[b]	13[d]
Côte d'Ivoire	14[b]	25[b]	50[e]	5	11	33	24	..	..	16
Democratic Republic of the Congo	..	..	38	2	6	26[c]	26	10	6[e]	..
Djibouti	17[b]	26[b]	42	2	3	40	26	24	17	..
Egypt	78[b]	82[b]	44[b]	..	..	..	56[b]	42[b]	..	36
Equatorial Guinea	..	..	20	2	4	30	34	4[b]	16	..
Eritrea	21	29	46	..	..	13	48	12	14	..
Ethiopia	19[b]	29[b]	44	1	4	25	28[e]	..	9	7
Gabon	..	..	34	5[e]	9[e]	36[e]	45[b]	16[b,e]	17[e]	25
Gambia	38	39	..	..	..	19	33	16	16	9
Ghana	43[b]	47[b]	50	4	8	34	33	22[b]	11	..
Guinea	22	37	14[b]	2	8	21	26	6[b]	3	6
Guinea-Bissau	6[b]	11[b]	27	..	..	16[b]	20[b]	7[b]	19[b]	..
Kenya	43[b]	47[b]	62	3	4	36	44[b]	40[b]	..	..
Lesotho	29[b]	19[b]	53	4	3	55	78	55	47	56
Liberia	12[b]	22[b]	40	13	18	43	27	26	16[b]	..
Libyan Arab Jamahiriya	..	..	53[b]	58[b]	53[b]	51[b]	..	..	13[b]	..
Madagascar	21[b]	21[b]	35	3	3	47	61	47[b]	30	35
Malawi	23	25	..	..	..	34	38	24	34	..
Mali	..	..	51	2	4	35[b]	27	13[b]	..	12
Mauritania	16[b]	18[b]	34[c]	2	5	26	35	10[b]	4	..
Mauritius	82[b]	81[b]	31[b]	18	16	53	65	56	26[b,e]	20[f]
Morocco	32[b]	37[b]	39	11	12	48	47	33[b]	19	28
Mozambique	2	3	31	1	2	33	34	16	21	34
Namibia	55[b]	44[b]	..	6	7	47	65[b]	50[b]	42	..

Table 3.B

Education: Secondary and tertiary education, teaching staff and researchers (*continued*)

	Secondary education			Tertiary education			Women's share among teaching staff, 2000–2007[a] (%)			Women's share among researchers, 2000–2007[a] (%)
	Secondary net enrolment rate, 2000–2007[a] (%)		Girls' share of enrolment in secondary TVET, 2000–2007[a] (%)	Tertiary gross enrolment ratio, 2000–2007[a] (%)		Women's share in total tertiary enrolment, 2000–2007[a] (%)				
Country or area	Girls	Boys		Women	Men		Primary	Secondary	Tertiary	
Africa (*continued*)										
Niger	7	11	17	1	2	29	43	17	6[b]	..
Nigeria	24[b]	30[b]	35	8	12	41	50	38	17	17
Rwanda	..	..	47[b]	2[b]	3[b]	39[b]	53	53	12[b]	..
Sao Tome and Principe	40	36	13	..	..	..	55[b]	13[b]	..	..
Senegal	19[b]	25[b]	40[b]	5[b]	9[b]	34[b]	28	15[b]	..	10
Sierra Leone	19	27	60	1[b]	3[b]	29[b]	26	16	15[b]	..
Somalia	..	..	..	..	..	..	35[e]	..	..	..
South Africa	76[b]	71[b]	39	17	14	55	77	53[b]	51	40
Sudan	..	..	21	6[b]	6[b]	47[b]	64	52	23[b,e]	40
Swaziland	27	32	26	4	4	50	70	48	40	..
Togo	14[b]	30[b]	38[b]	..	..	..	12	7[b]	11[b]	12
Tunisia	68[b]	61[b]	39	37	25	59	53	46	41	45
Uganda	18[b]	20[b]	33[b]	3	4	38	39	22[b]	19	41
United Republic of Tanzania	..	..	31[b,d]	1	2	32	49	..	18	..
Zambia	38	44	39	1[b]	3[b]	32[b]	48	39	..	27
Zimbabwe	36	38	..	3[b]	4[b]	39[b]	51	40	..	..
Asia										
Afghanistan	14[b]	37[b]	11	1	2	20	28	28	12	..
Armenia	88	83	33	37	31	55	100	84	47	45
Azerbaijan	82[c]	84[c]	28[b]	14[c]	16[c]	46	87	66	40	52
Bahrain	96	91	39	47	19	68	76[b]	54[b]	41[b]	..
Bangladesh	42	39	30	5	9	35	40	20	18	14[f]
Bhutan	39[b]	38[b]	36	3	7	31	50	41	27[b]	..
Brunei Darussalam	91	87	37	20	11	65	74	60	43	41
Cambodia	32[b]	36[b]	47	4	7	35	43	32	11	21
China	..	..	50	23	23	48	56	45[b]	43	..
China, Hong Kong SAR	79[c]	78[c]	15	34	33	50	78	56[b]	..	..
China, Macao SAR	79	76	44	55	59	49	88	59	31	22
Cyprus	96[c]	94[c]	15	36[c]	36[c]	50	82	62	40	32
Georgia	82[b]	82[b]	31	39	35	52	95[b]	82[b]	52	53
India	..	..	7	10	14	40	44[b]	34	40	13[d]
Indonesia	68	67	41	17	17	50	58	49	41	31
Iran (Islamic Republic of)	75	79	38	34	29	52	58	48	24	23
Iraq	32[b]	45[b]	32[b]	12[b]	20[b]	36[b]	72[b]	58[b]	35[b]	..
Israel	88	87	43	69	52	56	86	71	..	..
Jordan	87[b]	86[b]	35[b]	42	38	51	64[b]	58[b]	23	21

Table 3.B

Education: Secondary and tertiary education, teaching staff and researchers (*continued*)

| | Secondary education | | | Tertiary education | | | Women's share among teaching staff, 2000–2007[a] (%) | | | Women's share among researchers, 2000–2007[a] (%) |
| | Secondary net enrolment rate, 2000–2007[a] (%) | | Girls' share of enrolment in secondary TVET, 2000–2007[a] (%) | Tertiary gross enrolment ratio, 2000–2007[a] (%) | | Women's share in total tertiary enrolment, 2000–2007[a] (%) | | | | |
Country or area	Girls	Boys	(%)	Women	Men	(%)	Primary	Secondary	Tertiary	(%)
Asia (*continued*)										
Kazakhstan	86	86	31	61	42	58	98	85	63	51[g]
Kuwait	80[b]	80[b]	11	26	11	65	88	53[b]	27[b]	35
Kyrgyzstan	81	80	33	48	37	56	97	74	56	44
Lao People's Democratic Republic	33[b]	38[b]	35	10	13	42	47	43	33	23
Lebanon	77	69	41	56	47	54	85	54	38	..
Malaysia	72	66	43	33	27	54	68	63	48	38
Maldives	70[b]	64[b]	30	..	..	70[b]	71	35	67	..
Mongolia	85	77	46	58	37	61	95	74	56	48
Myanmar	..	..	..	..	..	58	83	83	82	85
Nepal	40[b]	44[b]	22	3	8	28	32	14	..	15
Occupied Palestinian Territory	91	86	34	51	42	54	67	49	17	..
Oman	79	78	..	28	23	53	63[b]	56[b]	29	..
Pakistan	28	37	35[b]	5[b]	6[b]	45[b]	46	51[b]	37[b]	27
Philippines	67	56	..	32	25	54	87	76	56[b]	52
Qatar	92	94	..	27	9	64	85	56	37	..
Republic of Korea	94	100	46	75	113	38	77	53	32	15
Saudi Arabia	68[b]	67[b]	9	36	25	58	52[b]	53[b]	33	17
Singapore	..	..	36	..	..	49	81	66	35	27
Sri Lanka	..	..	..	..	..	..	85	63[b]	..	42
Syrian Arab Republic	65	67	40	..	..	..	69	51[b]	..	..
Tajikistan	75	87	25	11	29	27	64	49	32	39
Thailand	81	72	45	55	44	54	60	54	53	50
Timor-Leste	..	..	40	11[c]	9[c]	53[c]	32	23	9[b]	..
Turkey	64[b]	75[b]	38	..	..	43	..	..	39	37
United Arab Emirates	84[b]	81[b]	..	37[b]	13[b]	66[b]	85	55[b]	27[b]	..
Uzbekistan	90	93	49	8	11	41	85	63	36	..
Viet Nam	..	..	56	8	11	49	78	64	44	43
Yemen	26[b]	48[b]	6	5[b]	14[b]	26[b]	20[b]	21[b]	16[b]	..
Latin America and the Caribbean										
Argentina	83	74	54	81	53	60	88	69	53	52
Aruba	85	80	39	39	27	58	..	..	..	..
Bahamas	89	84	..	..	..	..	85	70	..	..
Barbados	93	88	38	73	34	68	78	59	49	..
Belize	70	64	50	4	2	70	72	61	49[b]	..
Bolivia (Plurinational State of)	70	70	65	..	..	..	61[b]	53[b]	..	40
Brazil	83	75	58	34	26	56	91	69	44	50

Table 3.B
Education: Secondary and tertiary education, teaching staff and researchers (continued)

Country or area	Secondary education			Tertiary education			Women's share among teaching staff, 2000–2007[a] (%)			Women's share among researchers, 2000–2007[a] (%)
	Secondary net enrolment rate, 2000–2007[a] (%)		Girls' share of enrolment in secondary TVET, 2000–2007[a] (%)	Tertiary gross enrolment ratio, 2000–2007[a] (%)		Women's share in total tertiary enrolment, 2000–2007[a] (%)				
	Girls	Boys	(%)	Women	Men	(%)	Primary	Secondary	Tertiary	(%)
Latin America and the Caribbean (continued)										
Chile	87	84	47	52	52	49	78	63	39	30
Colombia	71	64	54	33	30	51	76	52	35[b]	36
Costa Rica	..	..	51	28[b]	23[b]	54[b]	80	58[b]	..	39
Cuba	87	85	42	143	77	64	76	56	56	46
Dominican Republic	68	55	60	42[b]	27[b]	61[b]	76[b]	60[b]	41[b]	..
Ecuador	60	59	51	39	32	54	70	50	28	45
El Salvador	56	53	53	24	20	55	68	48	33	31
Grenada	80[b]	78[b]	35	..	..	..	77	59	..	..
Guatemala	37[b]	40[b]	51	18	18	51	65	44	31	26
Guyana	..	..	31	17	8	68	88	57	50	..
Honduras	..	..	56	20[b]	14[b]	59[b]	75	55	38[b]	27
Jamaica	79	74	63	26[b]	12[b]	70[b]	89[b]	69	60[b]	..
Mexico	72	72	56	26	28	50	67	47	..	32
Netherlands Antilles	85[b]	77[b]	54[b]	25	17	60	86[b]	55[b]	46[b]	..
Nicaragua	49[b]	42[b]	55	19[b]	17[b]	52[b]	76	59	46[b]	42
Panama	67[b]	61[b]	48	56	35	61	76	58	46	41
Paraguay	59	56	47	27[b]	24[b]	52[b]	72[b]	62[b]	..	47
Peru	77	76	61	36[b]	34[b]	51[b]	65	45	..	..
Saint Lucia	88[b]	76[b]	29	12	5	71	87	66	54	33[e]
Saint Vincent and the Grenadines	71[b]	57[b]	34	..	..	..	77	58[b]	..	..
Suriname	79[b]	57[b]	51	15	9	62	92	60	48[b]	..
Trinidad and Tobago	66[b]	64[b]	28[b]	13[b]	10[b]	56[b]	77	62[b]	33[b]	39
United States Virgin Islands	..	..	..	..	..	..	..	..	..	18
Uruguay	71	64	43	82	47	63	92[b,e]	72[e]	..	42
Venezuela (Bolivarian Republic of)	73	64	50	41[b]	38[b]	51[b]	81	63	38	52
Oceania										
Fiji	83	76	34	17[b]	14[b]	53[b]	57[b]	50		..
Papua New Guinea	..	..	..	1[b,e]	3[b,e]	35[b,e]	43[b]	..	20[b,e]	..
Samoa	70[b]	62[b]	..	7[b]	8[b]	44[b]	78	60[b]	43[b]	..
Solomon Islands	25[b]	29[b]	..	..	..	..	41[e]	33[b]	..	..
Tonga	67[b]	54[b]	32	8[b]	5[b]	60[b]	63	52	23[b]	..
Vanuatu	35[b]	41[b]	30	4[b]	6[b]	36[b]	54	36[b]		..
More developed regions										
Albania	72[b]	74[b]	34	23	15	62	76[b]	56[b]	41[b]	..
Australia	89	87	44	85	66	55	..	..	..	..
Austria	..	..	44	56	46	54	89	62	32	25

Table 3.B

Education: Secondary and tertiary education, teaching staff and researchers (*continued*)

Country or area	Secondary education			Tertiary education			Women's share among teaching staff, 2000–2007[a] (%)			Women's share among researchers, 2000–2007[a] (%)
	Secondary net enrolment rate, 2000–2007[a] (%)		Girls' share of enrolment in secondary TVET, 2000–2007[a] (%)	Tertiary gross enrolment ratio, 2000–2007[a] (%)		Women's share in total tertiary enrolment, 2000–2007[a] (%)				
	Girls	Boys	(%)	Women	Men	(%)	Primary	Secondary	Tertiary	(%)
More developed regions (*continued*)										
Belarus	89[b]	87[b]	31	80	57	57	99	80	56	43
Belgium	85[b]	89[b]	44	70	55	55	80	57[b]	42	30
Bulgaria	87	89	38	55	45	54	93	78	45	45
Canada	..	..	36[b]	72[b]	53[b]	56[b]	68	68	43[b]	..
Croatia	88	86	47	51	41	54	91	68	41	45
Czech Republic	..	..	40	61	49	55	91	65	30	20
Denmark	91	88	44	94	67	58	64	48	..	30
Estonia	91	89	34	81	50	61	94	77	48[b]	44
Finland	97	97	46	104	84	54	77	67[b]	46[b]	31
France	99	97	42	62	49	55	82	59	39	28
Germany	..	..	42	..	..	..	84	57	36	21
Greece	91	91	35	95	86	50	65	58	35	36
Hungary	90	89	39	82	56	58	96	72[b]	37	34
Iceland	92	89	43	96	52	64	80[b]	65[b]	45	38[g]
Ireland	90	86	54	68	54	55	84	62	39	30
Italy	94	93	39	80	57	57	95	67	35	33
Japan	98	98	43	54	62	46	65[b]	31[b]	18[b]	13
Latvia	..	..	40	93	50	64	97	83	57	52
Lithuania	92	90	35	93	59	60	97	81	55	50
Luxembourg	86	83	48	11	10	52	72	47	..	18
Malta	90[b]	84[b]	33	36	27	56	86	57	23[b]	26
Montenegro	..	..	..	..	..	..	..	..	..	41
Netherlands	90[b]	88[b]	46	63	58	51	..	46	37	18
New Zealand	93	91	60	96	64	59	83	62	50	39
Norway	97	97	42	94	60	60	73[b]	58[b]	41	33
Poland	95	93	36	78	56	57	84	69[b]	42	40
Portugal	92	84	42	62	51	54	82	69	43	44
Republic of Moldova	82[c]	79[c]	43	48[c]	35[c]	57[c]	97	76	58[c]	45
Romania	72	74	43	67	50	56	87	67	44	45
Russian Federation	89	88	37	86	64	57	99	81	57	42
Serbia	..	..	47	..	..	..	..	..	..	47
Slovakia	..	..	46	61	41	59	85	74	43	42
Slovenia	..	..	42	102	70	58	98	72	35	35
Spain	96	93	50	76	62	54	72	57	39	37
Sweden	100	100	44	92	59	60	81	59	43	36
Switzerland	80	84	40	45	49	48	..	..	31	27
The former Yugoslav Republic of Macedonia	80	82	42	40	31	55	72	54	45	50

Table 3.B

Education: Secondary and tertiary education, teaching staff and researchers (continued)

Country or area	Secondary education			Tertiary education			Women's share among teaching staff, 2000–2007[a] (%)			Women's share among researchers, 2000–2007[a] (%)
	Secondary net enrolment rate, 2000–2007[a] (%)		Girls' share of enrolment in secondary TVET, 2000–2007[a] (%)	Tertiary gross enrolment ratio, 2000–2007[a] (%)		Women's share in total tertiary enrolment, 2000–2007[a] (%)				
	Girls	Boys		Women	Men		Primary	Secondary	Tertiary	
More developed regions (continued)										
Turkey	..	..	..	31	41	..	..	..	..	..
Ukraine	85[c]	84[c]	35	85	68	54	99[c]	79[c]	..	44
United Kingdom	93	90	50	69	49	57	81	61[c]	41	..
United States of America	89	87	30	96	68	57	89	62	45	..

Sources

Secondary net enrolment rate: UNESCO Institute for Statistics, correspondence in June 2009.

Girls' share of enrolment in secondary TVET: UNESCO Institute for Statistic, UIS Data Centre, *http://www.uis.unesco.org* (accessed in December 2009).

Tertiary gross enrolment ratio: UNESCO Institute for Statistics, UIS Data Centre, *http://www.uis.unesco.org* (accessed in December 2009).

Women's share in total tertiary enrolment: UNESCO Institute for Statistics, UIS Data Centre, *http://www.uis.unesco.org* (accessed in December 2009).

Women's share in teaching staff: UNESCO Institute for Statistics, correspondence in June 2009.

Women's share among researchers: UNESCO Institute for Statistics, correspondence in June 2009.

Definitions

Secondary net enrolment rate: The number of children of official secondary school age who are enrolled in secondary education as a percentage of the total number of children of official secondary school age.

Girls' share of enrolment in secondary TVET: Percentage of girls among the total enrolment in secondary technical and vocational education and training (TVET) programmes.

Tertiary gross enrolment ratio: The total enrolment in tertiary education, regardless of age, expressed as a percentage of the five-year age group population following secondary school leaving.

Women's share in total tertiary enrolment: Percentage of women among the total enrolment in tertiary education.

Women's share among teaching staff: Percentage of women among the teaching staff of a given level of education. Teaching staff includes persons employed full time or part time in an official capacity to guide and direct the learning experience of pupils and students, irrespective of their qualifications or the delivery mechanism, i.e. face-to-face and/or at a distance.

Women's share among researchers: Percentage of women among the total number employed in research and development. Data refer to the headcount of persons who are mainly or partially employed in research and development.

Notes

.. Data not available or not reported separately.

a Data refer to the latest year available in the given interval.

b UIS estimation.

c National estimation.

d Data measured not on the basis of headcount but on full-time equivalency (FTE), a method that adjusts for part-time or part-year participation.

e Data refer to year 1999.

f Data refer to year 1997.

g Data refer to year 2008.

Table 4.A

Work: Labour force participation, unemployment and economic sector of employment

Country or area	Adult (15+) labour force participation rate (%)				Women's share of the adult labour force, 2010 (%)	Adult (15+) unemployment rate, 2005-2007[a] (%)		Distribution of the employed population by economic sector, 2004-2007[a] (%)					
	1990		2010					Women			Men		
	Women	Men	Women	Men		Women	Men	Agriculture	Industry	Services	Agriculture	Industry	Services
Africa													
Algeria	23	75	39	76	34	..	..	22	28	49	20	26	54
Angola	74	90	76	88	47	..	..	..	..	..	..	..	..
Benin	51	88	59	85	41	..	..	..	..	..	..	..	..
Botswana	44	78	49	64	44	20	15	24	11	65	35	19	46
Burkina Faso	76	90	78	89	47	..	..	..	..	..	..	..	..
Burundi	91	90	89	90	51	..	..	..	..	..	..	..	..
Cameroon	53	79	53	75	42	..	..	72[b]	4[b]	24[b]	58[b]	15[b]	28[b]
Cape Verde	42	86	49	74	42	..	..	..	..	..	..	..	..
Central African Republic	69	88	67	87	45	..	..	..	..	..	..	..	..
Chad	57	84	72	77	49	..	..	..	..	..	..	..	..
Comoros	64	86	64	83	44	..	..	..	..	..	..	..	..
Congo	57	84	56	83	41	..	..	..	..	..	..	..	..
Côte d'Ivoire	42	89	39	85	31	..	..	..	..	..	..	..	..
Democratic Republic of the Congo	60	86	54	90	38	..	..	..	..	..	..	..	..
Djibouti	60	82	58	77	43	..	..	..	..	..	..	..	..
Egypt	24	74	25	71	26	25	7	43	6	51	28	26	46
Equatorial Guinea	42	91	43	92	33	..	..	..	..	..	..	..	..
Eritrea	55	88	55	86	41	..	..	..	..	..	..	..	..
Ethiopia	63	89	82	91	48	8	3	76	8	16	84	5	11
Gabon	63	83	62	80	44	..	..	..	..	..	..	..	..
Gambia	70	86	71	83	46	..	..	..	..	..	..	..	..
Ghana	73	74	72	73	49	..	..	..	..	..	..	..	..
Guinea	80	90	79	88	47	..	..	..	..	..	..	..	..
Guinea-Bissau	56	87	54	90	38	..	..	..	..	..	..	..	..
Kenya	75	90	75	87	47	..	..	..	..	..	..	..	..
Lesotho	68	85	68	74	52	..	..	..	..	..	..	..	..
Liberia	54	85	56	84	40	4	7	..	..	..	..	..	..
Libyan Arab Jamahiriya	17	78	27	77	25	..	..	..	..	..	..	..	..
Madagascar	79	85	84	89	49	3	2	83	2	16	82	5	13
Malawi	76	80	76	79	50	..	..	..	..	..	..	..	..
Mali	34	69	37	64	39	..	..	30	15	55	50	18	32
Mauritania	58	84	61	79	43	..	..	..	..	..	..	..	..
Mauritius	40	82	42	75	37	14	5	..	..	..	..	..	..
Morocco	24	82	25	80	25	10	10	61	15	24	37	22	41
Mozambique	86	84	88	77	56	..	..	..	..	..	..	..	..
Namibia	49	65	49	58	47	..	..	25	9	65	34	19	47
Niger	40	87	39	87	31	..	..	..	..	..	..	..	..
Nigeria	37	75	40	69	37	..	..	..	..	..	..	..	..

Table 4.A

Work: Labour force participation, unemployment and economic sector of employment (*continued*)

Country or area	Adult (15+) labour force participation rate (%) 1990 Women	1990 Men	2010 Women	2010 Men	Women's share of the adult labour force, 2010 (%)	Adult (15+) unemployment rate, 2005-2007[a] (%) Women	Men	Distribution of the employed population by economic sector, 2004-2007[a] (%) Women Agriculture	Women Industry	Women Services	Men Agriculture	Men Industry	Men Services
Africa (*continued*)													
Réunion	44	67	52	64	46	30	28	..	..	..	..	..	..
Rwanda	86	88	82	80	53	..	..	..	..	..	..	..	..
Sao Tome and Principe	37	78	45	70	40	25	11	..	..	..	..	..	..
Senegal	61	90	63	86	43	..	..	..	..	..	..	..	..
Sierra Leone	66	65	65	67	51	..	..	71	3	26	66	10	23
Somalia	52	89	55	89	39	..	..	..	..	..	..	..	..
South Africa	44	64	47	59	46	27	20	7	14	80	11	35	54
Sudan	24	78	32	71	31	..	..	..	..	..	..	..	..
Swaziland	66	79	62	68	50	..	..	..	..	..	..	..	..
Togo	53	89	52	87	38	..	..	..	..	..	..	..	..
Tunisia	21	76	27	71	27	17	13	..	..	..	..	..	..
Uganda	80	91	82	90	48	..	..	76[b]	5[b]	19[b]	62[b]	10[b]	28[b]
United Republic of Tanzania	89	93	87	90	50	..	..	80	2	18	73	7	21
Zambia	59	81	61	81	43	..	..	..	..	..	..	..	..
Zimbabwe	68	80	60	81	43	..	..	..	..	..	..	..	..
Asia													
Afghanistan	28	87	29	89	23	9	8	..	..	..	..	..	..
Armenia	66	79	57	69	50	..	..	46	10	45	46	21	33
Azerbaijan	66	78	60	72	48	..	..	42	4	54	35	21	44
Bahrain	28	88	33	83	22	..	..	—[b]	13[b]	85[b]	2[b]	32[b]	63[b]
Bangladesh	62	89	58	84	40	7	3	68	13	19	42	15	43
Bhutan	25	84	45	80	33	3	3	63	6	32	33	24	44
Brunei Darussalam	45	83	59	73	43	..	..	—[b]	11[b]	88[b]	2[b]	29[b]	69[b]
Cambodia	77	85	75	87	48	..	..	..	..	..	..	..	..
China	73	85	70	79	46	..	..	..	..	..	..	..	..
China, Hong Kong SAR	47	80	55	69	48	3	5	—	6	94	—	21	78
China, Macao SAR	45	73	60	73	47	3	3	—	15	86	—	27	73
Cyprus	48	81	54	70	46	5	4	2	10	88	6	33	60
Democratic People's Republic of Korea	51	79	60	78	45	..	..	..	..	..	..	..	..
Georgia	67	83	56	75	47	13	14	57	4	39	51	17	33
India	35	85	34	81	29	..	..	..	..	..	..	..	..
Indonesia	50	81	50	87	37	11	8	45	15	41	44	20	36
Iran (Islamic Republic of)	22	81	34	76	30	16	9	33	29	38	21	33	47
Iraq	11	74	15	68	18	..	..	33	7	60	14	20	66
Israel	41	62	51	60	47	8	7	1	11	88	3	32	65
Jordan	11	68	16	71	18	..	..	2[b]	12[b]	84[b]	4[b]	23[b]	73[b]
Kazakhstan	62	78	65	76	50	..	..	32	10	58	35	24	41
Kuwait	34	81	43	80	25	..	..	..	..	..	..	..	..

Table 4.A
Work: Labour force participation, unemployment and economic sector of employment (*continued*)

Country or area	Adult (15+) labour force participation rate (%)				Women's share of the adult labour force, 2010 (%)	Adult (15+) unemployment rate, 2005-2007[a] (%)		Distribution of the employed population by economic sector, 2004-2007[a] (%)					
	1990		2010					Women			Men		
	Women	Men	Women	Men		Women	Men	Agriculture	Industry	Services	Agriculture	Industry	Services
Asia (*continued*)													
Kyrgyzstan	58	74	53	76	43	9	8	35	11	54	37	26	37
Lao People's Democratic Republic	80	83	79	80	50	1	1	..	..	..	..	..	..
Lebanon	22	83	25	77	26	..	..	..	..	..	..	..	..
Malaysia	43	81	46	80	36	3	3	10	23	67	18	32	51
Maldives	20	78	58	78	42	24	8	..	..	..	..	..	..
Mongolia	66	66	69	61	50	11	11	37	15	48	43	19	38
Myanmar	69	88	70	86	46	..	..	..	..	..	..	..	..
Nepal	48	80	61	76	46	..	..	73[b]	14[b]	13[b]	60[b]	13[b]	25[b]
Occupied Palestinian Territory	10	67	15	67	18	19	22	36	10	53	11	27	61
Oman	20	81	27	76	21	..	..	..	..	..	..	..	..
Pakistan	11	86	23	85	20	8	5	72	13	15	36	23	41
Philippines	47	83	50	80	39	6	6	24	11	65	44	18	39
Qatar	30	93	42	91	16	..	..	—	4	96	4	48	48
Republic of Korea	47	73	49	72	41	3	4	8	16	76	7	33	60
Saudi Arabia	15	80	20	80	16	13	4	—	1	99	5	23	72
Singapore	51	79	54	75	42	4	4	1	18	82	2	26	72
Sri Lanka	46	79	44	74	38	9	4	37	27	34	30	28	43
Syrian Arab Republic	18	81	22	78	22	..	..	49[b]	8[b]	43[b]	23[b]	29[b]	48[b]
Tajikistan	75	84	58	70	47	..	..	75	5	20	42	27	31
Thailand	76	87	65	80	47	1	1	40	19	41	43	22	35
Timor-Leste	52	81	59	84	41	..	..	..	..	..	..	..	..
Turkey	34	81	24	69	25	10	10	47	15	38	19	29	52
Turkmenistan	63	75	60	71	47	..	..	..	..	..	..	..	..
United Arab Emirates	25	92	41	92	15	7	3	—	6	92	6	45	49
Uzbekistan	75	85	59	72	46	..	..	..	..	..	..	..	..
Viet Nam	74	81	69	76	48	..	..	60	14	26	56	21	23
Yemen	15	70	22	66	25	..	..	..	..	..	..	..	..
Latin America and the Caribbean													
Argentina	29	79	51	75	42	12	8	—[c]	11[c]	89[c]	1[c]	33[c]	66[c]
Bahamas	64	79	67	77	48	9	7	—	5	94	4	29	66
Barbados	62	78	67	79	48	..	..	..	..	..	..	..	..
Belize	23	81	47	81	37	17	7	3	10	86	28	22	50
Bolivia (Plurinational State of)	46	85	68	83	46	..	..	36[b]	11[b]	52[b]	42[b]	25[b]	33[b]
Brazil	39	85	61	81	44	..	..	15	13	72	23	28	50
Chile	32	77	40	70	37	7	5	6	11	84	16	31	53
Colombia	44	77	65	79	47	14	9	6	16	78	27	22	51
Costa Rica	36	85	44	78	35	7	3	5	13	82	18	28	54
Cuba	36	73	45	68	40	2	2	9	12	79	25	22	54

Table 4.A
Work: Labour force participation, unemployment and economic sector of employment (*continued*)

Country or area	Adult (15+) labour force participation rate (%) 1990 Women	1990 Men	2010 Women	2010 Men	Women's share of the adult labour force, 2010 (%)	Adult (15+) unemployment rate, 2005-2007[a] (%) Women	Men	Distribution of the employed population by economic sector, 2004-2007[a] (%) Women Agriculture	Women Industry	Women Services	Men Agriculture	Men Industry	Men Services
Latin America and the Caribbean (*continued*)													
Dominican Republic	26	82	58	72	45	29	11	3	15	82	21	26	53
Ecuador	33	78	54	79	41	11	6	4[d]	13[d]	83[d]	11[d]	28[d]	61[d]
El Salvador	51	80	47	78	39	4	8	5	19	76	29	26	45
French Guiana	52	75	54	64	45	35	24	..	..	..	..	..	..
Guadeloupe	53	68	56	62	51	31	24	..	..	..	..	..	..
Guatemala	28	89	46	83	38	..	..	..	..	..	..	..	..
Guyana	36	82	48	81	34	..	..	7[b]	12[b]	77[b]	27[b]	30[b]	39[b]
Haiti	49	81	39	83	33	..	..	..	..	..	..	..	..
Honduras	37	87	36	81	32	6	3	13	23	63	51	20	29
Jamaica	65	80	54	73	44	14	5	8	5	87	26	27	47
Martinique	54	66	54	60	51	27	23	..	..	..	..	..	..
Mexico	34	84	42	78	37	4	3	4	18	77	19	31	50
Netherlands Antilles	46	69	55	68	50	14	10	..	..	..	..	..	..
Nicaragua	39	85	40	87	32	5	5	8	18	73	42	20	38
Panama	37	81	48	80	38	9	5	3	10	87	21	25	54
Paraguay	52	83	72	84	46	8	4	24	9	68	33	24	43
Peru	48	75	65	83	45	8	6	6[d]	43[d]	51[d]	12[d]	41[d]	46[d]
Puerto Rico	31	61	39	57	43	10	12	—	10	89	2	26	72
Saint Lucia	47	78	52	79	41	..	..	..	..	..	..	..	..
Saint Vincent and the Grenadines	45	81	56	80	41	..	..	8[b]	8[b]	84[b]	21[b]	28[b]	50[b]
Suriname	37	67	38	66	37	..	..	5	8	82	10	31	55
Trinidad and Tobago	39	76	58	78	44	10	4	2	16	82	6	41	52
United States Virgin Islands	62	70	57	59	52	..	..	..	..	..	..	..	..
Uruguay	43	72	54	74	44	12	7	5	13	83	16	29	56
Venezuela (Bolivarian Republic of)	32	82	53	81	40	8	7	2	12	86	13	30	56
Oceania													
Fiji	29	84	39	78	33	6	4	..	..	..	..	..	..
French Polynesia	49	74	48	72	39	..	..	..	..	..	..	..	..
Guam	50	81	56	78	42	..	..	..	..	..	..	..	..
New Caledonia	47	74	43	71	38	..	..	..	..	..	..	..	..
Papua New Guinea	71	75	71	73	49	..	..	..	..	..	..	..	..
Samoa	40	77	41	75	34	..	..	..	..	..	..	..	..
Solomon Islands	59	82	53	80	39	..	..	..	..	..	..	..	..
Tonga	28	73	54	70	43	..	..	..	..	..	..	..	..
Vanuatu	79	89	80	88	47	..	..	..	..	..	..	..	..
More developed regions													
Albania	67	84	50	70	42	..	..	..	..	..	..	..	..
Australia	52	76	58	71	46	5	4	2	9	89	4	31	64

Table 4.A

Work: Labour force participation, unemployment and economic sector of employment (*continued*)

Country or area	Adult (15+) labour force participation rate (%)				Women's share of the adult labour force, 2010 (%)	Adult (15+) unemployment rate, 2005-2007[a] (%)		Distribution of the employed population by economic sector, 2004-2007[a] (%)					
	1990		2010					Women			Men		
	Women	Men	Women	Men		Women	Men	Agriculture	Industry	Services	Agriculture	Industry	Services
More developed regions (*continued*)													
Austria	43	70	54	67	46	5	4	6	13	81	6	39	55
Belarus	60	75	54	66	49	..	..	..	..	..	..	..	..
Belgium	36	61	46	59	45	9	7	1	11	87	3	36	61
Bosnia and Herzegovina	69	83	53	66	46	35	29	..	..	..	..	..	..
Bulgaria	57	64	46	57	47	9	9	6	29	66	9	42	49
Canada	58	76	64	73	47	6	6	2	11	88	3	32	65
Channel Islands	44	76	52	67	45	..	..	..	..	..	..	..	..
Croatia	52	75	44	59	45	11	8	14	19	67	12	40	48
Czech Republic	61	80	51	66	45	7	4	3	27	71	4	50	45
Denmark	62	75	60	70	47	4	3	2	12	86	4	33	63
Estonia	61	72	56	66	51	4	5	3	22	75	6	48	45
Finland	59	71	57	65	48	7	6	3	12	86	6	38	55
France	46	65	50	61	47	9	7	2	12	86	5	34	62
Germany	46	73	53	66	46	9	9	2	16	82	3	41	56
Greece	36	67	44	65	41	13	5	13	10	78	11	30	59
Hungary	47	65	43	59	45	8	7	2	21	76	7	42	51
Iceland	67	81	71	78	47	2	2	3	8	89	9	31	60
Ireland	35	69	56	73	44	4	5	1	11	87	9	39	51
Italy	36	66	40	60	42	8	5	3	17	80	5	39	56
Japan	50	77	47	70	42	4	4	4	17	77	4	35	59
Latvia	63	77	56	71	48	5	6	7	16	76	12	39	47
Lithuania	59	74	51	61	50	4	4	8	20	72	13	41	46
Luxembourg	34	68	50	63	45	4	4	..	..	..	..	..	..
Malta	22	74	34	66	34	7	5	—	13	86	2	32	65
Montenegro	..	..	..	..	..	36	26	9	9	82	9	26	65
Netherlands	43	70	57	70	46	4	3	2	8	89	4	31	65
New Zealand	53	74	61	74	46	4	3	5	10	85	9	32	58
Norway	57	73	62	70	48	2	3	1	8	91	4	33	63
Poland	55	72	46	61	46	10	9	14	18	68	15	41	44
Portugal	50	73	57	70	47	10	7	12	18	69	11	41	48
Republic of Moldova	61	74	45	46	52	4	6	30	12	58	36	25	39
Romania	55	67	46	58	46	5	7	31	25	44	28	37	35
Russian Federation	60	76	58	71	50	6	6	7	20	73	11	38	51
Serbia[e]	63	77	52	67	45	21	16	20	20	61	22	37	42
Slovakia	66	79	52	69	45	13	10	2	24	73	6	51	43
Slovenia	60	76	52	65	46	6	4	10	23	65	10	44	45
Spain	34	69	49	68	43	11	6	3	12	85	6	42	53
Sweden	63	72	61	69	48	6	6	1	9	90	3	33	64
Switzerland	49	79	60	73	47	5	3	3	11	86	5	33	62

Table 4.A

Work: Labour force participation, unemployment and economic sector of employment (*continued*)

Country or area	Adult (*15+*) labour force participation rate (%)				Women's share of the adult labour force, 2010 (%)	Adult (*15+*) unemployment rate, 2005-2007[a] (%)		Distribution of the employed population by economic sector, 2004-2007[a] (%)					
	1990		2010					Women			Men		
	Women	Men	Women	Men		Women	Men	Agriculture	Industry	Services	Agriculture	Industry	Services
More developed regions (*continued*)													
The former Yugoslav Republic of Macedonia	54	73	42	66	39	36	35	17	29	54	19	33	48
Ukraine	57	72	54	66	50	7	7	..	..	..	..	..	..
United Kingdom	53	75	56	69	46	5	6	1	9	90	2	33	65
United States of America	57	76	58	72	46	5	5	1	9	90	2	30	68

Sources

Adult labour force participation rate: ILO, Economically Active Population Estimates and Projections 1980-2020. 5th edition, revision 2008, available from *http://laborsta.ilo.org/applv8/data/EAPEP/eapep_E.html* (accessed in June 2009);

Women's share of the adult labour force: Computed by the United Nations Statistics Division based on data from ILO, Economically Active Population Estimates and Projections 1980-2020. 5th edition, revision 2008, available from *http://laborsta.ilo.org/applv8/data/EAPEP/eapep_E.html* (accessed in June 2009);

Adult unemployment rate: ILO, Key Indicators of the Labour Market (KILM), 5th edition, table 8a. Online version (accessed in July 2009);

Distribution of the employed population by economic sector: KILM, 5th edition, table 4a. Online version (accessed in October 2009).

Definitions

Adult labour force participation rate: The proportion of persons aged 15 years or over who furnish, or are able to furnish, the supply of labour for the production of goods and services in accordance with the System of National Accounts.

Women's share of the adult labour force: The proportion of women in the adult labour force.

Adult unemployment rate: The proportion of the labour force aged 15 or over that is unemployed. The unemployed are persons who are currently without work, who are available for work and who are seeking or have sought work recently.

Distribution of the employed population by economic sector: The share of each broad economic sector in the employed population, calculated separately for each sex. The three broad sectors are agriculture, industry and services. Agriculture covers farming, animal husbandry, hunting, forestry and fishing. Industry comprises mining and quarrying; manufacturing; electricity, gas, steam and air conditioning supply; water supply, sewerage and waste management and remediation activities; and construction. Services covers wholesale and retail trade; repair of motor vehicles; transportation and storage; accommodation and food service activities; information and communication; financial and insurance activities; real estate activities; professional, scientific and technical activities; administrative and support service activities; public administration and defence; compulsory social security; education; human health and social work activities; arts, entertainment and recreation; and other service categories. The percentage distribution may not sum to 100 due to rounding or the non-classification by economic sector of a significant portion of the employed population.

Notes

..   Data not available or not reported separately.

—   Magnitude nil or less than 0.5 per cent.

a   Unless otherwise noted, data refer to the latest year available in the given interval.

b   Data refer to a year between 2001 and 2003.

c   For 31 urban agglomerations.

d   Urban areas only.

e   Data for adult labour force participation rate and women's share of the adult labour force refer to Serbia and Montenegro.

Table 4.B
Work: Status in employment, occupation and wages

| Country or area | Distribution of the employed population by status of employment, 2004–2007[a] (%) | | | | | | | | Women's share of legislators, senior officials and managers, 2004–2008[a] (%) | Women's share of clerks, 2004–2008[a] (%) | Women's wages in manufacturing as a percentage of men's, 2006–2008[a] |
| | Women | | | | Men | | | | | | |
	Employ-ees	Employ-ers	Own account workers	Contrib-uting family workers	Employ-ees	Employ-ers	Own account workers	Contrib-uting family workers			
Africa											
Algeria	49.8	1.3	35.3	13.6	61.9	5.8	24.9	7.1	5	37	..
Botswana	74.9	3.2	16.3	5.5	84.1	6.5	6.4	2.9	30	70	66
Egypt	53.7	2.8	10.9	32.6	63.7	15.9	11.9	8.6	11	29	66
Ethiopia	6.2	0.2	24.8	68.5	9.3	0.9	54.8	34.6	20	55	..
Madagascar	10.8	—	16.1	73.0	16.0	—	51.8	32.1	22	43	85
Mali	11.4	—	78.4	10.2	15.2	—	66.4	18.4	..	..	..
Mauritius	83.8	1.1	10.4	4.4	78.0	4.4	16.2	0.9	23	60	..
Morocco	33.4	0.6	9.8	55.3	46.8	3.3	29.9	17.0	13	24	..
Namibia	67.7	4.3	22.3	5.7	76.0	6.6	13.7	3.2	36	73	..
Sierra Leone	3.7	—	74.7	21.6	11.3	—	73.9	14.8	..	..	..
South Africa	84.2	3.0	11.4	1.4	84.5	7.5	7.5	0.4	30	69	..
Uganda	..	..	..	..	..	..	..	..	33[b]	56[b]	..
United Republic of Tanzania	6.1	1.0	79.9	13.0	15.3	2.6	72.4	9.7	16	51	..
Asia											
Armenia	..	..	..	..	..	..	..	..	24[b]	73[b]	62
Azerbaijan	32.7	1.3	66.0	—	50.7	8.7	40.5	—	7	41	60
Bahrain	..	..	..	..	..	..	..	..	12[b]	27[b]	99
Bangladesh	11.7	0.1	26.4	60.1	14.5	0.3	74.8	9.7	23[b]	4[b]	..
Bhutan	18.0	0.7	23.9	51.7	51.9	1.7	17.6	21.3	..	..	..
Brunei Darussalam	..	..	..	..	..	..	..	..	26[b]	66[b]	..
Cambodia	..	..	..	..	..	..	..	..	14[b]	45[b]	..
China, Hong Kong SAR	94.0	1.7	3.2	1.1	84.2	6.2	9.5	0.1	29	73	60
China, Macao SAR	94.6	1.5	2.5	1.4	88.5	5.2	6.2	0.1	27	61	66
Cyprus	86.8	1.8	8.7	2.7	73.9	9.5	15.7	0.9	16	77	56
Georgia	34.5	0.4	25.8	39.0	34.3	1.6	44.7	19.0	34	64	60
Indonesia	30.7	1.4	34.4	33.6	35.9	3.8	52.5	7.8	22	42	68
Iran (Islamic Republic of)	42.2	0.9	23.4	32.7	53.4	6.4	34.4	5.4	13	26	..
Israel	91.8	1.7	5.1	0.4	83.5	6.3	9.0	0.1	32	74	..
Kazakhstan	60.2	0.6	37.2	1.3	64.1	1.6	32.2	1.0	38	73	68
Kuwait	..	..	..	..	..	..	..	..	14	26	..
Kyrgyzstan	51.7	0.6	27.8	19.3	50.2	1.5	38.6	8.8	35	74	..
Lebanon	..	..	..	..	..	..	..	..	8	47	..
Malaysia	77.3	1.3	12.5	8.8	72.5	4.6	20.1	2.7	24	70	..
Maldives	..	..	..	..	..	..	..	..	14	53	..
Mongolia	..	..	..	..	..	..	..	..	30[b]	74[b]	71
Myanmar	..	..	..	..	..	..	..	..	..	..	88
Nepal	..	..	..	..	..	..	..	..	14[b]	13[b]	..
Occupied Palestinian Territory	55.0	0.8	12.7	31.5	60.2	5.4	27.7	6.6	10	37	50

Table 4.B
Work: Status in employment, occupation and wages (*continued*)

| Country or area | Distribution of the employed population by status of employment, 2004–2007[a] (%) | | | | | | | | Women's share of legislators, senior officials and managers, 2004–2008[a] (%) | Women's share of clerks, 2004–2008[a] (%) | Women's wages in manufacturing as a percentage of men's, 2006–2008[a] |
| | Women | | | | Men | | | | | | |
	Employ-ees	Employ-ers	Own account workers	Contrib-uting family workers	Employ-ees	Employ-ers	Own account workers	Contrib-uting family workers			
Asia (*continued*)											
Oman	..	..	..	..	..	..	..	..	9[b]	14[b]	..
Pakistan	24.6	0.1	13.4	61.9	40.6	1.0	39.8	18.6	3	3	..
Philippines	51.0	2.4	28.6	18.0	51.1	5.3	34.6	9.0	55	64	..
Qatar	99.9	0.1	—	—	98.7	0.8	0.5	—	7	17	..
Republic of Korea	68.8	3.5	15.0	12.7	67.7	8.9	22.2	1.2	10	50	57
Saudi Arabia	..	..	..	..	..	..	..	..	8	9	..
Singapore	89.9	2.8	6.0	1.3	80.8	6.8	11.9	0.4	31	77	65
Sri Lanka	55.1	0.7	22.5	21.7	57.2	3.9	34.5	4.4	24	46	77
Syrian Arab Republic	..	..	..	..	..	..	..	..	10	19	..
Thailand	42.4	1.5	26.0	29.9	44.6	4.2	37.1	14.0	24	66	75
Turkey	48.5	1.3	12.0	38.2	61.5	6.9	25.9	5.6	10	42	..
United Arab Emirates	98.7	0.7	0.5	—	96.6	1.6	1.7	—	10	38	..
Viet Nam	21.2	0.3	31.3	47.2	29.8	0.7	50.7	18.9	22	50	..
Latin America and the Caribbean											
Argentina[c]	80.2	2.5	15.7	1.6	72.5	5.3	21.4	0.7	23	56	..
Aruba	..	..	..	..	..	..	..	..	40	69	..
Bahamas	87.4	..	11.5[d]	0.5	81.6	..	17.8[d]	—	..	..	..
Barbados	89.5	0.5	9.7	0.2	79.5	1.9	17.9	—	43	80	..
Belize	73.9	4.5	17.2	4.3	66.9	8.4	20.9	3.7	41	68	..
Bolivia (Plurinational State of)	..	..	..	..	..	..	..	..	29	54	..
Brazil	66.0	2.8	16.1	8.1	61.9	5.7	24.9	4.6	36	59	61
Chile	74.4	1.7	21.1	2.8	70.8	3.8	24.4	0.9	33[b]	50[b]	..
Colombia	56.1	3.1	34.6	6.1	53.0	5.7	37.9	3.2	..	..	60
Costa Rica	76.1	4.0	17.1	2.8	71.3	9.1	18.4	1.3	30	56	81
Cuba	93.5	—	4.2	—	76.7	—	16.6	—	..	..	..
Dominican Republic	66.5	2.9	25.7	4.9	45.7	5.5	46.0	2.8	31	68	..
Ecuador[e]	54.5	4.5	29.9	11.1	63.1	7.8	24.7	4.4	28	58	..
El Salvador	42.5	2.8	34.1	9.9	63.7	5.5	20.4	8.8	25	61	64
Guyana	..	..	..	..	..	..	..	..	25[b]	67[b]	..
Honduras	52.6	..	39.2[d]	8.3	48.7	..	39.2[d]	12.1	..	..	..
Jamaica	66.1	2.1	29.2	2.2	57.6	3.8	37.9	0.5	..	..	..
Mexico	65.1	2.5	22.3	10.0	65.7	6.5	22.8	4.9	31	61	72
Netherlands Antilles[f]	..	..	..	..	..	..	..	..	34	78	..
Nicaragua	51.7	2.5	36.4	9.1	49.7	5.3	32.4	12.2	41	60	..
Panama	74.6	1.8	19.6	4.0	65.9	4.0	27.8	2.3	48	68	..
Paraguay	46.8	2.8	41.4	8.9	49.0	6.5	33.7	10.8	34	46	86

Table 4.B

Work: Status in employment, occupation and wages (continued)

| Country or area | Distribution of the employed population by status of employment, 2004–2007[a] (%) | | | | | | | | Women's share of legislators, senior officials and managers, 2004–2008[a] (%) | Women's share of clerks, 2004–2008[a] (%) | Women's wages in manufacturing as a percentage of men's, 2006–2008[a] |
| | Women | | | | Men | | | | | | |
	Employees	Employers	Own account workers	Contributing family workers	Employees	Employers	Own account workers	Contributing family workers			
Latin America and the Caribbean (continued)											
Peru[e]	48.8	3.8	37.2	9.9	58.2	8.2	28.7	4.7	19	52	..
Puerto Rico	90.8	..	8.9[d]	—	79.5	..	20.5[d]	—	43	77	..
Trinidad and Tobago	83.0	2.8	11.4	1.7	76.4	5.5	17.0	0.3	43	76	..
Uruguay	72.7	2.9	21.0	3.0	67.7	6.3	25.1	0.9	40	61	..
Venezuela (Bolivarian Republic of)	60.6	1.9	31.3	1.6	58.5	5.6	27.3	0.6	..	..	..
More developed regions											
Australia	91.0	2.1	6.6	0.4	85.5	3.3	11.1	0.2	37	73	90
Austria	87.7	2.9	6.4	2.9	83.9	7.0	7.1	2.0	28	71	61
Belgium	88.2	2.4	6.4	2.9	82.4	6.4	10.8	0.4	33	64	86
Bosnia and Herzegovina	73.1	..	15.9[d]	11.0	72.2	..	25.0[d]	3.0	..	..	..
Bulgaria	90.6	2.3	5.4	1.6	84.9	5.6	8.8	0.7	32	76	69
Canada	88.6	2.8	8.4	0.2	80.8	7.1	12.0	0.1	36	76	..
Croatia	79.8	3.0	13.5	3.7	77.3	7.3	14.2	1.1	27	69	76
Czech Republic	89.2	1.8	7.6	1.1	79.2	5.2	15.0	0.2	28	74	65
Denmark	94.6	..	4.4[d]	1.0	88.1	..	11.6[d]	0.3	24	72	87
Estonia	94.6	1.5	3.6	—	87.5	4.8	7.5	—	36	74	..
Finland	91.8	..	7.8[d]	0.4	82.1	..	15.7[d]	0.6	30	80	84
France	92.7	2.3	4.0	1.0	86.0	6.2	7.5	0.3	39	76	85
Germany	90.8	..	7.5[d]	1.8	85.8	..	13.8[d]	0.4	38	67	76
Greece	68.9	4.1	16.3	10.7	61.0	10.8	24.5	3.7	28	60	..
Hungary	90.8	3.2	5.2	0.7	84.9	6.9	7.7	0.3	36	91	73
Iceland	91.9	2.7	4.7	—	81.1	6.6	12.0	0.1	33	79	72
Ireland	92.9	2.5	3.7	0.9	76.0	8.3	15.3	0.4	32	75	80
Italy	80.0	0.7	13.5	2.6	70.0	1.8	25.2	1.3	33	60	..
Japan	86.4	1.1	4.7	7.3	86.0	3.6	8.8	1.1	..	..	61
Latvia	91.8	1.9	4.7	1.6	87.1	4.4	7.0	1.5	41	85	81
Lithuania	89.0	..	8.6[d]	2.4	83.7	..	15.2[d]	1.1	40	80	70
Malta	93.0	1.6	5.5	—	82.9	6.0	11.0	—	17	60	89
Montenegro	85.4	..	11.9[d]	2.6	77.1	..	21.1[d]	1.9	..	..	..
Netherlands	89.6	..	9.4[d]	1.0	83.6	..	16.2[d]	0.2	27	70	83
New Zealand	87.2	3.2	8.0	1.5	78.7	7.1	13.3	0.8	40	78	81
Norway	95.3	1.3	3.0	0.3	89.1	2.9	7.8	0.2	31	64	90
Poland	79.1	2.8	12.2	6.0	74.5	5.1	17.7	2.8	36	66	..
Portugal	77.3	3.4	17.2	1.5	73.9	7.4	17.6	0.7	31	61	68
Republic of Moldova	69.7	0.7	26.3	3.4	63.7	1.1	33.9	1.3	38	88	..
Romania	66.6	0.7	12.8	19.9	66.0	2.1	25.4	6.5	29	70	75
Russian Federation	93.3	1.1	5.4	0.1	92.0	1.7	6.0	0.1	37	90	..

Table 4.B

Work: Status in employment, occupation and wages (continued)

Country or area	Distribution of the employed population by status of employment, 2004–2007[a] (%)								Women's share of legislators, senior officials and managers, 2004–2008[a] (%)	Women's share of clerks, 2004–2008[a] (%)	Women's wages in manufacturing as a percentage of men's, 2006–2008[a]
	Women				Men						
	Employ-ees	Employ-ers	Own account workers	Contrib-uting family workers	Employ-ees	Employ-ers	Own account workers	Contrib-uting family workers			
More developed regions (continued)											
Serbia	76.8	2.9	8.3	11.9	70.4	5.1	21.4	3.1	36	56	..
Slovakia	91.9	2.0	5.2	0.1	82.6	4.0	13.2	0.1	30	70	..
Slovenia	85.8	1.6	5.5	7.1	81.7	4.6	10.3	3.1	35	64	..
Spain	86.5	3.3	8.3	1.6	79.4	7.0	12.3	0.7	32	66	..
Sweden	94.2	..	5.5[d]	0.3	85.1	..	14.6[d]	0.3	32	69	91
Switzerland	86.0	3.3	7.4	3.2	82.0	8.2	8.1	1.7	30	70	77
The former Yugoslav Republic of Macedonia	76.9	3.3	4.8	14.9	69.3	7.0	16.7	7.0	29	49	..
Ukraine	79.5	..	20.2[d]	0.3	81.8	..	17.7[d]	0.4	39	85	71
United Kingdom	91.9	..	7.7[d]	0.5	82.4	..	17.4[d]	0.2	35	79	75
United States of America	94.2	..	5.7[d]	0.1	91.6	..	8.4[d]	0.1	43	75	..

Sources

Distribution of the employed population by status in employment: ILO, Key Indicators of the Labour Market (KILM), 5th edition, table 3. Online version (accessed in July 2009);

Women's share of legislators, senior officials and managers and women's share of clerks: Computed by the United Nations Statistics Division based on data from ILO, LABORSTA table 2c. Online database. *http://laborsta.ilo.org* (accessed in January 2010);

Women's wages in manufacturing as a percentage of men's: Computed by the United Nations Statistics Division based on data from ILO, LABORSTA tables 5a and 5b. Online database. *http://laborsta.ilo.org* (accessed in October 2009).

Definitions

Distribution of the employed population by status in employment: The share of each status in employment category in the employed population, calculated separately for each sex. Status in employment relates to the type of explicit or implicit contract of employment an individual has with his or her employer or other persons. Four status in employment groups are shown: employees, employers, own-account workers and contributing family workers. Employees refer to those who hold paid employment jobs and are typically remunerated by wages and salaries, but may also be paid by commission from sales, or by piece-rates, bonuses or in-kind payments such as food, housing or training. Employers are those who, working on their own account or with one or several partners, hold self-employment jobs and have engaged on a continuous basis one or more persons to work for them in their businesses as employees. Own-account workers are those who, working on their own account or with one or several partners, hold self-employment jobs and have not engaged any employees on a continuous basis. Contributing family workers refer to people employed in a market-oriented establishment (i.e., business or farm) operated by a relative living in the same household, who cannot be regarded as a partner because their degree of commitment to the operation of the establishment is not at a level comparable to that of the head of the establishment. The percentage distribution may not sum to 100 due to rounding or the presence of other categories of status in employment.

Women's share of legislators, senior officials and managers: The proportion of women among persons employed in this major occupation group. This group includes (a) legislators and senior officials; (b) corporate managers; and (c) general managers.

Women's share of clerks: The proportion of women among persons employed as clerks.

Women's wages in manufacturing as a percentage of men's: The ratio of the average earnings of men to the average earnings of women in manufacturing, expressed as a percentage. Data on average earnings are generally taken from establishment payrolls and usually cover cash payments received from employers, such as remuneration for normal working hours, overtime pay, incentive pay, earnings of piece-workers; remuneration for time not worked (annual vacation, public holidays, sick leave and other paid leave), bonuses and gratuities. Average earnings data generally cover wage earners without distinction as to age.

Notes

.. Data not available or not reported separately.

— Magnitude nil or less than 0.05 per cent.

a Unless otherwise noted, data refer to the latest year available in the given interval.

b Data refer to a year between 2000 and 2003.

c For 31 urban agglomerations.

d Employers and own-account workers.

e Urban areas only.

f Curaçao.

Table 4.C
Work: Time spent on paid and unpaid work

| Country or area | Year | Age group | Average time spent, by activity (*hours and minutes per day*) | | | |
| | | | Paid work | | Unpaid work | |
			Women	Men	Women	Men
Africa						
Benin						
Urban	1998	6–65	3:55	3:55	3:15	1:00
Rural	1998	6–65	5:05	4:45	3:15	1:05
Madagascar						
Urban	2001	6–65	2:55	4:50	3:45	0:55
Rural	2001	6–65	4:00	6:00	3:30	0:40
Mauritius	2003	10+	1:56	4:56	4:37	1:13
South Africa	2000	10+	1:56	3:10	3:36	1:23
United Republic of Tanzania	2006	15+	4:11	5:45	4:13	1:15
Asia						
Armenia	2004	15–80	1:44	5:18	5:46	1:06
Cambodia	2004	18–60	3:57	6:10	3:54	0:56
China	2008	15–80	4:23	6:00	3:54	1:31
Iraq	2007	10+	0:28	3:54	5:47	1:00
Kyrgyzstan	2005	20–74	3:30	5:53	5:42	2:19
Lao People's Democratic Republic	2002/03	10+	4:30	5:12	2:30	0:36
Mongolia	2000	16–54/59[a]	4:27	6:44	4:36	2:10
Occupied Palestinian Territory	1999/2000	10+	0:32	5:07	5:01	1:16
Oman	1999/2000	15+	1:35	4:47	4:56	1:46
Pakistan	2007	10+	1:18	5:21	4:47	0:28
Republic of Korea	2004	10+	3:01	5:14	3:31	0:44
Turkey	2006	20–74	1:08	4:27	6:11	1:28
More developed regions						
Australia	2006	15+	2:21	4:33	5:13	2:52
Belgium	2005	20–74	2:08	3:31	4:38	2:57
Bulgaria	2001/02	20–74	2:52	3:55	5:29	3:06
Canada	2005	15+	3:06	4:42	4:12	2:42
Denmark	2001	16–74	3:53	5:02	3:30	2:26
Estonia	1999/2000	20–74	3:26	4:55	5:29	3:11
Finland	1999/2000	20–74	2:48	4:06	4:34	2:51
France	1998/99	20–74	2:32	4:12	4:54	2:45
Germany	2001/02	20–74	2:10	3:54	5:01	3:07
Hungary	2000	20–74	2:19	3:34	4:57	2:39
Ireland[b]	2005	18+	2:44	5:46	5:07	1:42
Italy	2002/03	20–74	2:07	4:47	6:06	2:06
Japan	2006	10+	2:54	5:42	4:18	1:08
Latvia	2003	20–74	3:53	5:37	4:39	2:24
Lithuania	2003	20–74	3:50	5:13	5:08	2:46
Netherlands	2005	20–74	1:57	3:56	4:01	2:06
New Zealand	1999	12+	2:14	4:11	4:46	2:46
Norway	2000/01	20–74	2:56	4:30	4:19	2:53

Table 4.C

Work: Time spent on paid and unpaid work (continued)

| Country or area | Year | Age group | Average time spent, by activity (hours and minutes per day) | | | |
| | | | Paid work | | Unpaid work | |
			Women	Men	Women	Men
More developed regions (continued)						
Poland	2003/04	20–74	2:29	4:24	5:38	3:08
Portugal	1999	15+	2:40	4:29	5:02	1:17
Romania	2000	10+	1:36	2:54	5:12	2:42
Slovenia	2000/01	20–74	2:58	4:14	5:26	3:10
Spain	2002/03	20–74	2:24	4:52	5:32	2:00
Sweden	2000/01	20–74	3:11	4:34	4:21	3:07
The former Yugoslav Republic of Macedonia	2004	20–74	2:05	4:18	5:42	1:57
United Kingdom	2000/01	20–74	2:41	4:40	5:06	2:55
United States of America	2006	15+	3:01	4:32	4:19	2:40

Sources

Statistics Sweden, Harmonized European Time Use Survey: web application. *https://www.testh2.scb.se/tus/tus* (accessed in December 2009); UNECE, Work-life Balance, Gender Statistics Database. *http://w3.unece.org/pxweb/DATABASE/STAT/30-GE/98-GE_LifeBalance/98-GE_LifeBalance.asp* (accessed in November 2009); and national statistical sources (publications, reports and information from websites of national statistical offices).

Definitions

Average time spent: Total time spent by all individuals of given age group and sex on the indicated activity divided by the population subgroup regardless of whether they performed the activity or not.

Paid work: Activities that fall within the SNA production boundary. It covers all production for the market and certain types of non-market production including production and processing of primary products for own consumption, own account construction (owner-occupied dwellings) and other production of fixed assets for own use.

Unpaid work: Activities that fall outside the SNA production boundary and consists mainly of domestic work and community or volunteer work. Domestic work includes food preparation, dish washing, cleaning and upkeep of dwelling, laundry, ironing, handicraft, gardening, caring for pets, construction and repairs, shopping, installation, servicing and repair of personal and household goods, childcare, care of sick, elderly or disabled household members, etc. Community or volunteer work includes volunteer services for organizations, unpaid community work and informal help to other households.

Notes

a   16–54 for women and 16–59 for men.

b   Data refer to the average weekday. Paid work includes both employment and study.

Table 4.D
Work: Maternity leave benefits, as of 2009

Country or area	Length of maternity leave	Percentage of wages paid in covered period	Provider of benefit
Africa			
Algeria	14 weeks	100	Social security
Angola	12 weeks	100	Social security and Employer
Benin	14 weeks	100	Social security (1/2) and Employer (1/2)
Botswana	12 weeks	25	Employer
Burkina Faso	14 weeks	100	Social security (if necessary, the employer adds up to the full wage)
Burundi	12 weeks	50	Employer
Cameroon	14 weeks	100	National Social Insurance Fund
Cape Verde	60 days	90	Social insurance
Central African Republic	14 weeks	50	Social security
Chad	14 weeks	50	Social security
Comoros	14 weeks	100	Employer
Congo	15 weeks	100	50% Social security, 50% Employer
Côte d'Ivoire	14 weeks	100	Social insurance
Democratic Republic of the Congo	14 weeks	67	Employer
Djibouti	14 weeks	50, 100[a]	Employer
Egypt	90 days	100	Social security (75%) and Employer (25%)
Equatorial Guinea	12 weeks	75	Social security
Eritrea	60 days	..[b]	Employer
Ethiopia	90 days	100	Employer (for up to 45 days)
Gabon	14 weeks	100	National Social Security Fund
Gambia	12 weeks	100	Employer
Ghana	12 weeks	100	Employer
Guinea	14 weeks	100	Social security (1/2), Employer (1/2)
Guinea-Bissau	60 days	100	Employer (if women receive subsidy from social security, employer pays the difference between subsidy and full salary)
Kenya	3 months	100	Employer
Lesotho	12 weeks	..[c]	—
Libyan Arab Jamahiriya	50 days	50, 100[a]	Employer, Social security for self-employed women
Madagascar	14 weeks	100	50% Social insurance, 50% Employer
Malawi	8 weeks[d]	100	Employer
Mali	14 weeks	100	Social insurance
Mauritania	14 weeks	100	National Social Security Fund
Mauritius	12 weeks	100	Employer
Morocco	14 weeks	100	Social security
Mozambique	60 days	100	Social security
Namibia	12 weeks	100	Social security
Niger	14 weeks	100	50% Social insurance, 50% Employer
Nigeria	12 weeks	50	Employer
Rwanda	12 weeks	100, 20[a]	Employer (if women not covered by social security)
Sao Tome and Principe	60 days	100	Social security (Employer if women not covered by social security)
Senegal	14 weeks	100	Social security
Somalia	14 weeks	50	Employer
South Africa	4 months	60[a]	Unemployment Insurance Fund

Table 4.D
Work: Maternity leave benefits, as of 2009 (continued)

Country or area	Length of maternity leave	Percentage of wages paid in covered period	Provider of benefit
Africa (continued)			
Sudan	8 weeks	100	Employer
Swaziland	12 weeks	..[c]	–
Togo	14 weeks	100	50% Employer, 50% Social security
Tunisia	1–2 months[d]	67, 100[a]	National Social Security Fund
Uganda	60 working days	100	Employer
United Republic of Tanzania	12 weeks	100	National Social Security Fund
Zambia	12 weeks	100	Employer
Zimbabwe	98 days	100	Employer
Asia			
Afghanistan	90 days	100	Employer
Armenia	140 days	100	Social insurance
Azerbaijan	126 calendar days	100	Social insurance
Bahrain	45 days	100	Employer
Bangladesh	16 weeks	100	Employer
Cambodia	90 days	50	Employer
China	90 days	100[a]	Social insurance
China, Hong Kong SAR	10 weeks	80	Employer
Cyprus	18 weeks	75[a]	Social security
India	12 weeks	100	Social insurance or employer (for non-covered women)
Indonesia	3 months	100	Employer
Iran (Islamic Republic of)	90 days	67	Social security
Iraq	62 days	100	Social security
Israel	14 weeks	100[a]	Social security
Jordan	10 weeks	100	Employer
Kazakhstan	126 calendar days	100	Employer
Kuwait	70 days	100	Employer
Kyrgyzstan	126 calendar days	100[a]	Social security (Employer covers the first 10 working days)
Lao People's Democratic Republic	90 days	100[a]	Social security or employer
Lebanon	7 weeks	100	Employer
Malaysia	60 days	100	Employer
Mongolia	120 days	70	Social Insurance Fund
Myanmar	12 weeks	67	Social security
Nepal	52 days	100	Employer
Pakistan	12 weeks	100[a]	Social insurance
Philippines	60 days[d]	100	Social security
Qatar	50 days	100	Employer
Republic of Korea	90 days	100[a]	Employment Insurance Fund
Saudi Arabia	10 weeks	50, 100[a]	Employer
Singapore	12 weeks	100[a]	Employer and Government
Sri Lanka	12 weeks	86, 100[a]	Employer
Syrian Arab Republic	50 days	70	Employer
Tajikistan	140 calendar days	..[b]	Social security

Table 4.D
Work: Maternity leave benefits, as of 2009 (continued)

Country or area	Length of maternity leave	Percentage of wages paid in covered period	Provider of benefit
Asia (continued)			
Thailand	90 days	100, 50[a]	Employer and Social insurance system
Turkey	16 weeks	67[a]	Social security
Turkmenistan	112 days	100[a]	Social security
United Arab Emirates	45 days	100, 50[a]	Employer
Uzbekistan	126 calendar days	100	Social insurance
Viet Nam	4–6 months[d]	100	Social insurance fund
Yemen	60 days	100	Employer
Latin America and the Caribbean			
Argentina	90 days	100[a]	Family allowance funds (financed through state and employer contributions)
Bahamas	13 weeks	100[a]	National Insurance Board (2/3) and Employer (1/3)
Barbados	12 weeks	100	National insurance system
Belize	14 weeks	100	Social security or Employer (for women who are not entitled to receive benefits from social security)
Bolivia (Plurinational State of)	12 weeks	70–100[a]	Social insurance
Brazil	120 days	100	Social insurance
Chile	18 weeks	100	Social security
Colombia	12 weeks	100	Social security
Costa Rica	4 months	100[a]	50% Social security, 50% Employer
Cuba	18 weeks	100	Social security
Dominican Republic	12 weeks	100[a]	50% Social security, 50% Employer
Ecuador	12 weeks	100	75% Social security, 25% Employer
El Salvador	12 weeks	75	Social security for insured workers, otherwise Employer must pay
Grenada	3 months	100, 60[a]	60% for 12 weeks by Social security, 40% for 2 months by Employer
Guatemala	84 days	100[a]	Social security (2/3), Employer (1/3)
Guyana	13 weeks	70[a]	Social security
Haiti	12 weeks	100[a]	Employer
Honduras	12 weeks	100[a]	Social security (2/3), Employer (1/3)
Jamaica	12 weeks	..[e]	Social insurance
Mexico	12 weeks	100[a]	Social security
Nicaragua	12 weeks	60[a]	Social security
Panama	14 weeks	100[a]	Social Insurance Fund
Paraguay	12 weeks	50[a]	Social insurance system
Peru	90 days	100[f]	Social security system
Saint Lucia	3 months	65[a]	National Insurance Corporation
Saint Vincent and the Grenadines	13 weeks	65[a]	Social insurance
Trinidad and Tobago	13 weeks	100, 50[a]	Employer and National Insurance Board
Uruguay	12 weeks	100[a]	Social security system
Venezuela (Bolivarian Republic of)	18 weeks	67	Social insurance
Oceania			
Fiji	84 days	..[e]	Employer
Papua New Guinea	6+ weeks[d]	..[c]	–
Solomon Islands	12 weeks	25	Employer

Table 4.D
Work: Maternity leave benefits, as of 2009 (continued)

Country or area	Length of maternity leave	Percentage of wages paid in covered period	Provider of benefit
Oceania (continued)			
Vanuatu	3 months	50	Employer
More developed regions			
Albania	365 calendar days	80, 50 [a]	Social insurance system
Australia	12 months [d]	.. [e]	Social assistance system financed by the State
Austria	16 weeks	100	Statutory health insurance, family burden equalization fund, or employer
Belarus	126 calendar days	100	State social insurance
Belgium	15 weeks	82, 75 [a]	Social security
Bosnia and Herzegovina	1 year	50–100 [a]	..
Bulgaria	135 days	90	Public social insurance (the General Sickness and Maternity Fund)
Canada	17 weeks [d]	55 [a,f]	Federal and State Employment Insurance
Channel Islands	18 weeks	.. [e]	Social insurance and social assistance
Croatia	1+ year [d]	100 [a]	Health Insurance Fund (until the child reaches the age of 6 months), and the rest is paid from the State Budget
Czech Republic	28 weeks	69	Social security
Denmark	52 weeks [d]	100 [f]	Municipality and Employer
Estonia	140 calendar days	100	Health Insurance Fund
Finland	105 working days	70 [a]	Social insurance system
France	16 weeks	100 [f]	Social security
Germany	14 weeks	100 [f]	Statutory health insurance scheme, state, employer
Greece	119 days	50+ [a]	Social security/Employer
Hungary	24 weeks	70	Social insurance
Iceland	3 months [d]	80	Social security
Ireland	26 weeks	80 [a]	Social insurance
Italy	5 months	80	Social insurance
Japan	14 weeks	67 [a]	Employees' health insurance scheme or National health insurance scheme
Latvia	112 calendar days	100	State Social Insurance Agency
Lithuania	126 calendar days	100	State Social Insurance Fund
Luxembourg	16 weeks	100	Social insurance
Malta	14 weeks	100 [a]	Employer/Social security
Netherlands	16 weeks	100 [f]	Social insurance
New Zealand	14 weeks	100 [f]	State funds (Universal and social assistance system)
Norway	46–56 weeks [d]	80, 100 [a]	Social insurance
Poland	16 weeks	100	Social Insurance Fund
Portugal	120 days	100	Social insurance
Republic of Moldova	126 calendar days	100	Social insurance
Romania	126 calendar days	85	Social Insurance Fund
Russian Federation	140 calendar days	100 [a,f]	Social Insurance Fund
Serbia	365 days	100 [a]	Social insurance
Slovakia	28 weeks	55	Social Insurance Fund
Slovenia	105 calendar days	100	State
Spain	16 weeks	100	Social security
Sweden	480 days [d]	80 [a,f]	Social insurance

Table 4.D

Work: Maternity leave benefits, as of 2009 (*continued*)

Country or area	Length of maternity leave	Percentage of wages paid in covered period	Provider of benefit
More developed regions (*continued*)			
Switzerland	14 weeks[d]	80 [a,f]	Social insurance
The former Yugoslav Republic of Macedonia	9 months	.. [b]	Health Insurance Fund
Ukraine	126 days	100	Social security
United Kingdom	52 weeks[d]	90 [a]	Employer (92% refunded by public funds)
United States of America	12 weeks	.. [c]	–

Source

United Nations, Statistics and Indicators on Women and Men, table 5. *http://unstats.un.org/unsd/demographic/products/indwm/tab5g.htm* (accessed in February 2010).

Definitions

Length of maternity leave: The length of time for which maternity leave is provided, whether with or without pay.

Percentage of wages paid in covered period: The extent of compensation during the entire length of maternity leave or part thereof. In many cases, the cash benefit or wages paid during the covered period vary according to various criteria.

Provider of benefit: The institution or system responsible for providing the cash benefits related to maternity leave.

Notes

.. Not available.

– Not applicable.

a   Benefits may vary or may be subject to eligibility requirements. See source for details.

b   Paid amount not specified.

c   No legal obligation for paid maternity leave. Some cash benefits may be provided by the employer or at the state or other local level.

d   For additional information on the length of maternity leave entitlement, see source.

e   For description of coverage amount, see source.

f   Up to a ceiling.

Table 5.A
Power and decision-making

Country or area	Share of women in the parliament, 2009 (%)		Candidates to lower or single house of parliament, 2003–2008[a]			Whether gender quota for lower or single house of parliament exists	Share of women among ministers, 2008 (%)	Share of women among mayors, 2003–2009[a] (%)
	Lower or single house	Upper house	Share of women (%)	Proportion elected (%)				
				Women	Men			
Africa								
Algeria	8	3	..	..	..	✓	11	..
Angola	37	–	..	..	..	✓	6	..
Benin	11	–	10	5	7	•	22	5[b]
Botswana	11	–	..	..	..	✓	28	..
Burkina Faso	15	–	..	..	..	✓	14	5[b]
Burundi	31	35	23	41	27	✓	30	..
Cameroon	14	–	10	42	29	✓	12	6[b]
Cape Verde	18	–	..	..	..	•	36	6[b]
Central African Republic	11	–	9	14	11	•	13	..
Chad	5	–	..	..	..	•	17	..
Comoros	3	–	..	..	..	•	..	..
Congo	7	13	..	..	..	•	13	..
Côte d'Ivoire	9	–	..	..	..	✓	13	..
Democratic Republic of the Congo	8	5	14	3	6	•	12	..
Djibouti	14	–	11	50	50	✓	9	..
Egypt	2	7	..	..	..	✓	6	..
Equatorial Guinea	6	–	..	..	..	•	14	..
Eritrea	22	–	..	..	..	✓	18	..
Ethiopia	22	19	15	43	27	•	10	..
Gabon	17	18	..	..	..	•	17	..
Gambia	9	–	..	..	..	•	28	..
Ghana	8	–	7	26	20	•	16	11
Guinea	–[c]	–[c]	..	..	..	•	16	..
Guinea-Bissau	10	–	..	..	..	•	25	..
Kenya	10	–	11	6	8	✓	..	..
Lesotho	25	29	..	..	..	•	32	..
Liberia	13	17	..	..	..	•	20	..
Libyan Arab Jamahiriya	8	–	..	..	..	•	—	..
Madagascar	8	11	..	..	..	•	13	4
Malawi	13	–	..	..	..	•	24	..
Mali	10	–	..	..	..	✓	23	..
Mauritania	22	16	..	..	..	✓	12	..
Mauritius	17	–	10	19	10	•	10	40[b]
Mayotte	..	..	..	..	..	•	..	—[b]
Morocco	11	1	..	..	..	✓	19	..
Mozambique	35	–	..	..	..	✓	26	3
Namibia	27	27	..	..	..	•	25	..
Niger	12	–	..	..	..	✓	26	..
Nigeria	7	8	..	..	..	•	23	..
Rwanda	56	35	53	20	23	✓	17	..
Sao Tome and Principe	7	–	..	..	..	•	..	..
Senegal	22	40	..	..	..	•	18	..
Sierra Leone	13	–	..	..	..	•	14	..

Table 5.A
Power and decision-making (*continued*)

Country or area	Share of women in the parliament, 2009 (%)		Candidates to lower or single house of parliament, 2003–2008[a]			Whether gender quota for lower or single house of parliament exists	Share of women among ministers, 2008 (%)	Share of women among mayors, 2003–2009[a] (%)
	Lower or single house	Upper house	Share of women (%)	Proportion elected (%)				
				Women	Men			
Africa (*continued*)								
Somalia	6	–	..	..	..	✓	..	..
South Africa	44	30	..	..	..	✓	45	16
Sudan	18	6	..	..	..	✓	6	..
Swaziland	14	40	..	..	..	•	19	..
Togo	11	–	..	..	..	•	10	..
Tunisia	23	15	..	..	..	✓	7	2
Uganda	31	–	..	..	..	✓	28	3
United Republic of Tanzania	30	–	..	..	..	✓	21	..
Zambia	15	–	14	22	21	•	17	..
Zimbabwe	15	25	13	32	23	✓	16	..
Asia								
Afghanistan	28	22	..	..	..	✓	4	..
Armenia	8	–	21	4	11	✓	6	..
Azerbaijan	11	–	..	..	..	•	7	..
Bahrain	3	25	9	6	21	•	4	..
Bangladesh	19	–	..	..	..	✓	8	—
Bhutan	9	24	..	..	..	•	—	..
Brunei Darussalam	..	..	..	..	..	•	7	..
Cambodia	16	15	..	..	..	•	7	..
China	21	–	..	..	..	•	9	..
Cyprus	14	–	23	7	13	✓	18	3
Democratic People's Republic of Korea	16	–	..	..	..	•	—	..
Georgia	6	–	..	..	..	•	18	..
India	9	10	..	..	..	✓	10	..
Indonesia	12	–	..	..	..	✓	11	..
Iran (Islamic Republic of)	3	–	8	1	4	•	3	..
Iraq	26	–	..	..	..	✓	10	..
Israel	18	–	..	..	..	✓	12	..
Jordan	6	13	23	4	15	✓	15	1
Kazakhstan	16	4	..	..	..	•	6	..
Kuwait	3	–	10	—	23	•	7	..
Kyrgyzstan	26	–	..	..	..	✓	19	..
Lao People's Democratic Republic	25	–	23	73	64	•	11	..
Lebanon	5	–	..	..	..	•	5	—
Malaysia	11	29	..	..	..	•	9	1
Maldives	12	–	..	..	..	•	14	..
Mongolia	4	–	..	..	..	•	20	..
Myanmar	..	..	..	..	..	•	—	..
Nepal	33	–	9	54	10	✓	20	..
Occupied Palestinian Territory	13	..	..	..	..	✓	..	..
Oman	—	20	3	—	14	•	9	..
Pakistan	23	17	..	..	..	✓	4	1
Philippines	21	17	..	..	..	✓	9	15[b]

Table 5.A
Power and decision-making (*continued*)

Country or area	Share of women in the parliament, 2009 (%)		Candidates to lower or single house of parliament, 2003–2008[a]			Whether gender quota for lower or single house of parliament exists	Share of women among ministers, 2008 (%)	Share of women among mayors, 2003–2009[a] (%)
	Lower or single house	Upper house	Share of women (%)	Proportion elected (%)				
				Women	Men			
Asia (*continued*)								
Qatar	—	–	..	..	..	•	8	..
Republic of Korea	14	–	..	..	..	✓	5	..
Saudi Arabia	—	–	..	..	..	•	—	..
Singapore	25	–	..	..	..	•	—	..
Sri Lanka	6	–	..	..	..	•	6	..
Syrian Arab Republic	12	–	10	3	3	•	6	..
Tajikistan	18	24	16	31	27	•	6	9[b]
Thailand	12	16	..	..	..	✓	10	1
Timor-Leste	29	–	..	..	..	✓	25	..
Turkey	9	–	18	2	3	•	4	1
Turkmenistan	17	–	..	..	..	•	7	..
United Arab Emirates	23	–	14	2	5	•	8	..
Uzbekistan	18	15	..	..	..	✓	5	..
Viet Nam	26	–	..	..	..	•	4	..
Yemen	—	2	1	9	22	•	6	..
Latin America and the Caribbean								
Argentina	40	39	..	..	..	✓	23	7
Bahamas	12	60	..	..	..	•	8	..
Barbados	10	19	..	..	..	•	28	..
Belize	—	39	3	—	33	•	18	..
Bolivia (Plurinational State of)	17	4	..	..	..	✓	24	11
Brazil	9	12	..	..	..	✓	11	5
Chile	15	5	..	..	..	✓	41	13
Colombia	8	12	..	..	..	✓	23	3
Costa Rica	37	–	51	4	6	✓	29	11[b]
Cuba	43	–	..	..	..	•	19	..
Dominican Republic	20	3	..	..	..	✓	14	7
Ecuador	25	–	..	..	..	✓	35	3
El Salvador	19	–	..	..	..	✓	39	7
Grenada	13	31	..	..	..	•	50	..
Guatemala	12	–	..	..	..	✓	7	3
Guyana	30	–	..	..	..	✓	26	..
Haiti	4	–[d]	..	..	..	•	11	..
Honduras	23	–	..	..	..	✓	..	10
Jamaica	13	14	..	..	..	•	11	7[b]
Mexico	23	18	..	..	..	✓	16	5[b]
Nicaragua	19	–	..	..	..	✓	33	10
Panama	17	–	..	..	..	✓	23	16
Paraguay	13	16	30	3	13	✓	19	5
Peru	28	–	35	4	5	✓	29	3[b]
Puerto Rico	..	..	..	..	..	•	..	..
Saint Lucia	11	27	..	..	..	•	..	..
Saint Vincent and the Grenadines	18	–	..	..	..	•	21	..

Table 5.A
Power and decision-making (*continued*)

Country or area	Share of women in the parliament, 2009 (%)		Candidates to lower or single house of parliament, 2003–2008[a]			Whether gender quota for lower or single house of parliament exists	Share of women among ministers, 2008 (%)	Share of women among mayors, 2003–2009[a] (%)
	Lower or single house	Upper house	Share of women (%)	Proportion elected (%)				
				Women	Men			
Latin America and the Caribbean (*continued*)								
Suriname	26	–	..	..	..	•	17	..
Trinidad and Tobago	27	42	25	34	31	•	36	—[b]
Uruguay	12	13	..	..	..	✓	29	..
Venezuela (Bolivarian Republic of)	19	–	..	..	..	•	21	18[b]
Oceania								
Fiji	—[e]	—[e]	..	..	..	•	8	..
Micronesia (Federated States of)	—	–				•	14	
Papua New Guinea	1	–	..	..	..	•	4	..
Samoa	8	–	8	16	22	•	23	2[b]
Solomon Islands	—	–	6	—	12	•	—	
Tonga	3	–	11	—	45	•	..	..
Vanuatu	4	–	3	22	15	•	8	..
More developed regions								
Albania	7	–	..	..	..	✓	7	..
Australia	27	36	26	15	14	✓	24	15
Austria	28	25	..	..	..	✓	38	
Belarus	32	34	21	65	29	•	6	..
Belgium	35	38	49	15	23	✓	23	7
Bosnia and Herzegovina	12	13	39	2	9	✓	—	3[b]
Bulgaria	22	–	..	..	..	•	24	10
Canada	22	34	23	17	20	✓	16	..
Croatia	21	–	25	2	3	✓	24	5[b]
Czech Republic	16	17	28	2	5	✓	13	..
Denmark	38	–	32	22	17	•	37	9
Estonia	21	–	27	9	11	•	23	10
Finland	42	–	40	11	10	•	58	10
France	18	22	42	3	11	✓	47	11
Germany	32	22	28	19	16	✓	33	5
Greece	15	–	..	..	..	✓	12	2[b]
Hungary	11	–	17	9	15	✓	21	12
Iceland	43	–	47	6	11	✓	36	17
Ireland	13	22	17	27	37	•	21	..
Italy	21	18	..	..	..	✓	24	7
Japan	9	18	12	21	28	•	12	—
Latvia	20	–	26	7	11	•	22	25
Lithuania	18	–	..	..	..	✓	23	3
Luxembourg	23	–	..	..	..	✓	14	11
Malta	9	–	12	27	37	✓	15	8
Montenegro	6	–	..	..	..	•	6	..
Netherlands	41	35	35	71	67	✓	33	16
New Zealand	34	–	28	22	17	•	32	26
Norway	36	–	..	..	..	✓	56	14
Poland	20	8	23	7	8	✓	26	5

Table 5.A

Power and decision-making (*continued*)

Country or area	Share of women in the parliament, 2009 (%)		Candidates to lower or single house of parliament, 2003–2008[a]			Whether gender quota for lower or single house of parliament exists	Share of women among ministers, 2008 (%)	Share of women among mayors, 2003–2009[a] (%)
	Lower or single house	Upper house	Share of women (%)	Proportion elected (%)				
				Women	Men			
More developed regions (*continued*)								
Portugal	28	–	32	5	9	✓	13	6
Republic of Moldova	22	–	..	..	..	•	11	15[b]
Romania	11	6	..	..	..	✓	—	4[b]
Russian Federation	14	5	..	..	..	•	10	..
Serbia	22	–	31	6	6	✓	17	26[b]
Slovakia	19	–	23	5	7	✓	13	14
Slovenia	13	3	..	..	..	✓	18	5
Spain	36	30	..	..	..	✓	44	11
Sweden	47	–	43	7	6	✓	48	17
Switzerland	29	22	35	5	8	✓	43	5
The former Yugoslav Republic of Macedonia	28	–	35	7	6	✓	14	2
Ukraine	8	–	19	3	7	•	4	..
United Kingdom	20	20	20	18	18	✓	23	8[b]
United States of America	17	15	..	..	..	•	24	17[b]

Sources

Share of women in the parliament: Inter-Parliamentary Union, *http://www.ipu.org/wmn-e/classif.htm#1* (accessed in May 2009)

Candidates to lower or single house of parliament: Inter-Parliamentary Union, Women in Parliament: The year in perspective (2003, 2005, 2006, 2007 and 2008).

Gender quota for lower or single house of parliament: International Institute for Democracy and Electoral Assistance (IDEA) and others, Global datatabase of quotas for women, *http://www.quotaproject.org/index.cfm* (accessed in June 2010).

Share of women among ministers: Inter-Parliamentary Union and United Nations Division for the Advancement of Women. 2008. Women in Politics: 2008. Map. *http://www.un.org/womenwatch/daw/public/publications.htm.*

Share of women among mayors: United Cities and Local Governments, *http://www.cities-localgovernments.org* (accessed in June 2009), unless otherwise stated.

Definitions

Share of women in the lower or single house of the parliament: Proportion of seats held by women in the lower house of a bicameral national parliament or in the unicameral national parliament. The parliament is the legislative or deliberative assembly. Seats are usually won by members in general parliamentary elections, but may also be filled by indirect election, rotation of members, nomination, or appointment.

Share of women in the upper house of the parliament: Proportion of seats held by women in the upper house of a bicameral national parliament. This indicator is not applicable to countries with unicameral parliaments.

Share of women among candidates: Proportion of women among candidates in elections for the lower or single house of parliament.

Proportion of candidates elected: Proportion of women (or men) candidates in parliamentary elections who were successfully elected.

Gender quota for lower or single house of parliament: Any type of electoral quota for women adopted in a country either through legislation or on a voluntary basis. Three types of quota are covered by the indicator: 1) reserved seats for women in a legislative assembly; 2) legislated quotas on female candidates on electoral lists; 3) quotas for women as election candidates voluntarily adopted by political parties.

Ministers: Ministers include Deputy Prime Ministers and Ministers. Prime Ministers are also included when they hold ministerial portfolios. Vice-Presidents and heads of governmental or public agencies are not included.

Mayors: Heads of government of a city, town, borough, or municipality.

Notes

..   Data not available.

–   Not applicable.

—   Magnitude nil or less than 0.5 per cent.

✓   Yes

•   No

a   Latest available data in the given interval.

b   Data collected from national sources.

c   The parliament was dissolved following the December 2008 coup.

d   No winners had emerged from Senate elections in April 2009.

e   Parliament has been dissolved or suspended for an indefinite period.

Table 6.A
Prevalence of violence against women

Country or area	Year	Prevalence of physical violence against women (%)								Prevalence of sexual violence against women (%)			
				By intimate partner									
		All perpetrators		Lifetime			Last 12 months			All perpetrators		By intimate partner	
				Total	Severity of violence		Total	Severity of violence					
		Lifetime	Last 12 months	Total	Moderate	Severe	Total	Moderate	Severe	Lifetime	Last 12 months	Lifetime	Last 12 months
Africa													
Egypt	1995/96	35	..	34	..	..	13						
Ethiopia–province	2002	..	..	49	13	35	29	7	22	..	..	59	44
Mozambique	2004	48	17	36	..	..	15	..	..	24	9	12	6
Namibia–city	2001	..	..	31	11	20	16	5	11	..	..	17	9
United Republic of Tanzania–city	2001/02	..	..	33	16	17	15	6	8	..	..	23	13
United Republic of Tanzania–province	2001/02	..	..	47	22	25	19	8	11	..	..	31	18
Zambia	2001/02	59	..	48	..	..	27	..	..	..	..	..	..
Asia													
Azerbaijan	2006	13	8	13	..	..	10	..	..	4	..	3	2
Bangladesh–city	2001	..	..	40	21	19	19	9	10	..	..	37	20
Bangladesh–province	2001	..	..	42	22	19	16	7	9	..	..	50	24
Cambodia[a]	2000	23	..	18	..	..	15	..	..	..	..	..	..
China, Hong Kong SAR	2005	12	2	6	..	..	1	..	..	14	3	5	1
India[a]	1998/2000	21	..	19	..	..	10	..	..	..	..	..	..
Maldives	2006	..	..	18	..	..	..	..	..	..	..	7	..
Philippines	2005	15	5	10	..	..	3	..	..	6	2	3	1
Republic of Korea	2004	..	..	16	..	..	..	..	..	..	..	7	..
Thailand–city	2000	..	..	23	10	13	8	3	5	..	..	30	17
Thailand–province	2000	..	..	34	16	18	13	5	8	..	..	29	16
Turkey	2008	..	..	39	21	18	10	..	..	..	..	15	7
Latin America and the Caribbean													
Bolivia (Plurinational State of)[b]	2003	..	..	36	..	..	7	..	..	..	..	12	3
Brazil–city	2000/01	..	..	27	12	16	8	5	3	..	..	29	9
Brazil–province	2000/01	..	..	34	14	20	13	5	8	..	..	14	6
Colombia	2000	41	..	44	..	..	..	..	..	..	..	..	..
Costa Rica	2003	47	11	33	..	..	7	..	..	41	7	15	3
Dominican Republic	2002	24	..	22	..	..	11	..	..	..	..	..	..
Ecuador	2004	..	..	31	..	..	10	..	..	..	..	12	4
Haiti	2000	35	..	29	..	..	21	..	..	..	..	..	..
Mexico	2006	40	..	23	..	..	..	..	..	44	..	11	..
Nicaragua	1997/98	33	..	30	..	..	13	..	..	..	..	..	..
Paraguay	2004	..	..	19	..	..	7	..	..	..	..	8	3
Peru	2000	47	..	42	..	..	..	..	..	..	..	..	..
Peru–city	2000	..	..	49	23	26	17	7	10	..	..	23	7
Peru–province	2000	..	..	61	12	49	25	4	21	..	..	47	23
Oceania													
Samoa	2000	..	..	41	17	24	18	6	12	..	..	20	12
Solomon Islands	2008	..	..	46	..	..	..	..	..	..	..	55	..

Table 6.A

Prevalence of violence against women (*continued*)

Country or area	Year	Prevalence of physical violence against women (%)								Prevalence of sexual violence against women (%)			
		All perpetrators		By intimate partner						All perpetrators		By intimate partner	
				Lifetime			Last 12 months						
					Severity of violence			Severity of violence					
		Lifetime	Last 12 months	Total	Moderate	Severe	Total	Moderate	Severe	Lifetime	Last 12 months	Lifetime	Last 12 months
More developed regions													
Albania	2002	..	..	8	..	..	5	..	..	..	..	3	2
Australia	2002/03	48	8	25	..	..	4	..	..	34	4	8	1
Canada[c]	2004	..	..	7	..	..	2	..	..	..	..	..	..
Czech Republic	2003	51	12	35	..	..	8	..	..	35	5	11	2
Denmark	2003	38	4	20	..	..	1	..	..	28	2	6	—
Finland	2005/06	44[d]	12[d]	18[e]	..	..	..	..	..	..	..	4[f]	..
France	2003	17	..	..	..	..	..	..	..	5	..	..	..
Germany	2003	37	..	28	..	..	..	..	..	13	..	7	..
Italy	2006	19	3	12	..	..	2	..	..	24	4	6	1
Japan–city	2000/01	..	..	13	9	4	3	3	1	..	..	6	1
Lithuania	2000	..	..	33	..	..	..	..	..	..	..	8	..
New Zealand–city	2003	..	..	30	..	..	..	..	..	..	..	14	..
New Zealand–province	2003	..	..	38	..	..	..	..	..	..	..	22	..
Poland	2004	30	5	15	..	..	3	..	..	17	2	5	—
Republic of Moldova	2005	27	13	24	..	..	..	..	..	..	..	4	..
Serbia–city	2003	..	..	23	15	8	3	2	2	..	..	6	1
Switzerland	2003	27	1	9	..	..	1	..	..	25[g]	1	3	—
United Kingdom[h]	2006/07	..	..	19	15	14	3	2	2	..	..	24	3

Source

All indicators: Compiled by the United Nations Statistics Division from national and international reports (see table 6.E).

Definitions

Physical violence: An act that inflicts physical harm to the body of a woman.

Sexual violence: An act aimed to force the woman to engage in sexual acts against her will (or without her consent).

Notes

..   Data not available.

—   Magnitude nil or less than 0.5 per cent.

a   Data refer to ever-married women only.

b   Data refer to being hit by partner's hand. Not included are shoving, hits with hard objects and attempted strangulation.

c   Data refer to spousal assault only.

d   At least one form of violence or threat.

e   Data refer to current partnership only. The corresponding figure for previous partnership(s) is 45%.

f   Sexual violence and threatening behaviour. Data refer to current partnership only. The corresponding figure for previous partnership(s) is 17%.

g   Data refer to three categories of violence that may overlap: rape (5.6%), rape attempt (6.8%) and unwanted kisses or sexual touching (18.0%).

h   Data refer to England and Wales only.

Table 6.B

Physical and/or sexual violence against women by current or former intimate partner

		Proportion of ever-partnered women who experienced physical or sexual violence by current or former intimate partner (%)															
		In the last 12 months								During lifetime							
		Total	Age group							Total	Age group						
Country or area	Year	Total	15–19	20–24	25–29	30–34	35–39	40–44	45–49	Total	15–19	20–24	25–29	30–34	35–39	40–44	45–49
Africa																	
Egypt	1995/96	13	21	19	14	13	13	8	5	34	29	34	34	37	36	33	32
Ethiopia–province	2002	54	50	60	64	62	52	42	28	71	60	67	76	77	71	68	61
Namibia–city	2001	20	28	26	15	19	20	15	19	36	43	36	33	34	36	36	44
United Republic of Tanzania–city	2001/02	22	23	30	26	20	19	13	4	41	30	39	46	44	46	40	35
United Republic of Tanzania–province	2001/02	29	37	32	34	29	22	18	21	56	44	49	58	62	56	59	65
Zambia	2001/02	27	33	35	30	24	20	17	18	48	38	49	55	49	46	50	44
Asia																	
Azerbaijan	2006	10[a]	..	..	..	..	..	..	..	14[a]	14[a]	11[a]	15	14[a,b]	..	14[a,c]	..
Bangladesh–city	2001	30	48	37	36	28	19	16	10	53	59	56	57	55	49	48	34
Bangladesh–province	2001	32	41	34	40	33	26	19	26	62	53	53	68	67	63	57	62
Cambodia	2000	15	4	12	19	17	17	11	18	18	4	14	21	19	18	13	22
India	1998/2000	10	10	11	12	12	10	8	6	19	13	17	21	22	21	19	17
Maldives	2006	..	..	..	..	..	..	..	..	20	..	..	..	..	..	..	..
Thailand–city	2000	21	44	30	27	22	20	19	8	41	48	44	47	42	41	37	35
Thailand–province	2000	23	39	31	23	21	27	18	20	47	50	52	46	39	54	48	45
Turkey	2008	..	..	..	..	..	..	..	..	30	3[d]	..	30[e]	..	29[f]	..	26
Latin America and the Caribbean																	
Bolivia (Plurinational State of)	2003	..	..	..	..	..	..	..	..	53	44	50	51	55	55	58	54
Brazil–city	2000/01	9	19	12	10	11	7	4	9	29	24	22	30	30	30	28	38
Brazil–province	2000/01	15	20	25	15	12	13	14	6	37	27	39	33	36	45	42	32
Colombia	2000	..	..	..	..	..	..	..	..	44	39	43	43	44	45	43	48
Dominican Republic	2002	11	15	17	13	11	10	5	6	22	20	26	25	23	22	23	16
Ecuador	2004	10[a]	15[a]	15[a]	10[a]	11[a]	10[a]	6[a]	7[a]	31[a]	22[a]	29[a]	29[a]	32[a]	37[a]	29[a]	32[a]
El Salvador	2002/03	24[g]	..	..	..	..	..	..	..	..	..	..	..	..	..	..	..
Haiti	2000	13	25	31	19	26	22	13	13	29	26	33	25	31	27	22	36
Nicaragua	1997/98	13	18	16	14	14	11	12	7	30	27	27	29	32	33	33	30
Paraguay	2004	7[a]	12[a]	9[a]	7[a]	6[a]	5[a]	5[a]	..	19[a]	18[a]	20[a]	20[a]	21[a]	17[a]	20[a]	..
Peru	2000	..	..	..	..	..	..	..	..	42	31	37	41	43	45	45	44
Peru–city	2000	19	41	28	23	20	10	19	8	51	54	50	55	49	51	54	47
Peru–province	2000	34	49	44	36	34	35	26	24	69	60	68	64	70	72	71	76
Oceania																	
Samoa	2000	22	36	33	26	21	22	12	18	46	52	47	40	46	48	49	49
Solomon Islands	2008	42	..	..	..	..	..	..	..	64	..	..	..	..	..	..	..
More developed regions																	
Australia	2002/03	4	..	..	..	..	..	..	..	27	..	..	..	..	..	..	..
Canada	2004	2[i]	..	..	..	..	..	..	..	7[i,j]	..	..	..	..	..	..	..
Denmark	2005	1	..	..	..	..	..	..	..	22	..	..	..	..	..	..	..
Finland	2005/06	7[a]	15[a,k]	..	9[a,e]	..	7[a,f]	..	5[a,l]	30	26[a,k]	..	29[a,e]	..	27[a,f]	..	28[a,l]
France	2000	3[a]	4[a,k]	..	3[a,e]	..	3[a,f]	..	2[a,l]	..	..	..	..	..	..	..	..
Germany	2003	3	7	..	4	..	3	..	1	29	29[a,k]	..	31[a,e]	..	28[a,f]	..	25[a,l]
Italy	2006	2	..	..	..	..	..	..	..	14	..	..	..	..	..	..	..

Table 6.B

Physical and/or sexual violence against women by current or former intimate partner (*continued*)

Country or area	Year	Proportion of ever-partnered women who experienced physical or sexual violence by current or former intimate partner (%)															
		In the last 12 months								During lifetime							
		Total	Age group							Total	Age group						
			15–19	20–24	25–29	30–34	35–39	40–44	45–49		15–19	20–24	25–29	30–34	35–39	40–44	45–49
More developed regions (*continued*)																	
Japan–city	2000/01	4	4	3	6	3	6	3	2	15	7	13	14	17	18	14	16
Lithuania	2000	..	..	..	..	..	..	..	..	38	23[a,k]		31[a,e]		33[a,f]	..	45[a,l]
Norway	2004	6	..	..	..	..	..	..	..	27	..	..	..	..	..	..	..
Poland	2004	3								16							
Republic of Moldova	2005	..	..	..	..	..	..	..	..	25[h]	20[h]	18[h]	20[h]	25[h]	29[h]	27[h]	28[h]
Serbia–city	2003	4	14	6	2	4	3	2	3	24	20	19	19	26	24	26	28
Slovakia	2008	12	..	..	..	..	..	..	..	21[g]	..	..	..	..	..	..	..
Sweden	1999/2000	5[a]	5[a,k]	..	4[a,e]	..	5[a,f]	..	5[a,l]	21[a]	20[a,k]	..	20[a,e]	..	21[a,f]	..	21[a,l]
Switzerland	2003	1	..	..	..	..	..	..	..	11	..	..	..	..	..	..	..
United Kingdom[m,n]	2006/07	6	..	..	..	..	..	..	..	29	..	..	..	..	..	..	..

Source

All indicators: Compiled by the United Nations Statistics Division from national and international reports (see table 6.E).

Definitions:

Physical violence: An act that inflicts physical harm to the body of a woman.

Sexual violence: An act aimed to force the woman to engage in sexual acts against her will (or without her consent).

Notes

..   Data not available.

a   Data refer to physical violence only.

b   Data refer to the age group 30–39.

c   Data refer to the age group 40–49.

d   Data refer to the age group 15–24.

e   Data refer to the age group 25–34.

f   Data refer to the age group 35–44.

g   Data refer to violence by current partner only.

h   Data refer to violence by current or most recent partner.

i   Data refer to spousal assault only.

j   Data refer to the last five year only.

k   Data refer to the age group 18–24.

l   Data refer to the age group 45–59.

m   Data refer to England and Wales only.

n   Includes non-physical abuse (emotional, financial), threats, force, sexual assault or stalking.

Table 6.C
Female genital mutilation/cutting (FGM/C)

Country or area	Year	Proportion of women 15–49 years old who have undergone FGM/C (%)									
		Total	Place of residence		Age group						
			Urban	Rural	15–19	20–24	25–29	30–34	35–39	40–44	45–49
Africa											
Benin	2001	17	13	20	12	13	17	18	18	25	24
Benin[a]	2006	13	9	15	8	..	..	..	16	..	..
Burkina Faso	1998/99	72	82	70	64	71	75	74	74	77	74
Burkina Faso	2003	77	75	77	65	76	79	79	82	83	84
Cameroon	2004	1	1	2	—	3	2	1	1	2	2
Central African Republic	1994/95	43	40	46	35	43	44	44	48	51	53
Central African Republic	2000	36	29	41	27	34	36	40	43	42	42
Chad	2000	45	43	46	42	44	44	47	45	45	52
Chad[a]	2004	45	47	44	43	..	..	..	46	..	..
Côte d'Ivoire	1994	43	40	45	35	42	48	47	44	45	44
Côte d'Ivoire	1998/99	45	39	48	41	43	42	49	45	51	51
Côte d'Ivoire[a]	2006	36	34	39	28	..	..	..	44	..	..
Djibouti[a]	2006	93	93	96	..	..	..	..	..	..	..
Egypt	1995	97	94	100	98	98	97	96	97	97	97
Egypt	2000	97	95	99	99	97	97	97	97	97	98
Egypt	2003	97	95	99	97	97	97	97	96	97	98
Egypt[a]	2005	96	92	98	96	..	..	..	96	..	..
Eritrea	1995	95	93	95	90	94	95	96	97	96	97
Eritrea	2001/02	89	86	91	78	88	91	93	93	94	95
Ethiopia	2000	80	80	80	71	78	81	86	84	86	87
Ethiopia[a]	2005	74	69	76	62	..	..	..	81	..	..
Gambia[a]	2005/06	78	72	83	80	..	..	..	80	..	..
Ghana	2003	5	4	7	3	4	6	6	7	6	8
Ghana[a]	2006	4	2	6	1	..	..	..	6	..	..
Guinea	1999	99	98	99	97	99	99	99	99	99	100
Guinea[a]	2005	96	94	96	89	..	..	..	99	..	..
Guinea-Bissau[a]	2006	45	39	48	44	..	..	..	49	..	..
Kenya	1998	38	23	42	26	32	40	41	49	47	48
Kenya	2003	32	21	36	20	25	33	38	40	48	48
Mali	1995/96	94	90	96	93	94	94	95	94	94	92
Mali[b]	2001	92	90	93	91	91	92	92	92	91	91
Mali[a]	2006	85	81	87	85	..	..	..	85	..	..
Mauritania	2000/01	71	65	77	66	71	73	74	72	77	69
Niger	1998	5	2	5	5	5	4	5	4	3	3
Niger[a]	2006	2	2	2	2	..	..	..	3	..	..
Nigeria	1999	25	30	23	9	20	26	31	31	38	48
Nigeria	2003	19	28	14	13	17	21	19	22	22	28
Senegal[c]	2005	28	22	35	25	28	28	30	31	30	31
Sierra Leone[a]	2006	94	86	97	81	..	..	..	98	..	..
Somalia	2006	98	97	98	97	..	..	..	99	..	..
Sudan[d]	1989/90	89	93	87	87	90	89	90	89	89	91

Table 6.C

Female genital mutilation/cutting (FGM/C) (continued)

Country or area	Year	Proportion of women 15–49 years old who have undergone FGM/C (%)									
		Total	Place of residence		Age group						
			Urban	Rural	15–19	20–24	25–29	30–34	35–39	40–44	45–49
Africa (continued)											
Sudan[d]	2000	90	92	88	86	89	89	90	92	92	93
United Republic of Tanzania	1996	18	10	20	13	16	19	21	18	21	22
United Republic of Tanzania[a]	2004/05	15	7	18	9	..	..	..	16	..	..
Togo[a]	2006	6	4	7	1	..	..	..	9	..	..
Uganda[a]	2006	1	—	1	1	..	..	..	1	..	..
Asia											
Yemen	1997	23	26	22	19	22	21	23	24	25	25
Yemen[a]	2003	38	33	41	..	..	..	..	..	..	..

Sources

All indicators: UNICEF, *Female genital Mutilation/Cutting – A Statistical Exploration*, 2005; and Population Reference Bureau, *Female Genital Mutilation/Cutting: Data and Trends*, 2008. Both compilations have the DHS and MICS as their primary sources.

Definition

Female genital mutilation/cutting (FGM/C): Any procedure involving the partial or total removal of the external female genitalia or other injury to the female genital organs for non-therapeutic reasons.

Notes

.. Data not available.

— Magnitude nil or less than half of unit employed.

a Data from Population Reference Bureau, *Female Genital Mutilation/Cutting: Data and Trends,* 2008.

b Data for 2001 for Mali includes the district of Kidal, which was excluded in the 1996 DHS. This has increased the proportion of circumcised women from 9.3% in the districts of Tombouctou/Gao to 33.6% in Tombouctou/Gao/Kidal.

c Data for Senegal (2005) are preliminary.

d Data refer to the northern part of the country.

Table 6.D
Women's attitudes towards wife beating

| | | Proportion of women who agree that a husband is justified in hitting or beating his wife for specific reasons, by level of education (%) | | | | | | | | | | | | | | | | | | |
| | | Burning the food | | | | Arguing with him | | | | Going out without telling him | | | | Neglecting the children | | | | Refusing to have sex with him | | | |
Country or area	Year	Total	None	Primary	Secondary+	Total	None	Primary	Secondary+	Total	None	Primary	Secondary+	Total	None	Primary	Secondary+	Total	None	Primary	Secondary+
Africa																					
Benin	2001	29	35	24	12	39	46	34	17	44	51	39	20	51	58	46	26	17	21	13	6
Burkina Faso	2003	26	28	25	13	52	56	48	25	53	57	48	23	55	58	51	33	37	41	33	13
Cameroon	2004	19	30	21	11	27	35	31	17	34	41	39	24	45	44	51	40	20	36	23	10
Egypt	2005	19	31	23	10	37	57	46	21	40	59	50	24	40	57	50	25	34	51	41	19
Eritrea	2002	29	34	31	15	45	55	43	20	52	62	53	26	51	55	55	35	48	58	47	23
Ethiopia	2005	61	68	61	24	59	64	59	27	64	70	62	34	65	70	64	38	44	51	40	15
Ethiopia	2000	65	70	62	27	61	66	60	28	56	60	53	27	65	67	66	42	51	56	45	17
Ghana	2003	14	24	15	8	30	43	31	21	34	47	38	26	37	51	41	28	20	33	20	13
Guinea	2005	35	37	28	26	58	61	49	44	72	74	67	65	70	72	65	64	62	66	47	45
Kenya	2003	16	24	19	9	46	61	52	27	39	58	44	23	55	66	61	39	29	47	33	16
Lesotho	2004	13	24	16	8	36	46	43	26	24	43	30	14	37	49	42	29	20	40	25	11
Madagascar	2003/04	8	9	8	8	3	3	4	2	14	12	15	15	25	25	25	25	6	6	6	4
Malawi	2004	11	12	12	7	12	11	13	9	14	13	15	10	17	16	18	14	14	15	15	8
Malawi	2000	17	16	18	9	19	17	21	12	17	15	18	11	22	19	24	16	18	19	19	10
Mali	2001	34	34	37	21	62	64	63	42	75	77	75	56	71	72	76	61	74	76	75	52
Morocco	2003/04	24	36	20	5	51	66	52	25	50	68	50	20	49	65	49	23	43	59	41	18
Mozambique	2003	24	27	23	12	33	37	32	21	37	41	36	22	38	41	38	26	34	41	33	15
Nigeria	2003	31	43	30	18	44	56	44	30	53	71	51	33	49	61	50	37	38	54	36	20
Rwanda	2005	11	13	11	3	7	8	8	3	26	30	27	12	41	42	43	27	14	18	14	7
Rwanda	2000	22	28	22	10	12	15	11	6	37	46	36	17	56	63	57	37	33	43	32	17
Senegal	2005	23	27	20	15	49	56	44	30	50	58	43	28	49	55	43	31	45	54	37	24
United Republic of Tanzania	2004/05	20	22	20	9	46	48	48	27	43	45	45	23	47	47	50	29	29	33	30	12
Uganda	2000/01	22	28	23	14	37	44	39	23	56	60	58	45	67	71	69	59	24	32	25	13
Zambia	2001/02	45	49	51	33	52	54	58	41	79	75	83	72	61	62	65	52	47	50	54	32
Zimbabwe	1999	12	19	16	8	32	43	38	25	28	33	32	24	31	34	34	29	22	32	30	16
Asia																					
Armenia	2005	2	0	4	2	15	0	28	15	10	17	20	10	17	15	29	17	4	—	4	4
Armenia	2000	5	12	7	5	14	12	24	14	20	23	21	20	27	23	28	27	7	12	22	7
Jordan	2002	60	84	78	55	4	21	11	2	24	63	48	18	37	74	57	31	..	..	..	..
Turkmenistan	2000	22	33	26	22	34	45	36	34	40	58	50	40	44	48	45	44	21	34	30	21
Indonesia	2002/03	3	4	3	2	5	8	6	4	18	18	19	17	20	18	20	19	7	8	8	6
Nepal	2001	5	6	4	1	9	9	9	5	12	13	13	8	25	25	26	26	3	4	2	1
Philippines	2003	3	6	5	2	5	5	8	4	9	21	15	7	21	34	26	19	3	4	5	3

Table 6.D

Women's attitudes towards wife beating (*continued*)

Country or area	Year	Proportion of women who agree that a husband is justified in hitting or beating his wife for specific reasons, by level of education (%)																			
		Burning the food				Arguing with him				Going out without telling him				Neglecting the children				Refusing to have sex with him			
		Total	None	Primary	Secondary+	Total	None	Primary	Secondary+	Total	None	Primary	Secondary+	Total	None	Primary	Secondary+	Total	None	Primary	Secondary+
Latin America and the Caribbean																					
Bolivia (Plurinational State of)	2003	5	10	7	3	6	12	9	4	9	12	13	5	17	19	20	13	3	6	4	2
Dominican Republic	2002	2	7	4	1	1	3	2	1	3	9	5	1	7	12	10	4	1	3	1	0
Haiti	2000	11	13	14	5	11	14	13	4	29	36	33	17	28	33	31	18	14	21	14	6
Nicaragua	2001	5	10	6	1	4	10	6	1	6	12	9	2	9	17	12	5	3	6	4	1
More developed regions																					
Republic of Moldova	2005	4	4	17	4	5	9	24	5	7	12	19	7	18	26	32	18	3	9	19	3

Source

All indicators: Macro International, Demographic and Health Survey (DHS) STATcompiler (accessed in October 2009).

Notes

..   Data not available.

—   Magnitude nil or less than 0.5 per cent.

Table 6.E

Sources of data on prevalence of violence against women (*tables 6.A and 6.B*)

Country or area	Survey year	Source
Africa		
Egypt	1995/96	Kishor, Sunita and Kiersten Johnson, 2004. *Profiling Domestic Violence – A Multi-Country Study*. Calverton, Maryland: ORC Macro.
Ethiopia–province	2002	García-Moreno, C., H.A.F.M. Jansen, M. Ellsberg, L. Heise and C. Watts, 2005. *WHO Multi-country Study on Women's Health and Domestic Violence against Women: Initial results in prevalence, health outcomes and women's responses*. Geneva: WHO.
Mozambique	2004	Johnson, Holly, Natalia Ollus and Sami Nevala, 2008. *Violence Against Women. An International Perspective*. New York: Springer.
Namibia–city	2001	García-Moreno, C., H.A.F.M. Jansen, M. Ellsberg, L. Heise and C. Watts, 2005. *WHO Multi-country Study on Women's Health and Domestic Violence against Women: Initial results in prevalence, health outcomes and women's responses*. Geneva: WHO.
United Republic of Tanzania–city and province	2001/02	García-Moreno, C., H.A.F.M. Jansen, M. Ellsberg, L. Heise and C. Watts, 2005. *WHO Multi-country Study on Women's Health and Domestic Violence against Women: Initial results in prevalence, health outcomes and women's responses*. Geneva: WHO.
Zambia	2001/02	Kishor, Sunita and Kiersten Johnson. 2004. *Profiling Domestic Violence – A Multi-Country Study*. Calverton, Maryland: ORC Macro.
Asia		
Azerbaijan	2006	State Statistical Committee of the Republic of Azerbaijan and Macro International, 2008. *Demographic and Health Survey 2006*. Baku.
Bangladesh–city and province	2001	García-Moreno, C., H.A.F.M. Jansen, M. Ellsberg, L. Heise and C. Watts, 2005. *WHO Multi-country Study on Women's Health and Domestic Violence against Women: Initial results in prevalence, health outcomes and women's responses*. Geneva: WHO.
Cambodia	2000	Kishor, Sunita and Kiersten Johnson, 2004. *Profiling Domestic Violence – A Multi-Country Study*. Calverton, Maryland: ORC Macro.
China, Hong Kong SAR	2005	Johnson, Holly, Natalia Ollus and Sami Nevala, 2008. *Violence Against Women. An International Perspective*. New York: Springer.
India	1998/2000	Kishor, Sunita and Kiersten Johnson, 2004. *Profiling Domestic Violence – A Multi-Country Study*. Calverton, Maryland: ORC Macro.
Maldives	2006	Fulu, Emma. 2007. The Maldives Study on Women's Health and Life Experiences. Initial results on prevalence, health outcomes and women's responses to violence.
Republic of Korea	2004	Byun, Whasoon. 2007. Violence against women in Korea and its indicators. Invited paper, Expert Group Meeting on indicators to measure violence against women, Geneva, 8-10 October.
Thailand–city and province	2000	García-Moreno, C., H.A.F.M. Jansen, M. Ellsberg, L. Heise and C. Watts, 2005. *WHO Multi-country Study on Women's Health and Domestic Violence against Women: Initial results in prevalence, health outcomes and women's responses*. Geneva: WHO.
Turkey	2008	Henrice A.F.M. (Henriette) Jansen, Sunday Üner, Filiz Kardam and others, 2009. *National Research on Domestic Violence Against Women in Turkey*. Ankara.
Philippines	2005	Johnson, Holly, Natalia Ollus and Sami Nevala, 2008. *Violence Against Women. An International Perspective*. New York: Springer.
Latin America and the Caribbean		
Bolivia (Plurinational State of)	2003	Instituto Nacional de Estadística and others, 2004. *Encuesta Nacional de Demografía y Salud 2003*. Miraflores.
Brazil–city and province	2000/01	García-Moreno, C., H.A.F.M. Jansen, M. Ellsberg, L. Heise and C. Watts, 2005. *WHO Multi-country Study on Women's Health and Domestic Violence against Women: Initial results in prevalence, health outcomes and women's responses*. Geneva: WHO.
Colombia	2000	Kishor, Sunita and Kiersten Johnson, 2004. *Profiling Domestic Violence – A Multi-Country Study*. Calverton, Maryland: ORC Macro.
Costa Rica		Johnson, Holly, Natalia Ollus and Sami Nevala, 2008. *Violence Against Women. An International Perspective*. New York: Springer.
Dominican Republic	2002	Kishor, Sunita and Kiersten Johnson, 2004. *Profiling Domestic Violence – A Multi-Country Study*. Calverton, Maryland: ORC Macro.
Ecuador	2004	Centro de Estudios de Población y Desarrollo Social, 2009. Violencia contra la mujer. *www.cepar.org.ec/endemain_04/nuevo06/violencia/violencia_m.htm* (accessed in July 2009).
El Salvador	2002/03	Asociación Demográfica Salvadoreña and others, 2004. *Encuesta Nacional de Salud Familiar, FESAL 2002/03*.
Haiti	2000	Kishor, Sunita and Kiersten Johnson, 2004. *Profiling Domestic Violence – A Multi-Country Study*. Calverton, Maryland: ORC Macro.
Mexico	2003	Ramírez, Eva Gisela, 2007. ENDIREH-2006's achievements and limitations in determining indicators for measuring violence against women in Mexico. Invited paper, Expert Group Meeting on indicators to measure violence against women, Geneva, 8-10 October.
Nicaragua	1997/98	Kishor, Sunita and Kiersten Johnson, 2004. *Profiling Domestic Violence – A Multi-Country Study*. Calverton, Maryland: ORC Macro.
Paraguay	2004	Centro Paraguayo de Estudios de Población and others, 2005. *Encuesta nacional de demografía y salud sexual y reproductiva, 2004*.
Peru	2000	Kishor, Sunita and Kiersten Johnson, 2004. *Profiling Domestic Violence – A Multi-Country Study*. Calverton, Maryland: ORC Macro.
Peru– city and province	2000	García-Moreno, C., H.A.F.M. Jansen, M. Ellsberg, L. Heise and C. Watts, 2005. *WHO Multi-country Study on Women's Health and Domestic Violence against Women: Initial results in prevalence, health outcomes and women's responses*. Geneva: WHO.

Table 6.E
Sources of data on prevalence of violence against women (*continued*)

Country or area	Survey year	Source
Oceania		
Samoa	2000	García-Moreno, C., H.A.F.M. Jansen, M. Ellsberg, L. Heise and C. Watts, 2005. *WHO Multi-country Study on Women's Health and Domestic Violence against Women: Initial results in prevalence, health outcomes and women's responses.* Geneva: WHO.
Solomon Islands	2008	Secretariat of the Pacific Community for the Ministry of Women, Youth & Children's Affairs, 2009. *Solomon Islands Family Health and Safety Study: A study on violence against women and children.*
More developed regions		
Albania	2002	Albania Institute of Public Health, Ministry of Health, Institute of Statistics and others, 2005. *Reproductive Health Survey. Albania 2002.* Tirana.
Australia	2002/03	Johnson, Holly, Natalia Ollus and Sami Nevala, 2008. *Violence Against Women. An International Perspective.* New York: Springer.
Canada	2004	Statistics Canada, 2006. Measuring Violence Against Women: Statistical Trends 2006. Ottawa: Minister of Industry.
Czech Republic	2003	Johnson, Holly, Natalia Ollus and Sami Nevala, 2008. *Violence Against Women. An International Perspective.* New York: Springer.
Denmark	2003	Johnson, Holly, Natalia Ollus and Sami Nevala, 2008. *Violence Against Women. An International Perspective.* New York: Springer.
Finland	2005/06	Minna Piispa, Markku Heiskanen, Juha Kääriäinen and Reino Sirén, 2006. *Violence against Women in Finland.* Helsinki: National Research Institute of Legal Policy Publication and The European Institute for Crime Prevention and Control - affiliated with the United Nations (HEUNI).
	1997	Co-ordination Action on Human Rights Violations (CAHRV), 2006. *Comparative reanalysis of prevalence of violence against women and health impact data in Europe – obstacles and possible solutions.* December.
France	2003	Federal Ministry for Families, Senior Citizens, Women and Youth, 2003. *Health, Well-Being and Personal Safety of Women in Germany. A Representative Study of Violence against Women in Germany.*
		Co-ordination Action on Human Rights Violations (CAHRV, 2006. *Comparative reanalysis of prevalence of violence against women and health impact data in Europe – obstacles and possible solutions.* December.
Germany	2003	Federal Ministry for Families, Senior Citizens, Women and Youth, 2003. *Health, Well-Being and Personal Safety of Women in Germany. A Representative Study of Violence against Women in Germany.*
Italy	2006	ISTAT, 2006. *Violence and abuses against women inside and outside family*
Japan - city	2000/01	García-Moreno, C., H.A.F.M. Jansen, M. Ellsberg, L. Heise and C. Watts, 2005. *WHO Multi-country Study on Women's Health and Domestic Violence against Women: Initial results in prevalence, health outcomes and women's responses.* Geneva: WHO.
Lithuania	2000	Co-ordination Action on Human Rights Violations (CAHRV), 2006. *Comparative reanalysis of prevalence of violence against women and health impact data in Europe – obstacles and possible solutions.* December.
New Zealand–city and province	2003	García-Moreno, C., H.A.F.M. Jansen, M. Ellsberg, L. Heise and C. Watts, 2005. *WHO Multi-country Study on Women's Health and Domestic Violence against Women: Initial results in prevalence, health outcomes and women's responses.* Country Fact Sheets. Geneva: WHO.
Norway	2004	Haaland, Thomas, Sten-Erik Clausen and Berit Schei, 2005. *Couple Violence - different perspectives. Results from the first national survey in Norway.* NIBR Report.
Poland	2004	Johnson, Holly, Natalia Ollus and Sami Nevala, 2008. *Violence Against Women. An International Perspective.* New York: Springer.
Republic of Moldova	2005	Moldova National Scientific and Applied Center for preventive Medicine, Ministry of Health and Protection and ORC Macro, 2006. *Moldova Demographic and Health Survey 2005.* Chisinau.
Serbia - city	2003	García-Moreno, C., H.A.F.M. Jansen, M. Ellsberg, L. Heise and C. Watts, 2005. *WHO Multi-country Study on Women's Health and Domestic Violence against Women: Initial results in prevalence, health outcomes and women's responses.* Geneva: WHO.
Slovakia	2008	Bodnárová, Bernardina, Jarmila Filadelfiová and Barbara Holubová, 2009. *Representative Research on Prevalence and Experience of Women with Violence against Women in Slovakia.* Bratislava: Ministry of Labour, Social Affairs and Family.
Switzerland	2003	Johnson, Holly, Natalia Ollus and Sami Nevala, 2008. *Violence Against Women. An International Perspective.* New York: Springer.
Sweden	1999/2000	Co-ordination Action on Human Rights Violations (CAHRV), 2006. *Comparative reanalysis of prevalence of violence against women and health impact data in Europe – obstacles and possible solutions.* December.
United Kingdom	2006/07	Povey, David (Ed.), Kathryn Coleman, Peter Kaiza, Jacqueline Hoare and Krista Jansson. 2008. Homicides, Firearm Offences and Intimate Violence 2006/07, 3rd edition (Supplementary Volume 2 to Crime in England and Wales 2006/07). 31 January.

Table 7.A

Access to sources of drinking water and use of solid fuels for cooking

Country or area[a]	Year	Proportion of households within 15 minutes from a source of drinking water (%)		Proportion of households without water on premises by adult person usually collecting water (%)				Average time needed to collect water (*minutes per trip*)		Proportion of households using solid fuels for cooking (%)	
				Urban		Rural					
		Urban	Rural	Woman	Man	Woman	Man	Urban	Rural	Urban	Rural
Africa											
Algeria[b]	2006	..	..	..	..	..	..	..	..	—	3
Angola	2006/07	..	..	..	..	..	..	..	..	17	92
Benin	2006	73	50	..	..	..	..	..	..	86	98
Burkina Faso[b]	2006	45	23	45	14	87	4	29	37	77[c]	98[c]
Burundi[b]	2005	65	22	..	..	..	..	26	37	97	100
Cameroon[b]	2006	65	33	26	22	47	18	20	30	53	94
Central African Republic[b]	2006	62[d]	43[d]	..	..	..	..	..	..	98	99
Chad	2004	74	37	..	..	..	..	..	..	..	..
Comoros	1996	86	81	..	..	..	..	..	..	..	..
Congo	2005	73	34	..	..	..	..	..	..	70	96
Côte d'Ivoire[b]	2006	92	56	12	1	59	2	17	29	68	100
Democratic Republic of the Congo	2007	57	22	..	..	..	..	..	..	88	100
Djibouti[b]	2006	89	32	11	1	54	16	34	38	10	79
Egypt	2008	100	97	—	—	4	1	..	..	—[e]	1[e]
Eritrea	2002	69	8	..	..	..	..	..	..	28	91
Ethiopia	2005	76	27	39	7	81	6	..	..	69	100
Gabon	2000	83	52	..	..	..	..	..	..	14	83
Gambia[b]	2005/06	72	50	34	5	75	4	22	20	84	97
Ghana[b]	2006	80	47	60[f]	22[f]	67[f]	15[f]	13	21	80[c]	98[c]
Guinea	2005	81	55	..	..	..	..	..	..	94	100
Guinea-Bissau[b]	2006	71	48	54	1	83	1	18	23	96	100
Kenya	2003	84	43	..	..	..	..	..	..	36	96
Lesotho	2004	76	37	..	..	..	..	..	..	7	79
Liberia	2007	73	79	..	..	..	..	..	..	98	99
Madagascar	2003/04	73	65	..	..	..	..	..	..	96	99
Malawi[b]	2006	57	27	60	8	86	5	32	38	93	100
Mali	2006	87	81	..	..	..	..	..	..	96	99
Mauritania[b]	2007	85	33	10	7	57	11	47	71	37	82
Morocco	1992	90	44	..	..	..	..	..	..	..	..
Mozambique	2003	62	25	..	..	..	..	..	..	91	100
Namibia	2006/07	95	58	10	6	37	14	..	..	16	90
Niger	2006	77	36	..	..	..	..	..	..	96	100
Nigeria	2003	65	51	..	..	..	..	..	..	42	86
Rwanda	2005	48	27	..	..	..	..	..	..	97	100
Senegal	2005	91	54	..	..	..	..	..	..	21	87
Sierra Leone[b]	2005	67	53	33	13	76	6	17	17	98	100
Somalia[b]	2006	55	15	31	25	71	21	38	82	99	100
South Africa	2003	96	51	..	..	..	..	..	..	..	..
Swaziland	2006/07	91	51	15	7	49	12	..	..	13	79
Togo[b]	2006	74	39	62[f]	18[f]	65[f]	17[f]	14	30	95	100
Tunisia[b]	2006	..	..	..	..	..	..	..	..	—	1
Uganda	2006	63	15	46[f]	25[f]	68[f]	29[f]	..	..	85	98
United Republic of Tanzania	2004/05	68	30	..	..	..	..	..	..	87	99

Table 7.A

Access to sources of drinking water and use of solid fuels for cooking (*continued*)

| Country or area[a] | Year | Proportion of households within 15 minutes from a source of drinking water (%) | | Proportion of households without water on premises by adult person usually collecting water (%) | | | | Average time needed to collect water (*minutes per trip*) | | Proportion of households using solid fuels for cooking (%) | |
| | | | | Urban | | Rural | | | | | |
		Urban	Rural	Woman	Man	Woman	Man	Urban	Rural	Urban	Rural
Africa (*continued*)											
Zambia	2007	81	46	37	9	81	6	..	..	61	98
Zimbabwe	2005/06	99	39	4	1	63	11	..	..	12	96
Asia											
Armenia	2005	99	87	1	2	4	16	..	..	1	12
Azerbaijan	2006	95	68	6	3	35	7	..	..	1	23
Bangladesh[b]	2006	95	89	20	1	31	2	11	13	62[g]	99[g]
Cambodia	2005	92[h]	75[h]	..	..	..	..	..	..	69	96
Georgia[b]	2005	98	83	3	2	23	14	13	17	18	90
India	2005/06	86	70	22	6	48	6	..	..	31	90
Indonesia	2007	96	90	6	5	19	9	..	..	22	77
Iraq[b]	2006	96	72	2	5	32	13	13	24	1	13
Jordan	2007	100[i]	98[i]	..	..	..	..	..	..	—	1
Kazakhstan[b]	2006	93	70	4	8	16	33	18	20	7	41
Kyrgyzstan[b]	2005/06	95	72	7	4	31	19	13	17	12	56
Lao People's Democratic Republic[b]	2006	94	79	18	5	61	5	9	12	91	100
Mongolia[b]	2005	62	31	19	28	32	51	21	39	61	98
Nepal	2006	88	77	20	6	52	4	..	..	39	92
Pakistan	2006/07	93	85	..	..	..	..	..	..	22	90
Philippines	2003	93	81	..	..	..	..	..	..	..	..
Syrian Arab Republic[b]	2006	99	91	1	6	6	15	10	24	—	1
Tajikistan[b]	2005	89	60	16	2	57	7	24	27	8	48
Thailand[b]	2005/06	99	98	3	2	6	3	9	11	11	47
Turkey	2003	96	93	..	..	..	..	..	..	..	..
Turkmenistan	2000	96	89	..	..	..	..	..	..	—	1
Uzbekistan[b]	2006	94	70	6	4	34	20	16	15	1	25
Viet Nam[b]	2006	97	95	2	1	7	4	17	16	26	79
Yemen[b]	2006	92	43	2	5	47	6	45	65	1	52
Latin America and the Caribbean											
Belize[b]	2006	95	91	5	8	14	10	13	9	2	27
Bolivia (Plurinational State of)	2003	97	81	..	..	..	..	..	..	8	79
Colombia	2005	100	93	..	..	..	..	..	..	3	53
Cuba[b]	2006	95	82	4	8	12	27	15	17	..	..
Dominican Republic	2007	96	86	..	..	..	..	..	..	3	24
Guatemala	1998/99	92	89	..	..	..	..	..	..	..	..
Guyana[b]	2006/07	96	92	2	3	6	7	29	19	2	14
Haiti	2005/06	74	42	..	..	..	..	..	..	87	98
Honduras	2005	97	90	3	2	12	4	..	..	20	86
Jamaica[b]	2006	96	84	3	4	8	15	18	21	..	..
Nicaragua	2001	98	77	..	..	..	..	..	..	39	92
Peru	2004/05	96	86	..	..	..	..	..	..	11[h]	87[h]
More developed regions											
Albania[b]	2005	96	95	4	3	13	5	22	17	26	79
Belarus[b]	2005	99	96	..	..	..	..	9	7	0	9

Table 7.A

Access to sources of drinking water and use of solid fuels for cooking (*continued*)

Country or area[a]	Year	Proportion of households within 15 minutes from a source of drinking water (%)		Proportion of households without water on premises by adult person usually collecting water (%)				Average time needed to collect water (*minutes per trip*)		Proportion of households using solid fuels for cooking (%)	
				Urban		Rural					
		Urban	Rural	Woman	Man	Woman	Man	Urban	Rural	Urban	Rural
More developed regions (*continued*)											
Bosnia and Herzegovina[b]	2006	98	95	2	2	8	7	12	12	19	67
Montenegro[b]	2005/06	100	97	..	..	6	3	15	15	18	56
Republic of Moldova	2005	..	..	..	..	..	..	..	..	1	24
Serbia[b]	2005/06	99	96	1	1	4	4	33	19	14	61
The former Yugoslav Republic of Macedonia[b]	2005	98	98	1	1	4	1	29	10	24	55
Ukraine[b]	2005	98	91	2	4	36	35	20	8	2	25

Sources

All indicators: Macro International, Demographic and Health Survey (DHS) reports and STAT compiler, *http://www.measuredhs.com/* (accessed in August 2009); and UNICEF (United Nations Children's Fund), Multiple Indicator Cluster Survey (MICS) reports, *http://childinfo.org/* (accessed in August 2009).

Definitions

Households within 15 minutes from a source of drinking water: Households whose members need less than 15 minutes to go to the main source of drinking water, get water and come back.

Adult usually collecting water: Woman or man aged 15 years or over identified by a household member as the person usually going to fetch water from the household's main source of drinking water.

Average time needed to collect water: Average time needed to go to the main source of drinking water, get water and return home, calculated only for households without water on premises.

Households using solid fuels for cooking: Households using as main type of fuel for cooking wood, straw, shrubs, grass, crop residue, animal dung, coal, lignite or charcoal. These types of fuels are associated with increased indoor air pollution.

Notes

.. Data not available.

— Magnitude nil or less than 0.5 per cent.

a Data from Demographic and Health Survey (DHS) unless otherwise stated.

b Data from Multiple Indicator Cluster Survey (MICS) national reports.

c Data from 2003 DHS national report.

d Data from 1994/95 DHS national report.

e Data from 2005 DHS national report.

f Multiple response for the question on person usually collecting water.

g Data from 2007 DHS national report.

h Data from 2000 DHS national report.

i Data from 1997 DHS national report.

Table 8.A

Access to cash income and participation of women in intrahousehold decision-making on spending

Country or area	Year	Married persons aged 15–49 earning cash income in the last 12 months (%)		Married women aged 15–49 not participating in the decision on how own earned money is spent (%)			Married women aged 15–49 participating in the decisions on household purchases (%)					
							Purchases for daily household needs			Major household purchases		
		Women	Men	Total	Poorest quintile	Wealthiest quintile	Total	Poorest quintile	Wealthiest quintile	Total	Poorest quintile	Wealthiest quintile
Africa												
Benin	2006	77	89	4	5	1	62	56	67	44	43	45
Burkina Faso	2003	21	37	6	6	4	39	39	43	24	26	28
Cameroon	2004	52	..	9	13	4	51	39	67	36	29	48
Chad	2004	41	..	7	5	2	..	..	..	..	..	..
Congo	2005	66	89	5	7	2	..	..	..	..	..	..
Democratic Republic of the Congo	2007	56	74	28	36	12	57	56	65	44	42	48
Egypt	2008	14	..	3	9	1	78	69	85	55	39	64
Ethiopia	2005	9	30	5	8	2	83	77	88	57	48	67
Ghana	2008	79	86	6	13	4	80	74	83	62	52	67
Guinea	2005	66	64	8	11	6	53	54	53	45	47	42
Kenya	2003	50	89	13	17	8	60	53	68	36	31	43
Lesotho	2004	28	50	10	26	5	78	68	87	43	34	56
Liberia	2007	46	66	23	35	11	91	92	93	75	77	84
Madagascar	2004	52	76	10	13	7	92	92	95	82	80	88
Malawi	2004	18	57	34	47	14	33	30	48	18	17	27
Mali	2006	48	72	7	10	4	28	26	27	20	18	20
Morocco	2003	12	..	4	13	1	49	32	66	50	34	69
Namibia	2006/07	45	78	10	20	8	81	66	92	75	60	89
Niger	2006	30	60	3	2	2	19	21	19	13	12	16
Nigeria	2003	57	69	10	12	10	33	24	56	20	16	31
Rwanda	2005	22	47	22	22	13	67	67	74	58	60	60
Senegal	2005	37	84	6	13	5	25	18	36	16	10	23
Swaziland	2006	50	84	4	7	4	80	75	85	61	50	72
United Republic of Tanzania	2004	24	67	21	44	10	49	41	65	34	28	43
Uganda	2006	48	76	14	19	5	65	74	67	51	61	46
Zambia	2007	39	73	21	28	10	79	66	94	56	44	73
Zimbabwe	2005	32	71	6	14	3	88	84	93	90	86	92
Asia												
Armenia	2005	24	76	7	15	3	79	74	81	77	73	82
Azerbaijan	2006	19	84	7	9	1	52	49	58	53	49	60
Bangladesh	2007	27	..	13	17	9	64	68	64	56	60	57
Cambodia	2005	47	..	5	7	3	93	95	93	79	77	79
India	2005/06	27	90	18	21	8	60	59	67	53	51	61
Indonesia	2007	39	..	3	4	3	94	93	95	79	76	82
Jordan	2007	..	..	..	..	..	74	68	81	71	63	79
Nepal	2006	30	75	14	13	9	58	56	71	53	52	64
Philippines	2003	43	85	6	6	5	86	86	84	77	79	76
Turkey	2003	23	..	11	28	2	..	..	..	..	..	..

Table 8.A

Access to cash income and participation of women in intrahousehold decision-making on spending (continued)

Country or area	Year	Married persons aged 15–49 earning cash income in the last 12 months (%)		Married women aged 15–49 not participating in the decision on how own earned money is spent (%)			Married women aged 15–49 participating in the decisions on household purchases (%)					
							Purchases for daily household needs			Major household purchases		
		Women	Men	Total	Poorest quintile	Wealthiest quintile	Total	Poorest quintile	Wealthiest quintile	Total	Poorest quintile	Wealthiest quintile
Latin America and the Caribbean												
Bolivia (Plurinational State of)	2003	56	87	10	16	8	89	81	90	77	69	80
Dominican Republic	2007	49	..	3	3	3	83	78	87	76	70	82
Haiti	2005	62	..	3	2	3	78	82	74	65	70	63
Honduras	2005	43	..	2	4	1	78	59	91	66	48	81
Peru	2004	50	..	4	12	1	81	65	86	70	50	80
More developed regions												
Republic of Moldova	2005	57	76	2	3	2	97	97	95	96	95	94
Ukraine	2007	79	94	1	1	2	95	95	95	92	94	93

Source

All indicators: Macro International, Demographic and Health Survey (DHS) database, correspondence in November 2009.

Definitions

Married persons aged 15-49 earning cash income in the last 12 months: Currently married/in union women or men aged 15-49 who were employed at any time in the last 12 months and earned either cash income or cash and in-kind income.

Married women aged 15-49 not participating in the decision of how own earned money is spent: Currently married/in union women aged 15-49, with cash income in the last 12 months, who stated that the husband/partner alone, mainly the husband/partner or somebody else other than herself, usually decides on how the money she earned is used.

Married women aged 15-49 participating in the decision on household purchases: Currently married/in union women aged 15-49 who stated that usually they make decisions by themselves or jointly with their husbands/partners on a) purchases for daily household needs and b) major household purchases.

Wealth quintiles: Are defined by socioeconomic status rather than income or consumption. A wealth index is calculated based on data on a household's ownership of selected assets such as televisions or bicycles, materials used for housing construction and types of water access and sanitation facilities. The indicators presented in the table refer to women in the poorest quintile of the wealth index (the 20 per cent population with the lowest score) and women in the wealthiest quintile (the 20 per cent population with the highest wealth index score). For calculation of the wealth index see *http://www.measuredhs.com/topics/wealth/methodology.cfm.*

Note

..   Data not available.

Table 9
List of countries, areas and geographical groupings

Only countries or areas with a population of at least 100,000 in 2010 are included.

Africa	Southern Africa (continued)	South-Eastern Asia (continued)
Northern Africa	South Africa	Thailand
Algeria	Swaziland	Timor-Leste
Egypt	**Western Africa**	Viet Nam
Libyan Arab Jamahiriya	Benin	**Southern Asia**[b]
Morocco	Burkina Faso	Afghanistan
Tunisia	Cape Verde	Bangladesh
Western Sahara	Côte d'Ivoire	Bhutan
Sub-Saharan Africa	Gambia	India
Eastern Africa	Ghana	Iran (Islamic Republic of)
Burundi	Guinea	Maldives
Comoros	Guinea-Bissau	Nepal
Djibouti	Liberia	Pakistan
Eritrea	Mali	Sri Lanka
Ethiopia	Mauritania	**Western Asia**
Kenya	Niger	Armenia[c]
Madagascar	Nigeria	Azerbaijan[c]
Malawi	Senegal	Bahrain
Mauritius	Sierra Leone	Cyprus
Mayotte	Togo	Georgia[c]
Mozambique	**Asia**	Iraq
Réunion	**Central Asia**[b]	Israel
Rwanda	Kazakhstan[c]	Jordan
Somalia	Kyrgyzstan[c]	Kuwait
Sudan[a]	Tajikistan[c]	Lebanon
Uganda	Turkmenistan[c]	Occupied Palestinian Territory
United Republic of Tanzania	Uzbekistan[c]	Oman
Zambia	**Eastern Asia**	Qatar
Zimbabwe	China	Saudi Arabia
Middle Africa	China, Hong Kong Special Administrative Region	Syrian Arab Republic
Angola	China, Macao Special Administrative Region	Turkey
Cameroon	Democratic People's Republic of Korea	United Arab Emirates
Central African Republic	Mongolia	Yemen
Chad	Republic of Korea	**Latin America and the Caribbean**
Congo	**South-Eastern Asia**	**Caribbean**
Democratic Republic of the Congo	Brunei Darussalam	Aruba
Equatorial Guinea	Cambodia	Bahamas
Gabon	Indonesia	Barbados
Sao Tome and Principe	Lao People's Democratic Republic	Cuba
Southern Africa	Malaysia	Dominican Republic
Botswana	Myanmar	Grenada
Lesotho	Philippines	Guadeloupe
Namibia	Singapore	Haiti

Table 9
List of countries, areas and geographical groupings (continued)

Only countries or areas with a population of at least 100,000 in 2010 are included.

Latin America and the Caribbean (continued)

Caribbean (continued)

Jamaica

Martinique

Netherlands Antilles

Puerto Rico

Saint Lucia

Saint Vincent and the Grenadines

Trinidad and Tobago

United States Virgin Islands

Central America

Belize

Costa Rica

El Salvador

Guatemala

Honduras

Mexico

Nicaragua

Panama

South America

Argentina

Bolivia (Plurinational State of)

Brazil

Chile

Colombia

Ecuador

French Guiana

Guyana

Paraguay

Peru

Suriname

Uruguay

South America (continued)

Venezuela (Bolivarian Republic of)

Oceania

Fiji

French Polynesia

Guam

Micronesia (Federated States of)

New Caledonia

Papua New Guinea

Samoa

Solomon Islands

Tonga

Vanuatu

More developed regions

Eastern Europe

Albania[d]

Belarus

Bosnia and Herzegovina[d]

Bulgaria

Croatia[d]

Czech Republic

Estonia[e]

Greece[d]

Hungary

Latvia[e]

Lithuania[e]

Montenegro[d]

Poland

Republic of Moldova

Romania

Russian Federation

Serbia[d]

Eastern Europe (continued)

Slovakia

Slovenia[d]

The former Yugoslav Republic of Macedonia[d]

Ukraine

Western Europe

Austria

Belgium

Channel Islands[e]

Denmark[e]

Finland[e]

France

Germany

Iceland[e]

Ireland[e]

Italy[d]

Luxembourg

Malta[d]

Netherlands

Norway[e]

Portugal[d]

Spain[d]

Sweden[e]

Switzerland

United Kingdom of Great Britain and Northern Ireland[e]

Other more developed regions

Australia[f]

Canada[g]

Japan[h]

New Zealand[f]

United States of America[g]

Notes

a   Sudan is included in Northern Africa for the analysis presented in Chapter 1 – Population and families, and Chapter 3 – Education.

b   Central Asia and Southern Asia are combined into one region, South-Central Asia, for the analysis presented in Chapter 1 – Population and families, and Chapter 3 – Education.

c   Included in the group "CIS in Asia" for the analysis presented in Chapter 4 – Work.

d   Included in Southern Europe for the analysis presented in Chapter 1 – Population and families, Chapter 3 – Education, and Chapter 4 – Work.

e   Included in Northern Europe for the analysis presented in Chapter 1 – Population and families, Chapter 3 – Education, and Chapter 4 – Work.

f   Australia and New Zealand are included in Oceania for the analysis presented in Chapter 1 – Population and families, and Chapter 3 – Education.

g   Canada and the United States of America are included in Northern America for the analysis presented in Chapter 1 – Population and families, and Chapter 3 – Education.

h   Japan is included in Eastern Asia for the analysis presented in Chapter 1 – Population and families, and Chapter 3 – Education.

References

Chapter 1
Population and families

Jha, Prabhat, Rajesh Kumar, Priya Vasa, Neeraj Dhingra, Deva Thiruchelvam and Rahim Moineddin, 2006. Low male-to-female sex radio of children born in India: national survey of 1.1 million households. *The Lancet*, vol. 367, no. 9506 (21 January).

McCauley, A. P, and C. Salter, 1995. Meeting the needs of young adults. *Population Reports*, Series J, No. 41. Baltimore, Maryland: Johns Hopkins School of Public Health, Population Information Program (October).

OECD (Organisation for Economic Co-operation and Development), 2009. OECD Family Database PF11.2: Full-time equivalent participation rates for children under 3 years old. *http://www.oecd.org/els/social/family/database* (accessed in December 2009).

UNICEF (United Nations Children's Fund), 2001. Early marriage: child spouses. *Innocenti Digest*, no. 7 (March).

United Nations, 2008. *Demographic Yearbook 2006*. Sales No. E/F.09.XIII,1. New York: United Nations Statistics Division.

United Nations, 2009a. *World Population Prospects: The 2008 Revision*. Sales No. 09.XII.6. New York: United Nations Population Division.

United Nations, 2009b. *Trends in International Migrant Stock: The 2008 Revision*. New York: United Nations Population Division.

United Nations, 2009c. *World Marriage Data 2008*. New York: United Nations Population Division.

United Nations, 2009d. Demographic Yearbook data collections (accessed in June 2009).

Chapter 2
Health

American Cancer Society, 2007. *Breast Cancer Facts & Figures 2007–2008*. Atlanta, Georgia: American Cancer Society. *www.cancer.org/downloads/STT/BCFF-Final.pdf* (accessed in June 2009).

Bloomfield, Kim, Tim Stockwell, Gerhard Gmel and Nina Rehn, 2003. International comparisons of alcohol consumption. *Alcohol Research & Health* (Winter). *http://pubs.niaaa.nih.gov/publications/arh27-1/95-109.htm* (accessed in July 2009).

Boland, Reed and Laura Katzive, 2008. Developments in law on induced abortion: 1998–2007. *International Family Planning Perspectives*, vol. 34, no. 3, pp. 110–120.

Garcia, M, Jemal, A, Ward, EM, Center, MM, Hao, Y, Siegel, RL and Thun, MJ. 2007. *Global Cancer Facts & Figures 2007*. Atlanta, GA: American Cancer Society.

Grimes, David, Janie Benson, Susheela Singh, Mariana Romero, Bela Ganatra, Friday Okonofua and Iqbal Shah, 2006. Unsafe abortion: the preventable pandemic. *The Lancet Sexual and Reproductive Health Series*, October.

International Diabetes Federation (IDF), 2008. *Diabetes Atlas*. 3rd edition. Brussels: IDF. *http://www.eatlas.idf.org/index1397.html* (accessed in June 2009).

International Diabetes Federation (IDF), 2009. *Diabetes Atlas*. 4th edition. Brussels: IDF. *http:///www.diabetesatlas.org/* (accessed in March 2010).

International Obesity Task Force, 2009. *Global Prevalence of Adult Obesity*. London: International Association for the Study of Obesity. *http://www.iotf.org/database/documents/GlobalPrevalenceofAdultObesityJuly2009.pdf* (accessed in August 2009).

Jernigan, David, 2001. *Global Status Report: Alcohol and Young People 2001*. Geneva: World Health Organization. *http://whqlibdoc.who.int/hq/2001/WHO_MSD_MSB_01.1.pdf* (accessed in July 2009).

Mackay, Judith, Ahmedin Jemal, Nancy Lee and Maxwell Parkin, 2006. *The Cancer Atlas*. *http://apps.nccd.cdc.gov/dcpcglobalatlas/default.aspx* (accessed in May 2009).

Macro International, 2009. MEASURE DHS STATcompiler. *http://www.measuredhs.com* (accessed in July 2009).

Mashal, Taufiq, Takehito Takano, Keiko Nakamura, Masashi Kizuki, Shafiqullah Hemat, Masafumi Watanabe and Kaoruko Seino, 2008. Factors associated with the health and nutritional status of children under 5 years of age in Afghanistan: family behaviour related to women and past experience of war-related hardships. *BMC Public Health*, vol. 8, no. 301. *http://www.biomedcentral.com/1471-2458/8/301* (accessed in June 2009).

Matlin, Stephen and Nancy Spence, 2000. The gender aspects of the HIV/AIDS pandemic. Paper prepared for Expert Group Meeting on the HIV/AIDS Pandemic and its Gender Implications, Windhoek, Namibia, 13-17 November. *http://www.un.org/womenwatch/daw/csw/hivaids/matlinspence.html* (accessed in September 2009).

Meslé, France, 2004. Mortality in Central and Eastern Europe: long-term trends and recent upturns. *Demographic Research*, Special Collection 2. Article 3 (16 April).

Murray, C.J.L. and A.D. Lopez, eds, 1996. *The Global Burden of Disease: A Comprehensive Assessment of Mortality and Disability from Diseases, Injuries and Risk Factors in 1990 and Projected to 2010*. Cambridge, Massachusetts: Harvard University Press.

Notzon, Francis, Yuri M. Komarov, Sergei P. Ermakov, Christopher T. Sempos, James S. Marks and Elena V. Sempos, 1998. Causes of declining life expectancy in Russia. *JAMA*, vol. 279, no. 10, pp. 793–800.

Obaid, Thoraya Ahmed, 2009. Message of the UNFPA Executive Director on the International Day of the Midwife (5 May). *http://www.unfpa.org/public/cache/offonce/News/pid/2631* (accessed in May 2009).

Obot, Isidore and Robin Room, eds, 2005. *Alcohol, Gender and Drinking Problems*. Geneva: WHO.

Omran, Abdel R, 1971. The epidemiologic transition: a theory of the epidemiology of population change. *The Milbank Memorial Fund Quarterly*, vol. 49, no. 4, pp. 509–538.

Parkin, Max, Freehie Bray, J. Ferlay and Paola Pisani, 2005. Global cancer statistics: 2002. *CA Cancer J Clin*, vol. 55, no. 2, pp. 74–108. *http://caonline.amcancersoc.org/cgi/content/full/55/2/74* (accessed in June 2009).

Parkin, Max, Paola Pisani and J. Ferlay, 1999. Global cancer statistics. *CA Cancer J Clin*, vol. 49, no. 1, pp. 33-64.

Peasey, Anne, Martin Bobak, Ruzena Kubinova, Sofia Malyutina, Andrzej Pajak, Abdonas Tamosiunas, Hynek Pikhart, Amanda Nicholson and Michael Marmot, 2006. Determinants of cardiovascular disease and other non-communicable diseases in Central and Eastern Europe: rationale and design of the HAPIEE study. *BMC Public Health*, vol. 6, no. 255 (October).

Preston, Samuel and Haidong Wang, 2006. Sex mortality difference in the United States: the role of cohort smoking patterns. *Demography*, vol. 43, no. 4, pp. 631-646.

Room, Robin and Klara Krdailova Selin, 2005. Problems from women's and men's drinking in eight developing countries. In Obot, Isidore and Robin Room, eds. *Alcohol, Gender and Drinking Problems*. Geneva: WHO.

Rutstein, Shea and Iqbal Shah, 2004. Infecundity, infertility, and childlessness in developing countries. *DHS Comparative Reports No. 9*. Calverton, Maryland, USA: ORC Macro and the World Health Organization.

Sedgh Gilda, Stanley Henshaw, Susheela Singh, Arkinrinola Bankole and Joanna Drescher, 2007. Legal abortion worldwide: incidence and recent trends. *International Family Planning Perspectives*, vol. 33, no. 3, pp. 106–116

Singh, Susheela, Deirdre Wulf, Rubina Hussain, Akinrinola Bankole and Gilda Sedgh, 2009. *Abortion Worldwide: A Decade of Uneven Progress*, New York: Guttmacher Institute.

UNAIDS (Joint United Nations Programme on HIV/AIDS), 2008a. *2008 Report on the Global AIDS Epidemic*. Geneva: UNAIDS.

UNAIDS, 2008b. Caregiving in the context of HIV/AIDS. Background paper for the Expert Group Meeting on Equal Sharing of Responsibilities between Women and Men, including Care-giving in the Context of HIV/AIDS. EGM/ESOR/2008/BP.4 (October).

UNICEF (United Nations Children's Fund), 2007. *State of the World's Children 2008: Child Survival*. New York: UNICEF.

UNICEF, 2008a. *State of The World's Children 2009: Maternal and Newborn Health*. New York: UNICEF.

UNICEF, 2008b. *Progress for Children: A Report Card on Maternal Mortality*. No. 7 (September). New York: UNICEF.

UNIFEM (United Nations Development Fund for Women), 2009. MDGs & Gender: Goal 5. *http://www.unifem.org/progress/2008/mdgsGender5.html* (accessed in October 2009).

UNDP (United Nations Development Programme), 2005a. *Arab Human Development Report 2005: Towards the Rise of Women in the Arab World*. Regional Bureau for Arab States. New York: UNDP.

UNDP, 2005b. *En Route to Equality: A Gender Review of National MDG reports: 2005*. New York: Bureau of Development Policy.

United Nations, 1995a. *Report of the Fourth World Conference on Women, Beijing, 4–15 September 1995*. Sales No. E.96.IV.13.

United Nations, 1995b. *Report of the International Conference on Population and Development, Cairo, 5–13 September 1994*. Sales No.E.95.XIII.18.

United Nations, 2000. *The World's Women 2000: Trends and Statistics*. Sales No. E.00.XVII.14.

United Nations, 2001. *World Population Monitoring 2000*. Sales No. E.01.XIII.14.

United Nations, 2003. *World Contraceptive Use 2003*. Sales No. E.04.XIII.2.

United Nations, 2007. *World Abortion Policies 2007*. Sales No. E.07.XIII.6.

United Nations, 2009a. *World Population Prospects: The 2008 Revision*. Sales No. 09.XII.6.

United Nations, 2009b. *World Contraceptive Use 2009*. Sales No. E.09.XIII.7.

United Nations, 2009c. World Population Prospects DEMOBASE. Department of Economic and Social Affairs, Population Division.

United Nations, 2009d. MDG Database. Department of Economic and Social Affairs, Statistics Division.

United Nations, 2010. World Population Policies Data 2009. Department of Economic and Social Affairs, Population Division.

WHO (World Health Organization), Undated. Youth Violence and Alcohol Fact Sheet. *http://www.who.int/violence_injury_prevention/violence/world_report/factsheets/ft_youth.pdf* (accessed in July 2009).

WHO, 1948. Preamble to the Constitution of the World Health Organization as adopted by the International Health Conference, New York, 19–22 June, 1946 (entered into force 7 April 1948). *http://www.who.int/about/definition/en/print.html* (accessed in March 2009).

WHO, 2004. *Global Status Report on Alcohol.* Geneva: WHO.

WHO, 2005. *Health and the Millennium Development Goals.* Geneva: WHO.

WHO, 2006. Obesity and overweight. *Fact sheet No. 311. http://www.who.int/mediacentre/factsheets/fs311/en/index.html* (accessed in April 2010).

WHO, 2007. *Maternal Mortality in 2005: Estimates prepared by WHO, UNICEF, UNFPA and the World Bank.* Geneva: WHO.

WHO, 2008a. *Global Burden of Disease: 2004 Update.* Geneva: WHO.

WHO, 2008b. *World Health Statistics: 2008.* Geneva: WHO.

WHO, 2008c. *WHO Report on the Global Tobacco Epidemic, 2008: The MPOWER Package.* Geneva: WHO.

WHO, 2009a. *World Health Statistics: 2009.* Geneva: WHO.

WHO, 2009b. *World Malaria Report 2009.* Geneva: WHO.

Wilsnack, Richard, Sharon Wilsnack and Isidore Obot, 2005. Why study gender, alcohol and culture. In Obot, Isidore and Robin Room (eds). *Alcohol, Gender and Drinking Problems.* Geneva: WHO.

Wiredu, Edwin and Henry Armah, 2006. Cancer mortality patterns in Ghana: a 10-year review of autopsies and hospital mortality. *BioMed Public Health*, vol. 6, no. 159. *www.biomedcentral.com/1471-2458/6/159* (accessed in June 2009).

Yin, Sandra, 2007. *Gender Disparities in Health and Mortality.* Washington, DC: Population Reference Bureau (November). *http://www.prb.prg/Articles/2007/genderdisparities.aspx?p=1* (accessed in March 2009).

Zaridze, David, Paul Brennan, Jillian Boreham, Alex Boroda, Rostislav Karpov, Alexander Lazarev, Irina Konobeevskaya, Vladimir Igitov, Tatiana Terechova, Paolo Boffetta and Richard Peto, 2009. Alcohol and cause-specific mortality in Russia: a retrospective case-control study of 48,557 adult deaths. *The Lancet*, vol. 373, no. 9682, pp. 2201-2214.

Chapter 3
Education

Colclough, C., S. Al-Samarrai, P. Rose and M. Tembon, 2003. *Achieving Schooling for All in Africa: Costs, Commitment and Gender.* Aldershot, UK: Ashgate.

European Commission, 2006. *She Figures 2006 – Women and Science, Statistics and Indicators.* Luxembourg: European Commission.

EUROSTAT, 2009. Information society statistics database. *http://epp.eurostat.ec.europa.eu* (accessed in October 2009).

Hafkin, Nancy, 2003. Keynote Address: Gender issues in ICT statistics and indicators with particular emphasis on developing countries. (September).

Huyer, Sophia, Nancy Hafkin, Heidi Ertl and Heather Dryburgh, 2005. Women in the information society. In G. Sciadis, ed. *From the Digital Divide to Digital Opportunities: Measuring Infostates for Development.* Montreal: Orbicom.

ITU (International Telecommunication Union), 2009. *Information Society Statistical Profiles 2009: Americas.* Geneva: ITU.

Juma, Calestous and Lee Yee-Cheong, 2005. *Innovation: Applying Knowledge in Development: A Report of the UN Millennium Project's Task Force on Science, Technology and Innovation*. London: Earthscan.

Lopez-Carlos, Augusto and S. Zahidi, 2005. *Women's Empowerment: Measuring the Global Gender Gap*. Geneva: World Economic Forum.

Mehran, G, 1995. *Girls' drop-out from primary schooling in the Middle East and North Africa: challenges and alternatives*. Amman: UNICEF Middle East and North Africa Regional Office.

UNECE (United Nations Economic Commission for Europe), 2009. UNECE Statistical database. *http://www.unece.org/stats/* (accessed in October 2009).

UNESCO (United Nations Educational, Scientific and Cultural Organization), 2003. *EFA Global Monitoring Report 2003/4: Gender and Education for All: The Leap to Equality*. Paris: UNESCO.

UNESCO, 2005. *Towards Knowledge Societies*. Paris: UNESCO.

UNESCO, 2007. *Science, Technology and Gender: An International Report*. Paris: UNESCO.

UNESCO, 2008. *EFA Global Monitoring Report 2008: Education for All by 2015: Will we make it?* Paris: UNESCO.

UNESCO, 2010. *EFA Global Monitoring Report 2010: Reaching the marginalized*. Paris: UNESCO.

UNESCO Institute for Statistics, 2005a. *Children Out of School: Measuring Exclusion from Primary Education*. Montreal: UNESCO.

UNESCO Institute for Statistics, 2005b. *Global Education Digest 2005: Comparing Education Statistics Across the World*. Montreal: UNESCO.

UNESCO Institute for Statistics, 2008. *International Literacy Statistics: A Review of Concepts, Methodology and Current Data*. Montreal: UNESCO.

UNESCO Institute for Statistics, 2009a. Correspondence in June 2009.

UNESCO Institute for Statistics, 2009b. UIS Data Centre. *http://www.uis.unesco.org* (accessed in December 2009).

UNESCO Institute for Statistics, 2009c. *Global Education Digest 2009: Comparing Education Statistics Across the World*. Montreal: UNESCO.

UNESCO-UNEVOC International Centre for Technical and Vocational Education and Training, 2006. *Participation in Formal Technical and Vocational Education and Training Programmes Worldwide: An Initial Statistical Study*. Bonn: UNESCO-UNEVOC.

United Nations, 1995. *Report of the Fourth World Conference on Women, Beijing, 4-15 September 1995*. Sales No. E.96.IV.13.

United Nations, 2008. *The Millennium Development Goals Report 2008*. Sales number: E.08.I.18.

United Nations, 2009. Demographic Yearbook data collections (accessed in June 2009).

United Nations Human Settlements Programme, 2006. *The State of the World's Cities Report 2006/7: The Millennium Development Goals and Urban Sustainability: 30 Years of Shaping the Habitat Agenda*. Nairobi: Habitat.

Chapter 4
Work

Addati, L. and N. Cassirer, 2008. Equal sharing of responsibilities between women and men, including care-giving in the context of HIV/AIDS. Paper prepared for the Expert Group Meeting on Equal Sharing of Responsibilities between Women and Men, Including Care-giving in the Context of HIV/AIDS, organized by the United Nations Division for the Advancement of Women, Geneva, 6–8 October 2008.

Anker, R., H. Melkas and A. Korten, 2003. Gender-based occupational segregation in the 1990s. *Working Paper No. 16*. Geneva: ILO.

Anker, R, 2005. Women's access to occupations with authority, influence and decision-making power. *Working Paper No. 44*. Policy Integration Department. Geneva: ILO.

Antonopoulus, R. and I. Hirway, eds, 2010. *Unpaid Work and the Economy: Gender, Time Use and Poverty in Developing Countries*. Basingstoke, United Kingdom: Palgrave MacMillan.

Australia Bureau of Statistics, 2009. Work, family life and balance. *Australian Social Trends*, 4102.0 (September).

Bettio, F. and A. Verashchagina, 2009. Gender segregation in the labour market: Root causes, implications and policy responses in the EU. Brussels: European Commission, Directorate-General for Employment, Social Affairs and Equal Opportunities.

Bianchi, S. M, 2000. Is anyone doing the housework? Trends in the gender division of household labor. *Social Forces*, vol. 79, no. 1, pp. 191–228.

Blanco, F, 2009. Assessing the gender gap: evidence from SIMPOC surveys. Geneva: ILO-IPEC, SIMPOC. *http://www.ilo.org/ipecinfo/product/viewProduct.do?productId=10952*.

Cousins, C. and N. Tang, 2003. *Households, Work and Flexibility: HWF Comparative Reports. Volume 2: Thematic Reports*. Vienna: Institute for Advanced Studies, HWF Project.

European Commission, 2007. Tackling the pay gap between women and men. *http://europa.eu/legislation_summaries/employment_and_social_policy/equality_between_men_and_women/c10161_en.htm* (accessed in October 2009).

European Commission, International Monetary Fund, OECD, United Nations and World Bank, 2009. *System of National Accounts 2008*. Sales No. E.08.XVII.28.

Guarcello, L., B. Henschel, S. Lyon, F. Rosati and C. Valdivia, 2006. *Child Labour in the Latin America and Caribbean Region: A Gender-based Analysis*. Geneva: ILO.

Hagemann, F., Y. Diallo, A. Etienne and F. Mehran, 2006. *Global Child Labour Trends 2000 to 2004*. Geneva: ILO-IPEC Statistical Information and Monitoring Programme on Child Labour (SIMPOC).

Hakim, Catherine, 2004. *Key Issues in Women's Work: Female Diversity and the Polarization of Women's Employment*. 2nd edition. London: The GlassHouse Press.

Hussmanns, R, 2005. Measuring the informal economy: from employment in the informal sector to informal employment. *Working Paper no. 53*. Policy Integration Department. Geneva: ILO.

Hussmanns, R., F. Mehran and V. Verma, 1990. *Surveys of Economically Active Population, Employment, Unemployment and Underemployment: An ILO Manual on Concepts and Methods*. Geneva: ILO.

International Labour Office, 1993a. *Bulletin of Labour Statistics*, 1993–2. Geneva: ILO.

International Labour Office, 1993b. *Report of the Fifteenth International Conference of Labour Statisticians, Geneva, 19–28 January 2003*. Geneva: ILO.

International Labour Office, 2002. *Women and Men in the Informal Economy: A Statistical Picture*. Geneva: ILO.

International Labour Office, 2003a. *Yearbook of Labour Statistics 2003*. Geneva: ILO.

International Labour Office, 2003b. *Report of the Seventeenth International Conference of Labour Statisticians, Geneva, 24 November – 3 December 2003*. Geneva: ILO.

International Labour Office, 2004a. Employment in the informal economy in the Republic of Moldova. *Working Paper no. 41*. Policy Integration Department. Geneva: ILO.

International Labour Office, 2004b. Making work arrangements more family-friendly. Information sheet No. WF-5. Conditions of Work and Employment Programme. Geneva: ILO. *http://www.ilo.org/public/english/protection/condtrav/pdf/infosheets/wf-5.pdf* (accessed in November 2009).

International Labour Office, 2004c. Maternity protection. Information sheet No. WF-4. Conditions of Work and Employment Programme. Geneva: ILO. *http://www.ilo.org/public/english/protection/condtrav/pdf/infosheets/wf-4.pdf* (accessed in November 2009).

International Labour Office, 2005. Examples of leave provisions for fathers. Conditions of Work and Employment Programme. Geneva: ILO. *http://www.ilo.org/public/english/protection/condtrav/family/reconcilwf/specialleave.htm* (accessed in December 2009).

International Labour Office, 2007. Key Indicators of the Labour Market. 5th edition. Geneva: ILO. Online version (accessed July – October 2009).

International Labour Office, 2008a. *Global Wage Report 2008/2009*. Geneva: ILO.

International Labour Office, 2008b. Economically Active Population Estimates and Projections, 2008 revision, 1980–2020. 5th edition. *http://laborsta.ilo.org/applv8/data/EAPEP/eapep_E.html* (accessed in June 2009).

International Labour Office, 2008c. *Report of the Eighteenth International Conference of Labour Statisticians, Geneva, 24 November – 5 December 2008*. Geneva: ILO.

International Labour Office, 2009a. *Gender equality at the heart of decent work*. International Labour Conference, 98th Session, Report VI. Geneva: ILO.

International Labour Office, 2009b. Work and Family: The way to care is to share! March 2009 theme of the Gender Equality at the Heart of Decent Work Campaign, 2008–2009. Brochure. *http://www.ilo.org/gender/Events/lang--en/docName--WCMS_101758/index.htm* (accessed in March 2010).

International Labour Office, 2009c. *Global employment trends for women: March 2009*. Geneva: ILO.

International Labour Office, 2009d. Resolution concerning statistics of child labour. In *Report of the Conference, Eighteenth International Conference of Labour Statisticians, Geneva, 24 November – 5 December 2008*. Geneva: ILO.

International Labour Office, 2009e. Labour Statistics database (Laborsta). *http://laborsta.ilo.org* (accessed June 2009 – January 2010).

ILO-IPEC, Undated. Domestic labour: global facts and figures in brief, Child labour by sector. *http://www.ilo.org/ipec/areas/Childdomesticlabour/lang--en/index.htm* (accessed in April 2009).

ILO-IPEC, 2009. Child labour data country briefs: data from SIMPOC surveys. *http://www.ilo.org/ipec/ChildlabourstatisticsSIMPOC/lang--en/index.htm* (accessed in June 2009).

ILO, UNICEF and World Bank, 2009. Country reports from Understanding Children's Work (UCW), an inter-agency research project. *http://www.ucw-project.org* (accessed in June 2009).

L'Office fédéral de la statistique de Suisse (OFS), 2009. Modèles d'activité dans les couples, partage des taches et garde des enfants. *Actualités OFS, Situation économique et sociale de la population, 20*.

Oun, I. and G. Pardo Trujillo, 2005. *Maternity at work: A review of national legislation*. Geneva: ILO.

Plantenga, J. and C. Remery, 2006. The gender pay gap: origins and policy responses – a comparative review of thirty European countries. Report prepared for the European Commission, Brussels.

Razavi, S. and S. Staab, 2008. The social and political economy of care: contesting class and gender inequalities. Paper prepared for the Expert Group Meeting on Equal Sharing of Responsibilities between Women and Men, Including Care-giving in the Context of HIV/AIDS, organized by the United Nations Division for the Advancement of Women, Geneva, 6–8 October 2008.

Statistics Norway, 2002. More time for leisure activities. *http://www.ssb.no/english/publications* (accessed in October 2009).

Statistics Sweden, 2009. Harmonized European Time Use Survey: web application. *https://www.testh2. scb.se/tus/tus* (accessed in December 2009).

UNECE (United Nations Economic Commission for Europe), 2008. Work-life Balance, Gender Statistics Database. *http://w3.unece.org/pxweb/DATABASE/STAT/30-GE/98-GE_LifeBalance/98-GE_LifeBalance.asp* (accessed in November 2009).

United Nations, 1995. *Report of the Fourth World Conference on Women, Beijing, 4–15 September 1995.* Sales No. E.96.IV.13.

United Nations, 2000. *The World's Women 2000: Trends and Statistics.* Sales No. 00.XVII.14.

United Nations, 2009a. *International Standard Industrial Classification of all Economic Activities,* Revision 4. Sales No. E.08.XVII.25.

United Nations, 2009b. Statistics and Indicators on Women and Men. *http://unstats.un.org/unsd/demographic/products/indwm/tab5g.htm* (accessed in February 2010).

United Nations, 2009c. *World Survey on the Role of Women in Development.* Sales No. E.09.IV.7.

United States Bureau of Labor Statistics, 2009. Charts from the American Time Use Survey. *http://www. bls.gov/tus/charts/home.htm* (accessed in October 2009).

Chapter 5
Power and decision-making

Adams, Renée B. and Daniel Ferreira, 2008. Women in the boardroom and their impact on governance and performance. *Social Science Research Network (SSRN) Working Paper Series.*

Economist, The, 2009. Four women become MPs in Kuwait's election. *The Economist,* 19 May.

European Commission, 2008. *Women and Men in Decision-making 2007: Analysis of the Situation and Trends.* Belgium: European Commission.

European Commission, 2009. *Women in European Politics – Time for Action.* Belgium: European Commission.

European Commission, 2010. Database on women and men in decision making. *http://ec.europa.eu/social/main.jsp?catId=764&langId=en* (accessed in June 2010).

Fortune, 2009. Global 500. *Fortune,* 20 July 2009. *http://money.cnn.com/magazines/fortune/global500/2009/womenceos/* (accessed in June 2010).

Instituto Nacional de las Mujeres, Mexico, 2006. Subrepresentación política de las mujeres en América Latina. [Political underrepresentation of women in Latin America.] Press release 24, 4 May. *http://www.inmujeres.gob.mx/images/stories/comunicados/2006/20060504_024.pdf* (accessed in April 2010).

International Institute for Democracy and Electoral Assistance (IDEA), 2005. *Women in Parliament: Beyond Numbers, A Revised Edition.* Stockholm: IDEA.

International IDEA and others, 2010. Quota Project: Global database of quotas for women. *http://www. quotaproject.org/index.cfm* (accessed in June 2010).

International Labour Office, 1990. *International Standard Classification of Occupations: ISCO-88.* Geneva: ILO.

International Labour Office, 2009. Labour Statistics database (LABORSTA). Employment by sex and detailed occupational groups (SEGREGAT). *http://laborsta.ilo.org/* (accessed in June 2009).

Inter-Parliamentary Union, 2003. *Women in Parliament in 2003, The Year in Perspective.* Geneva: IPU. *http://www.onlinewomeninpolitics.org/beijing12/2003_wip_ipu.pdf.*

Inter-Parliamentary Union, 2005. *Women in Parliament in 2005, The Year in Perspective.* Geneva: IPU. *http://www.ipu.org/pdf/publications/wmn05-e.pdf.*

Inter-Parliamentary Union, 2006a. Progress and setbacks of women in national parliaments between 01.07.1995 and 01.02.2006. *Women in politics: 60 years in retrospect.* Data sheet no. 2. *http://www.ipu.org/PDF/publications/wmninfokit06_en.pdf.*

Inter-Parliamentary Union, 2006b. An overview of women in parliament: 1945–2006. *Women in politics: 60 years in retrospect.* Data sheet no. 5. *http://www.ipu.org/PDF/publications/wmninfokit06_en.pdf.*

Inter-Parliamentary Union, 2006c. *Women in Parliament in 2006, The Year in Perspective.* Geneva: IPU. *http://www.ipu.org/pdf/publications/wmn06-e.pdf.*

Inter-Parliamentary Union, 2006d. A chronology of women Heads of State or Government: 1945 – 02.2006. *Women in politics: 60 years in retrospect.* Data sheet no. 4. *http://www.ipu.org/PDF/publications/wmninfokit06_en.pdf.*

Inter-Parliamentary Union, 2007. *Women in Parliament in 2007, The Year in Perspective.* Geneva: IPU. *http://www.ipu.org/pdf/publications/wmn07-e.pdf.*

Inter-Parliamentary Union, 2008. *Women in Parliament in 2008, The Year in Perspective.* Geneva: IPU. *http://www.ipu.org/pdf/publications/wmn08-e.pdf.*

Inter-Parliamentary Union, 2009a. Women in National Parliaments database. *http://www.ipu.org/wmn-e/classif.htm#1* (accessed in May 2009).

Inter-Parliamentary Union, 2009b. Women speakers of national parliaments. *http://www.ipu.org/wmn-e/speakers.htm* (accessed in June 2009).

Inter-Parliamentary Union, 2009c. *Women in Parliament in 2009, The Year in Perspective.* Geneva: IPU. *http://www.ipu.org/pdf/publications/wmnpersp09-e.pdf*

Inter-Parliamentary Union and UN Division for the Advancement of Women, 2008. *Women in Politics: 2008.* Map. *http://www.un.org/womenwatch/daw/public/publications.htm.*

Joy, Lois, Nancy M. Carter, Harvey M. Wagner and Sriram Narayanan, 2007. The bottom line: corporate performance and women's representation on boards. *Catalyst. http://www.catalyst.org/file/139/bottom%20line%202.pdf.*

Norway, Ministry of Children, Equality and Social Inclusion. *http://www.regjeringen.no/en/dep/bld/Topics/Equality/rules-on-gender-representation-on-compan.html?id=416864* (accessed in May 2010).

Spencer Stuart, 2009. The 2009 Spencer Stuart Board Index. *http://content.spencerstuart.com/sswebsite/pdf/lib/SSBI2009.pdf* (accessed in June 2010).

United Cities and Local Governments, 2009. Local governments database. *www.cities-localgovernments.org* (accessed in June 2009).

UN Millennium Project, 2005. *Taking Action: Achieving Gender Equality and Empowering Women.* Task Force on Education and Gender Equality. London: Earthscan.

United Nations Division for the Advancement of Women, 1992. Women in Public Life. *Women 2000*, no. 2.

UNECE (United Nations Economic Commission for Europe), 2009. Gender Statistics Database *http://w3.unece.org/pxweb/Dialog/Default.asp* (accessed in June 2009).

UNIFEM (United Nations Development Fund for Women), 2009. *Progress of the World's Women 2008/2009: Who answers to women? Gender and Accountability.* New York: UNIFEM.

United Nations, 1946. *The Universal Declaration of Human Rights*. *http://www.un.org/en/documents/udhr/shtml* (accessed in May 2010).

United Nations, 1979. Convention on the Elimination of All Forms of Discrimination Against Women, 18 December. *Treaty Series*, vol. 1249, no. 20378. *http://www.un.org/womenwatch/daw/cedaw/text/econvention.htm*

United Nations, 1995. *Report of the Fourth World Conference on Women, Beijing, 4-15 September 1995*. Sales No. E.96.IV.13.

United Nations, 1998. Rome Statute of the International Criminal Court. 17 July. A/CONF.183/9. *http://www.icc-cpi.int/Menus/ICC/Legal+Texts+and+Tools/Official+Journal/Rome+Statute.htm*

United Nations, 2000. *The World's Women 2000: Trends and Statistics*. Sales No. 00.XVII.14.

United Nations Office of the Special Adviser on Gender Issues and Advancement of Women, 2009. *The Status of Women in the United Nations System and in the United Nations Secretariat, as of 30 June 2009 (Secretariat), as of 30 December 2008 (United Nations System)*. *http://www.un.org/womenwatch/osagi/ianwge/Factsheet%20as%20of%20FEB%202010.pdf*

Chapter 6
Violence against women

ILO (International Labour Organization), 2005. Forced labour key statistics. Factsheet. Geneva: ILO. *http://webdev.ilo.org/declaration/info/factsheets/lang--en/docName--WCMS_DECL_FS_20_EN/index.htm*.

Johnson, Holly, Natalia Ollus and Sami Nevala, 2008. *Violence against Women: An International Perspective*. New York: Springer Science+Business Media.

Macro International, 2009. MEASURE DHS STATcompiler. *http://www.measuredhs.com* (accessed 6 October 2009).

Mathews, Shanaaz, 2009. "Every six hours": intimate femicide in South Africa. In *Strengthening Understanding of Femicide: Using research to galvanize action and accountability*. Program for Appropriate Technology in Health (PATH), *InterCambios*, Medical Research Council of South Africa (MRC) and World Health Organization.

Merry, Sally Engle, 2009. *Gender Violence: A Cultural Perspective*. Malden, Massachusetts: Wiley-Blackwell.

OHCHR, UNAIDS, UNDP, UNECA, UNESCO, UNFPA, UNHCR, UNICEF, UNIFEM and WHO, 2008. *Eliminating Female Genital Mutilation – An Interagency Statement*. Geneva: WHO.

Population Reference Bureau, 2008. *Female Genital Mutilation/Cutting: Data and Trends*. Washington, DC: Population Reference Bureau.

United Nations, 2005. *Report of the Fourth World Conference on Women, Beijing, 4–15 September 1995*. Sales No. E.96.IV.13.

United Nations, 2006a. *The World's Women 2005: Progress in Statistics*, Sales No. E.05.XVII.7.

United Nations, 2006b. *Ending Violence against Women: From Words to Action, Study of the Secretary-General*. Sales No. E.06.IV.8.

United Nations, 2009a. United Nations Secretary-General's Campaign UNiTE to End Violence against Women, Framework for Action. New York: United Nations.

United Nations, 2009b. *Report of the Friends of the Chair of the United Nations Statistical Commission on the Indicators on Violence against Women*, E.CN.3/2009/13. New York: United Nations.

United Nations General Assembly, 2006. Intensification of efforts to eliminate all forms of violence against women. Resolution 61/143 (December).

United Nations Statistics Division, 2009. *Proposed draft outline for the Guidelines for Producing Statistics on Violence against Women, Part I: Statistical Survey,* ESA/STAT/AC.193/Item13, Aguascalientes, Mexico.

UNICEF, 2005. *Female Genital Mutilation/Cutting – A Statistical Exploration.* New York: UNICEF.

WHO, 2010. Female genital mutilation. Fact sheet no. 241. Geneva: WHO (February).

Chapter 7
Environment

Agarwal, Bina, 2001. Participatory exclusions, community forestry, and gender: an analysis for South Asia and a conceptual framework. *World Development,* vol. 29, no.10, pp.1623–1648.

Centre for Research on the Epidemiology of Disasters (CRED) and Université Catholique de Louvain, 2009. Emergency Events Database EM-DAT. *http://www.emdat.be/* (accessed in July 2009).

Coates, Lucinda, 1999. Flood fatalities in Australia, 1788–1996. *Australian Geographer;* vol. 30, no. 3, pp. 391–408.

Commission on the Status of Women, 2002. Agreed conclusions on environmental management and the mitigation of natural disasters. 46th session. *http://www.un.org/womenwatch/daw/csw/agreedconclusions/Agreed%20conclusions%2046th%20session.pdf.*

Commission on the Status of Women, 2008. Gender perspectives on climate change. Interactive expert panel on emerging issues, trends and new approaches to issues affecting the situation of women or equality between women and men. Issues paper. 52nd session. *http://www.un.org/womenwatch/daw/csw/csw52/issuespapers/Gender%20and%20climate%20change%20paper%20final.pdf.*

Confalonieri, U., B. Menne, R. Akhtar, K.L. Ebi, M. Hauengue, R.S. Kovats, B. Revich and A. Woodward, 2007. Human health. In M.L. Parry, O.F. Canziani, J.P. Palutikof, P.J. van der Linden and C.E. Hanson, eds, *Climate Change 2007: Impacts, Adaptation and Vulnerability. Contribution of Working Group II to the Fourth Assessment Report of the Intergovernmental Panel on Climate Change.* Cambridge, UK: Cambridge University Press.

Croatia Central Bureau of Statistics, 2008. *Women and Men in Croatia 2008.* Zagreb: Central Bureau of Statistics.

Dasgupta, Susmita, Mainul Huq, M. Khaliquzzaman, Kiran Pandey and David Wheeler, 2006. Who suffers from indoor air pollution? Evidence from Bangladesh. *Health Policy and Planning,* vol. 21, pp. 444–58.

Delaney, Patricia L. and Elizabeth Shrader, 2000. Gender and post-disaster reconstruction: the case of Hurricane Mitch in Honduras and Nicaragua. LCSPG/LAC Gender Team. Decision Review Draft. Washington, DC: World Bank.

Desai, Manish A., Sumi Mehta and Kirk R. Smith, 2004. Indoor smoke from solid fuels: assessing the environmental burden of disease at national and local levels. Geneva: World Health Organization. *Environmental Burden of Disease Series,* no. 4.

Ezzati, Majid and Daniel M. Kammen, 2002. Evaluating the health benefits of transitions in household energy technologies in Kenya. *Energy Policy,* 30, pp. 815–826.

Ezzati, M., A.D. Lopez, A. Rodgers and C.J.L. Murray, 2004. *Comparative Quantification of Health Risks. Global and Regional Burden of Diseases Attributable to Selected Major Risk Factors.* Geneva: WHO.

FAO (Food and Agriculture Organization of the United Nations), 2005. *Global Forest Resources Assessment 2005.* Rome: FAO.

Guha-Sapir, Debarati and Regina Below, 2002. Quality and accuracy of disaster data: a comparative analysis of three global datasets. Working document prepared for Disaster Management Facility. Washington, DC: World Bank.

IPCC (Intergovernmental Panel on Climate Change), 2007. *Climate Change 2007. Fourth Assessment Report. Summary for Policymakers.* http://www.ipcc.ch/pdf/assessment-report/ar4/syr/ar4_syr_spm.pdf.

Jackson, Cecile, 1993. Doing what comes naturally? Women and environment in development. *World Development*, vol. 21, no.12, pp.1947–1963.

Macro International, 2009a. Demographic and Health Survey (DHS) reports. Calverton, MD. *http://www.measuredhs.com/* (accessed in August 2009).

Macro International, 2009b. Demographic and Health Survey (DHS) STATcompiler. Calverton, MD. *http://www.measuredhs.com/* (accessed in August 2009).

Masika, Rachel, ed, 2002. *Gender, Development, and Climate Change.* Oxfam Focus on Gender Series. Oxford: Oxfam Publishing.

Michelozzi, P., F. de'Donato, L. Bisanti, A. Russo, E. Cadum, M. DeMaria, M. D'Ovidio, G. Costa and C.A. Perucci, 2005. Heat waves in Italy: cause-specific mortality and the role of educational level and socio-economic conditions. In W. Kirch, B. Menne and R. Bertollini, eds, *Extreme Weather Events and Public Health Responses.* New York: Springer.

Myanmar Government, Association of Southeast Asian Nations and the United Nations, 2008. *Post-Nargis Joint Assessment.* July. *http://www.aseansec.org/21765.pdf* (accessed in September 2009).

Nigeria National Bureau of Statistics, 2005. *Nigeria Social Statistics 2005.* Abuja: National Bureau of Statistics.

Nogueira P.J, J.M. Falcão, M.T. Contreiras, E. Paixão, J. Brandão and I. Batista, 2005. Mortality in Portugal associated with the heat wave of August 2003: early estimation of effect, using a rapid method. *Eurosurveillance*, vol. 10, no. 7. *http://www.eurosurveillance.org/ViewArticle.aspx?ArticleId=553.*

OECD (Organization for Economic Co-operation and Development), 2008. *Household Behaviour and the Environment. Reviewing the Evidence.* Paris: OECD.

Oxfam International, 2005. The tsunami's impact on women. *Oxfam Briefing Note.* March.

Pirard, P., S. Vandentorren, M. Pascal, K. Laaidi, A. Le Tertre, S. Cassadou and M. Ledrans, 2005. Summary of the mortality impact assessment of the 2003 heat wave in France. *Eurosurveillance*, vol. 10, no. 7. *http://www.eurosurveillance.org/ViewArticle.aspx?ArticleId=554.*

Prüss-Üstün, Annette, David Kay, Lorna Fewtrell and Jamie Bartram, 2004. Unsafe water, sanitation and hygiene. In M. Ezzati, A.D. Lopez, A. Rodgers and C.J.L. Murray, eds, *Comparative Quantification of Health Risks: Global and Regional Burden of Diseases Attributable to Selected Major Risk Factors.* Geneva: WHO.

Sri Lanka Department of Census and Statistics, 2005. *Sri Lanka Census on the Persons and Buildings Affected by the Tsunami 2004.* http://www.statistics.gov.lk/Tsunami/index.htm (accessed in June 2009).

Tschoegl, Liz, Regina Below and Debarati Guha-Sapir, 2006. *An Analytical Review of Selected Data Sets on Natural Disasters and Impacts.* UNDP/CRED Workshop on Improving Compilation of Reliable Data on Disaster Occurrence and Impact. 2–4 April, Bangkok, Thailand.

Uganda Ministry of Finance, Planning and Economic Development, 2003. *Uganda Poverty Status Report 2003.* Kampala: Ministry of Finance, Planning and Economic Development.

UNCCD (United Nations Convention to Combat Desertification), 2009. National reports on the implementation of the United Nations Convention to Combat Desertification. *http://www.unccd.int/cop/reports/menu.php* (accessed in June 2009).

UNDP (United Nations Development Programme), 2009. *Resource Guide on Gender and Climate Change.* Second edition. New York: UNDP. *http://www.un.org/womenwatch/downloads/Resource_Guide_English_FINAL.pdf.*

UNEP (United Nations Environment Programme), 2005. *GEO Year Book 2004/05. An Overview of Our Changing Environment.* Nairobi: UNEP. *http://www.unep.org/yearbook/2004/pdf/geo_yearbook_2004.pdf.*

UNEP, 2007. Gender Mainstreaming Among Environment Ministries. Government Survey 2006. *http://www.unep.org/civil_society/PDF_docs/UNEP-survey-reportJan-07.pdf* (accessed in June 2009).

UNESCO World Water Assessment Programme, 2006. *Kenya National Water Development Report 2005.* Prepared for the 2nd UN World Water Development Report, 'Water: A shared responsibility'. *http://unesdoc.unesco.org/images/0014/001488/148866E.pdf* (accessed in May 2009)

UNICEF (United Nations Children's Fund), 2009. Multiple Indicator Cluster Survey (MICS) reports. http://www.childinfo.org/ (accessed in August 2009).

United Nations, 1995. *Report of the Fourth World Conference on Women, Beijing, 4–15 September 1995.* Sales No. E.96.IV.13.

United Nations, 2004. Report of the Secretary-General. Review of the implementation of the Beijing Platform for Action and the outcome documents of the special session of the General Assembly entitled "Women 2000: gender equality, development and peace for the twenty-first century". 6 December. E/CN.6/2005/2.

United Nations, 2009. *The Millennium Development Goals Report 2009.* Sales No. E.09.I.12.

UN Millennium Project, 2005. *Taking Action: Achieving Gender Equality and Empowering Women.* Task Force on Education and Gender Equality. London: Earthscan.

UN Women Watch, 2009. Women, Gender Equality and Climate Change. Fact sheet. *http://www.un.org/womenwatch/feature/climate_change/* (accessed in September 2009).

USA National Weather Service, 2009. Natural hazard statistics. National Oceanic and Atmospheric Administration (NOAA). *http://www.nws.noaa.gov/om/hazstats.shtml* (accessed in July 2009).

WHO (World Health Organization), 2006. *Fuel for Life: Household Energy and Health.* Geneva: WHO.

WHO, 2009. *Global Health Risks. Mortality and Burden of Disease Attributable to Selected Major Risks.* Geneva: WHO.

WHO and UNICEF Joint Monitoring Programme for Water Supply and Sanitation (JMP), 2010. *Progress on Sanitation and Drinking Water. 2010 Update.* New York and Geneva: UNICEF and WHO.

World Bank, 2006. *Gender, Time Use, and Poverty in Sub-Saharan Africa.* Washington, DC: World Bank.

World Values Survey, 2009. Fifth wave of the World Values Survey. Online data analysis. *http://www.worldvaluessurvey.org/* (accessed in June 2009).

Chapter 8
Poverty

Bardone, Laura and Anne-Catherine Guio, 2005. In-work poverty: new commonly agreed indicators at the EU level. *Statistics in Focus,* 5/2005. Luxembourg: EUROSTAT.

Case, Anne and Angus Deaton, 2002. Consumption, health, gender and poverty. *Center for Health and Wellbeing Working Paper no. 21.* Princeton University.

CEDLAS and The World Bank, 2009. Socio-Economic Database for Latin America and the Caribbean (SEDLAC). *http://www.depeco.econo.unlp.edu.ar/sedlac/eng/index.php* (accessed in December 2009).

Chant, Sylvia, 2007. *Gender, Generation and Poverty: Exploring the 'Feminization of Poverty' in Africa, Asia and Latin America.* Cheltenham UK: Edward Elgar.

Deaton, Angus, 1989. Looking for boy-girl discrimination in household expenditure data. *The World Bank Economic Review,* vol. 3, no. 1, pp.1–15.

Deere, Carmen Diana and Magdalena Leon, 2003. The gender asset gap: land in Latin America. *World Development*, vol. 31, no. 6, pp. 925–947.

EUROSTAT, 2009. Living Conditions and Social Protection database online. *http://epp.eurostat. ec.europa.eu/portal/page/portal/living_conditions_and_social_protection/introduction* (accessed in October 2009).

EUROSTAT, 2010. Living Conditions and Social Protection database online. *http://epp.eurostat.ec.europa. eu/portal/page/portal/living_conditions_and_social_protection/introduction* (accessed in April 2010).

FAO (Food and Agriculture Organization of the United Nations), 2005. A System of Integrated Agricultural Censuses and Surveys, vol. 1: World Programme for the Census of Agriculture. *FAO Statistical Development Series 11*. Rome: FAO.

Fuwa, Nobuhiko, 2000. The poverty and heterogeneity among female-headed households revisited: the case of Panama. *World Development*, vol. 28, no. 8, pp. 1515–1542.

Fuwa, Nobuhiko, Seiro Ito, Kensuke Kubo, Takashi Kurosaki and Yasuyuki Sawada, 2006. Gender discrimination, intrahousehold resource allocation, and importance of spouses' fathers: evidence on household expenditure from rural India. *Developing Economies*, vol. XLIV, no. 4 (December), pp. 398–439.

International Labour Office, 2010. Key Indicators of the Labour Market (KILM). 6th edition. Geneva: ILO. Online version (accessed in April 2010).

Jackson, Cecile, 1996. Rescuing gender from the poverty trap. *World Development*, vol. 24, no. 3, pp. 489–504.

Kabeer, Naila, 1994. *Reversed Realities. Gender Hierarchies in Development Thought*. London: Verso.

Lampietti, Julian A. and Linda Stalker, 2000. Consumption expenditure and female poverty: a review of the evidence. World Bank Policy Research Report on Gender and Development. *Working Paper Series* no. 11. Washington, DC: World Bank.

Macro International, 2009. Demographic and Health Survey (DHS) database (correspondence in November 2009). Calverton, MD.

Marcoux Alain, 1998. The feminization of poverty: claims, facts and data needs. *Population and Development Review*, vol. 24, no. 1.

Nepal Central Bureau of Statistics, 2003. *Population Monograph of Nepal*. Volume I and II. Kathmandu: Ramshah Path.

OECD (Organisation for Economic Co-operation and Development) Development Centre, 2009. Gender, Institutions and Development Database. *http://stats.oecd.org/Index.aspx?DatasetCode=GID2* (accessed in December 2009).

Palestinian Central Bureau of Statistics, 2002. *Ownership and access to resources in Occupied Palestinian Territory*. Ramallah: Palestinian Central Bureau of Statistics.

Sen, Amartya, 1999. *Development as Freedom*. New York: Knopf.

UNESCO (United Nations Educational, Scientific and Cultural Organization), 2010. *Education for All Monitoring Report. Reaching the Marginalized*. Paris: UNESCO.

United Nations, 1995a. *Report of the Fourth World Conference on Women. Beijing. 4–15 September 1995*. Sales No. E.96.IV.13.

United Nations, 1995b. *Report of the World Summit for Social Development. Copenhagen. 6–12 March 1995*. Sales No. E.96.IV.8.

United Nations, 2008a Official list of MDG Indicators. *http://mdgs.un.org/unsd/mdg/Host. aspx?Content=Indicators/OfficialList.htm*.

United Nations, 2008b. *Principles and Recommendations for Population and Housing Censuses. Revision 2.* Sales No. E.07.XVII.8. New York: United Nations Statistics Division.

United Nations, 2009. *Rethinking Poverty: Report on the World Social Situation 2010.* Sales No. E.09. IV.10. New York: Department of Economic and Social Affairs.

United Nations, 2010. Population Ageing and Development 2009. Wall Chart. Sales No. E.09.XIII.10. New York: United Nations Population Division.

Viet Nam Ministry of Culture, Sports and Tourism, General Statistics Office, UNICEF and Institute for Family and Gender Studies, 2008. *Results of Nation-wide Survey on the Family in Viet Nam 2006. Key Findings.* Hanoi: General Statistics Office.

World Bank, 2003. *Gender Equality and the Millennium Development Goals.* Gender and Development Group. Washington, DC: World Bank.

World Bank, 2009. *World Development Indicators.* Washington, DC: World Bank.